SYMBOLS
OF POWER

AT · THE · TIME · OF · STONEHENGE

SYMBOLS OF POWER

AT · THE · TIME · OF · STONEHENGE

D V CLARKE, T G COWIE AND ANDREW FOXON

with contributions by

JOHN C BARRETT, IAN A G SHEPHERD, JOAN TAYLOR AND CAROLINE WICKHAM-JONES

Photographs by

IAN LARNER, MICHAEL BROOKS AND DOREEN MOYES

NATIONAL MUSEUM OF ANTIQUITIES OF SCOTLAND

EDINBURGH

HER MAJESTY'S STATIONERY OFFICE

Designed by HMSO Graphic Design · J Cairns
Produced in Scotland for HMSO by the
following contractors:
Typesetting: Holmes McDougall Ltd
Colour Reproduction: Reproscan (Scotland) Ltd.
Printing: Waddies of Edinburgh
Binding: Paterson Bookbinding

ISBN 0 11 492455 4

CONTENTS

LIST OF ILLUSTRATIONS

Note that numbers given in parenthesis in the captions with the illustrations represent the catalogue numbers of the objects. Page numbers are italicised.

LENDERS TO THE EXHIBITION

Ulster Museum, Belfast
Art Gallery and Museum, Brighton
Moyse's Hall Museum, Bury St Edmunds
University Museum of Archaeology and Anthropology, Cambridge
Public Library and Museum, Campbeltown
National Museum of Wales, Cardiff
Art Gallery and Museum, Cheltenham
Wiltshire Archaeological and Natural History Society, Devizes
Dorset County Museum, Dorchester
Manx Museum, Douglas
Rougemont House Museum, Exeter
Art Gallery and Museum, Glasgow
Hunterian Museum, University of Glasgow
City Museums and Art Galleries, Kingston upon Hull
Museum and Art Gallery, Kirkcaldy
British Museum, London
The Museum, Malton
The Manchester Museum, Manchester
Museum of Antiquities of the University and the Society of Antiquaries of
    Newcastle upon Tyne
Castle Museum, Norwich
Ashmolean Museum, Oxford
Pitt Rivers Museum, Oxford
North East of Scotland Library and Museum Service, Peterhead
Salisbury and South Wiltshire Museum, Salisbury
City Museum, Sheffield
Royal Institution of Cornwall, Truro
Yorkshire Museum, York
National Museum of Ireland, Dublin
Musées Royaux d'Art et d'Histoire, Brussels, Belgium
Laboratoire d'Anthropologie, Université de Rennes, France
Museen der Lutherstadt Eisleben, German Democratic Republic
Landesmuseum für Vorgeschichte, Halle, German Democratic Republic
Museum für Ur- und Frühgeschichte, Potsdam, German Democratic Republic
Rheinisches Landesmuseum, Bonn, Federal Republic of Germany
Gemeentemuseum Arnhem, The Netherlands
Provinciaal Museum van Drenthe, Assen, The Netherlands
Biologisch-Archaeologisch Instituut, Groningen, The Netherlands
Rijksmuseum van Oudheden, Leiden, The Netherlands
Centraal Museum der Gemeente Utrecht, The Netherlands
Historisches Museum des Kanton Thurgau, Frauenfeld, Switzerland
And material from two private collections

ACKNOWLEDGEMENTS

Thanks are due to a large number of individuals whose help has enabled us to prepare this volume and the exhibition which it accompanied. We particularly wish to acknowledge the assistance and co-operation of the following:—

Lieutenant-General Sir Alexander Boswell, KCB, CBE

The Rt Hon the Lord Emslie

Cardinal Gordon J Gray

The Rt Hon Dr John McKay

Sir George Meyrick

J W F Stals

W G M Sutherland, QPM, Chief Constable, Lothian and Borders Police

Staff of the various lending Museums, particularly Laurence Flanagan (Belfast); Caroline Dudley (Brighton); Elizabeth Owles (Bury St Edmunds); Mary Cra'ster (Cambridge); Stephen Green and George Evans (Cardiff); Annette Carruthers and Alan Saville (Cheltenham); Paul Robinson (Devizes); Roger Peers and Rodney Alcock (Dorchester); S Harrison (Douglas); Michael Ryan, Mary Cahill and Nessa O'Connor (Dublin); John Allan (Exeter); Helen Adamson (Kelvingrove Art Gallery & Museum, Glasgow); Euan MacKie (Hunterian Museum, Glasgow); Jay Butler and Jan Lanting (Groningen); Dieter Kaufmann (Halle); David Crowther (Kingston upon Hull); Helen Bass (Kirkcaldy); Ian Longworth, Ian Kinnes, Ray Waters and Bob Walls (British Museum, London); Mr and Mrs F A Wiggle (Malton); John Prag (Manchester); Lindsay Allason-Jones (Newcastle); Barbara Green and Bill Milligan (Norwich); Arthur MacGregor (Ashmolean Museum, Oxford); Linda Cheetham (Pitt Rivers Museum, Oxford); Bernhard Gramsch (Potsdam); Jacques Briard (Rennes); Clare Coneybeare (Salisbury); Pauline Beswick (Sheffield); Roger Penhallurick (Truro); Elizabeth Hartley (York).

the production staff of Her Majesty's Stationery Office, especially Gavin Turner, Norrie Veitch, Jim Cairns, Gordon Campbell and Angus McKinnon.

all colleagues in the National Museum of Antiquities of Scotland, particularly Tom Bryce, Mary Bryden, Sheila Collins, Betty Curran, David Hogg, Helen Jackson, Anne O'Connor, Alex Quinn, Ian Scott, Theo Skinner, Ruth Wilson and Rosanna Zaccardelli.

Marion O'Neil, who preparedd the following line illustrations: 3.42, 3.43, 4.67, 4.69, 4.75, 4.80, 5.31a and the original work for illustrations 5.1, 5.2, 5.3, 5.4, 5.3b-c, 7.21.

numerous friends and professional colleagues for favours, guidance and advice, including Richard Bradley, Colin Burgess, Aubrey Burl, Roy Canham, George Eogan, David Fraser, Lesley Gray, Danny Miller, Stuart Needham, Brendan O'Connor, Graham Ritchie, Niall Sharples, Colin Wallace and Simon White.

. . . and finally, we are especially grateful to all the partners, spouses and friends who took part whether they wanted to or not.

Photographic Acknowledgements

Gemeentemuseum Arnhem 7.33; Provincial Museum van Drenthe, Assen 4.82, 4.83, 5.64; Ulster Museum, Belfast 5.24; Rheinisches Landesmuseum, Bonn 4.47; Roy Canham (Wiltshire Library & Museum Service) 3.2; Crown copyright 1.12; Crown copyright: Royal Commission on the Ancient and Historical Monuments of Scotland 3.4, 3.5; Manx Museum, Douglas 7.12; Historisches Museum des Kantons Thurgau, Frauenfeld 4.48; Biologisch-Archaeologisch Instituut, Groningen 4.66, 4.76; Landesmuseum für Vorgeschichte, Halle 4.24, 4.78, 4.79; Rijksmuseum van Oudheden, Leiden 4.3, 4.81; British Museum, London 4.44; Ashmolean Museum, Oxford 3.47, 7.14; Pitt Rivers Museum, Oxford 7.34; Museum für Ur- und Frühgeschichte, Potsdam 4.23; Rijksdienst voor het Oudheidkundig Bodemonderzoek/J W F Stals 7.35; Irvine Rusk 1.2; Scotsman Publications 1.7; Ian A G Shepherd 3.10; West Air Photography 3.40, 3.41.

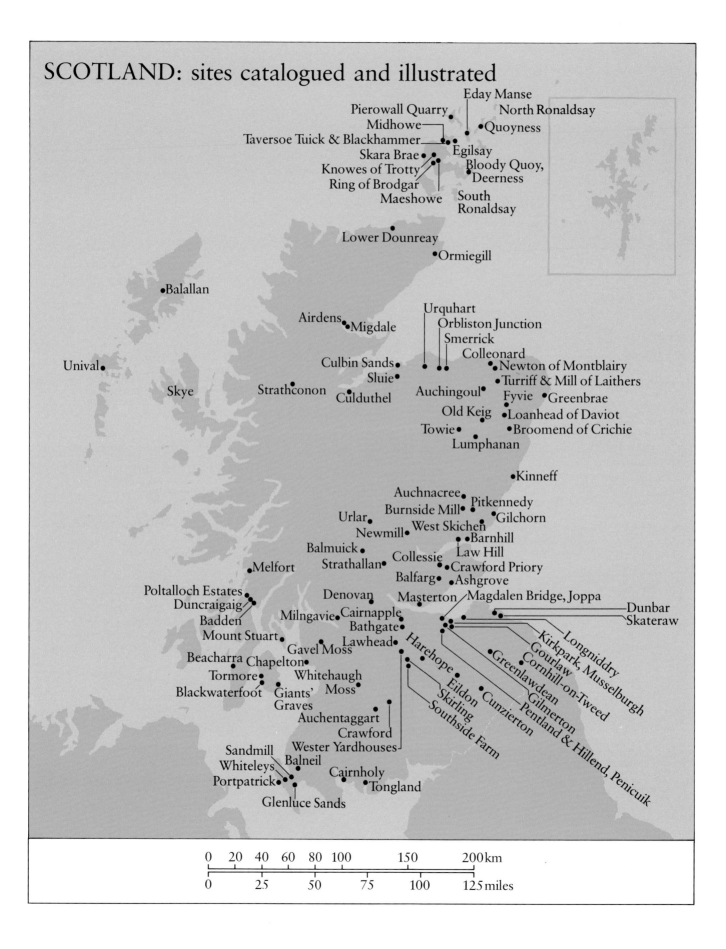

SCOTLAND: sites catalogued and illustrated

Eday Manse
Pierowall Quarry
North Ronaldsay
Midhowe
Quoyness
Taversoe Tuick & Blackhammer
Egilsay
Skara Brae
Bloody Quoy,
Knowes of Trotty
Deerness
Ring of Brodgar
Maeshowe
South
Ronaldsay

Lower Dounreay
Ormiegill

Balallan

Airdens
Urquhart
Migdale
Orbliston Junction
Smerrick
Colleonard
Unival
Culbin Sands
Newton of Montblairy
Sluie
Turriff & Mill of Laithers
Skye
Auchingoul
Fyvie
Greenbrae
Strathconon
Culduthel
Old Keig
Loanhead of Daviot
Towie
Broomend of Crichie
Lumphanan

Kinneff

Auchnacree
Pitkennedy
Burnside Mill
Gilchorn
Urlar
West Skichen
Newmill
Barnhill
Balmuick
Law Hill
Melfort
Strathallan
Collessie
Crawford Priory
Balfarg
Ashgrove
Poltalloch Estates
Denovan
Masterton
Magdalen Bridge, Joppa
Duncraigaig
Cairnapple
Dunbar
Badden
Milngavie
Bathgate
Skateraw
Mount Stuart
Lawhead
Longniddry
Gavel Moss
Harehope
Kirkpark, Musselburgh
Beacharra
Chapelton
Gourlaw
Cornhill-on-Tweed
Tormore
Whitehaugh
Eildon
Greenlawdean
Blackwaterfoot
Giants'
Moss
Skirling
Cunzierton
Gilmerton
Graves
Southside Farm
Pentland & Hillend, Penicuik
Auchentaggart
Crawford
Sandmill
Wester Yardhouses
Whiteleys
Balneil
Portpatrick
Cairnholy
Tongland
Glenluce Sands

0   20   40   60   80   100   150   200km

0   25   50   75   100   125 miles

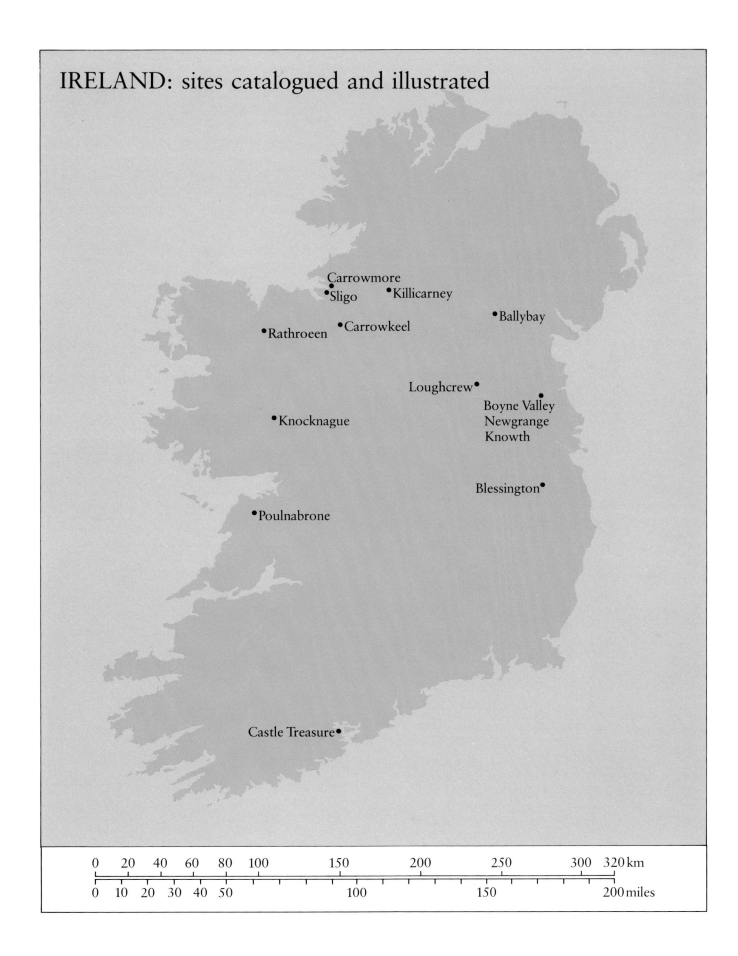

IRELAND: sites catalogued and illustrated

Carrowmore
•
•Sligo   •Killicarney
                                    •Ballybay
•Rathroeen   •Carrowkeel

                        Loughcrew•
                                    •
        •Knocknague   Boyne Valley
                                 Newgrange
                                 Knowth

                        Blessington•

•Poulnabrone

Castle Treasure•

0   20   40   60   80   100   150   200   250   300 320 km

0   10 20 30 40 50   100   150   200 miles

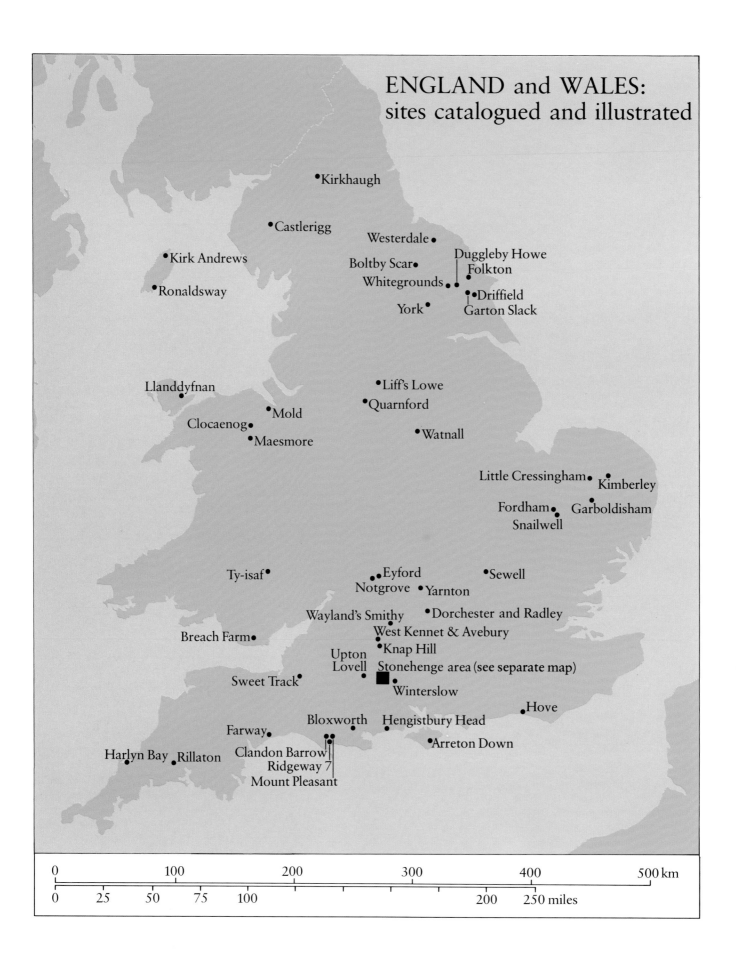

ENGLAND and WALES:
sites catalogued and illustrated

•Kirkhaugh

•Castlerigg

Westerdale•

•Kirk Andrews

Boltby Scar•

Duggleby Howe
Folkton

•Ronaldsway

Whitegrounds•

•Driffield

York•

Garton Slack

Llanddyfnan•

•Liff's Lowe

•Quarnford

•Mold

Clocaenog•

•Maesmore

•Watnall

Little Cressingham•

•Kimberley

Fordham•

Garboldisham

Snailwell

Ty-isaf•

••Eyford

•Sewell

Notgrove

•Yarnton

Wayland's Smithy

•Dorchester and Radley

Breach Farm•

West Kennet & Avebury

•Knap Hill

Upton
Lovell

Stonehenge area (see separate map)

Sweet Track•

Winterslow

•Hove

Bloxworth

Hengistbury Head

Farway•

Harlyn Bay •Rillaton

Clandon Barrow
Ridgeway 7
Mount Pleasant

•Arreton Down

| 0 | | 100 | | 200 | | 300 | | 400 | | 500 km |

| 0 | 25 | 50 | 75 | 100 | | | 200 | 250 miles |

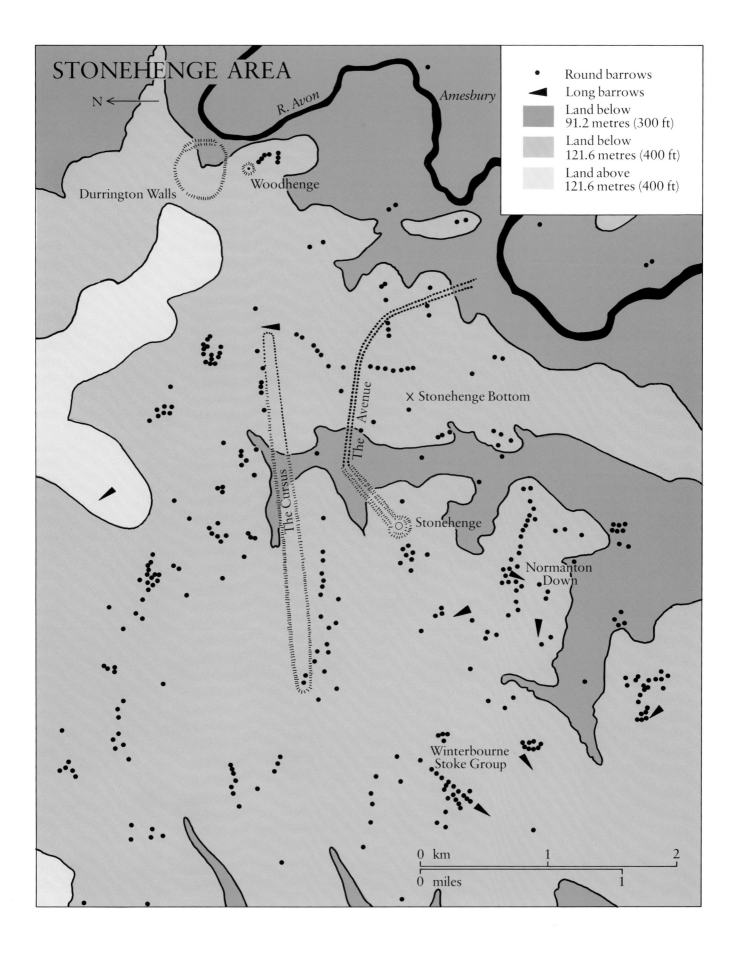

STONEHENGE AREA

N

R. Avon

Amesbury

Durrington Walls

Woodhenge

Round barrows

Long barrows

Land below
91.2 metres (300 ft)

Land below
121.6 metres (400 ft)

Land above
121.6 metres (400 ft)

× Stonehenge Bottom

The Avenue

The Cursus

○ Stonehenge

Normanton
Down

Winterbourne
Stoke Group

0   km   1   2

0   miles   1

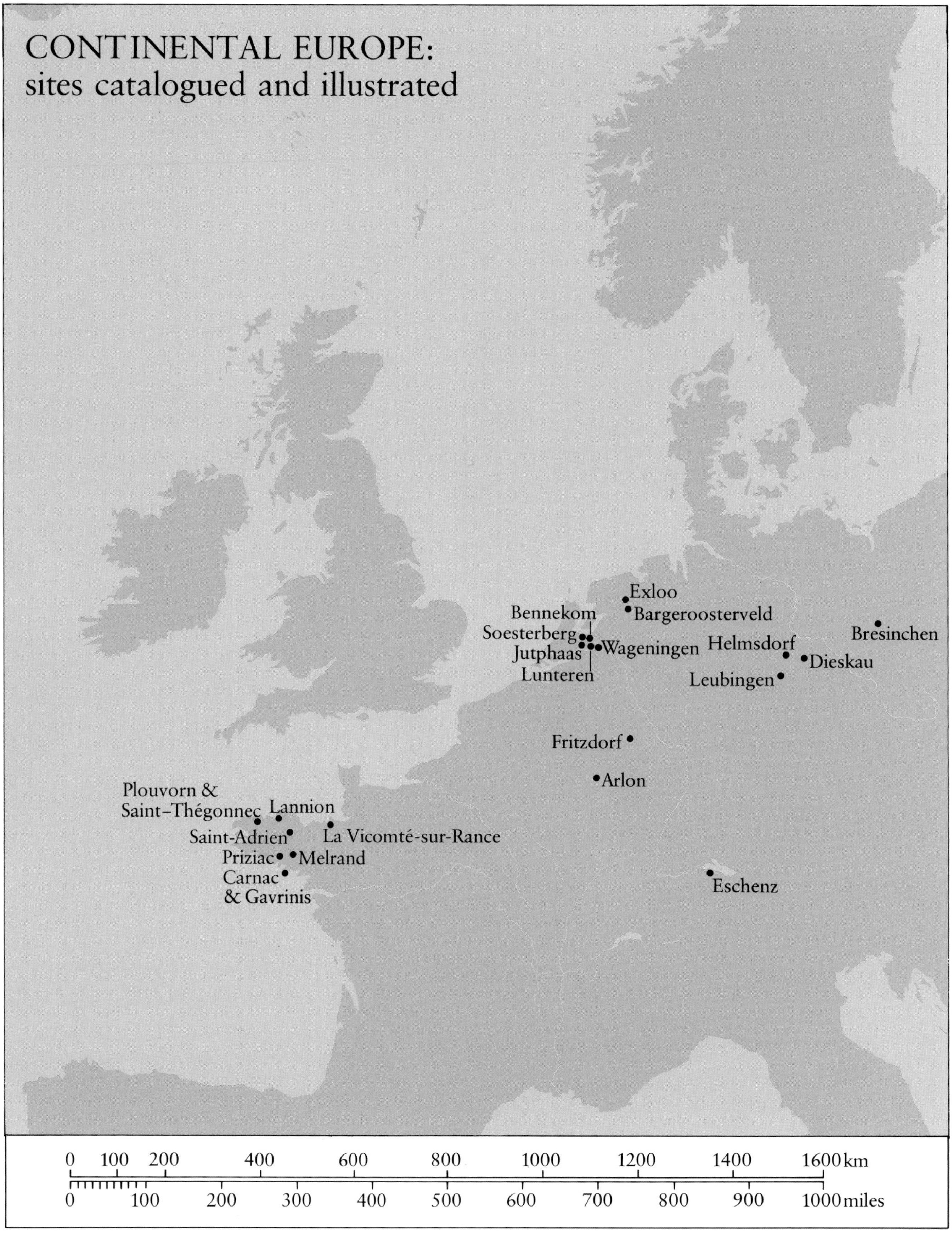

CONTINENTAL EUROPE:
sites catalogued and illustrated

Exloo

Bargeroosterveld

Bennekom

Soesterberg

Jutphaas   Wageningen   Helmsdorf   Bresinchen

Lunteren   Dieskau

Leubingen

Fritzdorf

Arlon

Plouvorn &
Saint–Thégonnec   Lannion

Saint-Adrien   La Vicomté-sur-Rance

Priziac   Melrand

Carnac   Eschenz
& Gavrinis

0	100	200		400		600		800		1000		1200		1400		1600 km

0		100		200		300		400		500		600		700		800		900		1000 miles

1

INTRODUCTION

THIS VOLUME was conceived from the outset to accompany an exhibition with the same title to be held in Edinburgh in 1985. It was nevertheless designed as an independent unit which, within the frames of reference, aims to be reasonably comprehensive. Hence the illustrations include not only the vast majority of the objects shown in the exhibition but also selected relevant material which, for various reasons, was not available for display. Rather than being primarily a record of the objects gathered together in Edinburgh, the catalogue section is to be regarded as a selection of some of the relevant evidence which supports and documents the points made in the main text. Much of the material is superficially well known, at least to specialists, but assembling even basic descriptions and other data is a work of some considerable labour. Archaeology must be one of the few remaining academic disciplines in which research is much more concerned with assembling basic information than with assessing the implications of that information. The overall approach was, however, prompted by the ideas for an exhibition, not a book and it is that thinking which must first be explained if the intentions and limitations of the present volume are to be properly understood.

Most archaeologists who study the prehistoric past rather than our more recent history have experienced discussions with non-specialists in which it quickly becomes apparent that there is a widespread view of prehistoric peoples as squat, grunting savages. This is particularly pronounced in the case of those groups without names except those which are the product of archaeological jargon; Celts and Picts evoke an emotional response never accorded to the 'Windmill Hill Culture' or the 'Grooved Ware Sub-Culture'. Such designations apparently destroy any sense that the peoples thus labelled were in any meaningful way part of our past. The importance of the role of terminology in forming our images of past peoples has long been recognised but attempts to humanise assemblages of material culture were once more vigorous than they are today. 'Beaker people' and 'Urn folk' or variations on this theme regularly appeared in the archaeological literature of a generation or two ago although curiously those most confident that such groups could be identified and labelled displayed in their subsequent descriptions the strongest commitment to the concept of prehistoric peoples as primitive and savage. It is only recently that archaeologists have more and more eschewed such nomenclature in favour of names which are descriptive of the objects but shorn as far as possible of implications for our understanding of the makers and users of those objects. This may have contributed a greater sense of theoretical purity and responsibility although it has added little to the wider understanding which earlier workers were seeking with their descriptions. Certainly, hand in hand with these developments has gone some searching for alternative approaches to understanding the detritus of the prehistoric past in terms of the people alive at the time but the importance of such searches to a balanced view of the past, as the immediate meaning of our terminology becomes more obscure, is often poorly appreciated. Inevitably perhaps, these attempts have as much to tell us about our use of the past in contributing to explanations of the present as they do in conjuring up prehistory but they represent nevertheless a significant turning away from the idea of prehistoric peoples as different in their broad aims, attitudes and motivations from individuals in the present day. By putting the emphasis on the fundamental similarity of some social issues at both periods, indeed all periods, it is possible to provide explanations which can combine a recognition of the variety of solutions to those issues through space and time with an understanding that is rooted in our own experience.

Very little of this work has yet filtered out of the specialist journals into the literature intended for the general reader. Nor is the situation much different in television presentations with their overwhelming concern with discovery rather than explanation. Here information is still structured in terms of concepts, ultimately rooted in late 19th-century social Darwinism, that postulate that human cultural development can be measured in terms of technological achievement. Such ideas are, of course, prominent in politics today and not at all exclusive to archaeology but they have proved particularly attractive to archaeologists faced with interpreting the past through the medium of material culture. Discussions in the 1950s concerning the limits of inference open to archaeologists (Hawkes 1954; Smith, M A 1955) laid considerable stress on the belief that technology was the area about which the most assured and reliable statements could be made. It would perhaps be unfair to suggest that such views only found widespread acceptance because they were underpinned by the ideas of progress in which technological achievement was by far the easiest form of measurement. It is difficult otherwise to explain the near-absence of studies of technological processes in the archaeological literature, most of which was dominated by broader cultural and historical interpretations. Indeed, it is rather paradoxical that archaeologists' reaffirmation of the importance of technological developments as a basis for their cultural interpretations should occur at a time of accelerating ignorance about the practical processes which are essential to our lives. Most of us would not know how to kill and butcher a cow to maximum effect in terms of the yield of food and raw materials even within a modern slaughterhouse let alone in the open countryside. Yet we quite liberally heap pejorative terms such as savage and primitive onto prehistoric peoples to whom such matters were second nature. In an attempt to redress the balance one section of this volume is devoted to examining some aspects of prehistoric craftsmanship. Much of this work is not readily explicable in terms of societies engaged in the short, squalid and brutish struggle for subsistence so characteristic of the popular images.

Equally powerful among our assumptions about prehistoric peoples has been the idea that existence was a simple round of unaltering toil in which change was an imperceptibly slow process. This gradualist view of prehistory is again in marked contrast to our own experiences where life is characterised as complex and rapid technological change is seen as threatening social disruption (cf. Schon 1971). Prehistory is perhaps too remote and too little understood to have figured in most recent 'golden age' philosophies: popularising attempts to explain some prehistoric monuments in terms of extra-terrestial visitors are symptomatic of the difficulties involved for many in relating to the distant past. Even direct experience of prehistoric monuments and objects does not appear to shake our fundamental images of the people who constructed or made them, perhaps because those images are reassuring and at the same time too bland and nebulous to provide a proper context for the items being viewed. All of this has encouraged the idea that archaeological books or exhibitions, which are not in themselves intended to be specialist productions, should embrace a broad spectrum of activities within a particular period. The recent exhibitions on the Vikings, held in London, New York and Stockholm, are a good example of this trend.

This book, and its accompanying exhibition, tries to present a contrary approach concentrating on aspects of a single theme, the manifestation of power, prestige and status in the third and second millennia bc. Influenced, however indirectly, by the views of Marx it is not perhaps unexpected that we should choose to look at the material in terms of the ideology of domination but in selecting this particular aspect we would not attempt to deny either that the evidence we have chosen is capable of alternative interpretations or that its contribution to our understanding of the past is limited to this particular theme. Nor, despite the reference to Marx above, should anyone expect our text to follow a particular doctrinal approach. Although influenced by anthropological studies and archaeologists familiar with that work (eg. Miller & Tilley 1984a) this volume has few pretensions towards theoretical evaluations but tries instead to provide explanations which seem to the authors consistent with the archaeological evidence as it is presently known while at the same time couching those explanations in terms which are hopefully intelligible to the general reader. We have chosen a long time-span embracing some 2000 years, the equivalent of the period from the Roman Conquest to the present day, and concentrated on what we believe to be major transformations. There are, of course, regional variations which are only hinted at here but to come to grips with them all would have required a much larger volume and a wealth of detail which might well have served only to bury our general conclusions.

Power is a concept with which we are all to some degree familiar. At the very least we are passive observers of it every day when we see policemen directing traffic or traffic wardens sticking tickets on illegally parked cars (illustration 1.1). Anthropological considerations of power tend to fall into two areas of investigation. The first is orientated towards study of personal or impersonal mystical energy, a belief in the existence of which modifies or controls an individual's thoughts or actions. Essentially, this is power derived from religious beliefs of which the prevailing Christian

1.1 *The bottom line of power*

ethics in our own society are but an example. The second involves political processes and decision making, an area more in accord with our normative use of the word 'power' (Fogelson 1977, 185). This duality, of course, reflects our own expectations of a firm divide between religious and political power but in many societies this division is and has been much less clear-cut. One has only to look at the role of the Roman Catholic Church in Irish politics or the involvement of the Dutch Reformed Church in South Africa to realise that this is the case even in societies in which in many respects one would not necessarily feel particularly alien. Among the prehistoric peoples with whom we are here concerned it is quite likely that the distinctions between types of power could never have been neatly drawn and for much of the period would have appeared quite meaningless.

But we are here concerned with the use of material culture as symbols of power for it is this aspect that provides archaeologists with access to the strategic patterns involved in the creation, maintenance and collapse of power among groups. Elitism is reflected in two types of symbol in the sphere of portable artefacts. Both reflect their control and authority but are acquired in different ways. The first is that in which the act of acquisition is itself the means by which status is obtained whereas the second is merely the outward confirmation of position achieved by less tangible means. A third form of symbolic statement is, of course, embodied in the design and form of immoveable monuments and

1.2 *Hairstyle by Irvine Rusk*

buildings. All of these types abound in the present day even though many institutions and groups now believe it to be more expedient not to indulge in overt displays of power and prestige. Moreover, many status symbols are now subject to rapid democratisation. Thirty-odd years ago owners of television sets had considerable prestige within their local community, today they are so commonplace that many families have several sets and not possessing one is largely a matter of choice. Indeed, some would interpret such a choice as an attempt to establish status through the absence of acquisition. We may be confident that such considerations were not a factor with prehistoric prestige symbols.

Our first type of symbol involves objects whose acquisition conferred status on the individual either within a particular group or vis-à-vis other groups. This system of ambitious competition now involves many members of our society and much advertising is based on projecting the image that purchasing a particular item will enhance one's prestige or at the very least is mandatory for the preservation of existing status. The item may be a particularly expensive car, a piece of jewellery or even something as transient as a particular hairstyle (illustration 1.2) but its potency will depend upon the degree of exclusiveness within established norms of taste. These norms will, of course, vary from group to group and indeed the whole structure is rooted in fundamental needs for material expressions of group identity. The decisions we make about which clothes to buy and which to wear on different occasions say a lot

1.4 *W G M Sutherland, QPM, Chief Constable, Lothian and Borders Police*

1.3 *Badges: symbols of affiliation from a varied group of organisations*

1.5 *Lieutenant-General Sir Alexander Boswell, KSB, CBE, General Officer commanding the Army in Scotland 1982-85*

1.6 *Cardinal Gordon J Gray, Archbishop of St Andrews and Edinburgh*

1.7 *The 1984 Moderator of the Church of Scotland, Rev John Paterson, with the outgoing Moderator, Rev J Fraser McLuskey*

1.9 *facing page: The Right Hon the Lord Emslie, Lord Justice General of Scotland and Lord President of the Court of Session*

1.10 *facing page: The mace of the former Town Council of Castle Douglas, Kirkcudbrightshire*

1.11 *facing page: The Right Hon Dr John McKay, Lord Provost of Edinburgh, wearing his chain of office. He wishes to state: 'Of course, the chain of office was once a symbol of power and authority, but today I see it more as a symbol of service to the community'*

about our social status and our commitment to particular values. Badges, ties and scarfs with specific motifs (eg. political party, company logo or football club) are used as more deliberate statements of affiliation (illustration 1.3). But within these patterns of use are endless opportunities for more subtle reflections of position and status — silk ties rather than woollen ones, gold badges rather than those of silver or bronze. Many of the choices will be instinctive reflections of basic perceptions of ourselves and if asked to explain them we might well attempt to disguise the reasons with a series of rationalisations that beg the question. Of course, in a capitalist consumer society, competition is centred on the consumption of material whereas in the pre-capitalist societies of prehistory the choice would have been very restricted from our point of view. It might also have involved the acquisition of non-material things like knowledge or skill for these too have a role at all times in enhancing prestige. Nevertheless, although the situation in prehistory can not be considered closely analogous to our experience the basic points remain applicable. Group identity can be fostered and enhanced by material symbols and the acquisition of exclusive or limited items will contribute to increased status and power for individuals within the group.

The second type of symbol which we identified were those which act as the concrete confirmation of acquired power. This group embraces the most obvious symbols of power in the modern world, such as police or military uniforms, and they occur across a broad spectrum of religious and secular life. Considered in the broadest sense, uniforms encompass much of the group and provide interesting insights into the variety of roles in which such symbols play a significant part. There are, it would be claimed, quite practical reasons for uniforms, recognising friend from foe in the case of military examples for instance, but they are an overt statement of group membership and effectively they define the associated power. Furthermore, there is always a degree of elaboration or significant

detailing intended to convey the wearer's position in a particular hierarchy. One is unlikely to confuse a chief constable (illustration 1.4) with a police sergeant or a general (illustration 1.5) with a private. Such distinctions are as prevalent in religion (illustrations 1.6-1.7) as they are in secular organisations and are invariably exaggerated in clothes and other insignia for ceremonial or special occasions (illustration 1.8). In some instances, the ceremonial and traditional aspects are allowed to take total precedence over practical considerations as in the wigs and robes of judges (illustration 1.9). Quite interestingly, such clear symbols of power are now largely restricted to those groups who are not required to submit themselves to the democratic process. Having to stand for election and regularly to seek renewal of one's right to govern has caused politicians to abandon overt symbols of power or prestige even when in office. Yet the symbols are never very far away. Parliament and councils have maces (illustration 1.10) and the leading officers, particularly of the former, are bedecked with symbols (illustration 1.11). We do not directly elect the Speaker of the House of Commons and although he is drawn from the elected members his elevation to this position involves the wearing of a uniform. His normal dress involves a black silk robe with train over a black cloth court suit with white linen bands, stiff white evening dress collar, a full-bottomed wig and a three-cornered black hat. Not surprisingly for State occasions the dress is much more elaborate: black satin robe trimmed with gold over a court suit of black velvet with a white lace jabot, white lace frills at his cuffs, full-bottomed wig, three-corned black hat and white gloves (illustration 1.12). None of this is, of course, strictly necessary to enable the Speaker to perform his duties but as a material expression of power, founded upon tradition and precedence, there could be no finer example. Certainly, many objects in prehistory were used in wholly analogous ways.

Finally, we must turn to the symbolism expressed in monuments and buildings. This is perhaps a less obvious manifestation of the symbols

1.8 Wooden baton for the Commissioners for Solicitors in the Supreme Court (left) and a special constable's baton (right), both c.1830 AD

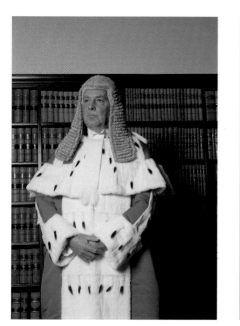

1.12 *The Speaker of the House of Commons, the Rt Hon Bernard Weatherill, MP*

1.13 *St Andrew's House, Edinburgh*

associated with power and prestige than the previous two groups since buildings have such strong practical aspects and monuments are seen primarily as commemorative. Further, clear statements of corporate power in the design of a building are now often regarded as insensitive and contributing to a poor image of the organisation involved. Indeed the near-universal steel and glass buildings of the 'modern movement' impress with their scale, altogether belittling, even intimidating, to human scales, but they do so in an impersonal and anonymous fashion. Power through limiting access to information is still strongly reflected, however, in many central government buildings. A recent commentator wrote of New St Andrew's House, the centre of government in Scotland, that 'the image of system-built bureaucracy conveyed by [it] is suitably frightening' and although its predecessor, St Andrew's House, is architecturally much more distinguished the same writer found its entrance 'unashamedly authoritarian' (Gifford, McWilliam & Walker 1984, 329, 441). Viewed from the south (illustration 1.13), the older building provokes thoughts of fortresses and prisons, the latter a presumably unconscious irony since it occupies the site of the former Edinburgh bridewell. More explicit statements of prestige and importance are to be found in many nineteenth-century commercial buildings. The Royal Bank of Scotland building (illustration 1.14) in George Street, Edinburgh, originally the headquarters of the Commercial Bank, was opened in 1847. The site was originally occupied by the grand and impressive Physician's Hall but only rebuilding on the largest possible scale could satisfy the needs of the Bank to impress its customers and potential customers with feelings of its importance, power and solidity. A counterpoise to this is provided by the statements of individual or family status embodied in the elaborate funerary monuments of the same period (illustration 1.15). No major aspect of life is immune from

1.14 *Royal Bank of Scotland, George Street, Edinburgh formerly the headquarters of the Commercial Bank*

1.15 *Nineteenth-century funerary monument in Warriston Cemetery, Edinburgh*

such images in buildings. Whether they be dwelling-houses or cathedrals, all involve themselves to some extent in the expression of hierarchy and status. Much of this volume is concerned with comparable approaches, using different designs and to some extent media, in prehistory.

We have tried in these brief remarks to show that our central themes are as much a part of life today as we believe them to have been in prehistory. The study of the past can enliven and broaden our perceptions of the present but it is not some distant mirror image of life today. It had its own images, values and structures which may perhaps be better understood if an outline of our major interpretations is provided at the outset. It should be borne in mind throughout that the dates for the period with which we are here concerned derive almost exclusively from the technique of radiocarbon dating. It has been shown in recent years that the dates obtained by this method when compared with those produced by counting tree-rings are not the equivalent of calendar years. The radiocarbon dates are invariably too young and at the beginning of the period the discrepancy may be more than half a millennium. Although the existence of this discrepancy is now generally accepted there remain considerable difficulties in establishing a procedure for accurate correction. We have chosen, therefore, to use a chronology of radiocarbon years, conventionally expressed as bc, and only occasionally have we indicated what the corrected date might be, expressed as BC. To present the overall picture both sets of dates are presented in the chart at the end of this section.

At the beginning of the third millennium bc, life for most people was lived within a small settlement satisfying most of its needs through the exploitation of the local environment. These settlements were linked through networks of reciprocal exchange based on the individual settlement's control of raw materials and locally available resources. One may, for instance, have had access to good fishing ground while another to readily available sources of flint. Such contact between groups inevitably fostered a sense of regional identity. But the groups still interpreted the consequent framework of shared beliefs in terms of their available resources and reflected their continuing need to express individual settlement identity within this wider framework. Hence, although we can determine regional patterns in the design of chamber tombs, no two tombs are exactly alike. These differences are reasonably explained as reflecting the varying resources, both in terms of manpower and surplus production, available to individual communities and the elaborations may well indicate the incipient growth of competition between those communities. Although we may suppose that much decision making in these settlements was communal there would nevertheless undoubtedly be leaders in each generation, though not invested with power which automatically transferred to their heirs. Individual aspirations for enhanced prestige would necessarily focus on the development of regional integration, using the power derived from leadership within individual communities to forge links with other comparable individuals and ultimately to create high-status groups. The earliest evidence of such trends is to be seen in southern England where causewayed enclosures seem to have combined the roles of settlements for such groups and regional centres. Such developments did not invariably occur but the frustration of them, seen most markedly in areas peripheral to southern England such as Derbyshire and Yorkshire, caused individual leaders to seek alternative but more personalised expressions of status. The early individual burials and perhaps large hoards of stone tools are the most obvious manifestations of this.

Nevertheless, the continuing contact between groups did create the momentum for coalition as regional identity was re-inforced through time and information about developments in other areas increased. Indeed, the formation of tighter regional structures may have been a pre-requisite to negotiating access to the wider exchange networks that were developing for the distribution of materials such as the products of the axe factories. Certainly, regional coalitions would have weakened the communal decision making processes that were customary within individual settlements by expanding the number of potential participants beyond an effectively manageable figure. The consequences would have been twofold. First, authority would have been delegated to smaller but more powerful groups and second, there would have been a perceived need to provide tangible expressions of the regional groups in order to foster the loyalty of those now effectively excluded from decision making. This need was satisfied by the construction of communal monuments for the living who were brought for the first time into a more immediate relationship with the gods, without the previous buffer of the ancestors. The convenient consequence was that, by downgrading the importance of the ancestors, the settlement-based structures of legitimation which had relied heavily upon them were considerably weakened. The labour and effort involved in the construction of these new monuments, henges and stone circles, was considerably greater than that required for the building of chamber tombs and the opportunities for them to be expressions of group prestige relative to the monuments of other groups was considerably enhanced. Indeed, the widespread distribution of such monument types, from Orkney to southern England, is best explained in such competitive terms, for effective competition in such matters requires an implicit but acceptable set of parameters. Choosing to buy an expensive car or work of art may enhance the prestige of individuals in their respective groups but they can hardly be said to form an effective basis for assessing the status of those groups relative to one another. A particularly clear and recent example of the use of buildings in this particular competitive way is to be found among the town halls built in the late nineteenth and early twentieth centuries (cf. Cunningham 1981).

In the new order promoted by these regionalising tendencies leaders sought to legitimise their wider authority through these communal monuments. They would have exercised control over both the design and construction of the monuments but maintenance of continuing power would have required that they play influential roles in the attendant rituals. These monuments were, after all, created to facilitate mediation with the intangible aspects of the natural and spirit worlds. Such developments seem to have encouraged, if not actually required, the acquisition of recognisable symbols of status. Jadeite and other stone axes made more for appearance than use, maceheads and carved stone balls are all examples found in the archaeological record. Some of these items were even embellished with designs that united the symbols of the living and the dead. These social elaborations promoted divergent trends with considerable implications for the future course of events. First, they furthered the formation of oligarchies, increasingly withdrawn from the practical aspects of daily life and drawing their authority from their restricted access to techniques for mediating with the feared unknown. But second, and more important, the increasing emphasis on portable symbols of power emphasised to those excluded from this oligarchy that access to positions of authority and importance might be had through the control of raw materials, craftsmen and objects in limited supply.

Towards the end of the third millennium bc, a major disruption of these social systems occurred provoked by the first appearance in Britain of the earliest metal objects made of copper and bronze. To those without access to modern scientific explanations, metal working is inherently a magical transformation of aspects of the natural world. By selecting certain stones and heating them in certain conditions a liquid is produced which can be poured into moulds of varying shapes and forms. Left to cool, the liquid becomes a solid which is at the same time bright, shiny and attractive as well as stronger and more durable than the hardest stone. Further, tools could be made with cutting edges which blunted less quickly and were more easily sharpened than stone tools. It is hardly surprising in these circumstances that individuals capable of controlling such processes should have acquired considerable prestige. Their skills cut at the basis of power exercised by those who had habitually claimed sole control of relationships with the natural world. Further, the metal workers not only created new status items but they introduced new styles of pottery, called by archaeologists beakers, which seem by their fineness of manufacture to have constituted status items in their own right. The consequent emergence of 'Big Men' exploiting a new technology not envisaged or understood by the established order seems to have promoted the collapse of the old regime in some areas. In others, however, with greater power and resources there was a variety of responses. In most, this involved the limited use of the new materials to elaborate existing prestige styles of object or to create new ones. The elaborate designs on the carved stone ball from Towie, Aberdeenshire may well have been carved with a metal tool and the gold collars or lunulae, often decorated with patterns borrowed from the new pottery styles, are perhaps to be interpreted as an attempt to upstage the new metal work in a comparable, indeed superior, material which can, of course, be worked by techniques more akin to those of stone tool production. By far the most powerful response occurred in Wessex with the construction of huge new impressive complex monuments. All of these activities served only to postpone and not avoid the transference of power to the new elites.

Power now seems to have been much more related to the control of raw materials and the technology and craftsmanship that are required to manipulate those materials. It sees, moreover, the final abandonment of the fiction that decision making rests in the hands of the whole community. Individual burial becomes the norm and the associated grave goods provide clear signs of social stratification. All of this finds its ultimate expression in the extravagantly rich graves of Wessex, and to a more limited extent other areas, which demonstrate not only control of rare resources such as amber and gold but also of the craftsmen who can combine these materials in virtuoso pieces without utilitarian function and probably made specifically for burial. Similarly rich burials occur in Brittany and Central Europe and the objects contained within them suggest that networks of contact existed across much of northern Europe. Alternative methods of expressing wealth and power, again indicative of authority over resources, can be seen in the deposition of early bronze hoards. Here, as with grave goods, the emphasis is on disposal and the prestige that accrues from being able to afford to abandon such wealth. By making such offerings to the gods the leading participants not only acquire status but also deny to potential competitors access to material. With the exception of Stonehenge, attempts are made to neutralise the potency of the large communal monuments as symbols of a past order by depositing on them the material culture of the new elite, often accompanied by practices reflecting the current traditions as in the case of the beaker burial at Balfarg, Fife. The new burial mounds, and indeed the rare ritual sites such as that at Bargeroosterveld in the Netherlands, are very much more human, more individual in scale. Their 'monumentality' is now heavily dependent on groupings into cemeteries or the use of spectacular siting. In effect it is the creation of a ritual landscape rather than a ritual monument.

We are aware that in advancing these interpretations we have, in company with all other commentators, made selective use of the evidence available to us. By concentrating on a single theme, however wide-ranging, we have ignored many aspects of life in the third and second millennia bc. Much of the material has been the subject of different interpretations in the past and will no doubt continue to be in the future. Nevertheless we hope that the material contained in the following pages will have sufficient interest to give even the sceptic pause for thought.

RADIOCARBON DATES bc	Long barrows and Chamber tombs	Early individual burials	Communal monuments	Beakers	Rich graves	Food vessels and urns	Metalwork	Bargeroosterveld timber 'temple'	CALENDAR BC DATES
1000									1250
									1835
1500									
2000									2520
2500									3245
3000									3785

2

THE USE OF THE ANCESTORS

THE ARRIVAL of the first farmers in the early centuries of the fourth millennium bc marks the beginning of a major transformation of the British landscape. Although in particularly favourable localities, notably around the coasts, sedentary groups of hunter-gatherers were probably already established, the introduction of agriculture created for the first time the possibility of settled occupation in much of Britain. While all are agreed that this involved colonisation from the European mainland, understanding the nature and source of this colonisation remains fraught with difficulty. Case (1969) has outlined some of the practical problems involved in transporting the basic elements of an agricultural lifestyle, domesticated animals and seeds, across the sea in open skin boats and maintaining that lifestyle following a successful journey. The problems were of sufficient magnitude, he believed, that it must be supposed that the early settlers devoted all their time and energy to survival. The consequence of this view is that large burial monuments 'are unlikely to have belonged to the period of early settlement but rather to stable adjustments of mature and fully extended economies in favourable environments' (Case 1969, 181). An alternative interpretation has been proposed by Bradley (1981, 11-15), who suggests that the difficulties have been over-stressed and that insufficient consideration has been given to the possibilities of their amelioration through contacts with indigenous hunter-gatherer communities. He further notes that there are documented examples which, while not providing close analogies to the situation in fourth millennium bc Britain, do nevertheless demonstrate that some communities use a different set of priorities from those we would find reasonable or sensible:

> Funeral rituals are the most important cultural institutions in traditional Malagasy societies. The expenditure of time and resources for death rituals and the maintenance of tombs are considerable, especially in the light of the often meagre economic base. The conspicuous burial of the dead is the central activity in Malagasy systems of religion, economics and social prestige (Huntington & Metcalf 1979, 95).

Clearly, if the ancestors are seen as mediators with the gods who control the natural elements on which the survival of farming communities are heavily dependent, the importance attached to making proper provision for them will be considerable.

The complex issues involved in our understanding of the establishment and development of the earliest farming groups are not central to our concerns in this volume. By the beginning of the third millennium bc we may reasonably suppose that settled agricultural communities were spread throughout the length and breadth of Britain. Yet curiously, apart from the causewayed enclosures of southern England discussed below (see pp 38-39) traces of actual settlement are rare and our principal evidence for the existence of these communities comes from their conspicuous burial monuments. Although widespread, these monuments are by no means universal, the most notable blank areas being much of East Anglia, the alluvial river gravels and South-West England. Such monuments, in the form either of long earthen mounds (barrows) or chamber tombs (usually contained within stone cairns), were designed as communal *not* individual tombs. But, as we shall see, they fulfilled a variety of roles extending well beyond those immediately connected with burial and fundamental to the activities of the living. Their sheer size and elaboration must have represented a considerable investment of resources and thereby reflected their importance to the communities that built them.

The idea that tombs should play an integral part in the activities of the living is something which we are not particularly familiar with today. It may be helpful, therefore, to look at some more recent uses of the past and in particular the past portrayed in terms of ancestors. This will not, of course, provide close analogies for the situation in the fourth and third millennia bc but may perhaps provide a general framework in which the significance of the ancestors in these earlier societies appears a good deal less unexpected and unusual.

For most of us the explicit invoking of ancestry to legitimise some action or position is rarely encountered. Nowadays such matters are subsumed by 'tradition' and it is our collective not individual ancestors to whom we resort. Although familiar justifications of action such as 'we've always done it this way' now convince less readily than was once the case, the appeal to past (ie. ancestral) practices remains a recurrent theme. It is seen most clearly in advertising where the clear implication is often that traditional approaches provide a guarantee of quality not available through modern processes. This is no more than the extreme expression of Golden Age philosophies expressed in vague calls for a return to Victorian values or appeals to the virtues of the 'good old days'. Such elements are now only a single strand influencing the exercise of political power but the fact that the majority of the members of the House of Lords occupy their places solely on the basis of ancestry provides a vivid demonstration of its continuing importance.

Control and manipulation of situations through the appeal to past circumstances remains then a continuing element of contemporary life but it is not nowadays reflected in the construction of monuments. We have noted that the monuments of the third millennium bc were for communal not individual burial. This finds no parallel in modern practices where even large family vaults maintain the identity of the individual in their disposition of the bodies. We might, however, better understand the wider roles of these prehistoric monuments by considering a modern feature embodying some aspect of them: war memorials. Again we must emphasise that there are no immediate comparisons to be drawn between the two; the prehistoric tombs do not, as far as we can tell, contain the remains of those slain in battle nor do they commemorate such individuals. However, war memorials are a rare example of a contemporary communal commemoration of the dead. Although the names of individuals often appear on them they were quite clearly constructed as monuments to a particular group. It is interesting to note, in this context, that towards the end of the Second World War and immediately after it there was considerable debate about the form of such memorials and particularly whether they should 'serve important and vital purposes to the living' (Whittick 1946, 1). Many people wished them to have a practical aspect, hospitals or libraries for instance, and not to be 'absolutely useless and often ugly memorials' but others argued that to combine practical considerations with commemoration would remove the spiritual value of such monuments and lead in time to the dilution of the commemorative element. In retrospect we can see the force of the latter argument for we remain aware of what the monuments represent but often do not know what memorial halls and the like commemorate. It is in these terms of a continuing and explicit reflection of the dead with the power to communicate across the generations that prehistoric monuments must be viewed.

The important position occupied by ancestors in the belief systems of farming communities is now generally acknowledged. Such views owe much to the work of Meillassoux who suggested (1972; 1973) that distinctions between hunter-gatherers and agriculturalists were to be explained by the different modes of subsistence employed by each group. Basically, hunter-gatherers exploit the various natural resources available in an area and collect them as members of relatively informal groups. This involves a degree of seasonal migration, immediate consumption of the food collected and a consequent absence of the need for long-term methods of storing food. Since these processes do not permanently alter the environment or take place within closely defined areas, hunter-gatherers have only a limited sense of territory. Further, their activities give great emphasis to the present, demand only a short-term view of the future and require no concern with the past. Agriculturalists, on the other hand, must of necessity have a very different time-scale and their sense of territory will be much more clearly defined. Their activities are heavily involved in an investment for the future which nevertheless reflects the successes or failures of the past. The results of one year's harvest will affect the potential of the next and it may take a considerable time to recover from particularly disastrous years. Moreover, after the initial clearance of land there will be constant reminders, in the form of the shape, size and location of the cultivated area, of the contributions of past generations. It is in this context that the ancestors become important in agricultural groups.

Several writers (eg. Chapman 1981, 73; Bradley 1984, 15-16) have commented on the difficulties of applying these rather idealised types, based on anthropological data, to the evidence from prehistory. In particular, they are concerned about the difficulties of explaining changes through time in terms of this particular model. These changes seem to suggest that the appearance of formal disposal of the dead, that is in cemeteries or similar well-defined areas, is related to pressure on critical resources. Such pressures create the need for more formal symbols of one's right to control those resources and the ancestors become a principal means of demonstrating that right. Of course, formal disposal of the dead is not necessarily the only reflection of the importance of the ancestors; in less competitive times, when the requirement for overt and permanent symbols was perhaps perceived to be less necessary, the use of oral tradition may well have been a sufficient commemoration of the past. Moreover, our knowledge of burial practices among early farming communities might well be constricted by the comparative ease of recognition and high survival rate of monumental tombs relative to flat graves and timber structures. The recent discovery of a cemetery of flat inhumations associated with the late hunter-gatherer settlement at Vedbaek in Denmark (Albrethsen & Brinch Petersen 1976) demonstrates that formal disposal is not restricted to agricultural groups. Although explained by Chapman (1981, 75) in terms of control of restricted resources, it is nevertheless a striking demonstration of how much our information is restricted by our conceptual frameworks and expectations.

Of course, there is a considerable difference in terms of investment of energy and resources between a flat cemetery such as Vedbaek and the monumental structures associated with agriculturalists in third millennium bc Britain. Whether or not the absence of recognised burials of the earliest farmers in Britain represents the practices prevailing at the time or a failure of recognition on the part of archaeologists, there is good reason to suppose that the monuments with which we are here concerned reflect in some measure increasing stress among the communities who

2.1 *Facade of the chamber tomb at Wayland's Smithy, Berkshire*

built them in terms of the demand for resources (cf. Goldstein 1981). These monuments are complex structures showing a bewildering variety of forms and are found over much of northern and western Europe. In Britain, a distinction has sometimes been drawn, on the basis of the materials used in their construction, between earth and timber long barrows and stone cairns containing chamber tombs. The former have sometimes been assumed to be earlier than the latter, largely on the basis of the unsupported belief that the earliest settlement by farming communities would have been restricted to lowland England. Certainly, at Wayland's Smithy, Berkshire the chamber tomb (illustration 2.1) is later than an earthen long barrow (Atkinson, R J C 1965) but at Lochhill, Kirkcudbrightshire (Masters 1973), for example, the techniques and materials of both groups are combined in a single structure. Allowing for the differences inherent in the use of these various materials, there are striking resemblances in terms of design between the two groups (Kinnes 1981, 84, figure 6.1) which suggests that distinctions based on architectural materials have little meaning for style or function.

It is important to recognise this basic unity since chamber tombs do provide, through the greater durability of the materials employed in their construction, a good deal more information regarding the architectural aspects of these monuments. At the most basic level they consist of a chamber enclosed by a mound or cairn. In attempts to document contacts or influences from area to area or even actual movements of people, the plans of the chambers have been subjected to endless typological analyses but with little in the way of firm conclusions as answers to these broad questions. Some regional groupings are reasonably well defined by their architectural features (eg. Henshall 1963; 1972) and in this more restricted compass the observed variety within the region is best explained in terms of competition between groups. But uniting essential similarities at a more general level with diversity of form has proved altogether more difficult. Kinnes (1976, 19-20) has suggested that a simple scheme of modular manipulation can help to resolve some of these problems by regarding the simplest form of chamber as the basic modular unit which can then be multiplied and combined in a variety of permutations dependent only on the resources and wishes of the builders. Applying this approach there do seem to be broad architectural trends in the north to linear extension and in the south to agglomeration and dispersal. A general sequence from simple to developed is, of course, implicit in this analysis although it cannot be used to establish comparative chronologies; the adoption of a long mound rather than a round one may in some instances be necessitated by the planned form of the chamber (Fleming 1973a, 190). Indeed, most of the key morphological aspects of these tombs, such as facades and forecourts, can be similarly interpreted in this modular fashion (Fleming 1972). This proposed sequence fits well with the available evidence (Scott, J G 1969, 181; Kinnes 1976, 18-19) although it needs to be emphasised that very few tombs have been properly excavated. At some sites, both chamber tombs and earthen long barrows, a process of remodelling leading to increasing elaboration can be observed (Kinnes 1981, 85-89, figures 6.2-7) while at others we must suppose replacement by an entirely new monument. Some, at least, will have required no alterations to fulfil the continuing needs of the communities that built them.

Today our normal experience of burial is that it takes place very soon after death and is usually preceded by a minimum of ceremony. If the grave has not been used for previous burials, the erection of any permanent monument will follow the interment, often involving a delay of some time. Almost all of the attitudes which we derive from such experiences are inappropriate to understanding the role of long barrows or chamber tombs in the early third millennium bc. This is because contemporary disposal of the dead, whether by inhumation or cremation, is a single final act accorded to each individual. Nothing in the evidence from the prehistoric monuments suggests that the process was either so cursory or so concerned with the individual although the available information is not as extensive as might be expected given the number of monuments known. Beyond the simple fact that these monuments act as communal graves in which very little attention is paid to maintaining the integrity of the individual body the variety seen in the burials is quite remarkable. This variety may perhaps be regarded as equivalent in terms of burial ritual of the variation in architectural design which we have already noted. But while this may be part of the explanation there are discrepancies which are not so easily dismissed.

To help illustrate the problems it is worthwhile to look in some detail at a single group of closely related cairns. The long stalled cairn is a type virtually restricted to Orkney and was described by Fleming (1973a, 180) as 'among the most effective ever devised, since they combine maximum internal space while maintaining minimum, though impressive mounds'. Several occur on Rousay, one of the most northerly islands in the Orkney archipelago, and were the subject of excavations during the 1930s. While not up to modern standards, these excavations were the work of the same archaeologists, Callander and Grant, so that the information obtained reflects a unified set of biases and approaches which in turn renders the evidence highly suitable for comparative purposes.

It will be sufficient for our purposes to concentrate on four tombs, Blackhammer (Callander & Grant 1937), Knowe of Ramsay (Callander & Grant 1936), Knowe of Yarso (Callander & Grant 1935) and Midhowe (Callander & Grant 1934). These tombs lie within 5 km of one another on the south coast of Rousay overlooking Eynhallow Sound, which divides that island from the north coast of Mainland. The best preserved of these is the tomb of Midhowe (illustration 2.2) where the chamber is divided into twelve compartments by the projecting side slabs. Low shelves were constructed between the slabs on the more northerly wall in compartments 5-11 and on these were nine articulated crouched skeletons placed so that their backs were against the wall. These skeletons appeared to the excavators to be largely complete although three had had their skulls placed upright. The remains of an additional fifteen individuals represented by only parts of their skeletons were found piled in heaps. The heaps were mostly located on or under the shelves but two skulls were found against the wall in compartment 12 and 'the scanty remains of an adult skeleton' lay on the floor of compartment 8 on the opposite side from the shelf. Six of the individuals appeared to be represented only by their skulls. No human remains were found in compartments 1-4, where shelves were also absent, or in compartment 11, where a shelf was present (for a diagram illustrating the arrangement of the burials in this tomb see Henshall 1985, 100, figure 5.3). The chamber at Knowe of Yarso is less than a third of the length of that at Midhowe and is divided into only three compartments but the end compartment appears to have two sections. Although at least twenty-nine individuals are represented, a number marginally greater than that found in Midhowe, there were no articulated skeletons. Groups of bones representing four individuals were found in the entrance passage and the first two compartments but the remaining twenty-five individuals were represented by bones packed into the third compartment forming a deposit some 0.5 m deep; twenty-two skulls without their lower jaws were placed close to the walls. The chambers at Knowe of Ramsay and Blackhammer have fourteen and seven compartments respectively but the contrast they provide in terms of the numbers of burials with Knowe of Yarso and Midhowe is very marked. At Ramsay there were the incomplete remains of only three individuals, one represented solely by fragments of an arm and a leg bone, while at Blackhammer the human remains were restricted to the 'much decayed and scanty fragments of two adult male skeletons'. It could, of course, be argued that this discrepancy reflects the greater damage that these two monuments had suffered since they were abandoned but the discovery of considerable

2.2 *Interior of the chamber tomb at Midhowe, Rousay, Orkney*

quantities of animal bone in both tombs makes this explanation difficult to sustain.

These Rousay monuments are as closely related, in terms of design and physical proximity to one another, as any group of chamber tombs in Britain and considerably more so than most. It might be expected, therefore, that they would demonstrate a more unified approach to mortuary practices than is actually the case. The difficulties in understanding are further exaggerated if we consider the recently excavated tomb at Isbister, South Ronaldsay, Orkney (Hedges, J W 1983; 1984). Here, in a tomb closely related architecturally to the stalled cairns of Rousay, detailed investigation of the skeletal material has shown that it represents the remains of at least 341 individuals contained in a chamber half the size of that at Midhowe. This is an order of magnitude greater than we see in the Rousay monuments and cannot be explained solely by appeals to the better quality of analysis employed on the Isbister material. Callander, Grant and their workmen were particularly concerned to recover fragments of skull but even in the most productive of the Rousay tombs, Yarso, less than a third of the number of skulls recovered at Isbister, in a state sufficient for detailed measurements, were found. However, despite the diversity documented here, some points of more general relevance are discernible.

The most obvious is that complete skeletons are very rare. Several explanations have been advanced although they do not in themselves provide an understanding of the criteria involved in selecting those bones found in the tomb. All are agreed that incorporation in the tomb is but one aspect of a complex series of mortuary practices, probably spread over a considerable time, to which the bodies of the deceased were subjected. Recent work by Chesterman at Quanterness (Renfrew 1979) and Isbister in Orkney and at Ascott-under-Wychwood, Berkshire (Chesterman 1977 but see also Benson, D & Clegg 1978) has led to the conclusion that the bones were in either skeletal or near-skeletal state when they were brought into the chamber. This presupposes that the bodies were stored elsewhere while the various processes of decay took their course (for a particularly fanciful interpretation of how this was achieved see the Endpapers in Hedges, J W 1984). This does not, of course, explain the subsequent selection procedures by which some individuals were represented by more bones of their skeleton than others for since very few of the bones show gnaw marks we may reasonably suppose that they were protected from predation by animals and birds. Others, however, most notably Wells in his discussion of the material from West Kennet, Wiltshire (in Piggott, S 1962, 80-81), felt that some bones had been selectively removed subsequent to interment in the tomb for other purposes. 'The conditions', he noted, 'are quite different from those which result simply from skeletons being moved aside to make room for new burials, nor do they correspond with the findings in cases where secondary deposition of remains already in skeleton form has taken place'. The selective removal of bones, particularly skulls and long bones, following their incorporation in the tomb is not perhaps as inconsistent with prior reduction of the body to skeletal form elsewhere as Wells appears to imply, especially if the initial processes were rigorously controlled. Some of the timber structures found beneath earthen long barrows, such as those at Fussell's Lodge, Wiltshire (Ashbee 1966; 1970), Nutbane, Hampshire (Morgan, F de M 1959), Kilham, Yorkshire (Manby 1976) and Dalladies, Kincardineshire (Piggott, S 1972) all seem to have served this purpose. Moreover, the timber structure on Normanton Down, Wiltshire (Vatcher 1961), which is generally interpreted as a mortuary enclosure, emphasises that the site of these initial practices need not be located at a place where a more permanent monument was built. Such separate areas would, of course, have been necessary in the case of chamber tombs which provided, in theory at least, the opportunity of use on several occasions. Indeed, the mortuary structure at Dalladies had all the bone material apart from one fragment removed from it before it was burnt and a mound subsequently built over it. While at Penywyrlod, Brecknock a timber-framed mortuary platform may have existed at the site in the area subsequently occupied by the forecourt of the chamber tomb (Britnell & Savory 1984, 35).

It is equally clear from our survey of the Rousay tombs that the size of the chamber in no way reflects the number of individuals buried within it; Knowe of Ramsay, the largest of the tombs considered, contained only the remains of three individuals. Even allowing for the removal of bones the motives behind the construction of large chambers can hardly have been the accommodation of more skeletons. A similar situation was noted by Kinnes (1976, 26) to exist among the tombs in the Severn-Cotswold area of southern England: 'an increased number of chambers or enlargement of the floor area involves no significant extension of the burial privilege, but rather a diversification of deposit'. Areas devoid of human remains were noted at Ascott-under-Wychwood (Chesterman 1977, 24) and at Lugbury, Wiltshire (Thurnam 1857) just as in the case of compartments 1-4 at Midhowe. Although many early excavators of these monuments described the arrangement of the bones as haphazard and confused, this judgment is based solely on the expectation that formal disposal of the dead should involve the maintenance of the unity of the indivdual body or, at the very least, the ordered arrangement of individual bones found in ossuaries.

The evidence is still very limited but more recent studies have suggested that spatial patterning is recognisable within some tombs, although what we may be seeing is a palimpsest of different patterns superimposed one on another. We have already noted the concentration of skulls in the end compartment at Knowe of Yarso and comparable groupings of skulls and long bones have been noted in Clyde cairns (Piggott, S 1954, 165). At . West Kennet long bones and a large cache of vertebrae were arranged against the wall of the north-west chamber and three skulls had been similarly set at the rear of the south-west chamber (Piggott, S 1962, 21). On the basis of this sort of evidence, Kinnes rather cautiously suggested that 'there is some reason to postulate the reservation of particular areas for sex- or age-linked groups' (1981, 85, 91, figure 6.10) but Shanks & Tilley (1982), using information from both Britain and Scandinavia, have made more wide-ranging assertions about the patterns present in the arrangement of the bones. Essentially, they suggest the possibility of four major contrasts: between articulated and disarticulated skeletons;

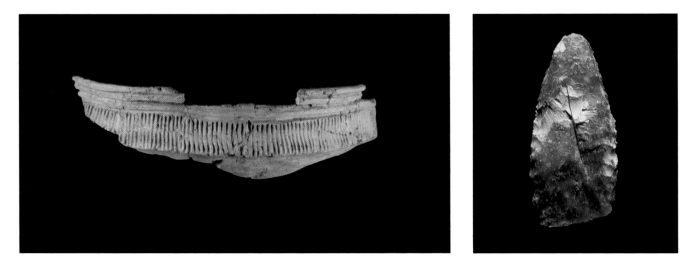

2.3 *The most complete pot from Midhowe (6.2)*

2.4 *Flint knife from Midhowe (6.1)*

between adult and immature individuals; between left and right parts of the body; and between male and female. They further propose that there is deliberate marking of the boundaries of burial deposits. The patterns and the boundaries associated with them are, they claim, 'an assertion of the collective, a denial of the individual and of differences between individuals' which, at the same time, emphasise 'the exclusiveness and solidarity of the local social group using the tomb' (Shanks & Tilley 1982, 150). Such concern with the collective and unified nature of the group would have been important for communities living in dispersed settlements (Bradley 1984, 20).

Related patterns might be expected in the location of objects and animal bones found in many tombs but as yet there is little in the way of published work. Certainly, the finds from Midhowe, consisting of parts of six pots and a flint knife (illustrations 2.3-4), were all found in one compartment in the area not occupied by the burials and at Isbister a similar concentration of pottery was noted (Hedges, J W 1983, 5, illustration 4). Given the nature of the human remains the objects found in the tombs are not readily associated with any one individual and, although objects of considerable craftsmanship do occasionally occur (illustrations 2.5-8), the overall impression is that their quality was not a significant factor in their deposition. Pottery is the commonest find but it is rare for complete pots or anything approaching such a state to be recovered. The factors involved in the selection of items for inclusion in the tombs clearly varied from region to region but they are unlikely to have been a mere reflection of domestic items. Many more beads, for instance, are known from the limited assemblage at West Kennet (illustration 2.9) than from the apparently contemporary but much larger assemblages found at the nearby causewayed enclosure at Windmill Hill (Smith, I F 1965, 134-35). Animal bones, though a recurrent feature, are equally difficult to interpret. Recent suggestions by Fraser (1983, 396-401) that the concentration of particular species found in some Orkney tombs represents totemism have not won universal acceptance. It is possible, however, that the emphasis given to particular species in some of these tombs reflects particular local activities and, as such, is a mechanism for fostering group identity.

THE USE OF THE ANCESTORS 25

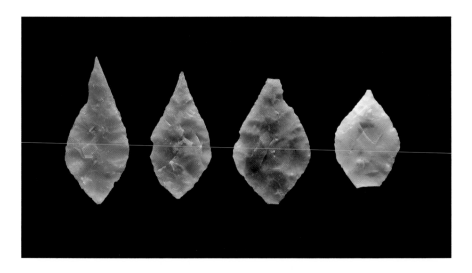

2.5 *Flint arrowheads from the chamber tomb at Giants' Graves, Arran (5.1-4)*

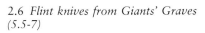

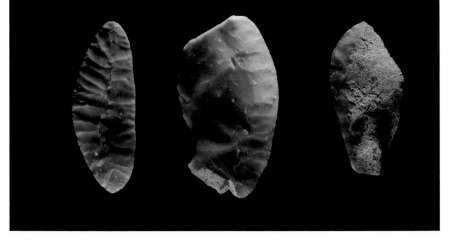

2.6 *Flint knives from Giants' Graves (5.5-7)*

2.7 *bottom left: Flint knives from the chamber tomb at Tormore, Arran (9.1-3)*

2.8 *bottom right: Flint arrowheads and a scraper from the chamber tomb at Ormiegill, Caithness (7.1-5)*

2.9 Beads and other objects from the chamber tomb at West Kennet, Wiltshire (2)

2.10 (Facing page) Chamber tomb at Poulnabrone, Co Clare, Ireland

The evidence points then to a complex series of mortuary practices in which the incorporation of some bones from an individual in or under a monument was but one aspect. Nor was this, in the case of chamber tombs, necessarily the final act in the sequence, for bones brought in could just as easily be removed. It remains to be considered, therefore, just who qualified for such treatment as a prelude to becoming part of the ancestral traditions. On the basis of the recent excavations at the chamber tomb of Quanterness, Orkney, Renfrew argued that the tomb contained the remains of an entire human community (1979, 162-66). In claiming this, he assumed an average age at death of just over 20 years, that the tomb was in use for 550 ± 180 years and that the total number of individuals represented in the tomb was at least 394. This figure for the total number of burials is an extrapolation from the 80 per cent of the main chamber and the one side chamber (out of six) excavated but, as we have seen in our discussion of the spatial patterns within tombs, to assume a uniform distribution of burials on the basis of limited excavation is not easily justified. Even so, there are difficulties in reconciling the settlement evidence from Orkney with his idea of communities as small as twenty. The pottery from Quanterness suggests that its users lived in village sites like those known at Skara Brae, Rinyo and Links of Noltland, all of which seem to have been extensive

settlements where one would expect populations in excess of twenty. Renfrew's ideas were supported by Hedges in a discussion of the material from Isbister (Hedges, J W 1982) where he suggested that the size of the community using the tomb was 'somewhere between 7 and 43'. Whether or not one finds these ideas plausible (see Fraser & Kinnes 1982 for examples of those who did not) the evidence from these two tombs cannot, at the moment, be regarded as typical even of Orkney and is certainly in marked contrast to discoveries elsewhere in Britain (Saville 1984, 22). Even R J C Atkinson, who appeared to accept the possibility that earthen long barrows were the tombs of individual families even though this involved an absurdly low figure for the population of lowland England, inclined 'to the view that chambered tombs in lowland England were used for the burial of selected members of the population only and not for the population at large' (1968, 92). Certainly, this remains the interpretation most consistent with the evidence from the whole of Britain. We have little in the way of information about how these individuals were selected but an untouched chamber in the tomb at Lanhill, Wiltshire (Keiller & Piggott, S 1938) produced burials which appeared to be those of closely related individuals.

Whatever the basis for selecting the individuals who would ultimately be interred in the tomb, it seems clear that the monument itself reflected specific needs of the community as a whole. Indeed, Fleming (1972, 62) has suggested that the design of many chamber tombs reflects the social organisation of the communities who built and used them. He notes that the area available for burial is not an undifferentiated chamber but often divided structurally into a number of separate areas which are nevertheless unified into a single monument by the surrounding mound. It is the mound or cairn, often far greater than is necessary to enclose the chamber, which would have created the visual impact of these monuments for the living. Certainly, some tombs seem never to have been surrounded by a mound and yet still remain powerful symbols (illustration 2.10) but it is the presence of a mound that normally greatly enhances the effect of the monument. This is particularly the case with the long trapezoidal mounds which are often embellished with carefully built kerbs (illustration 2.11) and elaborate forecourts (illustration 2.12) and the enhanced opportunities for ceremonial display which this form offered may well have been the reason for its widespread adoption (Fleming 1973a). That the mounds of these monuments were significant in their own right is confirmed by four sites in Wessex (the long barrows at Horslip, Beckhampton Road and South Street in Wiltshire: Ashbee, Smith & Evans 1979; and at Thickthorn Down, Dorset: Drew & Piggott, S 1936a) where elaborately constructed mounds covered no burials at all.

Many of the mounds, although impressive in terms of their sheer size, are made even more dominant features in the landscape by their siting. Fraser (1983, 298-303) has tried to investigate this element among the tombs in Orkney and, despite the inherent difficulties in defining adequately the concepts involved, it does seem that many of them were placed in positions which overlooked, and consequently could be seen from, extensive areas of land up to a distance of 5 km. Such locations have encouraged some (eg. Renfrew 1976) to see the tombs as territorial

2.11 *Decorative dry-stone kerb of the chamber tomb at Blackhammer, Rousay, Orkney*

2.12 *Facade of the chamber tomb at Cairnholy, Kirkcudbrightshire*

2.13 *Interior of the chamber tomb at Maeshowe, Orkney viewed from the entrance passage*

2.15 *View along the entrance passage at Maeshowe*

markers, placed strategically in the land controlled by a community. If we ignore the difficulties (on which see Kinnes 1981, 87) the approach appears plausible in a limited number of areas like the islands of Rousay and Arran but it is much harder to understand its operation even in adjacent areas. Nevertheless, without resorting to rigidly defined territories, the tombs do appear to be foci for territorial loyalties and their strong links to the past, achieved through their contents, would have served to legitimise the use of the land by the resident community. This would have been an important source of power to those communities in their relations with neighbouring groups and many of the elaborations seen at the monuments may well have been prompted by competition between groups. Equally though, they would have been major symbols of power for the leaders within the communities. These individuals would probably have controlled the rituals associated with the tombs and based their claim to power, in part at least, on an alleged relationship with the ancestors contained within the tombs.

Finally, we must consider that small group of sites whose size, architectural sophistication and quality of workmanship transcend the concept of community-based tombs which we have hitherto been considering. Sites such as Newgrange in Ireland and Maeshowe in Orkney (illustrations 2.13-18) are numbered among the finest of Europe's prehistoric monuments. Such radiocarbon dates as are available suggest that they were built around the middle of the third millennium bc,

2.14 *(Facing page) Interior of Maeshowe looking towards the entrance passage*

2.16 *The mound of a chamber tomb near Newgrange, Co Meath, Ireland with the River Boyne in the foreground*

2.17 *Roof of the chamber at Newgrange*

2.18 *A decorated stone at the junction of the end recess and chamber at Newgrange*

at a time when regional groupings, more commonly represented by the construction of henges and stone circles, were beginning to be established in many areas in Britain. Significantly enclosed in round mounds, echoing earlier forms but on a scale hitherto unknown, they occupy sites with little concern for visibility as if reflecting control of an area too large for a single place to meet that requirement. Moreover, they embody features which leaders could use to manipulate the living. Lynch (1973, 152) has suggested that the roof box at Newgrange 'could have been used as some form of oracle'. 'People', she thought, 'might seek the advice of their ancestors by asking their questions through the slot and their distorted words would come back to them as an answer, of which they could make what they liked'. The slot of 0.45 m created by the gap between the top of the stone door and the bottom of the lintel at Maeshowe could have served a similar function. Lynch notes other sites where similar features occur and more recently Henshall (1985, 113-15) has added further Scottish examples but none were likely to have created an effect comparable to that produced by the massive chambers at Newgrange and Maeshowe. This kind of access to the ancestors is likely to have been strictly controlled. It is not too fanciful then to regard these monuments as among the earliest to reflect regional groupings. They are monuments for the living which demonstrate the power of the ideologies rooted in the ancestors.

FROM ANCESTORS TO GODS

D URING THE late third millennium bc there were complex relationships between communities at different levels. We have seen how the ancestors were used as a way of claiming territorial rights and controlling land and the people on it. But ancestors are important only for a specific small area. How did these areas relate and what were the relationships between the communities within them? Renfrew (1973; 1979, 217-23) has argued on the evidence from Wessex and Orkney that during the late third millennium bc there was a change from isolated communities of roughly equal status to larger units which encompassed several of these smaller communities. The nature of the processes involved and the actual history of this development are not, however, clear from his argument.

Several general points have to be reviewed in any consideration of social relationships and social development. Individuals belong to several groups — on the basis of gender, age, lineage, status by birth, acquired status, place of birth, place of dwelling, philosophical view, etc. Different societies place different import on these groups. By the late third millennium bc, colonising expansion of farming communities had ceased for perhaps 600 years. These communities are thought to have been associated through ancestral claims with particular areas of land and the extent to which individuals moved from group to group is likely to have been restricted to, at one level, marriage arrangements and at another movements of craftsmen and people of high status. All of this is in good agreement with the stable communities of the type envisaged by Renfrew.

It is accepted here that there was a change in the centuries after 2500 bc to an emphasis on the larger community but looking back, it seems inherent in the structure of neolithic society. Whilst this was a general trend it did not happen throughout Britain at the same rate or in the same way. The small communities associated with ancestral burial places should not be seen as equal but as continually competitive. This may be in terms of access to important resources where one group has good fishing grounds and another has good sources of flint or it may also be in terms of political strength. These are unlikely to be contradictory types of power but it would be simplistic to suggest that political power derives solely from control of scarce or valuable resources. What is important is to note that through competition unequal power relations are established and some groups will be dominant over other groups. Their fortunes will wax and wane as those in power wield that power for better or worse and as the signs and symbols of that power are changed.

What we see happening is that this potential in late neolithic society for powerful groups to dominate others and to control areas larger than can be justified through the local ancestors was finally realised. How was this legitimised? We must examine two areas. First, there were the actual relations of power and domination which have been discussed above — what resources, human, natural or in combination, were important for control. Hand in hand with this runs the second area: ideology (discussed by Larrain 1979 & 1982 where this approach is considered to be Marxist and in Miller & Tilley 1984b). Through ideology actual relationships of power are given legitimacy and masked by reference to some 'natural order' which makes these relationships of power seem fundamental, unchallengeable and themselves natural. There are two principal ways in which this was achieved. The first was through competition between lineages. The claim seems to have been made that some ancestors were more important than others. In Orkney some tombs were deliberately slighted (Sharples forthcoming) and others had bones removed from them (Richards, C: pers comm). The first instance would suggest deliberate removal of the rights of a local group and its control by another. The removal of bones from a tomb, probably but not certainly to be placed in another tomb, seems again to suggest the subsuming of one group by another. Both were essentially a deliberate attempt to

3.1 *Stone circle at Castlerigg, Cumberland*

re-write the history of the lineage and show that claims through the ancestors were being manipulated. The 'facts' of who had rights to what were consequently changed. The second means by which dominant groups legitimised their rule was at a regional level and to understand this we must re-examine group affiliation. Someone from Kirkcaldy, Fife, Scotland nowadays has allegiances to those three increasingly larger areas — local, regional and national. In the late third millennium bc the importance of this larger regional area was emphasised and regional identities seems to have been deliberately developed. It had always been there, seen most obviously in the coherency of the styles of tombs that were built — Clyde cairns (Henshall 1972, 15-110), Cotswold-Severn tombs (Darvill 1982), etc. The new element is the construction of large communal monuments — henges, cursūs and stone circles — which reflect regional not local groups. It will be shown that some of these monuments incorporate aspects which are attempts to merge them with the 'natural' landscape, to encourage in effect the idea that they are themselves natural. They are open-air monuments, large in scale and often located in stunning positions where their relationships to land, water or sky can hardly have been avoided by their users (illustration 3.1). It is through these regional monuments that the leaders justified their power. Local problems could be controlled by re-writing the history of the ancestors but real power now required the control of a larger area and the ancestors were too localised. Claims had now, therefore, to be made to the 'gods', the 'natural' powers of the world, who were ranked above human and ancestral claims. By encouraging and structuring regional identity, individual leaders gained control of larger areas and greater human and natural resources. By claiming authority higher than that of the ancestors and, no doubt, restricting and controlling access to the gods by presenting themselves as appropriate mediators, leaders became more powerful and perhaps distanced themselves more and more from everyday work.

Communal monuments for the living

The modern belief that the sacred and secular are two separate areas of life is not one which elucidates the past. Most religious and spiritual groups regard life as a unity and even those who do not participate in organised religion regard their own lives as a whole. In order to understand the past it is necessary to assume that all the activities of life were conceived within a cosmology alien to our own but which, nonetheless, treated all its aspects as unified. We must then look to see whether there are 'ritual' objects, monuments or places set apart from settlement sites or within them and investigate whether and how they are different.

Communal burial places are for the dead and the ancestors but it is only within the *living* community that such ideas exist. The dead cannot bury themselves; the ancestors do not exist without being called upon by the living. Thus the communal tombs are monuments for the living and for their beliefs about and use of the dead (cf. Fleming 1973a, 189). There are, however, other monuments alluded to, stone circles, henges and cursūs which are not primarily burial places. These are usually described as 'ritual' sites. This term is sometimes used to encompass activities which have nothing to do with the production of food but here we use it to describe activities which relate to the reinforcement of cosmology/world view, the continuation of power and its legitimation, and the movement of a person from one status in society to another.

As will be discussed later the scale of these monuments can be astonishing. The amount of time, effort and co-ordination involved is massive and this has clear implications for the power of the leaders, their ability to motivate those doing the physical work and the acceptance of their authority and special relationship with the gods. It is assumed here that the wider community was willing to work on these projects but there may also have been some form of coercion involved. This need not necessarily have taken the extreme form of forced labour or slavery but perhaps involved the employment of more subtle means, such as finding favour with the gods or appeasing them in order to improve or maintain fertility or superiority over other communities. Different strategies seem to have been adopted in different regions of Britain and some of these will be discussed below.

Monumentality

It has been suggested that the building of communal monuments was a deliberate strategy by those holding power to maintain and increase control over larger areas. Some work has been undertaken to look at other societies and investigate when such monumentality becomes important (Bradley 1984, 73-74; Cherry 1978). Two occasions are suggested: first, while societies are forming and developing and secondly when a society is collapsing. Both are viewed as times of crisis when communal effort is used to weld society together. It must be noted that such long term ideas as 'development' and 'collapse' can only be discussed after an event and analysed in retrospect. They do not form part of the conscious and deliberate strategies of the individuals or groups involved although this is not to deny that contemporaries in any society often perceived them as collapsing or developing. There are always people who will take this view. For example, the government of the day see their policies as development while the opposition perceive them to be collapse and this is the case whatever party is in power. In a sense, things are always in a state of crisis since the potential directions that social organisation (and disorganisation) can take are myriad. What we see, then, at times when large monuments were built is a particular ideology beoming dominant within which such monuments are believed to be necessary. Viewed in retrospect their building does seem to coincide with periods of change.

Our earliest examples of such monuments are the causewayed enclosures (illustration 3.2). These consist of a roughly circular area of land surrounded by one or more ditches and usually banks which both have breaks in them, the causeways. Their distribution is concentrated in southern England, East Anglia and the Midlands (Palmer 1976), some have clear evidence of settlement (eg. Hembury: Liddell 1935 and Orsett:

3.2 *Causewayed enclosure at Knap Hill, Wiltshire*

Hedges, J & Buckley 1978) and a number had been attacked during their occupation (eg. Crickley Hill: Dixon 1981). These were probably high status settlements and although smaller scale settlements also existed they are now represented in the archaeological record only by scatters of worked flint, pottery and the occasional pit or post hole. The causewayed enclosures would have acted as a focus for the larger community, perhaps in the way that a market town does for the surrounding area. Several have a 'ritual' aspect. Hambledon Hill, Dorset, England (Mercer 1980, 30) has skulls placed in the bottom of the ditches and some complete burials. Refuse too had been thrown into the ditch and on other sites (eg. Windmill Hill: Smith, I F 1965, 9) it has been suggested that this is not ordinary domestic rubbish but the product of ritual feasting and other activities. These English sites seem to be the first manifestation of an emerging regional identity, acting as ceremonial centres as well as settlements and places where goods were brought for exchange. Several are situated near to quarry sites for lithic raw materials (Care 1982). Renfrew has argued (1973, 547-49) that in Wessex they seem to be located in such a way that they are surrounded by definable territories with several long barrows within this territory, although not all find his arguments convincing (Braithwaite 1984, 96). Whether or not they had definable territories, these enclosures do seem to show the first development of a hierarchy which stands above ancestral claims and it is not altogether surprising, therefore, to find human burials and in particular the most potent of human bones, the skull, placed in them in order to legitimate such developments.

Individual areas of Britain developed in a variety of ways and at different rates. It is very important to realise this is nothing to do with backwardness but is the result of people with access to different resources following alternative strategies in order to maintain control. In some areas there were major challenges from other groups and this is presumably what is reflected in the attacks on some of the causewayed enclosures and related complexes (eg. Crickley Hill: Dixon 1981 and Carn Brea: Mercer 1981a, 67-69). Warfare is not the only type of challenge for then, as now, economic activity and control of important resources proved a most effective way of competing. We see such attitudes in the proximity of some of the enclosures to quarry sites for flint and the apparent control of the distribution of particular types of pottery (Peacock 1969).

Late Third Millennium bc Developments

The deliberate manipulation of regional identity meant that different areas sought to control the present and future through various solutions. In Scotland there is no evidence for causewayed enclosures comparable to those we have just been discussing but instead from *c.* 2600 bc there was developed a type of monument known as a henge. These monuments, which also occur in areas of England, are now defined as being a roughly circular area surrounded by a ditch with an external bank and having one or more breaks in the ditch and bank forming entrances. Frequently there are additional internal features such as circles of timber or stone, pits or sometimes burials. The name derives from the most famous example, Stonehenge (although the word actually means 'hanging stone' it has been adopted as a technical archaeological term). Stonehenge is discussed below for its history is long and complex and quite atypical for most communal monuments. Suffice to say at this stage that in its earliest days it was a simple monument in comparison with the later elaboration made on the site.

In order to understand these developments better we shall focus on Orkney. Recent studies (Renfrew 1979; 1985; Fraser 1983; Hedges, J W 1983; 1984) have looked in detail at the island group and our knowledge of the archaeology of this geographically and socially defined region is comparatively good. Bradley (1984, 58-59)) has argued that Orkney was an innovating area which influenced developments throughout Britain, even regions like Wessex which were physically remote from the Orcadian perspective.

At present there are 77 known chamber tombs on Orkney (Henshall 1985, 115-17) although this must be lower than the original number. Fraser (1983, 324) argues that some may well be buried under peat and the examples of The Howe (Smith, B: pers comm) and Pierowall Quarry (Sharples forthcoming) show that others have been destroyed, incorporated in later monuments or not yet discovered. Despite this number of tombs there are only two henges, the Stones of Stenness (Ritchie, J N G 1976) and the Ring of Brodgar (Renfrew 1979, 39-43), both with stone circles inside. They are located in the West Mainland, in close proximity to one another on promontories which jut out at the junction between the Lochs of Stenness and Harray. There are only 1.4 km apart and the peninsulae are now joined by a short bridge (illustration 3.3). Several important points should be noted about these henges. Their location is central to some of the richest agricultural land in the West Mainland. They command distant views of the surrounding country. They are near the most elaborate chamber tomb in Orkney, Maeshowe, a virtuoso construction. The amount of effort involved in their construction is estimated as *c.* 50000-80000 worker hours some 5-8 times that estimated for a large chamber tomb (summarised in Fraser 1983, figure 14.1). The date of the construction of the Stones of Stenness is *c.* 2400 bc. The placing of burials in tombs seems to tail off from *c.* 2250 bc (cf. Renfrew & Buteux 1985). All this implies that around 2400 bc the regional identity of Orkney was confirmed through a major communal effort to create monuments in important places in the physical landscape

3.3 The Stones of Stenness (on the left)
and the Ring of Brodgar (on the right)
with Maeshowe in the foreground,
Orkney (lithograph by A Gibb 1861)

(illustration 3.4). They represent the whole island group, not just a particular island, and they are at a level above the ancestors. Open to the sky and with spectacular stone settings they appeal to the 'natural order' and the 'gods'.

In Orkney this development took place without any need to challenge the ancestors directly, the power that derived from them was simply superseded and outmanoeuvred. In other areas a different strategy was followed. At Newgrange, Co Meath, Ireland a spectacular chamber tomb was surrounded with a stone circle/henge and the astonishing circle and complex of stone alignments at Callanish, Lewis, Scotland (illustration 3.5-7) was centred on a chamber tomb (see O'Kelly 1982, 82-83 and Ashmore 1984, 27-28 for the paucity of evidence concerning these sequences). Such actions represent the re-writing of history, a re-interpretation and manipulation of the old order to justify the new. It is the same sort of deliberate manipulation that we see in the re-naming of towns and cities (St Petersburg/Petrograd — Leningrad; Salisbury — Harare) or even in the streets and bridges (in Lisbon, the Salazar Bridge became the 25th April Bridge). Two alternatives are possible in such circumstances. A monument can be destroyed, as at Pierowall Quarry,

3.4 *Aerial view of the Ring of Brodgar, Orkney*

3.5 *Aerial view of the stone circle, chambered cairn and alignments at Callanish, Lewis*

3.6 The central area at Callanish

Westray, Orkney, or it can be incorporated in a new structure and the new ideology. The name changes mentioned are one example of modern manipulation. In prehistory we can only note these changes which involve the physical re-interpretation of monuments. Stonehenge and its numerous re-buildings and re-designs must be the classic example.

Later still in some areas, for example Wessex (RCHME 1979, ix-x; Richards, J 1982), the Boyne Valley, Ireland, and Kilmartin, Scotland, there seem to have developed 'ritual landscapes'. These are areas where virtually all the activity is non-domestic and related to the gods. There are henges, stone circles and standing stones, built near earlier burial places, and which become the focus for later burial mounds. Such a development would seem to be a natural extension of the idea of a henge which has a central area separated off and in part obscured by the external bank. In contrast to the causewayed enclosures henges are not of the people but are of the gods and those powerful groups who draw their authority from them. These ritual landscapes seem to be a similar special area, set apart and perhaps 'holy'. Such things do not come through claims on the ancestors but from the deliberate control of the land and people at a regional level. Note, for example, the expression of regional as well as

individual power in Glasgow's Necropolis, a nineteenth-century AD ritual landscape (illustration 3.8).

There has been considerable debate about the astronomical significance of stone circles and standing stones (Thom 1971; MacKie 1977, 71-105; Ruggles & Whittle 1981; Thorpe, I J 1983). What is clear is that some monuments are located and aligned on important solar and lunar events. The midsummer sun shines down the passage at the tomb of Newgrange through a specially built box (O'Kelly 1982, 123-26), Maeshowe is reported to have its passage aligned on the midwinter sunset and the Clava Cairns in the Inverness area of Scotland are aligned on major phases of the moon (Burl 1981). In other monuments particular parts of the landscape are the focus of attention. The recumbent stone circles of North East Scotland (Burl 1970) have a horizontal stone with two upright flankers while the stones forming the circle tend to diminish in height towards the side opposite the recumbent. This directs attention towards particular parts of the landscape viewed from inside the circle, quite often a distant range of hills fronted by prime agricultural land (illustration 3.9-10). All this seems to be a re-inforcement of the claim on the gods of nature by placing monuments and in some cases symbols (illustration 3.11) in areas with views of important places and by aligning stones on major astronomical events. It is an attempt to establish the monument as part of the status quo, as part of the natural timeless universe.

However we view them, the people who designed these monuments and exercised the authority to have them built must have had a special status in society. MacKie (1977, 222-26) has written of a 'theocracy' which may well be an appropriate way of conceiving of them although the evidence he uses to support his argument is dubious. That there were leaders of some sort throughout the third and second millennia bc is likely but the way they claimed their authority varied. The call on the gods and the mediation and control of special understanding and knowledge that goes with it marked these people as separate. Whether access to the group was by lineage, age, sex, training or some combination of these, the consequence was that a society which had cohered because of ancestral claims was now held together because of the power of a group of individuals or an individual. In this way power was gradually seen as in the hands of individuals and was later acknowledged as such.

Symbols for the Living and Symbols for the Dead

We have seen in the Introduction how objects and designs are used to signal group affiliations and status. Indeed such elements are important features in our capitalist consumer society. In pre-capitalist societies, such consumerism is not seen. This is not to say that there was no competition for symbols in the third and second millennia bc nor is it to be assumed that variety or a range of choice about what to wear or what to do was absent. It is simply that the scale of choices available was very restricted. We do not know how easy it was to move from one community to another. Marriage partners would certainly have been

3.7 (facing page) Part of the stone alignments at Callanish

3.8 *(facing page) A modern ritual landscape: The Necropolis, Glasgow*

3.9 *Recumbent stone circle at Loanhead of Daviot, Aberdeenshire. General view from outside the circle looking towards the recumbent*

exchanged but we must not think of mobility in modern terms. Equally, we do not know how power was transferred, whether by lineage (as in the case of our monarchy) or by convincing one's 'equals' that one was the best and most suitable person (our democracy). Whatever actual system was involved it is clear that at this time there was a developing social stratification.

A distinction between types of symbol as we now observe them was proposed in the Introduction between those where the acquisition conferred status and others which were reflections of the authority vested in the individual but not the means by which that authority was established. The circumstances in the third and second millennia bc are not directly comparable since, as has already been said, it was not a consumer society like our own but the analogy works if we view access to symbols in terms of access to raw materials, technology and ideas. One of the phenomena of the neolithic which has sometimes confused archaeologists is the axe trade. Polished stone axes are characteristic of this period and they are frequently made from locally available stone or flint. There were, however, axe factories throughout Britain. The products of some of these factories are found tens and hundreds of miles from their geological source (Cummins 1979, 1980). Large numbers of axes from Langdale Pike in Cumbria are found in Yorkshire and there is a concentration of Cornish axes in Essex. At Cairnpapple Hill, West Lothian, Scotland fragments of two axes were found, one from North

Wales and the other from Cumbria (catalogue number 24). Bradley (1984, 55-56, figure 3.4) has shown that axes from these three sources (Cornwall, North Wales and Cumbria) have high concentrations in areas towards the limits of their distribution. Since we believe that the movement of the axes was probably from hand to hand and group to group, perhaps in gift exchanges, and that the organisation of the production of the axes was not under direct political control, it seems

3.10 *Recumbent stone circle at Old Keig, Aberdeenshire. View over the recumbent of the surrounding countryside*

likely that the final location of the axes represents political control either
of the movement of the axes or deriving from the areas acting as a magnet
for these exotic items (Bradley 1984, 55; Renfrew 1977, 86).

The example of the distribution of axes makes it clear that long
distance networks existed in Britain which did not rely on
producer-consumer relations as we view them. What it seems to represent
is the deliberate and selective acquisition of particular types of axes by

groups in specific regions. This is analogous with the first type of symbol. Changing styles of pottery can be seen in a similar way but in this case the ability to innovate, develop and acquire high status goods is more open to the ambitious. If a certain form of vessel is associated with those holding power, an ambitious group can make use of local clay sources and local skills to copy the product and enhance itself by association. The difference with axes is that to get an exotic axe one would have to be of sufficient status in the first place to merit a position in the exchange network.

The symbolic aspect of objects whose distribution is controlled is relatively secure whereas those which can be copied can be manipulated by anyone with the courage and ability to break into the system. But both these examples are to do with acquisition. What of those objects which embody authority? There may well be some confusion between the two if, for example, a symbol of authority can be copied. This, however, is less important provided that it is realised that authority is not simply imposed but has to be acknowledged by those over whom authority is taken. A five year old boy wearing field marshal's clothing is unlikely to be acknowledged as a field marshal by soldiers. There is a sense in which the symbols carry the authority and give it to the wielder of the symbols but only if certain conditions are met.

There are two important aspects to these symbols in the third millennium bc. First the development of complex and prestigious artefacts and second, the use of decoration which consists of non-representational art. It is interesting to see how these two groups were used and deposited. The title of this section is intended to show that the two areas are not separate but there are variations. Some objects are known only from settlement sites and as isolated finds but others occur only in burials. Some have been found in both situations. As for the decorative art, this falls into two categories: the use of spiral designs and the use of linear geometrical motifs. These two elements of objects and design link the worlds of the living and the dead in important ways.

First we shall examine decorative art. The use of curvilinear, in some instances spiral, designs is well known from Irish and Breton tombs eg. Newgrange and Gavrinis and is well illustrated in such monumental art (illustration 3.12-13). Apart from decorated stones within the chambers there are also stones which carry these motifs in a kerb around the outside of the Irish tombs. These seem to delineate and emphasise the sacred area and perhaps the best interpretation of the art is that it enhances the boundaries between the living world and that of the dead. We do not know the meaning of the motifs used but we can gain an idea of their significance by studying how they were used. Spiral decoration is also known from chamber tombs in Orkney at the tombs of Eday Manse (illustration 3.14) and Pierowall (catalogue number 56). The large decorated slabs have both been interpreted as lintels — the former at the entrance to a cell within the tomb and the latter at the entrance to the whole tomb itself. Entrances are, of course, very important features since they are boundaries between two areas and that these were sometimes specially marked should be no surprise. What is unusual is that spirals are also used on a number of smaller objects (illustrations 3.15-17) such as

3.11 *(facing page) Highly decorated stone surface in a spectacular location at Ormaig, Kilmartin, Argyll*

3.12 *The decorated kerb stone at the entrance to the chamber tomb at Newgrange, Co. Meath, Ireland*

3.13 *Detail of the decoration on stones within the chamber tomb at Gavrinis, Morbihan, France*

3.14 *Decorated stone from Eday Manse, Eday, Orkney (55)*

3.15 *Antler macehead from Garboldisham, Norfolk (45)*

3.16 *(below) Stone ball from Towie, Aberdeenshire (42)*

3.17 *(facing page) Decorated flint macehead from the chamber tomb at Knowth, Co Meath, Ireland*

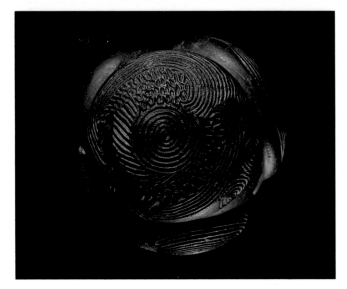

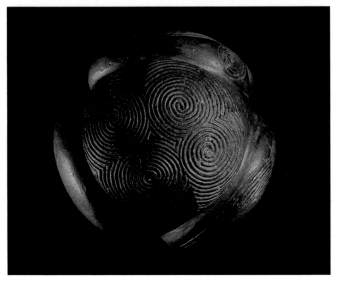

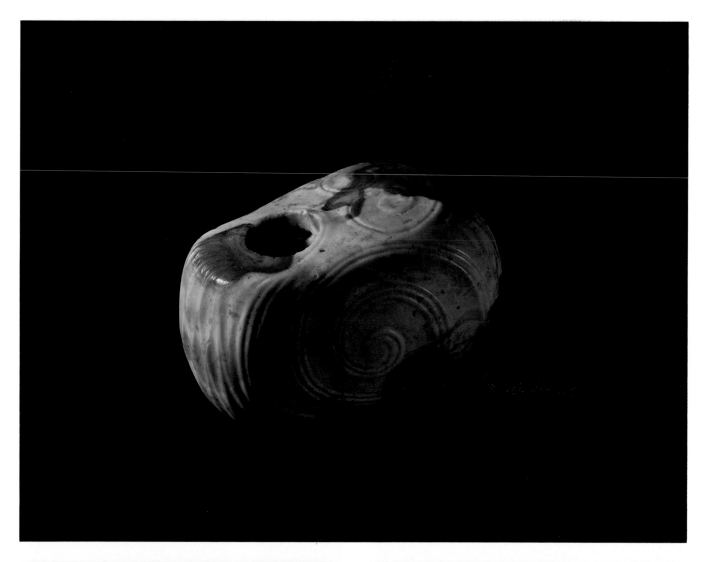

3.18 Decorated stone from Skara Brae, Orkney (26.6)

3.19 Decorated pottery from Durrington Walls, Wiltshire (20.7)

3.20 Decorated pottery from Skara Brae, Orkney (26.7)

3.21 (facing page) Stone objects from Quoyness, Sanday, Orkney (8.1-2)

3.22 (facing page) Stone object from Skara Brae, Orkney (26.5)

the Garboldisham macehead, the Towie stone ball and the Knowth macehead (Eogan 1983; Eogan & Richardson 1982). All are exceptionally well made and the Towie ball and Knowth macehead in particular are both outstanding pieces of craftsmanship. None are likely to have been utilitarian objects and all appear to be ceremonial symbols enhanced by the use of spiral decoration.

A similar case can be made for linear geometric art. This is known from several large decorated stones from Skara Brae (illustration 3.18) and from smaller objects at the same site (catalogue numbers 26.1, .3-.4). The use of triangles, lozenges and squares is also known from the chamber

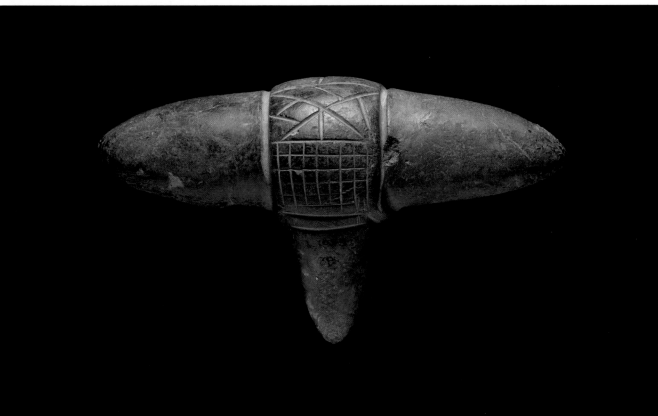

tombs and, indeed, grooved ware pottery carries some of the same motifs (illustration 3.19). There does tend to be a concentration of linear decoration on settlement and other sites, with spiral ornament being associated with tombs and communal monuments. Such items as the spirally decorated pottery from Skara Brae shows, however, that this is not a strict division (illustration 3.20).

Other, more unusual objects, are represented on both sites for the living and the dead. For example, the T-shaped stone object, the cylindrical stone object and the bone pin from the cairn at Quoyness, Sanday, Orkney find their closest parallels in material from the settlement at Skara Brae (illustrations 3.21-22). Again, the best known associations for pestle maceheads from Orkney are from the settlements at Rinyo, Rousay, Orkney (Childe & Grant 1947, 41) and Skara Brae and the chamber tomb at Taversoe Tuick, Rousay, Orkney (Turner 1903, 77; Grant 1939, 164 — illustration 3.23).

It is not that objects and types of art are simply being used by the living for themselves and then for the dead. These are very special things and would have been accessible only to a few people. Since the design of the cairns and the associated communal monuments was in the control of restricted groups of people, surely we are seeing here an attempt to represent this control and at the same time establish authority over the world of the dead and the natural world. To put it more simply, types of decoration are associated with the natural and spirit worlds. When these are used on quite small artefacts and in settlements, they are being used by individuals as symbols of power and authority over those worlds and, through this legitimising authority, over the temporal world. The symbols of the gods can only safely be entrusted to those who have favour with the gods and can mediate with them.

The development of this particular trend is really the culmination of the production of symbols of status which can be traced back to the early third millennium bc and perhaps before that. Symbols of status are objects which represent the position of the wearer or wielder of the symbol. These may be representative or abstract. Jadeite axes and finely polished or edge polished flint axes are not utilitarian items (illustrations

3.23 Macehead from the chamber tomb at Taversoe Tuick, Rousay, Orkney

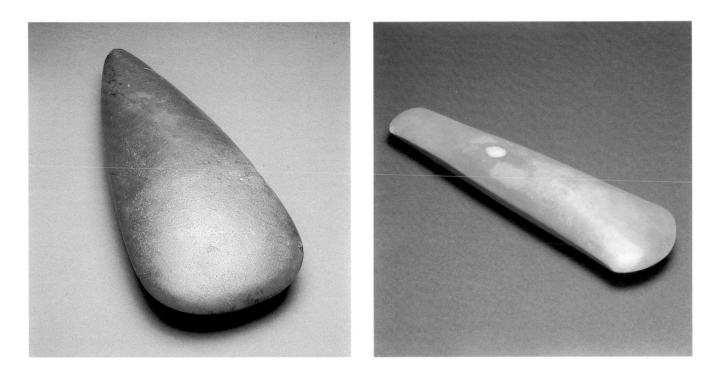

3.24 *Jadeite axe from Cornwall (35)*

3.25 *Flint axe from Gilmerton, East Lothian (36)*

3.26 *Carved stone balls from Balallan, Lewis (left: 40), Fyvie, Aberdeenshire (centre: 41) and Turriff, Aberdeenshire (right: 43)*

3.24-25). They are high class versions of the everyday axe but made in special materials and finely finished. They often have blunt edges and shapes which would have made them totally impractical for use in chopping wood or digging the ground. They do, therefore, represent utilitarian axes but are of such a high grade that they are practically useless except as deliberate statements of status. The carved stone balls are decorative abstract items (illustration 3.26). They were not intended as practical objects but seem to embody the power of the individual who held them. The range of highly decorated objects from Skara Brae should be seen in the same way.

We have, therefore, a range of prestigious objects set aside from those used in daily work by being made from rare materials, worked with elaborate skill or being of a form which is non-utilitarian. Clearly, for these to retain their symbolic meaning of power, access to them must have been restricted. These objects allowed those who possessed them to

3.27 *Carved stone objects from Skara Brae, Orkney (from left to right 26.1, 26.3, 26.4)*

3.28 *Bone and ivory pendants from Skara Brae, Orkney (26.11 left and 26.10 right)*

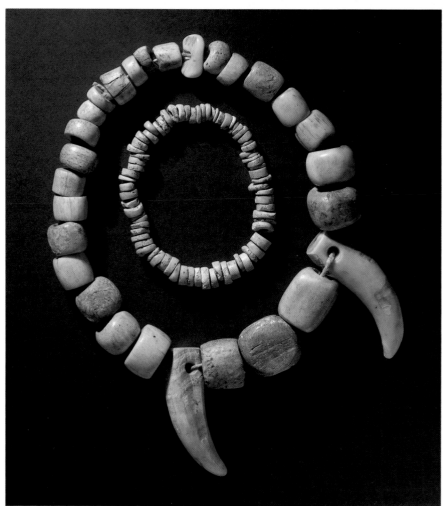

3.29 *Bone and ivory beads from Skara Brae, Orkney (26.8 outer and 26.9 inner)*

legitimise their position of power and are the symbols of mediation with the gods and control over such things as marriage alliances, decision making, exchange contacts, etc.

When we examine the circumstances in which these objects are found, there are interesting and consistent differences between the various types of objects and the place of their deposition. Jadeite axes are known both as isolated finds and hoards, although interestingly a fragment from such an axe was found in the forecourt blocking at the chambered tomb of Cairnholy I, Kirkcudbrightshire, Scotland (Piggott, S & Powell 1949, 121, 137-39).

Stone maceheads are known from some settlement sites, communal tombs and as isolated finds. Carved stone balls have been found in some settlements but mainly as isolated finds. It seems clear from the way these particular objects were deposited that the jadeite axes and stone balls were not seen as objects which could be placed with burials. The only settlement which has stone balls is Skara Brae and, as has already been said, there are other prestigious items from that site notably carved stone objects as well as fine pendants and necklaces of bone beads. The major group of stone objects was found together as was the vast bulk of the beads and pendants (illustrations 3.27-29). This seems to represent either hoarding of the objects or some other form of deliberate control over them to restrict access.

It is useful to consider two examples of finds of jadeite axes, the two found together at Cunzierton and the one found under a board beside the

3.30 Jadeite axes from Cunzierton, Roxburghshire (35.1 left and 35.2 right) and Greenlawdean, Berwickshire (centre: 37)

3.31 Jadeite axe from Sweet Track, Somerset (34)

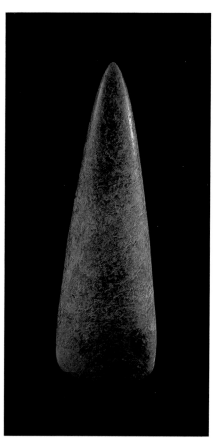

Sweet Track, Somerset (illustrations 3.30-31). In both circumstances they are fine unused objects and they seem to have been deliberately buried in a pristine state. These are not accidental losses nor does it seem that they were hidden in times of danger. Although as symbols of power these objects were restricted to a small number of individuals, they were probably held on behalf of the community since it is clear they were not buried with individuals and are not therefore to be considered as private possessions. Nevertheless, these people with power were the ones who determined how they were used and what happened to them. What we see at Skara Brae is the control of prestigious items within the settlement by keeping them in particular places. They were not accessible to the whole community. As for the jadeite axes and their deposition, there are circumstances of great display and ritual where conspicuous consumption and ritual destruction of wealth takes place. We believe that social status between groups was maintained by the exchange of prestigious gifts but even greater status can be achieved by giving things up to the gods, either by destroying them or rendering them totally inaccessible. People still give gifts of money and fine objects to the church. What is happening here is that the status of an individual is enhanced not by keeping prestigious objects but by giving them away. The ultimate form of this is to give it away to the gods where it is not an exchange of an axe for an axe or a feast for feast but one in which the return is understood, perhaps fertility or success. Such depositions of votive goods must have been spectacular for they are not something which would be hidden but would require the presence of the whole community to witness and acknowledge the power of one who could talk with the gods and gain power by conspicuously removing from circulation the very objects which symbolise that power. This is a theme to which we shall return.

Thus from the finds at Skara Brae and the examples of early hoards, we see how the symbols of power can be restricted or even totally removed from the networks of exchange. Maceheads seem to have been used in a different way and represent the clearest beginning of a trend towards the personal control of such prestige items. Some are known from the settlement sites of Skara Brae and Rinyo and were presumably used in the same way as necklaces and stone balls. But maceheads seem to be the first high status artefacts which are also regularly included with burials both in communal tombs and in individual burials. Maceheads have been found in the communal tombs at Ormegill, Caithness and Tormore, Arran (illustration 3.32). An especially elaborate one comes as we have seen from the tomb at Knowth, Co Meath, Ireland. It belongs to a decorated group of maceheads called the Maesmore type after the first one found. The one from Knowth is particularly important as it has not only the faceted lozenge decoration typical of the series but also spiral symbols on it. It seems clear that when such symbols of power are deposited in tombs they are no longer being viewed as communal property but the possession of individuals buried in the tombs. In the next section we shall discuss individual burials and the importance of the maceheads will be stressed.

This trend for special objects to be included in the tombs has already been mentioned and it seems that, in the later tomb burials at least, the

3.32 *Maceheads from chamber tombs at Ormiegill, Caithness (left: 7.6), and Tormore, Arran (right: 9.4)*

artefacts included with the burials were identified with individuals. The pumice pendant from Unival, North Uist (catalogue number 11) and the jet beads from Eyford and Notgrove, Gloucestershire (catalogue numbers 3-4) are all attributable to particular bodies — specific grave goods placed with one body. This contrasts strongly with the communal goods of the ancestors and reflects the authority of those individuals within the community.

Early Individual Burials

Kinnes (1979) has shown that the individual burial tradition was already well established in the third millennium bc. There was always a choice as to whether to bury the dead in communal places or separately. In areas such as Orkney, around the Severn and in Ireland, the communal tradition was very strong. In Derbyshire and Yorkshire, however, there was more emphasis on individual burial and this at a time when in other regions communal tombs were still being built. Clearly different strategies were being followed by the leaders in Derbyshire and Yorkshire. Their personal power was not of the kind which had to be masked behind the ancestors.

At the time when causewayed enclosures were being built in Southern England and the Midlands, we might expect to see in Northern England the development of similar types of regional identity and controlled access to resources. The course it took was different. It is difficult to say whether the amalgamation of groups was less successful in the North but this seems possible. What does seem to have happened is that the individuals were able to control power themselves, no doubt using the ancestors and then the gods as legitimation, but did not need to be seen as representing the wider group. It is therefore, in Yorkshire and Derbyshire

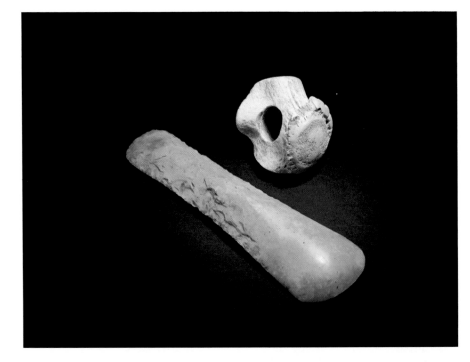

3.33 *Early individual burial, Burial 5, Duggleby Howe, Yorkshire (28.1-2)*

3.34 *Part of the grave group from an early individual burial at Liff's Lowe, Derbyshire (comprising from left to right, foreground 30.2, 30.1, 30.6, 30.9 and background 30.8, 30.9)*

that individual burials in shafts, pits or cists covered by mounds are seen to develop most quickly and these individuals are buried with prestigious objects. These must be seen as the personal property of the individual representing their status and power in the community.

It is interesting to examine the objects which were included with these individual burials; some of them are already familiar from other types of deposits in other areas.

Maceheads have already been mentioned. Roe (1968) has argued that stone maceheads developed from crown antler examples. The decorated antler macehead from Garboldisham has already been discussed but the regular associations of antler maceheads are in these early individual burials eg. Duggleby Howe burial 5, and Liff's Lowe (illustrations 3.33-34). These are not practical objects but symbols of status. Included in both these burials were also examples of the polished-edge axes/adzes. These again are types of object not intended for everyday work. They are high quality pieces of craftsmanship of the status which elsewhere were being ceremonially deposited in hoards but in the North and East of England were disposed of in a different way through burial. The inclusion of boar's tusks in individual graves is also prestigious: symbols of a wild, fierce animal, triumphs of the hunt and by analogy, statements of the power and prestige of the individual buried.

It must be emphasised that there are very important distinctions between the burial of an individual with grave goods in a barrow and the incorporation of a body with others in a communal tomb. The fact that the body remains intact after death and is not joined with others suggests that the individual is seen as retaining personal existence and does not merge with the ancestors. The inclusion of objects with the burial implies that they were seen as personal items and when these are symbols of power they indicate the status of the individual. There is also the question of scale in the burial places. Communal tombs are usually much larger than the individual burial mound but they were built to house the dead and the ancestors of a community. A barrow or cairn raised over a single burial is much smaller but it represents a far greater effort for one person. Liff's Lowe seems to have contained a single burial. Duggleby Howe (catalogue number 28) had 68 (Kinnes *et al* 1983), and 53 of these formed a later cremation cemetery dug into the top of the mound. Of the remaining 15, 4 are important burials with grave goods. The primary burial was an adult male who had a pottery vessel and flint objects interred with him. This burial was placed at the bottom of a shaft which was refilled and had three other burials placed in it. On top was placed burial 5 with an adze, arrowhead and antler macehead. Beside this was an adult with a fine, highly polished flint knife. Another adult was placed in a shallow hollow nearby and had a flint arrowhead, flaked knife, a bone pin, boar's tusks and beaver teeth. The rest of the burials are children or infants apart from one adolescent and an adult. The mound itself is in the centre of what appears to be a causewayed enclosure. Kinnes (in Kinnes *et al* 1983, 96) argues that the mound itself is a late feature. How are we to interpret such complexity in burial rites? It is tempting to argue that the primary burial and those low in the shaft represent the very beginning of single burial tradition and that it indicates the course of subsequent developments in Yorkshire and Derbyshire. The other three important burials at Duggleby Howe have rich and prestigious grave goods and are exactly the type of burial we would expect if individual leaders were in control of a system which recognised their personal authority and power.

The burial from Whitegrounds, Yorkshire is another important example (illustration 3.35). This adult male was placed in the centre of a previously existing burial cairn and had a jet slider and a Duggleby/Seamer axe with him. A barrow was subsequently raised to cover this body and the previous cairn. A radiocarbon date of 2570 bc ± 90 (Har-5587) has been obtained from the bone. This makes it quite clear that in Derbyshire and Yorkshire individual power was manifested in a way which was hidden elsewhere in Britain for a further few hundred years. A jet slider, for example was associated with the late phases in the chamber tomb at Beacharra, Argyll but not with a particular individual and the majority of such sliders (illustration 3.36) outwith North East England are not associated with burials at all except for that at Stanton Harcourt, Oxfordshire.

Other burial mounds have contained astonishing finds like the child burial with highly decorated drum-like objects of chalk from Folkton, Yorkshire (illustration 3.37). In other areas, occasional individual burials of the same general sort are known although the finds from Greenbrae, Aberdeenshire did not certainly accompany a burial (illustration 3.38).

Kinnes (1979) has shown that individual burial traditions were far more widespread than was previously appreciated. If we are to interpret this properly we must, however, concentrate on the particular regions in which this happens since the meaning and importance of the use of individual burial will vary over time and from place to place according to the strategies taken by the small groups who held and controlled power. The particular circumstances in North East England have been discussed.

3.35 Early individual burial from Whitegrounds, Yorkshire (31)

3.36 Jet sliders from Beacharra, Argyll (top: 12) and Skye (bottom: 13)

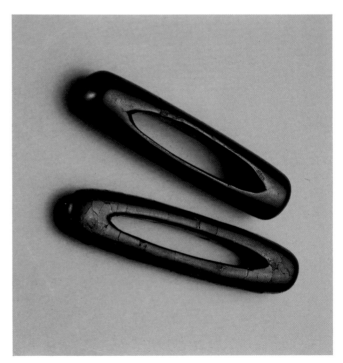

Elsewhere different solutions were being found to similar types of problems. One area where things seem to have been quite exceptional is Wessex. Since its place in the later third millennium and in the second millennium bc is important, it will be useful to examine what happened there and how its history varied from that of other regions.

Wessex and the Wessex Henges

Wessex has already been mentioned in terms of its early development of regional groups and the building of causewayed enclosures as well as other types of monument. It seems that the combination of causewayed enclosures, burial in non-megalithic long barrows and the later megalithic barrows and tombs were elements in a system which was strong and provided a secure basis for long term control of the area. The development of ritual landscapes in this area and the creation of massive ceremonial monuments, such as bank barrows and cūrsus, form a combination which reinforced this structure. Some reference has been made to Stonehenge and the development of henges in this area. This took a particularly striking course towards the end of the third millennium bc with the building of immense henge monuments. What was it in this area that was so different?

3.37 *Early individual burial from Folkton, Yorkshire (from left to right: 29.1, 29.3, 29.2)*

The soils of Wessex make rich agricultural land. There are good sources of flint and it is situated in the middle of a number of routes along which axes, pottery and other goods were moved. There are two ways of controlling important resources, one to control production and the other to control distribution. Clearly, the leaders in Wessex were able to control local agricultural production and the manufacture of implements made from the local flint. Because of its location, its inhabitants were also able to control the distribution of prestige *exotica* from other areas, thereby enhancing the importance of Wessex by comparison with nearby regions. The early development of large communal monuments where, no doubt, much of the overt power was shown, was instrumental in gaining and controlling these resources.

Such developments in Wessex meant a strong power base for the leaders there but it also tended to fossilise the system to such an extent that when changes took place elsewhere they constituted a real threat. The building of monuments like bank barrows and cūrsus show a scale of expenditure of effort unprecedented in Britain, indicating the amount of labour upon which the leaders could call. The early henge phase at

3.38 *? Early individual burial from Greenbrae, Cruden, Aberdeenshire (32)*

Stonehenge shows this type of monument was also being built there. The change from ancestors to gods noted in other areas of Britain was also taking place in Wessex but it seems that there was little development towards the individual control of symbols of power (Bradley 1984, 46). We have mentioned the early nature of such a system in Derbyshire and Yorkshire but one of the other areas where this happens is in the Thames Valley. Surely such a change in the ideology used to justify the control of power must have been a challenge to the social structure in nearby Wessex. What we see happening, then, in the late third millennium bc in Wessex is an intensification of monument building and in the scale of these monuments. The best examples are the five large henges — Durrington Walls (Wainwright & Longworth 1971), Mount Pleasant (Wainwright 1979), Marden (Wainwright, Evans & Longworth, 1971) Avebury (Burl 1979) and Dorchester, Dorset (Woodward, P: pers comm). These are monuments of staggering size and scale. The ditch alone at Durrington Walls, for example, is estimated to have taken 500,000 worker hours to dig. That at Avebury was $c.$ 15 m wide at the top and $c.$ 8 m deep (illustration 3.39) and the circumference of the circle is in the order of 1.5 km. Excavations at Durrington Walls and Mount Pleasant have shown that there were substantial wooden structures within these monuments as well. The stone circles at Avebury (illustration 3.40) were, of course, already known (cf. labour estimates in Startin & Bradley 1981).

The best way to view these monuments is as a backlash response of

3.39 *Modern re-excavation of the ditch at Avebury, Wiltshire in 1922, under the direction of H St George Gray, indicated just how much work was involved in digging it*

exceptional scale to the challenges to the system which were coming from nearby areas and perhaps also from continental Europe. The Wessex solution was to reinforce the prevailing ideology by maximising the control of labour and investing in the massive henges. Not long before, the major elaborations at Stonehenge had begun and the huge mound at Silbury Hill was started (Atkinson, R J C 1970).

Associated with the large Wessex henges is a type of pottery known as grooved ware. It has already been said that pottery as a symbol of status is a dangerous thing since it can be copied and can thus be taken over by groups who have little status in order to enhance themselves. From the middle of the third millennium bc to the end of it, grooved ware was a prestigious style of pottery taking over from the earlier important Peterborough styles (cf. Bradley 1984, figure 4.2). Grooved ware is well known from Orkney, Yorkshire, Essex and is also found in other areas of

3.40 *Aerial view of Avebury, Wiltshire with the stone avenue which runs from one of the entrances and, beyond, Silbury Hill*

Britain (Wainwright & Longworth 1971, 268-306; Manby 1974). It seems that in Wessex the leaders not only responded to challenge with a massive building programme but also with the adoption of a new style of pottery, both of which seem to have been earlier developments outside the region. This was the deliberate manipulation of symbols.

It seems clear that the Wessex problem was a challenge from other groups claiming a different type of authority. It has been suggested here that it was due to the effect of nearby developments but this is only part of the story. Contacts with the continent saw the introduction of objects of metal and of the pottery style known as beakers. These contacts were finally to provide an unstoppable challenge to the control of the Wessex oligarchies and to have a radical effect on the course of events in the rest of Britain.

STONEHENGE

Stonehenge (illustration 3.41) has been a source of interest, fascination and pilgrimage for thousands of years. It is one of the most famous prehistoric monuments in the world and has caught the modern imagination so much that in 1984 it attracted 639,604 visitors (almost 1½ times the population of Edinburgh 439,721), who came to study, marvel or 'feel the power' (figures supplied by Historic Buildings and Monuments Commission, England and Edinburgh District Council). Our decision to use it in the title of this book was not simply to relate our theme to a famous monument, but because the history of the building of Stonehenge is in many ways a reflection of the events we are here concerned with. We have already mentioned some monuments which were deliberately destroyed in the past because they did not fit the new ideology and others which had additions made to desanctify or reinterpret them. Stonehenge is the example *par excellence* of this since the first structure was built there *c.* 2410 bc and the last phase was finished *c.* 1240 bc. Moreover, it is still being interpreted in terms that are concerned with current attitudes and have nothing to do with those of its prehistoric creators — druidical site, source of earth power, etc.

Chippindale (1983) has studied the influence of and interest in the site through the centuries but far greater importance was accorded it in prehistory. That no other monument was of greater significance in the third and second millennia bc is reflected in the number of times it was re-planned and re-built and the ambitious nature of its designs. This is not to say that other henges, cairns or barrows were not major features in the landscape but in the case of Stonehenge it was *so* important that as power and its associated ideologies changed, this monument had to be re-built. It could not be ignored or simply re-interpreted without re-design. What follows is a brief summary of the complex story of the building of Stonehenge. Current views on the site are summarised by Professor R J C Atkinson (1978; 1979). Further study by Atkinson, Ehrenberg and Berridge is likely to change some of our ideas about the details. Other research (RCHME 1979; Richards, J 1982) has shown that the area around the monument forms an important ritual landscape of other

3.41 *Aerial view of Stonehenge, Wiltshire with the Avenue running from the entrance*

monuments from this period. Stonehenge itself became the focus for these and the people who controlled Stonehenge were masters of the worlds of the living, the dead and the gods.

The various stages of building and re-design are usually described in sequence as I-IV. These are not of equal duration but represent different structural phases (illustrations 3.42-43).

Period I. A penannular ditch was dug enclosing an area 90 m in diameter and the soil and chalk was made into a bank *c.* 1.8 m high, on the inside of the ditch. At the entrance, two stones were erected, one on each side, and beyond the entrance were placed a line of four timber posts with a lintel on top to act, perhaps, as a ceremonial gateway. A little further out a single stone, known as the 'Heel Stone' (illustration 3.44) was put up. Immediately inside the bank and running right round the interior were dug 56 pits *c.* 1 m wide and the same depth known as the

'Aubrey Holes'. These seem to have been dug and then almost immediately filled in. Several radiocarbon dates indicate that the outer ditch, at least, was dug around 2410 bc ± 40 (Evans, J G *et al* 1984; I-2328; BM-1617; BM-1583). A further radiocarbon date, 1848 bc ± 275 (C-602) suggests that, much later, the Aubrey Holes were cut into and had human cremations placed in them. Four stones which form the corners of a very accurate rectangle — the 'station stones' — were set up in Period I or perhaps slightly later. Two of them had ditches dug round them.

Period II. Around 1750 bc (1770 bc ± 100: HAR-2013; 1728 bc ± 68: BM-1164) the entrance was completely re-designed and the whole axis of the henge changed slightly, providing a better alignment with the rising of the midsummer sun. The entrance was widened by filling up part of the ditch with soil from the bank and a ditched 'Avenue' was constructed, running for 530 m in a straight line away from the henge. The two entrance stones and the timber gateway were removed and two single stones placed in line in the centre of the Avenue. A small ditch was dug round the Heel Stone and then filled up again. In the centre of the henge, work began on a double circle of bluestones which also gave greater prominence to the midsummer solstice by having additional stones inside the circle and a large single stone at the back of it, both in line with the Avenue. Less than three-quarters of the work was completed when the stones were removed and the holes filled in (1620 bc ± 110: I-2384).

Period III. Almost immediately work began on a new design (IIIa). This was itself changed twice (IIIb, IIIc), before the final monument as we know it was finished.
IIIa Large blocks of sarsen were dressed to make a circle of uprights linked by lintels kept in place by mortice and tenon joints (illustration 3.45). Within this were five trilithons (two uprights and a single lintel each) placed in a horseshoe-shape with its open end towards the Avenue. The radiocarbon date for the construction of the trilithons is 1720 bc ± 150 (BM-1720). In addition, two new stones were set up, side by side, in the entrance to the henge.
IIIb was an elaboration of IIIa. At least 20 of the bluestones which had previously been removed at the end of Period II were dressed and then erected in an oval setting within the sarsen horseshoe and at least two smaller versions of the trilithons were set up. Around the large sarsen circle, two additional circles of holes were dug, apparently to take rings using the rest of the bluestones which had earlier been removed. But again this work was never completed. A radiocarbon date for the abandonment of this project is 1240 bc ± 105 (I-2445).
IIIc (illustration 3.46)   The final re-organisation of the design saw the removal of the bluestone oval and the re-erection of 60 bluestones in a circle between the sarsen trilithons and circle. A very large bluestone slab was then set up in line with the Avenue at the back of the trilithon horseshoe. Some of the sarsen uprights were decorated with images of axes comparable to those from the Arreton hoard (catalogue number 142) and daggers.

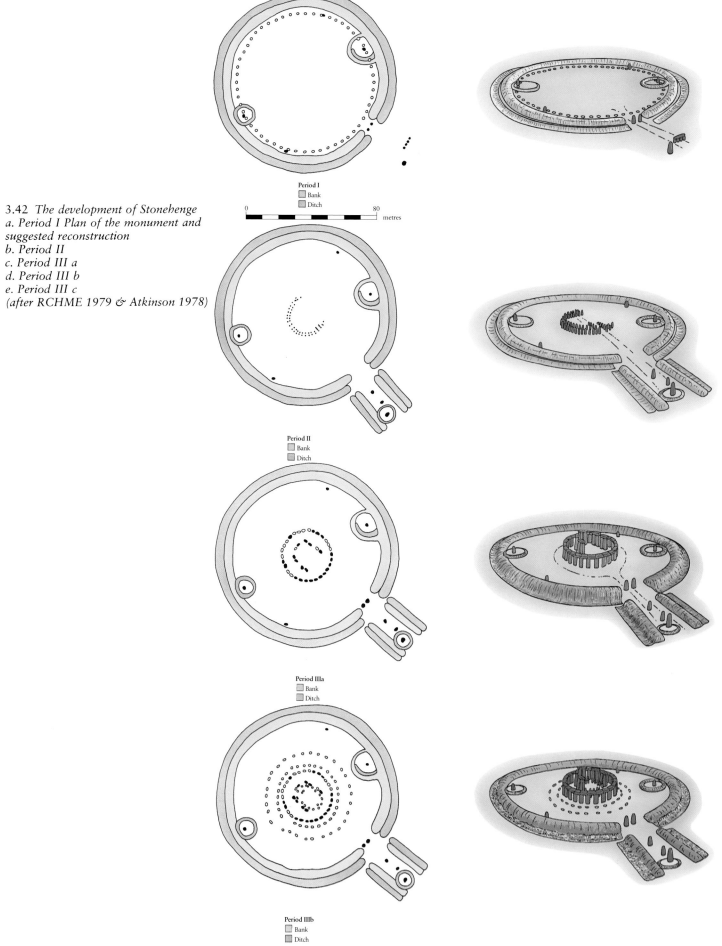

3.42 *The development of Stonehenge*
a. Period I Plan of the monument and
suggested reconstruction
b. Period II
c. Period III a
d. Period III b
e. Period III c
(after RCHME 1979 & Atkinson 1978)

Period I
☐ Bank
☐ Ditch

0   80
▬▬▬▬▬▬▬▬▬
metres

Period II
☐ Bank
☐ Ditch

Period IIIa
☐ Bank
☐ Ditch

Period IIIb
☐ Bank
☐ Ditch

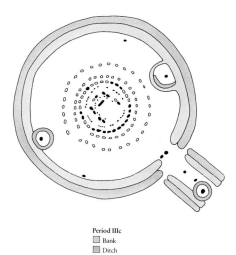

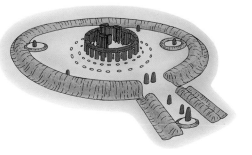

Period IIIc
☐ Bank
☐ Ditch

*3.43 Stonehenge: plan of the monument
as it survives today (after RCHME 1979)*

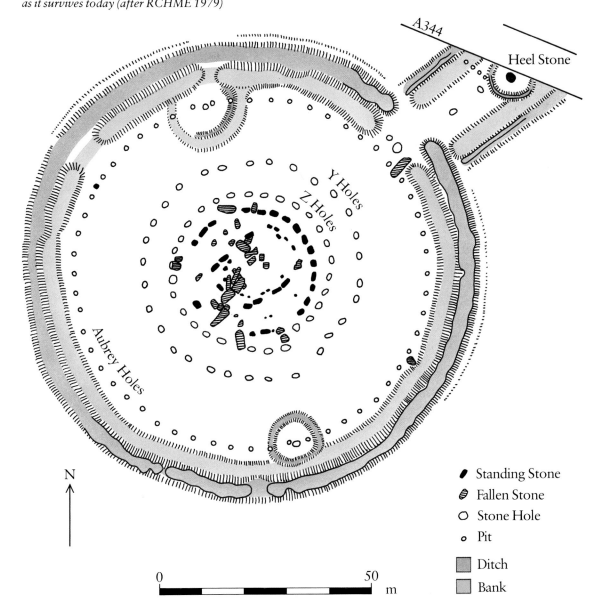

A344

Heel Stone

Y Holes

Z Holes

Aubrey Holes

N

🝙 Standing Stone

🝙 Fallen Stone

○ Stone Hole

· Pit

▨ Ditch

▨ Bank

0   50
m

3.44 Stonehenge: view from the centre of the circle towards the Heel Stone

3.45 Stonehenge: the exterior of the sarsen circle

3.46 (facing page) Stonehenge from outside the ditch

Period IV Much later (the relevant radiocarbon dates are 1070 bc ± 180: BM-1079 and 800 bc ± 100: I-3216) the Avenue itself was extended. This was not a continuation of its original line, but instead formed an angle with it.

Two important points must be discussed about Stonehenge: the nature of the re-building and the effort and skill involved. We must not see the changes in plan as reflections of incompetence or indecision. They were deliberate re-designs made by those in control of the area, people who could mobilise a massive labour force and the expertise needed to create such a monument. The simplest way of viewing the changes is in terms of competition, first with other groups by building the most spectacular and complex stone construction seen in Britain and second, with preceding generations by surpassing the vision of those who had been in control before. It is no coincidence that the major re-buildings of Periods II and III took place at a time when the large henge at Durrington Walls (catalogue number 20) was fading in significance while Mount Pleasant (catalogue number 21) underwent substantial re-building involving the replacement of the timber circle in stone. This was the time when groups using late forms of beakers were in power and what happened at Stonehenge, as at other monuments, reflected the assertion of their control. As Burgess (1980, 333) has observed in discussing the change from Period II to III: 'New leaders emerged, and what more natural act could there be for a new regime than to demolish the great unfinished project of the old order, and institute an even more ambitious design?'.

The amount of labour involved in the construction of Stonehenge was immense. The largest of the bluestones weighed 4 tonnes and the sarsens up to 51 tonnes. The bluestones originally came from South Wales and were once thought to have been brought specifically for the building of

3.47 *Aerial view of the barrow cemetery at Winterbourne Stoke, Wiltshire*

Stonehenge, but finds of bluestones at earlier sites imply that they may have been brought to Wessex before the first bluestones were used at Stonehenge itself (Atkinson, R J C 1979, 214). The sarsens must have been brought a distance of *c.* 30 km to Stonehenge, probably using logs as rollers with human strength and, perhaps also animal traction, to pull them (Atkinson, R J C 1979, 116-22). The squaring and dressing of the stones was itself a very time consuming job while even more skill was required to make the mortice and tenon joints and to shape the curved lintels to follow the line of the circle. Raising the stones can have been no simple feat. Burgess (1980, 336) gives an estimate of 50 million worker hours for raising the sarsen monument alone and when we consider what was involved in planning and putting into practice the design and re-design of the site, we can gain a crude estimate of the importance of the project and the strength of the authority of those in power.

Many overwhelming claims have been made for the astronomical importance of Stonehenge. What is clear at the very least is that the later periods of the site were deliberately aligned on the midsummer sunrise. The four station stones mark a right angle to this line and at Stonehenge the midsummer full moon rises perpendicular to the rising midsummer sun. Since these do not coincide even within a few miles to the north or

3.48 *Decorated chalk plaques from near Stonehenge Bottom, Wiltshire (53)*

3.49 *Chalk axes from Woodhenge, near Amesbury, Wiltshire (22)*

south, the location was *very* carefully chosen. This is a perfect example of the siting of a communal monument in a position which was natural and belonging to the gods. Indeed, it may not be too extreme to say that Stonehenge was being promoted as the centre of the universe.

Some mention has been made of the ritual landscape in this area (cf. Richards, J 1984). Within a 4 km radius of Stonehenge there are at least 10 long barrows, 2 cursūs, the henges at Durrington Walls and Woodhenge, 321 round barrows, some in large cemeteries (illustration

3.47), and many unmarked burials. These are by no means all contemporary but do date to the third and second millennia bc. They constitute the highest concentration of monuments in Britain (Atkinson, R J C 1978, 3) and as such confirm the long-term importance of this place. Two groups of objects found in the area are worth particular mention. In a pit near Stonehenge Bottom, less than 1 km from the henge, were found two decorated chalk plaques (illustration 3.48) and at Woodhenge (another communal monument comprising a bank and ditch surrounding rings of wooden posts) 2 symbolic axes, both made of chalk, were found in post holes (illustration 3.49). Woodhenge is only 120 m from Durrington Walls and c. 3 km from Stonehenge. This concentration of communal monuments of the dead and the living, individual burial places and points of deposition for symbolic objects shows how the importance of this area spans the whole of the mid-third to second millennia bc in a way not seen elsewhere. Stonehenge itself should be seen as the dramatic and developing focus for this activity since, above all other monuments, it strength was such that it had to be controlled by those in power. It could not be ignored.

THE ACKNOWLEDGEMENT
OF INDIVIDUAL POWER

TRADITIONALLY, THE appearance of new pottery forms, characterised as beakers in the archaeological literature, just before the beginning of the second millennium bc and the introduction of metallurgy have been seen as the reflections in material culture of the arrival of new immigrants from the Continent. These immigrants, it was believed, were physically different from the indigenous population, who were rapidly condemned to a subservient role in the new social order. Changes in ideology resulted in the wholesale transformation of existing institutions. No better or more widely accepted symbol of power was known from British prehistory; the evidence appeared so irrefutable that such interpretations of beakers remained untouched by the wholesale attack on the concept of invasions as explanatory models for events in prehistoric Britain (eg. Clark, J G D 1966). D L Clarke's monumental study of British beakers (1970)

4.1 *AOC beaker from Bathgate, West Lothian (78)*

4.2 *Grave group from Newmill, Perthshire (76)*

dramatically reaffirmed this view by proposing successive waves of immigrants, mainly from the Rhineland and the Low Countries, to account for the variety of styles. Indeed he implied that the influence of the users of beakers was so pervasive as to provide a basis for explaining most of the available evidence from the second millennium bc. In a widely accepted criticism of this work, Lanting & van der Waals (1972) suggested that only the earliest beakers, Maritime and All-over-cord (AOC: the example from Bathgate, West Lothian (illustration 4.1) shows this type's form), need represent actual immigrants; to these types we must now add the All-over-ornamented (AOO) beaker from Newmill, Perthshire (illustration 4.2: cf. Lanting & van der Waals 1976).

More recently, this view has been challenged, most notably by Burgess (Burgess & Shennan 1976; Burgess 1980, 62-64). He has argued that, although beakers have been discovered in a wide area from North Africa to Norway and Czechoslovakia to Ireland, there is no equivalent uniformity of house or settlement types, ritual or burial traditions to support the idea of a widespread folk movement. Further, he finds the evidence from Britain for a new physical type questionable and suggests that many of the practices, for example individual burial, habitually ascribed to the arrival of users of beakers were already present in the traditions of the indigenous population. Instead he suggests that beakers and associated material are better viewed as a cult package in which the ideas and objects fundamentally linked to the central beliefs spread relatively rapidly but without major movements of people. By way of analogy he cites the Peyote Cult which expanded from Mexico to Canada in the decades after AD 1850. He acknowledges, however, that 'whether Beakers represent a cult, a fashion or something quite different, they were special prestige vessels, requiring a technology and skill much higher than that used in normal potting' (1980, 63).

All then accept that beakers were prestige vessels even though they may disagree about the mechanisms by which they arrived in Britain. We have seen already that the adoption of individual burial traditions, accompanied by high status material on rare occasions, had already taken place in the third millennium bc in some area. Nevertheless, the predominant form of burial still involved the use of communal tombs and no amount of special pleading on Burgess's part that many of the unaccompanied single burials, normally now ascribed to the second millennium bc, may be earlier (Burgess & Shennan 1976, 319) alters our perception that the widespread change to individual burial, especially crouched inhumation, coincides with the appearance of the beakers. These graves occur in flat cemeteries, in cists and under round barrows. For this reason alone, we would find it difficult to accept that 'people continued to live in the same settlements, farming as their forebears had for generations, with the same beliefs, burial customs and ritual monuments, and persisting with much of their old material culture' (Burgess 1980, 62).

The leadership of the regional groups of the late third millennium bc found expression of their power in the construction of large communal monuments (eg. henges and stone circles) and to a lesser extent the acquisition of prestige items. An essential component of this power, however, involved the control of the rituals associated with the monuments for mediation with the gods. They were in effect a priestly hierarchy. But, as Douglas observes (1982, 8), 'if all the decision-making members of society were located behind the barriers which constitute inner compartments and hierarchical layering, they will have a problem of communicating with the outside and so of getting information and adapting to new external conditions'. It is precisely this lack of information and failure to adapt to changed circumstances which led ultimately to the collapse of the hierarchy's power and its replacement by those controlling the new resources of beakers and metallurgy, a more entrepreneurial form of leadership in which emphasis on the individual was altogether more acceptable and desirable. Such a transfer of power does not require invasion to explain it but it is something more than the adoption of cult practices which left the lives of most people unchanged.

There are problems in establishing the precise relationship between the appearance of beakers and metallurgy, not least the relative absence of beakers in Ireland and the lack of coincidence between their distribution and areas of presumptive early metalworking (Harbison 1973, 99;

4.3 A metalworker's grave group from Lunteren, Gelderland, Netherlands (159)

1980). Some have reconciled these difficulties (eg. Case 1966, 166-68) by regarding the mechanisms that brought beakers to Ireland as the same as those that prompted the first metalworking. Certainly, the evidence for close links between the two developments in the Netherlands is particularly strong (Butler & van der Waals 1966), exemplified by the metalworker's tools found in the grave at Lunteren, Ede (illustration 4.3), and this is an area where the beakers show a strong stylistic relationship with many found in Britain. What is clear is that the earliest associations of metalwork are with beakers, for example the copper dagger from Winterslow, Wiltshire and the spiral-headed pin of central European metal from Sewell, Totternhoe, Bedfordshire (illustrations 4.4-5), although, as the latter example indicates, not all the objects need be of indigenous manufacture. If, then, beakers and metallurgy did not arrive in Britain as components of a single ideology they rapidly became merged after their arrival.

4.4 *Grave group from Winterslow, Wiltshire (72)*

Of the two, metallurgy was by far the more threatening to the established order for it represented a form of control over the natural world, powers that had hitherto been restricted to the ruling elites. Initially, production seems to have been heavily concentrated on axes which, as we have seen, had long had significance far in excess of their importance as a tool. It seems probable that the earliest copper and bronze axes would not have shown any marked advantage in terms of functional efficiency over good quality stone ones. But as an item for gift exchange and enhancement of prestige and status a metal axe would surely have been more than a match for even the finest jadeite and flint axes, given the magical aura that must have surrounded its manufacture. Were this not so, copies in stone of metal axes would be difficult to explain (illustration 4.6). Moreover, metalworkers or their patrons seem to have acquired not only a knowledge of the technical skills involved but also an awareness of new forms for display, knife-daggers and earrings

4.5 *Grave group from Sewell, Bedfordshire (71)*

4.6 *Stone axe from Hillend, Penicuik, Midlothian imitating the form of early copper and bronze axes*

(illustration 4.7) for example. One has only to review the metal types known from the first 500 years or so of metalworking — predominantly axes, halberds, knives and daggers, spearheads and ornaments of various forms — to appreciate that their use was rooted primarily in the search for prestige and status, not in the development of a more efficient tool-kit to enhance subsistence opportunities. Apart from the axe which undoubtedly had a symbolic aspect, almost the only tool type to occur in any quantity is the awl and it is by no means a common find. Moreover, its use in the manufacture of gold and jet items is well documented (see below, chapter 5) and was perhaps restricted to the production of prestige objects.

Beakers themselves may have posed a more insidious and less obvious threat to traditional practices and structures. The finest of them were apparently the work of specialist potters and may well have been exchanged over considerable distances (Clarke, D L 1976). As we have noted, their position as prestige vessels is widely recognised. Yet it would not have been easy for established regional leaders to have acknowledged them as such since they did not conform to accepted norms. The skill and craftsmanship involved in their manufacture made them desirable and prestigious but their form and decoration reflected an alien ideology. The art-style, in particular, with its sophisticated use of filled areas and voids, symmetry and mirror imaging was part of a set of international symbols quite at odds with indigenous concepts. It and the craftsmen responsible were not controllable at a regional level through the imposition of ritual authority, and, whatever the means were for effecting the exchanges, the

4.7 *Gold earring from Kirkhaugh, Northumberland (80)*

widespread distribution of beakers suggests they were prosecuted with some vigour. Having promoted the idea of other prestige objects as a means of bolstering their own power, the leaders must have twisted a great deal on the horns of this dilemma. It is certainly not surprising that the new items should have appealed to ambitious individuals whose exclusion from the hierarchy must have engendered a much weaker commitment to the accepted ideology. By controlling the exchanges and, in some instances, the craftsmen working in both pottery and metal such individuals would have acquired the status of 'Big Men' with a power and prestige quite separate from the ruling elites.

It is not easy to see how the inevitable conflicts were handled and such evidence as we have suggests that the situation varied from region to region. In some areas, such as Yorkshire and perhaps Aberdeenshire, where communal monuments were relatively small in scale and the participation in wide-ranging exchange networks well established, links with the new beaker networks must have been more easily forged. Indeed, the appearance of different prestige items in groups already heavily involved in their use may not have greatly exacerbated the tensions between such groups and those with power rooted in ritual authority.

In southern Wessex, however, the situation was very different. This is an area, as we have seen, which contains major communal monuments producing objects associated with ritual authority which were not available to lower ranking groups (Bradley 1982). The power derived from the control and use of ritual was considerable but the exclusive focusing on this particular aspect of life seems to have resulted in a degree of spatial separation matching that found in the material culture. In peripheral areas, a measure of autonomy permitted the emergence of 'Big Men' with limited power fostered by activities such as feasting, marriage alliances and gift giving. Such individuals would have found beakers and their associated objects particularly attractive, not least for the enhanced prestige that participation in a wider exchange network represented. The resultant conflict between secular power and ritual authority was not easily or quickly resolved. The first rich individual burials, for example that from Winterslow (illustration 4.4), all avoid the areas of the major monuments but are indicative of the growth of secular power. Relatively soon after 1800 bc, the power invested in ritual authority seems to have diminished to the point where the functioning of the large communal monuments could no longer be sustained. Power was now in the hands of groups competing in terms of the control and consumption of prestige goods. It did, however, require the take over of the communal monuments to legitimise and secure it. These were, after all, significant symbols of the past order in the landscape. A small number, in the longer term only Stonehenge, were so important that only wholesale transformation and re-modelling was appropriate — a more recent analogy might be the treatment of Sancta Sophia in Istanbul, for long the largest Christian church in the world where, after the Turkish conquest, minarets were added at each of the four external angles and the interior adapted to the requirements of Moslem worship, mainly by the destruction or concealment of most of the mosaics, replete with Christian symbols, which adorned the walls (Talbot-Rice 1959, plates 54-56). The rebuilding in stone of some of the timber monuments in Wessex between 1700 and 1600 bc (Wainwright 1979, 232) may reflect the same processes. But at other sites, for example Durrington Walls and Woodhenge, the presence of beaker pottery and burials (Wainwright & Longworth 1971, 71-73; Cunnington 1929, 42, plates 40-41, 50.4) may indicate no more than acts of de-sanctification, confirming the power of the new order (many of these points are discussed in greater detail in Thorpe, I J & Richards 1984).

It is in this context that the widespread occurrence of beakers and related material on a large number of earlier sites should be interpreted. There is nothing to suggest that the users of beakers were involved in the construction of *new* communal monuments, rather the emphasis of their ritual was directed towards the reflection of individual power and prestige through burial practices. In these circumstances, the burials in the henge at Balfarg, Fife (illustration 4.8) or under a round barrow superimposed on the funerary end of a long barrow at Garton Slack, Yorkshire (illustration 4.9: Mortimer 1905, 209-11; Brewster 1980, 81-83) are better interpreted as meaningful acts of desecration rather than as any attempt to legitimise power through association with past

4.8 *Handled beaker from Balfarg, Fife (23)*

4.9 *Grave group from Garton Slack, Yorkshire (69)*

centres of ritual activity. A wide variety of sites seem to have been treated in this way although not always apparently involving burials — examples range from causewayed enclosures at Hambledon Hill, Dorset (Mercer 1980, 37) and Knap Hill, Wiltshire (Connah 1965, 14), cursus A at Rudston, Yorkshire (Dymond 1966, 91-92) to the recumbent stone circles at Loanhead of Daviot, Aberdeenshire (Kilbride-Jones 1935, 175, 182-84) and Broomend of Crichie, Aberdeenshire where a battle-axe (illustration 4.10) was buried inside the circle. There appears to have been a general concern with major monuments in the landscape, which, no matter what their significance for former ideologies, might have formed a focus for a resurgence of past beliefs. Nothing in the evidence from chamber tombs (eg. Henshall 1972, 187-91) prevents us from interpreting the presence of beakers there in similar terms. We are not suggesting that such events occurred synchronously throughout Britain although the networks of competitive exchange will probably have encouraged the process. But the deciding factor is likely to have been the requirement that individuals or lineage groups felt sufficiently secure in their own power to risk interfering with monuments which might still remain potent symbols to some.

4.10 *Battle-axes from Broomend of Crichie, Aberdeenshire (left: 87), Chapelton, Lanarkshire (back: 89) and Longniddry, East Lothian (front: 90)*

Two major areas, Orkney and Ireland, seem to have resisted the social

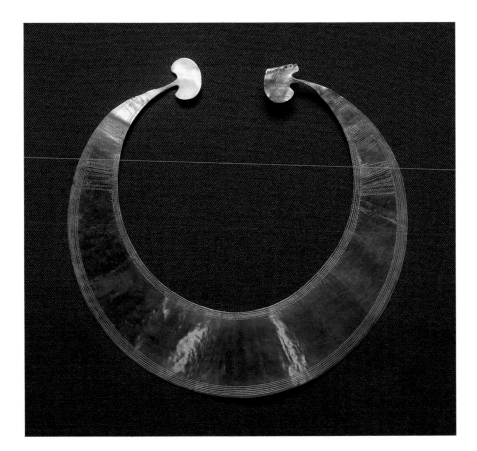

4.11 *(facing page) Gold lunula from Blessington, Co Wicklow, Ireland (63)*

4.12 *Gold lunula from Auchentaggart, Dumfriesshire (59)*

changes brought about by the appearance of beakers and metallurgy. Certainly, Ireland became a major region for metalworking but we have already noted the relatively small number of beaker finds. There are some but the rite of individual burial accompanied by beakers appears absent, something which Burgess attributes to the absence of a long inhumation tradition in Ireland (1980, 65). However, large communal monuments for the living of the kind developed in Britain, do not occur to any extent for this particular role seems to have been fulfilled by large and elaborate chamber tombs such as the passage grave cemeteries at Newgrange and Knowth, perhaps reflecting networks stretching south down the Atlantic seaboard rather than across the Irish Sea. This alternative structure may have meant that the controlling elites were less vulnerable to the pressures of the new situation. A more combative and vigorous response to them can be seen in the production of items such as lunulae (illustration 4.11). These gold collars are an Irish development but their decoration involves skilled and sophisticated use of motifs and design from the beaker art-style (Taylor 1970a). Yet their distribution in Britain avoids all the areas where beakers are commonly found; Scottish examples do occur but their decorative motifs show much less effective use of beaker styles (illustration 4.12). None are unequivocally associated with a burial and Taylor (1970a, 44) thought them to be the property of 'a larger unit like the family or clan'. All of this is difficult to explain, especially in view of the undoubted appeal of gold ornaments for the users of beakers in Britain (illustration 4.13), unless we see lunulae as a deliberate attempt by the old order to appropriate the symbols of the new with the clear intention of neutralising their power.

Orkney presents a very different situation in which the power of the existing leaders seems to have been sufficient to prevent any effective challenge to their authority. Remarkably, given the evidence for the range of third and early second millennia bc occupation (reviewed in Renfrew 1985, 36-130), only two sites, Rinyo and Links of Noltland, have produced incontrovertible beakers (parts of one vessel from Rinyo and two from Links of Noltland — the so-called S4/hybrid from Birsay: Clarke, D L 1970, number 1733 is unacceptable as a beaker). Finds of early metalwork are equally rare. This scarcity is a considerable contrast with the rich settlements, the tombs and the ritual landscape of henges containing stone circles at Brodgar and Stenness allied to the outstanding passage grave at Maeshowe, all dating to the late third millennium bc. The explanation appears to be that the elite controlling these monuments were strong enough to prevent the adoption of an alien ideology but the success of that ideology elsewhere in Britain caused a disjuncture in the networks on which the Orkney leaders relied. In these circumstances, the power structure merely atrophied with the result that for most of the second millennium bc there is nothing except the rich grave group from Knowes of Trotty (illustrations 4.39 & 5.44) to suggest that Orkney formed part of any wider networks.

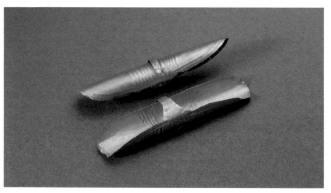

4.13 *a. Grave group from Radley, Berkshire (70); b. Detailed view of the earrings*

The exceptions provided by these two areas are striking but they serve to emphasise just how wide-ranging the success of the new ideologies was. Initially, the prestige of the beaker itself was sufficient to mark out the powerful and important individual at the time of burial but, as Bradley has observed (1984, 71-73), pottery is particularly subject to loss of status as a prestige item. The ease of copying and its identification with powerful groups caused aspiring individuals lower in the hierarchy to seek to emulate those groups by acquiring comparable pots (the importance of emulation even in a stable hierarchy is stressed in Miller 1982). Since beakers were a prestige item which could not be easily controlled, it is not surprising that the important individuals soon turned to the use of other objects in combination with the beaker to denote their status. On rare occasions, gold objects are found as at Radley, Berkshire (illustration 4.13) although these often occur as isolated finds (illustration 4.14) but more usually it is the range, quality and number of objects included with the burial that were used to make the distinctions (illustrations 4.15-16). We should not, however, suppose that ranking

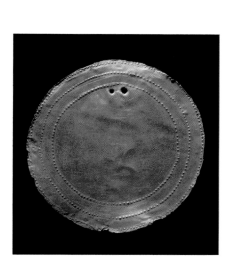

4.14 *Gold disc from Kirk Andrews, Isle of Man (82)*

4.15 *Grave group from Driffield, Yorkshire (68)*

4.16 *Grave group from Culduthel,*
Inverness-shire (74)

4.17 *Grave group from Crawford,*
Lanarkshire (73)

burials, and hence the individuals buried, is a matter of simple number counts. The burial from Crawford, Lanarkshire (illustration 4.17) contained only a beaker and a bronze armlet but both are in their individual way exceptional pieces and may for the period of their deposition and in the context of their locality have been appropriate for a high status individual. Many other factors including the age and sex of the individual may have influenced the nature and number of items included in the grave.

What is clear is that the graves of the early second millennium bc mark the wholesale adoption of individual burial as the dominant tradition. In this situation beakers and the products of early metalworking constituted the key elements in a society where power was vested in the control of prestige items. For some this meant access to exchange networks reaching far into Continental Europe. These fundamental features established the pattern which was to be elaborated and refined until late in the millennium.

Hoards and related metalwork

John C Barrett

Hoards, like grave goods, are made up of objects deliberately buried in the ground. Archaeologists distinguish between hoards, as groups of more than one object, and single finds, believing that whilst hoards have been deliberately deposited many single finds may result from more casual loss or discard. However, a brief comparison between the objects which occur in hoards and those which occur as single finds dispels the idea of establishing a firm distinction between the two. It is difficult to believe that it is casual loss that accounts for the occurrence of bronze axes (such as the decorated example from Cornhill Farm, Berwickshire or the spectacularly large axe from Lawhead, Lanarkshire: illustrations 4.18-19), spearheads (eg. Whitehaugh Moss, Ayrshire: illustration 4.20), or halberds (eg. Whiteleys, Wigtownshire: illustration 4.21), let alone one of the remarkable Ommerschans rapiers (eg. Beaune, France: illustration 4.22). It is altogether more profitable to consider the reasons behind the deposition of all objects which we believe have been deliberately buried outside the context of a grave or settlement.

Hoards (a term which can embrace, therefore, both multiple or single deposits) are like grave goods in being deliberately buried but the reasons for such burial are more difficult to ascertain. We assume that grave goods were intended to be left in the ground although there is good evidence that many graves were later re-opened. However, in the case of hoards, archaeologists have attempted to distinguish between votive hoards, deposited without any intention of later recovery, and other hoards which may have been valuables hidden for safekeeping but never recovered. If this distinction is valid the major problem confronting us is in deciding how to differentiate between the two types of hoard. A clearer understanding of this problem is possible if we begin with a consideration of how objects may have circulated in these societies before they were buried. The reasons for depositing material in hoards presumably had

4.18 *Decorated bronze axes from
?Banffshire (middle: 151), Cornhill-on-
Tweed, Berwickshire (lower: 152) and
near Eildon, Roxburghshire (upper: 153)*

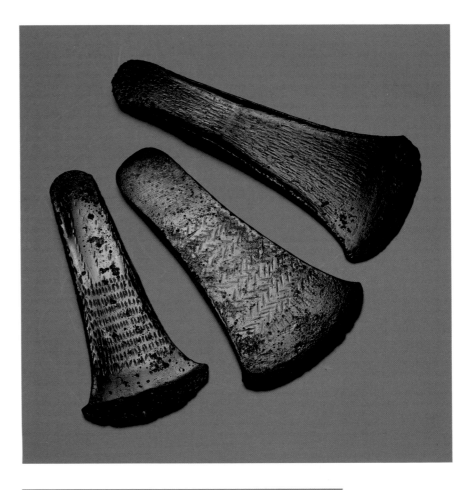

4.19 *Massive bronze axe from
Lawhead, Lanarkshire (154)*

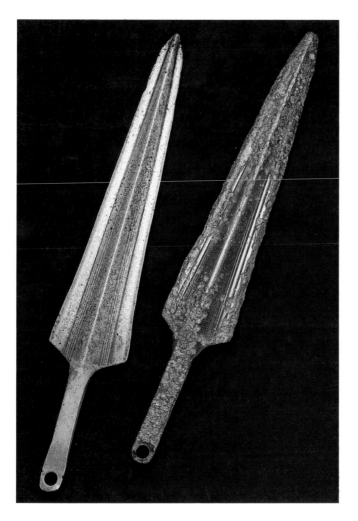

4.20 *Tanged bronze spearheads from Crawford Priory, Fife (right: 157) and Whitehaugh, Moss, Ayrshire (left: 158)*

4.22 *Bronze 'swords' (Ommerschans rapiers) from Kimberley, Norfolk (left: 150) and Beaune, France (right: 178)*

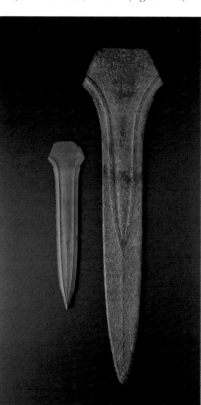

4.21 *Copper halberds from Poltalloch Estates, Argyll (front: 155) and Whiteleys, Wigtownshire (back: 156)*

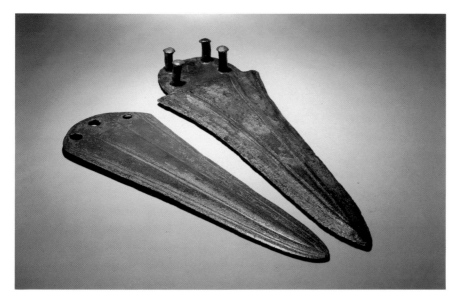

something to do with circulation since it is the mechanisms of production and circulation which define the value of an object and the nature of property.

When we begin to look at the small-scale, pre-capitalist societies which archaeologists study we must begin by putting aside many of the assumptions which we make about contemporary economic activity. Today, economic activity takes place between people who would normally be classed as 'strangers'. Apart from the payment for a commodity no other particular social obligations need tie the participants of an economic deal. Commodities are given a value, which is determined by forces that we do not normally consider, and that value is met by money which allows us to buy and sell commodities. When we buy, the commodity become ours, when we sell, we relinquish control over it: such procedures are known as the alienation of property. Economic power involves the accumulation of either property, which can be converted into money, or money, which can be converted into property.

Living as we do under such economic conditions it is natural that on first sight large hoards, such as those from Bresinchen or the second hoard from Dieskau (illustrations 4.23-24), appear to indicate the accumulation of wealth which was itself a source of power and prestige. Yet when we look at the past very little is as it seems. Anthropologists have found the production and exchange of artefacts in the non-industrial, so-called primitive, world difficult to understand because the exchanges which take place do not conform to the logic of our own economic experience. In these societies what appear to be economic relations seem more concerned with establishing and maintaining other kinds of social relations, such as marital ties, kinship bonds and alliances. This has led some people to distinguish between situations where economic relations are embedded in other social institutions and those (as in our own world) where economic relations have become separate, existing as economic institutions in their own right. Nevertheless, in societies where such processes seem to be embedded, there are situations where 'pure' economic exchanges can take place between strangers. These occur as barter relations at the edge of social groups (Sahlins 1974). In barter the values of commodities are established in relation to each other at the moment the bargain is struck, and once the exchange has taken place no further obligations exist between the people involved. For example, if you and I meet as strangers and I barter a pig for a bronze axe from you, then we establish, at that moment, an agreed equivalence of value between two commodities. That agreement need lead to no further obligations between us, and at some later date I may barter the same bronze axe for two pigs from someone else. This kind of exchange appears close to what we would accept as economic activity, although we may regard it as 'primitive' as it does not use the intermediary of money which we tend to believe has an absolute value of some kind notwithstanding the effects of inflation. However, this is a kind of exchange which is likely to be a marginal aspect in the European societies of the third and second millennia bc. In other social exchanges very different rules apply. Far from the accumulation of objects being an end in itself because it confers power and prestige upon an individual, it is

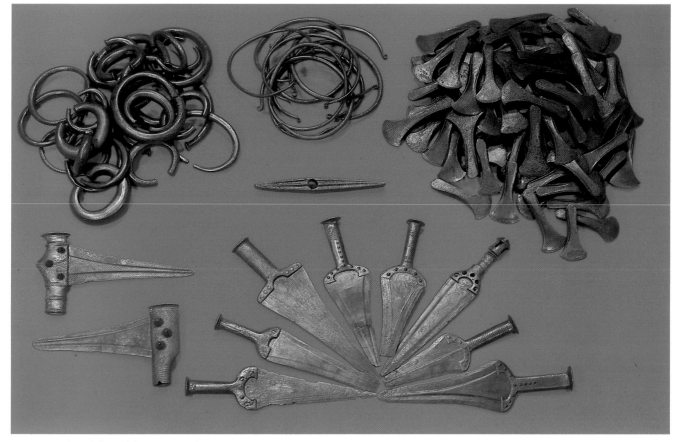

4.23 *Metalwork hoard from Bresinchen,*
Guben, German Democratic Republic
(175)

4.24 *Metalwork hoard from Dieskau,*
Saalkreis, German Democratic Republic
(176)

often the ability to give which matters. By giving things away obligations are established and it is these which are the means of maintaining a social position. If I give you an axe, or invite you to a feast, then I have established an obligation which you will at some stage have to meet in equal or greater degree. And when objects are exchanged at a marriage ceremony, it is because one group is perceived to be receiving the gift of a marriage partner from another group. Gifts have always to be repaid. This means that objects do not become alienated by exchange, instead they remain connected to the person who gives the gift, an obligation is in effect carried by the gift (Mauss 1970). The ability to give rather than accumulate is therefore a means of establishing social position but debt obligations can rarely be permanently maintained. There is always the demand that the gift be returned, together with the possibility that its return will be in a greater quantity which in itself will create new obligations. Unlike social authority which is established through genealogical links with ancestors or gods, gift exchange is competitive and an unstable means of establishing rank. There is, however, one strategy which brings two of these systems together and that is in gifts to gods (Gregory 1982).

Gifts are inalienable; they return. But if gifts are directed to gods, by perhaps destroying them, burying them, or throwing them into a lake or river, then two things happen. First, a gift is seen to be given to a supreme being, acknowledging the relations and obligations of the giver to that being. Second, the artefacts used in that particular process of gift-giving are removed from circulation. They will not be returned by the gods and they are no longer available for gift-giving between humans. A strain may thus have been put upon the cycle of gift-giving between the living because the overall stock of gifts has been diminished.

This discussion of exchange systems can now return to consider the archaeological remains. Archaeologists are much concerned with artefacts and we must now, when considering social rank, distinguish between two different classes of material. The first class acts in the way we have been discussing here in that they are a means of establishing social rank. In our society social position depends upon accumulating alienable property but in pre-capitalist societies rank through artefacts depends much more upon giving away gifts and thereby accumulating the obligations of others. The second class of artefacts do not act in this primary way in establishing social rank but instead they are secondary to an established rank, symbols which mark out a position which has been achieved by some other means. They may, for example, be items of clothing worn by someone who has some ritual or genealogical status. These distinctions can be identified in the archaeological record.

Various factors must however be taken into account. The first is value and how it is determined. Value is not something which is the natural property of an artefact but is instead the product of a very complex set of forces which are particular to the prevalent conditions of production and exchange. We cannot, therefore, look at an archaeological object and say that it has some intrinsic value but must alternatively consider the kind of relations within which the artefact was circulated. This brings us back to the assumptions archaeologists normally employ when studying hoards and which we outlined at the beginning of this section. The normal explanation for hoarding, that it either represents gifts to gods or personal property accumulated and hidden for security could lead us to assume that artefacts were used in two ways — either as gifts or as commodities to be accumulated. Yet, as we have seen, these strategies are contradictory. When we approach the archaeological information on hoards we must remember that the reasons for deposition were in some way connected with the preceding processes of production and circulation.

Elsewhere in this volume the level of craft expertise demonstrated in the artefacts is examined in greater detail (see below, Chapter 5). The degree of skill is often considerable as is the amount of time and energy spent in procuring the raw materials and in the processes of production. Nonetheless it would not be safe to assume that time spent in these ways was itself the measure of the exchange value of the artefact. At first sight the position of the producers would seem to be very powerful for they actually make and then exchange the objects which may subsequently circulate as gifts. However, time and again, anthropologists, economists and historians are able to demonstrate how the producers are in fact placed in a far more ambiguous relationship to the product of their labours by the processes which alienate the products from them. Metalworkers often appear as social outcasts, both powerful and dangerous. We do have evidence for craft techniques and, in some parts of Europe, the quarry sites and mines which provided the raw material. Hoards of smithy debris and scrap are not known from the period under discussion here. It was not until the first millennium bc when major changes were taking place in the organisation of the production that we find large hoards of scrap metal and raw copper ingots occurring in some parts of Europe.

Having considered value and production we must now turn to circulation. While the relationship between production and circulation is difficult to understand on our present evidence, that between circulation and deposition is of vital importance for our understanding of hoards. Clearly, the types of objects which were accessible must in some way have determined the selection of material for burial and the quantity of available items would have controlled the frequency with which hoarding took place. Moreover, deposition, which rendered material inaccessible, must itself have had a direct impact upon the circulation process.

The hoard evidence usually represents the exchange of complete finished artefacts and, by definition, marks the end of the line for the circulation of a particular object. Occasionally, we can tell how far an object has been carried from the source of production to the place of its final deposition. The most detailed work on this question has, of course, been the petrological analysis of stone axes but chemical sourcing has been attempted on metal ores and artefacts in the hope of linking the two. As a result it has been suggested that Alpine ores were providing the metal for a large number of western European artefacts. In central Europe a number of hoards have been recovered which contain large numbers (often several hundred) of so-called ingot torcs (Bath-Bílková 1973). These objects have generally been taken to represent the production of a standard metal form for use in exchange, with the hoards constituting the accumulation of ingots prior to such an exchange. However, it may well be that far from representing stock for trade these hoards are the result of massive local consumption in the form of sacrifice; a consumption which might itself have driven forward the exploitation of local metal resources. A particularly good indicator of the geographical distances over which some objects may have been carried is provided by the distribution of the Ommerschans rapiers which, it has been suggested, could be the product of a single smith (Greenwell 1902, 5; Butler & Bakker 1961, 201; Butler & Sarfatij 1971, 305, 308, 309, fn 2). Five of these ceremonial rapiers or swords are known, two from the Netherlands (Ommerschans & Jutphaas), two from France (Beaune & Plougrescant), and one from Norfolk (Kimberley). Indeed, the type takes its name from a remarkable hoard found at Ommerschans in the Netherlands which contained besides the sword a Sicilian bronze razor, two bronze chisels, two pins or needles, a bronze rod, a spiral of bronze wire, four fragments of bronze and a variety of flint and stone objects including three chisels, a whetstone and a tablet (Butler & Bakker 1961). A somewhat earlier example of long distance exchange is provided by the Irish axe in the second hoard from Dieskau (illustration 4.24). The exchange networks which carried these artefacts across Europe were likely to have been largely local so that items travelling considerable distances may well have passed through many hands. At some stage they would have begun to appear exotic because of their unfamiliarity and might then have started to acquire a different value from that involved in the initial exchanges.

Perhaps the most important point to make about circulation and the way it affects the hoard record is that different kinds of artefact might circulate through different kinds of exchange network. Again, a comparison with the modern world emphasises the distinction with the past. The medium of money allows us, by buying and selling, to convert one kind of commodity into another: Commodity 1 → Money → Commodity 2 → Money → Commodity 3 . . . . However, in a non-money using society, where artefacts circulate through particular social channels converting one kind of artefact into another is a far more complex process. Particular sets of artefacts are likely to have carried particular 'meanings' closely related to the types of social exchange which carried them.

The final factor to be examined is consumption. Not all objects circulated in the same way or meant the same thing with the result that a single concept of value, to which all objects could be reduced, did not exist within the societies of the third and second millennia bc. Only at moments of barter, between strangers, was it necessary to establish such a value. In such circumstances, hoards will not represent a random assortment of material available at any one time, as we might expect if they were collections of valuables stored for safekeeping. Instead we should find different classes of artefact treated in different ways and included in different kinds of deposits. This is exactly what seems to occur.

In metalwork hoards there is considerable emphasis upon the inclusion of axes, for example Colleonard, Banffshire (illustration 4.25). Indeed

the axe appears the most common element to be found in hoards of more than one object, as at Auchnacree, Angus (illustration 4.26), almost as if it represented the core symbol about which the other objects came to be arranged. This is significant because throughout the preceding third millennium bc stone axes appear to have been a widely exchanged item although hoards including several axes are rare in comparison to the number of isolated finds. Axes, as items of exchange, seem to have become a focus of competitive gift exchange at various times in different local exchange systems, leading to their sacrifice in the way we have already described. Nowhere in Britain do we see the size of deposit represented by, for example, the third Dieskau hoard which contained 293 flanged metal axes as well as 10 arm-rings of various types, two shaft-hole axes and a halberd (von Brunn 1959, 56). Operating in this way the axe became not only a practical tool for cutting wood, etc but also an item whose gifting could have accrued debt obligations. It is, therefore, an artefact which may have had a primary role to play in establishing social position.

Not all objects operated in the same way. The primary role of the dagger seems to have been display and it is best seen alongside items of

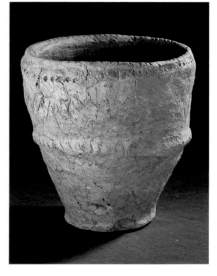

4.25 a. Metalwork hoard from Colleonard, Banffshire (145); b. The pot which contained the axes

dress such as buttons and beads. In putting daggers among the symbols whose primary purpose was display we are perhaps better able to understand why, in some parts of Europe, daggers are more normally found in graves rather than in hoards. If daggers are seen as overt statements of rank and status they would not play the same primary role as the axe in competitive exchange and we should expect the two types of artefact to be deposited in different circumstances. One will be connected with the rank of an individual entering a world of ancestors and the other employed in gifting to the gods.

Hoards contain particular artefacts which represent a core of symbols which may be contrasted with the symbols found in graves. Each type of deposit is concerned with establishing or signalling social rank but they act in rather different ways. The archaeological record does not produce, nor should we expect it to, an absolute distinction between the types of artefact in each of these contexts. Even in Wessex where the emphasis is very much on the reflection of power and prestige through burials axes are occasionally found in some graves. Yet on two occasions, at Bush

4.26 *Metalwork hoard from Auchnacree Lodge, Angus (144)*

Barrow, Wiltshire (Annable & Simpson 1964, pl, number 178) and Ridgeway barrow 7, Dorset (illustration 4.57), these axes preserve in their corrosion products the traces of textiles. Such traces will only be preserved in exceptional circumstances but they do suggest that the axes entered the graves wrapped or sheathed indicating that they were not in this context items of display. Instead, they were perhaps particularly important gift exchanges. Similar evidence has been found in Brittany,

4.27 Metalwork hoard from Arreton Down, Isle of Wight (142)

where axes more commonly occur in graves, at Kernonen, Plouvorn (Finistère) and Tossen-Maharit, Trévérec (Côtes-du-Nord) (Briard 1984, 77-79). Equally, daggers do occur on occasions in hoards as at Auchnacree, Angus and Knocknague, Co Galway, Ireland (illustration 5.11). Moreover, the Arreton Down hoard from the Isle of Wight, which is the hoard of the period found closest to the Wessex heartland, contains only two daggers but 4 axes and 11 spearheads (illustration 4.27).

As well as these core assemblages of grave and hoard there are other items such as spearheads and halberds which are more frequent inclusions in hoards as at Sluie, Moray (illustration 5.15) than graves but which are often found as single deposits or as single type hoards as at Auchingoul, Banffshire (illustration 4.28).

Patterns do, therefore, occur but not as rigid statements of inclusion and exclusion. People do live their lives by formulae but they employ the cultural values available to them, sometimes in an imaginative way.

Rich Graves

We have shown in the previous two sections how individual burial became the norm and suggested that hoards of metalwork are best interpreted as displays of power involving the conspicuous disposal of wealth. We now wish to consider three areas in which individual power was expressed, in part, through the lavish provision of exotic grave goods to accompany the corpse. Each of the three areas — Wessex, Brittany and central Europe — displays particular features but they nevertheless provide the clearest evidence of the widespread inter-regional contacts throughout Europe that characterised the middle centuries of the second millennium bc.

4.28 Metalwork hoard from Auchingoul, Banffshire (143)

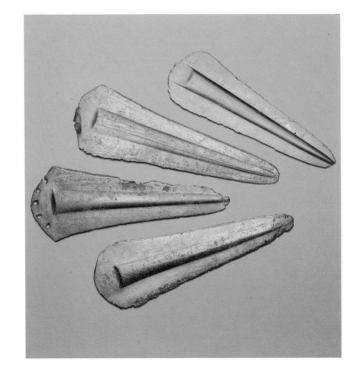

Wessex

The rich graves of this area, known as the Wessex culture since Piggott's now classic study of them (Piggott, S 1938), provide evidence of a display of wealth unparalleled in burials elsewhere in Britain. This is not to say that individual grave groups in regions outside of Wessex do not on occasion come close to matching the range and quality of the objects in the Wessex graves, that from Little Cressingham, Norfolk (illustration 4.29) being a case in point, but nowhere else do we observe the same concentration of such burials. Yet there is an air of provincialism about even the richest of the non-Wessex material, examples of local interpretations of Wessex ideas just as Wessex, in the finest grave groups, demonstrates its individuality by creating its own translations of European ideas and symbols. Little Cressingham, for example, would rank alongside the richest graves in Wessex with its daggers, amber beads and goldwork but the gold objects are not of the same quality as those produced by a master craftsman and buried in Bush Barrow (Wilsford G5), Wiltshire (illustration 4.30). Equally, the gold discs from Barnhill, Angus (illustration 4.31) have been seen as interpretations of the more elaborate gold-bound amber discs found in several Wessex graves (illustration 4.32: Taylor 1980, 45). The status and prestige expressed in these Wessex burials quite clearly involved competing on an equal footing with other European groups in terms of shared symbols, regionally interpreted. Individuals in other areas of Britain who chose to adopt this mode of expressing their power could do no more than construct their displays in terms of the Wessex idiom. There was for these people, it seems, no independent access to the wider networks. Moreover, those with such access, particularly in north Britain and Ireland through involvement in the exchange of metalwork, preferred not to compete in this way, displaying their power with the use of alternative methods like the deposition of hoards. The find from Migdale, Sutherland (illustrations 4.33-37) is perhaps the best example of this with its single bronze axe, armlets, earring, tubular beads, cones and V-bored jet buttons. The beads and cones may well have come from the Únĕtice groups in central Europe (Butler 1963, 200) but, if the interpretation of the beads and some of the sheet metalwork as part of a crescentic necklace is correct (Stevenson 1956), they were then used to create forms emphasising prestige and status in local terms. None of the objects from Migdale have close parallels in Wessex but they are the kinds of personal ornaments which would there have been deposited in a grave and not a hoard. Indeed close parallels for the bronze beads were found in a burial at the Mound of the Hostages, Tara, Co Meath with jet, amber and faience beads and two bronze fragments, tentatively identified as a knife and an awl (Ó Riordáin 1955).

Equally important as the distinction between grave and hoard in the consumption of wealth is the adoption of different sets of symbols which are nevertheless internationally meaningful. Migdale has eight bronze armlets and armlets certainly appear in both hoards and graves in central Europe but not in Wessex. Nor are armlets confined to hoards in Scotland for they accompany some of the richest burials — the cist at

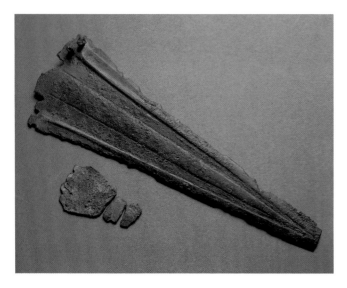

4.29 *Grave group from Little Cressingham, Norfolk (95): a. the daggers; b. the amber; c. the goldwork*

4.30 *The gold objects from Wilsford G5 (Bush Barrow), Wiltshire (101)*

4.31 *Grave group from Barnhill, Angus (103)*

4.32 *The gold objects from Wilsford G8, Wiltshire (102)*

4.33 *Metalwork hoard from Migdale,*
Sutherland: bronze axe and armlets
(147.1; 147.9-14)

4.34 *Metalwork hoard from Migdale,*
Sutherland: bronze armlets (147.15-16)

4.36 *Metalwork hoard from Migdale,*
Sutherland: fragment of bronze earring
(147.8)

4.35 *Metalwork hoard from Migdale,*
Sutherland: bronze cones and beads
(147.2-7; 147.17-18)

4.37 *Metalwork hoard from Migdale,*
Sutherland: jet buttons (147.19-24)

Melfort, Argyll (illustration 4.38) contained an extended inhumation, a pair of identical bronze armlets of superlative craftsmanship and parts of two jet necklaces while that at Masterton, Fife (illustrations 5.14 & 5.50) contained a pair of bronze armlets, a bronze dagger, a bronze knife and a jet necklace. In contrast to Wessex, Scottish graves contain only a small amount of goldwork; apart from Barnhill and the remarkable gold discs from Knowes of Trotty, Orkney (illustration 4.39) its use is restricted to

4.38 *Bronze armlet from Melfort, Argyll (119.1)*

three pommel mounts accompanying daggers from Blackwaterfoot, Arran, Collessie, Fife and Skateraw, East Lothian (illustration 4.40). It may well be that the greater use of bronze for important objects was a conscious reflection of the major source of power in that region.

What then were the symbols used in Wessex to denote power and prestige and which have caused it to be seen as the richest area in Britain at this period? First and foremost, of course, it is the exquisite goldwork

4.39 *Gold discs from the Knowes of Trotty, Orkney (104.1-4)*

4.40 *Grave group from Blackwaterfoot, Arran (112)*

present in the finest grave groups. Gold remains to this day one of the most potent symbols of power so it is hardly surprising that its presence in the Wessex graves should have attracted so much attention. Although it occurs in only some 15% of the burials which Piggott defined as representing the Wessex culture the concentration in the area is still remarkable. Fifteen findspots are known for Wessex, all certainly or presumptively graves, compared to five findspots in four other southern English counties (Cornwall, Devon, Essex and Norfolk — the latter has two sites) and a complete absence from the rest of England (figures based on Taylor 1980, 136). Only the gold cape from Mold, Flintshire (illustration 4.41), perhaps the ultimate British symbol of power at this period, truly competes with the Wessex material for it involves

4.41 *Gold cape from Mold, Flintshire (98)*

symbolism not seen in Wessex. Much of the Wessex goldwork appears to be the work of a single master craftsman and all may have been the product of his workshop (Taylor 1980, 46-48). If this is the case then the *floruit* of the Wessex culture was relatively short and this has indeed been proposed (Coles, J M & Taylor 1971). Nevertheless, this suggestion does not diminish the power of the patrons of that workshop for many of the graves contain more than one gold object and its products were, as we shall see later, not restricted to Wessex.

The major arguments against this short time-scale derive from the second significant symbol in the Wessex graves, the daggers (ApSimon 1954; Britton 1961; Gerloff 1975; Burgess 1980, 106). As we have seen earlier the dagger has been an important symbol of power and status from the appearance of the earliest metalwork, at least in terms of reflecting individual prestige through grave goods. Two major types of dagger are known from the Wessex graves: the Armorico-British (eg. Bush Barrow: illustration 4.42) and Camerton-Snowhill (eg. Winterbourne Stoke G4: illustration 4.43), the latter apparently succeeding the former as the burial rite changed from inhumation to cremation. Once again the concentration in Wessex is particularly

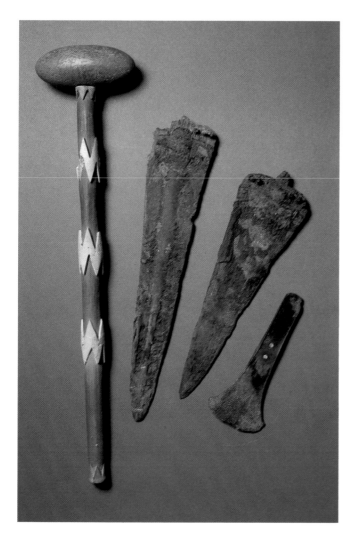

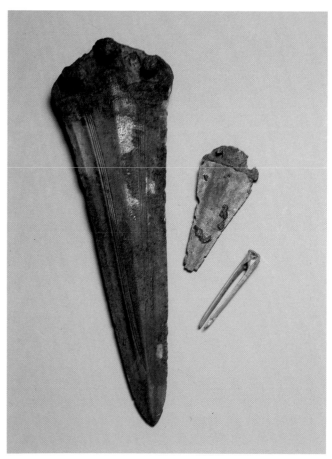

marked (Gerloff 1975, plates 34-37) with outliers being largely restricted to areas in the south and east of England. Indeed, apart from a few early types in Yorkshire, their absence from there and Derbyshire is, as with the finds of goldwork, quite striking. This contrast between these areas and Wessex was noted as early as the first individual burials and although there seems to have been no diminution in the tradition of leadership and control being reflected in burials in either Derbyshire or Yorkshire it does not seem to have involved any need for attempts to emulate Wessex.

One particular type of object illustrates particularly well the development of these divergent trends within the burial tradition. A rare but important component of the rich graves was small cups made of gold as at Rillaton, Cornwall (illustration 4.44) and Cuxwold, Lincolnshire (if one accepts Gerloff's interpretation of a now lost piece: 1975, 180-81), amber as at Hove, Sussex (illustration 4.45) and Clandon, Dorset (catalogue number 94), and shale as at Farway Down, Devon (illustration 4.46) and two unprovenanced Wiltshire examples (Newall 1929). All of them must have been major items of craftsmanship when new, involving considerable mastery of materials and technique — the amber and shale pieces, for example, appear to have been turned on a lathe. Their small

4.42 Bronze daggers and axe stone macehead and dentated bone mounts from Wilsford G5 (Bush Barrow), Wiltshire. The macehead and bone mounts are parts of separate objects and not, as shown here, one item

4.43 Grave group from Winterbourne Stoke G4, Wiltshire (111)

size does not suggest that they were produced primarily as functional objects but rather that they were to be admired for their aesthetic qualities reflecting the skill required for their creation. Just the sort of thing, in fact, that one would expect the rich and powerful members of the community to seek to acquire. The appeal of such cups in exotic materials was by no means restricted to Wessex as the gold examples from Fritzdorf, FRG (illustration 4.47) and Eschenz, Switzerland (illustration 4.48), and the silver one from Saint-Adrien, France (illustration 4.68) amply demonstrate. Indeed Gerloff has sought to show that handled cups were a feature of many assemblages throughout Europe at this period (1975, 177-96). Eastern areas of England, including Yorkshire, do not seem to have been totally immune from this development but there it is seen in much larger handled beakers and food vessels. This variation in size may only be reflecting the requirements of the different medium to achieve the desired effect for the pottery version of the Rillaton cup from Balmuick, Perthshire (illustration 4.49) is also much larger. Some of these such as the

4.44 *Gold cup from Rillaton, Cornwall*

4.45 *Grave group from Hove, Sussex (97)*

4.46 *Shale cup from Farway Broad Down, Devon (105)*

4.47 *Gold cup from Fritzdorf, Federal Republic of Germany (173)*

4.48 *Gold cup from Eschenz, Switzerland (171)*

4.49 *Handled beaker from Balmuick, Perthshire (106)*

example from Fordham, Cambridgeshire (illustration 4.50) have every bit the same aura of prestige and exclusivity that attaches to the Wessex cups. Certainly, the distribution of these large pottery cups (Clarke, D L 1970, 566, map 10) shows them to be virtually absent from the areas acquiring the smaller cups in exotic materials. Those from Wessex are, of course, concerned to present images that can be readily understood throughout Europe whereas although the pottery cups may be reflecting these wider concerns they are doing so in terms of long-established local traditions of how power and prestige should be expressed.

In concentrating on these three forms of symbol we have tried to emphasise the innovative qualities represented in the Wessex graves and the contrast they present with much of the rest of Britain. There are, of course, many more groups of objects with the burials serving the same general purposes ranging from amber crescentic necklaces (illustration 4.51) and segmented faience beads to bronze pins acquired from Europe (illustration 4.52), or local copies in other materials such as bone, and new types of accessory cup, particularly grape cups (illustration 4.53) and Aldbourne cups (Piggott, S 1938, 69-77). Only occasionally are there overt symbols of authority such as the macehead and staff decorated with dentated bone mounts in the Bush Barrow grave (illustration 4.42) or the equally remarkable gold and shale macehead from Clandon (illustration 4.54). Nor was the innovation restricted to the grave goods as the new

4.50 *Handled beaker, side-view and base, from Fordham, Cambridgeshire (77)*

barrow forms, bell and disc, demonstrate (Piggott, S 1973, 354-56; Fleming 1971; Grinsell 1974); Piggott has further suggested (1973, 357) that the burial in Amesbury 15, Wiltshire was covered by a wooden mortuary structure comparable to the rich Únětice burials at Leubingen and Helmsdorf discussed below (pp 142-44) although not in this instance accompanied by the same wealth of grave goods. This is an important point for although the overall impression is that power and prestige were

4.51 *Amber necklace from Upton Lovell G2(e), Wiltshire*

4.52 *Grave group from Wilsford G23, Wiltshire (110)*

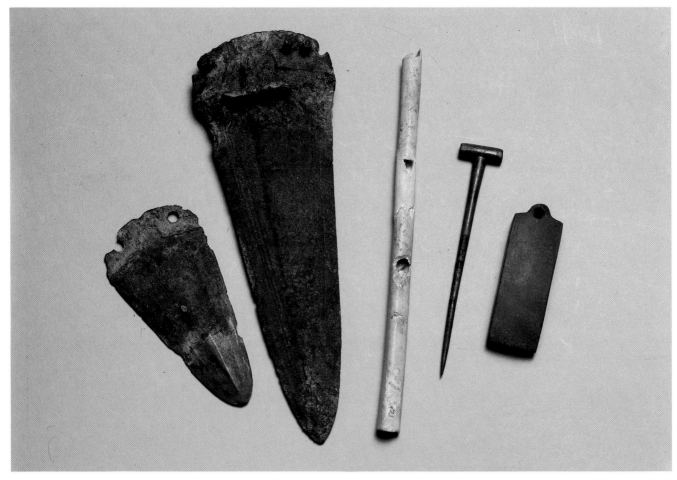

4.53 *Grape cup, cinerary urn and fragment of bronze dagger from Upton Lovell G2(e), Wiltshire*

primarily demonstrated through the burial ritual in Wessex at this period, the range and quality of the objects accompanying any particular individual is extremely variable. Even the use of one of the special barrow types or a barrow of exceptional size shows no clear correlation with the richness of the burials covered (Fleming 1973b, 572-73; Burgess 1980, 99). It may well be that these outward displays were considered by some a more appropriate manner of reflecting status and wealth than burial with a rich array of grave goods.

Despite this diversity, which appears to be the product of a complex series of interrelating factors involving sex, age and lineage (to isolate only the most obvious), there are some unifying themes observable in the essentially dynamically competitive situation. Perhaps the most obvious example is the practice of miniaturisation alluded to in our discussion of the handled cups. The regular use of accessory cups in preference to other large pottery types is not seen elsewhere in Britain to anything like the same extent. But it remains possible to interpret them in functional terms although a convincing explanation is still wanting. However, other objects, most notably the halberd pendants (illustrations 4.55-56) but including the bronze axe, 45 mm long, from Collingbourne Kingston G4, Wiltshire (Annable & Simpson 1964, number 387) suggest that the accessory cups are best seen in the context of a deliberate use of small items. Another aspect of this phenomenon appears to be represented by the tokenism involved in the deposition of only a small number of beads to represent a necklace or bracelet for even in the richest graves complete necklaces are rare, the Upton Lovell gold barrow being the most obvious exception. These token beads show another element consistently present in Wessex graves, the combination of a variety of materials to create a

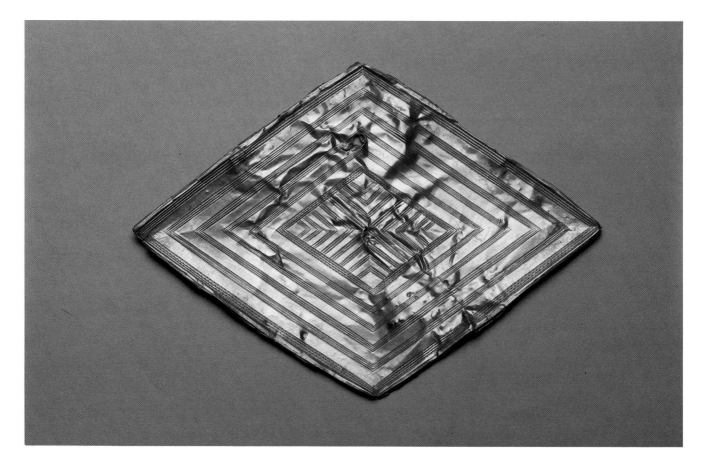

4.54 *facing page: Grave group from Clandon, Dorset (94): a. gold plate; b. shale and gold macehead, accessory cup and fragments of an amber cup*

4.55 *Grave group from Hengistbury Head, Hampshire (96): a. cinerary urn and accessory cup; b. the gold cones, amber beads and halberd pendant*

4.56 Accessory cup and halberd pendant from Wilsford G8, Wiltshire

single object. In the case of Winterslow 21, Wiltshire (Stone 1934, 219, 222-24), which may be taken as a fairly typical example, the eight beads are made of three different materials (faience, amber and jet) and have four different forms (segmented, biconical, barrel-shaped and annular). Of course, necklaces or bracelets do not require much virtuosity in their production but the items in the richest graves are of an altogether different order. There, halberd pendants imitating central European types never found in Wessex, gold-bound amber discs, gold and shale buttons, a wooden dagger hilt inlaid with minute gold pins and even a gold-covered bone disc (illustrations 4.32 & 57) all show a positive delight in the skill of the craftsmen to create composite objects of considerable delicacy. These are the ultimate expressions of the appeal of craftsmanship expressed through small but undoubtedly costly objects.

It should be clear from these brief remarks that the individuals buried in the rich Wessex graves were both powerful and wealthy with the confidence to adopt innovative practices and modes of expression. Indeed this basic point has been widely accepted from the beginnings of serious study of the objects in the eighteenth century. To say this, of course, raises a number of related questions concerning the origins of the individuals involved, the extent of their foreign contacts and the sources of their wealth. None of these issues has been explained in terms which have met with widespread endorsement among archaeologists (the various positions are reviewed in Piggott S, 1973; Fleming 1973b; Burgess 1980, 98-111).

Turning first to the question of origins we find that recent considerations have largely polarised around two different views. Some (eg. Clark, J G D 1966; Burgess 1980, 99-103) would see the graves as no more than those of the leaders of the indigenous population who in times

4.57 *The gold objects from Upton Lovell G2(e), Wiltshire (100)*

of economic and social change consolidated their position at the head of a more structured society. On the other hand, others (eg. Hawkes 1966; Clarke D L 1970, 279) have interpreted the evidence in terms of invasion from continental Europe; Clarke's proposals involved 'an alien aristocracy, probably from the Middle Rhineland' travelling with metalworkers trained in Únĕtice techniques subsequently reinforced by 'a second wave, possibly from North Germany'. Even those supporting the concept of invasion would find the details of this proposal difficult to accept today. The problem revolves around the importance that is to be attached to the new material in the assemblages. There are clearly strong echoes of indigenous traditions among which individual inhumation under barrows and cremation are particularly important. Equally, the continued use of maceheads and battle-axes as symbols of prestige and the presence of V-bored buttons all have antecedents in local practices. Certainly, there is a degree of elaboration (eg. the shape of the buttons are exaggerated and they are covered with gold) but this is no more than one would expect in the circumstances. Moreover, it is curious that if there was an invasion by people from any likely area in continental Europe they should have abandoned key symbols from their homeland: axes are certainly more prevalent in Breton graves and halberds were important in Únĕtice areas although neither appears to be particularly significant in Wessex.

We have tried to suggest that the innovative material seen in the Wessex graves results from the leaders in that area being part of an interregional network of contacts between widespread European groups. Whilst there were shared views and accepted symbols for demonstrating power and prestige there remained the need to interpret these things in terms of individual groups. The objects in the Wessex graves are to be seen as the particular selections of the powerful individuals in that area from a wider international range. Some, of course, may represent objects received through gift-exchange but most must be the work of craftsmen

4.58 Bronze dagger and axe from Ridgeway barrow 7, Dorset (99.1-2)

operating under local patronage: the pattern is well illustrated by the finds from Ridgeway barrow 7, Dorset (illustrations 4.58-59). There does seem to have been more contact with Brittany and central Europe in the early phase (Burgess 1980, 104-06) and with northern Germany and Switzerland in the later but it would be a mistake to see these foci as in any way exclusive. Whether these wide-ranging contacts extended as far as the Aegean is not clear. Leaving aside the vexed question of faience beads where it seems the techniques of manufacture were exported rather than the beads (see below p 219-20) there are a number of items in the area with claims to manufacture in Wessex: notably the gold-bound amber disc at Knossos on Crete (Cunnington 1925, 69-70) and fragments of amber crescentic necklaces in three Mycenaean contexts (Shaft-Grave IV and Grave Omicron at Mycenae and a chamber-tomb at Kakovatos: Piggott, S 1973, 365). Equally important are the dentated bone mounts from Bush Barrow paralleled only by examples in Shaft-Grave Iota at Mycenae (Piggott, S 1966, 119) and the technical comparisons between the northern European gold cups and Mycenaean examples. Contacts between central and Eastern Europe and the Myceaean world were more substantive (Piggott, S 1966) and it may be that these areas acted as intermediaries in promoting gift-exchanges and a sharing of technical expertise. Renfrew (1968), however, argued on the basis of radiocarbon dates that the Wessex graves were too early for any link with Mycenae to be possible. This view was soon challenged (McKerrell 1972) and recent radiocarbon dates from graves with Camerton-Snowshill daggers have further weakened his arguments (Burgess 1980, 106).

Finally, it remains to consider what was the source of the wealth and power expressed in the Wessex burials. By far the commonest explanation has been that the Wessex leaders were acting as middlemen for Irish gold and bronze objects in their distribution to the European mainland (originally proposed by Piggott, S 1938, 94). There is, however, very litttle evidence to support this proposition. Very little Irish metalwork has been found in Wessex and Ireland in common with Scotland seems to have been using alternative modes for displays of prestige, which suggest that leaders there were directly linked to the inter-regional networks we have been proposing. The problem is, as Burgess rightly recognised (1980, 103), to identify what was peculiar to Wessex and absent in other apparently important areas. The explanation, he felt, could not lie with the major ceremonial monuments since these

4.59 Gold pommel-mount from Ridgeway barrow 7, Dorset (99.3): a. top view; b. side view

were also to be found, although not perhaps in quite such concentrations, in other areas and he chose instead the direct and easy access to the Continent afforded by the harbours of Wessex. The beginnings of an answer may well lie in these suggestions, although not quite in the way formulated by Burgess. Fleming's study of the barrow distributions in Wessex (1971) showed two major concentrations, one around Stonehenge and one on the Dorset Ridgeway. As he points out there is no equivalent to Stonehenge on the Ridgeway but it is nevertheless a spectacular setting in which not only do the barrows appear impressive when seen from the lower ground but it also provides 'splendid views . . . over much of S Dorset and the adjacent English Channel' (RCHME 1970, 426). We have then evidence for Wessex burials being concentrated around and reflecting control of the most important ceremonial site in Britain (demonstrated by its continuing use after other large communal monuments had been abandoned) and on a major ridge commanding extensive views of the English Channel, the means of access to the Continent. Both settings are in their own way spectacular and entirely consistent with the choice of individuals wishing to express their power and prestige in the most flamboyant burial practices in Britain during the second millennium bc.

Brittany

The connections between the rich graves of Brittany and Wessex have been commented on since the Wessex graves were first recognised as a coherent group. None would wish to challenge the idea that in Brittany, as in Wessex, these graves represent a powerful elite expressing their prestige and status through burial practices. But it would be a mistake to over-emphasise the strength of the relationship between the two areas. Certainly, it was stronger than either area's links with central Europe but this is not surprising given their proximity to one another and the ease of contact afforded by the English Channel. Nevertheless the evidence is limited to a small number of objects of specific types and while the leaders in Brittany drew on the same set of internationally acknowledged symbols, they showed quite as much individuality in their interpretation of these symbols as their peers in other areas.

The graves with which we are primarily concerned are contemporary with those in Wessex and usually described as the Armorican First Series graves. The division of second millennium bc burials in Brittany into First and Second Series was first proposed over 30 years ago (Cogné & Giot 1951) and remains a convenient descriptive shorthand. The two groups are defined by the types of object occurring in the graves. The First Series normally contain high quality flint arrowheads commonly accompanied by bronze metalwork, particularly daggers and, to a lesser extent, axes. The Second Series are characterised by the presence of a pottery vessel, usually a jar with four handles. Although often the only grave goods, the pottery is in a number of cases accompanied by a bronze dagger or, exceptionally, other artefacts such as faience beads. Both types occur in elaborately constructed graves under burial mounds. Although the largest of these mounds, 50-60 m in diameter and 5-6 m high, covers First

Series burials, there is no clear distinction in size between the two Series. Most of these barrows lie west of a line drawn from the Bay of Saint Brieuc to the mouth of the Villaine. Within this area, however, there is quite marked spatial separation between the mounds of the two Series: the First Series have primarily a coastal distribution concentrated in Finistère and Morbihan with only a few sites in the interior whereas the Second Series, although more widely distributed, are concentrated inland, particularly along the valley of the River Blavet and on the southern slopes of the Monts d'Arrée. In almost every instance the barrows cover a single grave.

The First Series burials are generally earlier in date, even though the chronological separation between the two Series envisaged when the scheme was first proposed can no longer be sustained, and mark a dramatic shift in emphasis towards the use of individual burial. Briard (1976b, 34) while acknowledging this, has drawn attention to earlier instances of individual interments in closed cists or under mounds (eg. Kerméné, Guidel, Morbihan). These instances are, however, rare compared to the 400 or so barrows of second millennium bc date known from western Brittany and both are in marked contrast to the vigorous chamber tomb traditions of the preceding two millennia. Unlike the situation in Britain the impetus of these developments does not seem to have been caused by the appearance of beakers. Although Brittany is one of the few areas in northern and western France where beakers occur in any quantity (Harrison 1984, 202-04, figures 1-3) their acquisition seems largely to have been in the hands of leaders whose power derived from control of the major communal monuments. Monuments for the living seem to have taken the form of stone alignments, seen at their most spectacular in the area around Carnac, and single standing stones (menhirs), often of considerable height (illustrations 4.60-64). Much alteration and disturbance, particularly in the form of 19th-century AD restoration, combined with the absence of the carefully defined areas seen in the British monuments make interpretation difficult. The introduction of beakers and associated artefact types must, however, have given emphasis to the idea of power expressed through prestige items and involved Brittany in wider international networks. Although beakers do not occur in First Series graves, Briard drew attention to several links between their contents and beaker-associated artefacts representing perhaps a developing ideology. Although no continuous development can be traced, the technological background of the distinctive Armorican arrowheads lies most convincingly among earlier forms of ogival barbed and tanged arrowheads associated with beaker pottery (Briard 1976b, 38-40). These links are reinforced by the presence of stone wristguards in First Series graves at Lothéa, Forest of Carnoët (Briard & Mohen 1974, 49) and Coatjou-Glas, Ploneis, Finistère (Briard 1984, 250) and by the presumptively symbolic representation of such wristguards in amber at Saint-Fiacre (illustration 4.65) and in gold at 'La Motta' (illustration 4.66).

The basic features of First Series burials can best be illustrated in brief descriptions of one or two graves. One of the most impressive assemblages recovered in recent years is that from the barrow at

4.61 *Stone alignments at Carnac*

Kernonen, Plouvorn, Finistère (Briard 1970; 1984, 262-63). The mound, originally 50 m in diameter and 6 m high, was largely composed of local yellow loam containing a thick layer of grey clayey loam which appears to have been brought from a source at least a kilometre away from the site. The central grave, protected by a cairn some 11 m in diameter, consisted of a rectangular chamber with dry stone walls and measuring 4.7 × 1.4 m. The floor of the grave had been paved and covered with wooden flooring. Some of the grave goods had been placed directly on the floor but a large proportion of the items had been deposited in three oak boxes arranged along the north wall of the grave (illustration 4.67). The box at the north-west end contained the remains of four bronze axes, one of them with traces of textile, probably linen, and fragments of worked wood adhering to it. Beside the central box there was a line of 10 overlapping arrowheads which may originally have involved a further 8 found dispersed in the grave.

These 18 arrowheads appear to have been placed in the burial with their shafts still intact. The large central box itself contained the remains of two bronze daggers laid across a short bronze 'sword'. All three blades

4.60 *facing page Stone alignments at Carnac, Brittany*

4.62 *Stone alignments at Carnac*

4.63 *Stone alignments at Carnac*

4.64 *Le Grand Menhir, Brittany: now fallen but once the largest standing stone in the region*

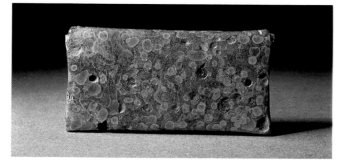

4.65 *Amber pendant from Saint-Fiacre, Morbihan, Brittany (166.12)*

4.66 *Gold 'box' and arrowheads from 'La Motta', Côtes-du-Nord, Brittany (163.1 & 12)*

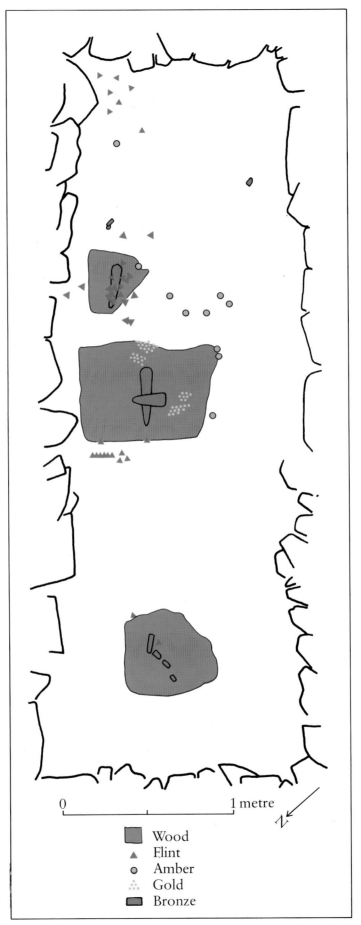

4.67 *Plan of the grave at Kernonen, Finistère, Brittany showing the arrangement of the grave goods (after Briard 1984)*

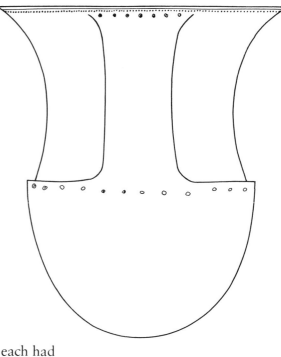

0   5
⊢━━━━━━━━━━┴━━━━━━━━━━┤ c m

had once had wooden hilts ornately inlaid with gold pins and each had been placed in a composite sheath also containing bronze ring-headed pins. To the south of this box lay a dispersed series of 11 amber pendants of discoidal and trapezoidal form. The third box held a further bronze dagger with a bone pommel and traces of its sheath, 42 arrowheads and an amber pendant in the form of an archer's wristguard. The decayed remains of another bronze axe lay near the southern wall.

4.68 *Silver cup from Saint-Adrien, Côtes-du-Nord, Brittany (165.5)*

4.69 *Reconstruction drawing of the silver cup from Saint-Adrien (after Briard 1984)*

The barrow of Brun-Bras at Saint-Adrien, Côtes-du-Nord (Briard 1978, 13-16; 1984, 225-26) was only about 30 m in diameter and covered a cairn 6 × 4 m, which had been built over a wooden mortuary structure. On the floor of the grave were found traces of what appears to have been an oak coffin or box. Like Kernonen, no skeletal remains survived but the disposition of the grave goods suggested that the burial had consisted of an inhumation deposited with the head to the east. Near the presumed position of the head were found fragments of a single-handled silver cup (illustrations 4.68-69). At about waist-level lay a small bronze dagger with traces of a wooden hilt ornately inlaid with gold pins and two long bronze blades or 'swords', one of them with traces of a composite sheath of wood and animal skin. Very fragmentary traces of a second dagger lay dispersed about the floor of the grave. Lying on the traces of the coffin were a series of 45 flint arrowheads (illustration 4.70), placed overlapping and side by side in a position which strongly suggests they were deposited with shafts and flights in place, an interpretation re-inforced by the discovery of traces of wood on one of the tangs (Briard 1984, 226). Finally, towards the west end of the grave, was a bronze axe with low flanges lying on its own (illustration 4.71).

Between them these two burials amply demonstrate the range of material found in Armorican First Series graves although both are rich in comparison with other members of the Series. Within the Series, Briard has distinguished a limited group of 5 or 6 large mounds, such as 'La Motta', Saint-Fiacre, Saint-Adrien and Kernonen, which he regards as being of 'princely' status (1974, 140). These are, in fact, the Breton equivalent of the richest graves found in Wessex, for example at Bush

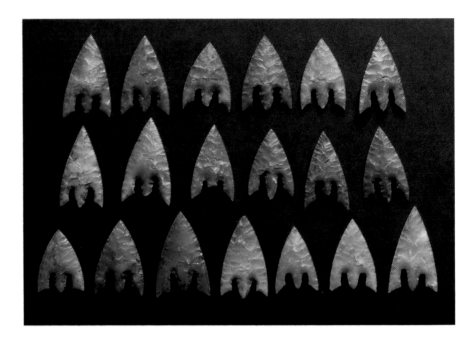

4.70 *Arrowheads from Saint-Adrien (165.1)*

Barrow, or in central Europe, for example at Leubingen and Helmsdorf. While in a general sense the comparisons may well be valid there are, nevertheless, considerable differences in the manner chosen by leaders in particular areas to express their power and prestige. All of this is consistent with elites seeking to combine the new international symbols with those traditionally regarded as reflecting prestige and status in a particular region.

Nowhere is this process better demonstrated than in the flint arrowheads from Breton graves. As we have already noted these arrowheads are a defining feature of First Series graves and probably reflect traditions introduced with beakers. Three types are discernible: short ogival, long ogival and triangular (Giot 1960, 131-32; Briard 1979, 78-80; 1984, 97-106). The short ogival variety are the most common, occurring in twenty-four graves, often in impressive deposits of between twenty-five and fifty, for example Brun-Bras, Saint-Adrien (illustration 4.72). The long ogival arrowheads are superlative pieces of craftsmanship in flint and unsurpassed in quality anywhere in prehistoric Europe. Their extreme thinness, finely serrated edges and elegantly drooping barbs are the product of superbly controlled flaking (eg. Creac'h Morvan, Saint Thégonnec: illustration 4.73). These arrowheads are peculiar to Brittany, where over 150 are known from some sixteen burials, often in conjunction with the short ogival variety. The triangular arrowheads are much less common having been found at only three sites. Arrowheads were clearly an important component of the suite of material considered appropriate for deposition in graves. Indeed, the long ogival arrowheads appear to have been made exclusively for burial since only one has been recovered in a non-funerary context at Saint-Nicholas-du-Pélem, Côtes-du-Nord (Le Provost Giot & Onnée 1972). But they were not always treated in the same manner for as we have seen at Kernonen one

4.71 *Bronze daggers, 'sword' and axe from Saint-Adrien (165.2-4): a. the bronzes; b. some of the minute gold pins which decorated the wooden hilt of the dagger*

group was placed unmounted in one of the wooden boxes while the other retained their shafts and at Kerguéverac, Plouyé, Finistère the arrowheads had been arranged in a circle around a jet spacer-plate (Piggott, S 1939, 193-95, figure 1). In some of the larger assemblages the work of individual craftsmen can be seen. Briard suggested that several of the Kernonen arrowheads were the product of a single flint-knapper (1970,

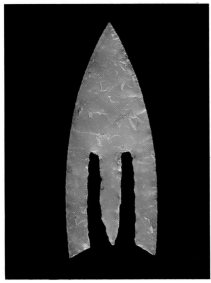

24) and the group of long ogival arrowheads from 'La Motta' also appear to be the work of one hand (illustration 4.66: Butler & Waterbolk 1974, 127). Control of such skilled craftsmen using imported materials, in this case high quality flint from Touraine (Briard 1970, 40; 1984, 103), reflects a situation common to the production of items for rich graves throughout Europe but the absence of arrowheads in other areas, particularly Wessex, suggests that in this case they were producing a local symbol.

Gold, on the other hand, demonstrates very effectively the workings of wider networks. Although much rarer than in Wessex graves comparable remarkable technical skills are evident in its use, principally as a means of decorating weapons, in particular the wooden hilts of bronze daggers and swords and occasionally their blades (eg. Cosqueric, Priziac, Morbihan: illustration 4.74). At Kernonen (Briard 1970, 24-32), the hilts of the two bronze daggers and the 'sword' had been elaborately decorated with as many as 5000 tiny gold nails (cf. illustration 4.71). The average length of these nails was less than 1 mm and they were arranged to emphasise the outlines of the hilt plate and the pommel and to encircle the bronze rivet heads. In addition, the central part of the hilt had been ornamented on each side with a triangular arrangement of gold 'tacks' or mock rivets, each group designed and made specifically for the dagger concerned. Daggers with hilts ornately decorated in this fashion are known from a dozen sites in Brittany, over half of them in the Côtes-du-Nord (including the barrow at Brun-Bras, Saint-Adrien). Two examples of this technique are known from southern England, the best known being the wooden handle of one of the daggers from Bush Barrow, and both may represent the products of Breton craftsmen (illustration 4.75). However, the gold pendant in the form of a wristguard from 'La Motta' appears to be the

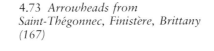

4.74 *Fragment of bronze dagger inlaid with gold roundels from Priziac, Morbihan, Brittany (164)*

4.72 *The two main types of arrowhead: a. short ogival; b. long ogival*

4.73 *Arrowheads from Saint-Thégonnec, Finistère, Brittany (167)*

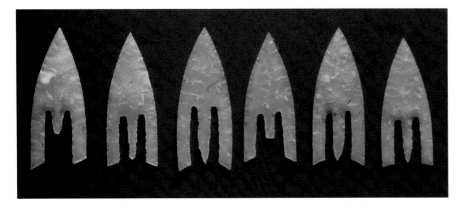

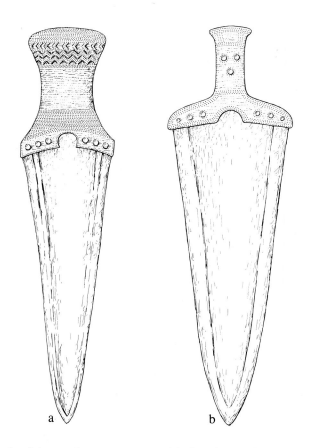

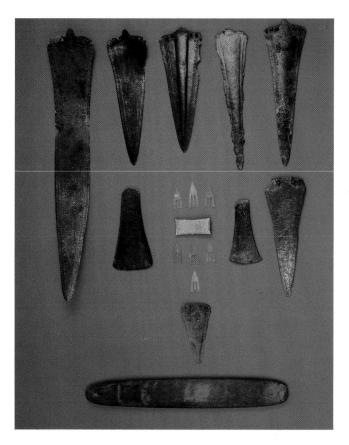

work of the craftsman responsible for the gold work in the Wessex graves at Bush Barrow, Wilsford G8, Upton Lovell G2(e) and Clandon (Taylor 1974, 160-62; 1980, 47).

Links with Wessex are seen equally clearly in the Armorico-British type of daggers found in graves in both areas but there is a marked contrast in terms of the numbers deposited with each burial (illustration 4.76). The occurrence of several daggers is a common feature of the richest Armorican First Series graves, often accompanied by 'swords' which do not occur at all in Wessex. Such 'swords', reflecting ideas seen also in the Ommerschans rapiers (Butler & Bakker 1961; Butler & Sarfatij 1971), can only have been for display or ceremonial purposes, if indeed they were not made especially for burial. Three of these 'swords' formed part of the exceptionally rich grave group from the Lothéa barrow, Forest of Carnoët, Finistère and their blades appear to have been given a deliberate arsenic-rich coating in order to create a silvered effect. Comparable weapons are known from contemporary contexts in Iberia (Briard & Mohen 1974, 57-59).

This emphasis on quantity, seen most conspicuously in the case of arrowheads but also as significantly in terms of bronze weapons, gives the richest graves in Brittany many of the characteristics of British hoards. Certainly, hoards are known from Brittany but they are by no means common. It would not be altogether surprising in such a metal-rich area if the ideologies reflected in graves and hoards which we have seen as separate in Britain should have here become more intertwined. In this context it is interesting to note that the Breton graves reflect the

4.75 *Drawing of daggers with wooden hilts decorated with gold pins: a. Bush Barrow (Wilsford G5), Wiltshire; b. Kernonen, Finistère, Brittany (after: a. Thurnam 1871; b. Briard 1984)*

4.76 *Grave group from 'La Motta', Côtes-du-Nord, Brittany (163)*

differentiation between daggers and axes which we have already noted. Axes occur more commonly in graves here than in Wessex and may be of considerable size (eg. Tossen Maharit, Trévérec, Côtes-du-Nord: 202 mm; Saint-Fiacre, Melrand, Morbihan: 174 mm: illustration 4.77). They appear to be made specifically for burial and differ in size and more especially form from the axes recovered in hoards or as isolated finds (Briard 1965, 59-60; 1984, 77-78). They were, moreover, placed apart from other material in the grave, as we have seen at Saint-Adrien and Kernonen, and there is some evidence that they were on occasion wrapped in textiles.

It is hard to avoid associating the appearance of the Breton rich graves with the exploitation of Armorican mineral resources at a time when the expansion of full bronze metallurgy was underway in western Europe. In this respect Brittany's location on the Atlantic seaboard may well have been a significant factor. The power and wealth acquired by the individuals controlling these resources is reflected both in the elaborate construction of the barrow and the contents of the graves. As with Wessex, we see participation in wide-ranging networks existing alongside a strong concern to develop symbols of power promoting regional identity.

4.77 *Grave group from Saint-Fiacre, Morbihan, Brittany (166)*

Central Europe

During the third and second millennia bc the development of copper and bronze industries in areas which had access to important ores did not take place in isolation. Not only were there connections which resulted in the movement of objects, but there was also movement of ideas. Barrett *(supra)* has argued that an axe made in one area and moved from its source of manufacture by exchange becomes gradually more 'exotic' the farther it gets. During the second millennium bc there are finds of bronze axes of Irish form in central Europe. In Ireland, Scotland and central Europe, halberds are used as objects of display and ceremony. Amber from the Baltic and Denmark was used, particularly in Wessex and central Europe (and even farther afield in Greece), to make necklaces, beads and buttons. Traditionally, the appearance in several distant places of similar objects and the use of materials whose sources are few have been seen in terms of long-distance trade. We have suggested that this is not a useful way in which to approach the evidence and that it should be seen in terms of exchange and the two ways in which prestige goods may be controlled — production and distribution. In central Eruope, the Únětice group shows the development of a locally controlled bronze industry which could acquire objects ultimately from as far afield as Ireland and had an important influence on the movement of amber. Clearly several mechanisms of control are represented here in terms of both production and distribution. In this chapter we shall concentrate on the European Únětice group and explore its importance for understanding the similarities and differences with Britain and Ireland and the connections which existed between it, other areas of Continental Europe and the British Isles.

From *c.* 1800-1500 bc there flourished in what is now southern East Germany, south-west Poland, Czechoslovakia and parts of neighbouring countries, a society known by the modern name of one of its rich cemeteries — Únětice (Aunjetitz) in Czechoslovakia (Gimbutas 1965, 245-70; Coles, J M & Harding 1979, 38-50). Closely related groups (eg. Straubing and Adlerberg) inhabited southern West Germany. It is impossible to discuss these groups in the same detail as we have given for Britain. To talk of a society covering such a large area is a statement of sufficient generality that it hides major differences which must have existed between its constituent parts and indeed from site to site. Here we shall concentrate on those Únětice groups who inhabited Saxo-Thuringia and occasionally mention other areas. Únětice graves are, in general, well supplied with grave goods, but in Saxo-Thuringia there are two particularly rich graves — Leubingen and Helmsdorf — and a great concentration of large hoards. It is the importance of this area in particular which elucidates developments in Wessex and the British Isles.

The origins of the Únětice society lie in the earlier inhabitants of this area. These people are identified by the use of two types of pottery — corded ware and bell beaker. The latter we have already discussed in terms of its importance in Britain. The beaker phenomenon was one which dramatically influenced many areas of Europe, but in no two areas does it seem to have had exactly the same effect (cf. Harrison 1980).

Certainly, as in Britain, the appearance of beakers coincides with the development of metal technology, but there was a long European tradition of copper-working before the manufacture of bronze increased in scale. Gold was also an important resource and we might mention the gold cups from Fritzdorf, Bonn, FRG, (illustration 4.47), Eschenz, Switzerland (illustration 4.48) and Golenkamp bei Hannover, FRG (Hardmeyer & Bürgi 1975, 116, Abb 11) as examples of the sheet gold technology which was developing.

It is from such traditions that the power and strength of the Únetice groups grew. Within a radius of 120 km of Prague there are major sources of copper, tin and gold (eg. the Erzgebirge (Ore Mountains) were important for copper mining). A wide range of objects were made in copper — spiral arm rings, spiral beads, neckrings/ingot torcs, large pins, double-spiral pendants, hair rings etc — and, in gold, pins and beads (Gimbutas 1965, 251-60). The richness of the range of objects for personal decoration is impressive. Most of the finds are known from burials, the vast majority of which are in cemeteries of individual flat graves (ie. without large barrows built over them) and these often comprise over 60 graves (Coles, J M & Harding 1979, 38). The cemetery of Grossbrembach, Sömmerda, GDR had a long history (Ullrich 1972; Coles, J M & Harding 1979, 38-40) producing 81 graves with 108 skeletons. On the basis of the order of burial and detailed anatomical analysis, Ullrich was able to distinguish 'family groups' buried in particular areas of the cemetery and argued that the position of the burial represented family ties rather than the date of the burial. During the early Únětice period the goods buried with the dead were quite small in number, but later on in the 'Classical' period, greater numbers of objects and, at times, richer objects were included. There are clear indications of social differentiation, seen in the varying quality and quantity of the objects included in the graves. Different interpretations have been put upon this evidence, but what is certain is that as the later tin-bronze technology developed, there was a marked increase in differentiation in grave goods as well as the ritual disposal of masses of bronze objects in hoards.

As Champion et al (1984, 211) point out (following Shennan 1982b, 159), there are important distinctions between the changes seen here and those in Wessex and Brittany. The development of very rich graves in Britain and north west France happened at a time of ideological change. In Saxo-Thuringia, however, there was no such change and the rich graves are an extension of the local burial tradition with the addition of more and better quality grave goods. Two exceptional burials are known from Leubingen, Sömmerda, GDR (illustrations 4.78-79) and Helmsdorf, Hettstedt, GDR. Both were within large mounds and had massive wooden grave chambers covering the burial. Neither of these is part of the known earlier Únětice traditions. At Leubingen (Höfer, 1906) a triangular-sectioned timber chamber was built in oak (illustration 4.80). On the floor was placed the extended body of a mature male and at right angles across his hips was the extended body of an adolescent or a child. The grave goods were carefully placed; a pot surrounded by stones, a stone pick and a cushion stone placed side by side, a halberd with a

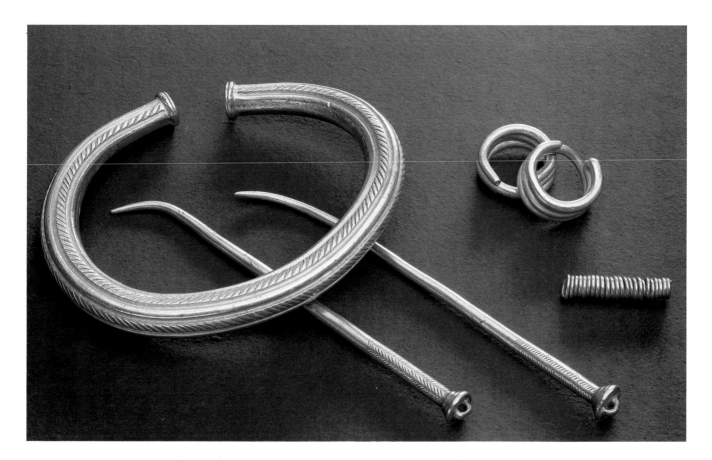

4.78 *The gold objects from Leubingen, Sömmerda, German Democratic Republic (169.12-17)*

4.79 *The other objects from Leubingen: a. stone and bronze (169.1-11), b. pottery (169.18)*

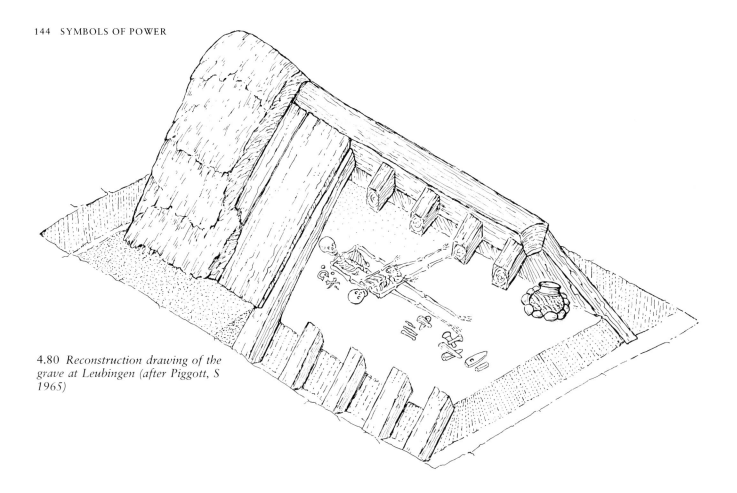

4.80 *Reconstruction drawing of the grave at Leubingen (after Piggott, S 1965)*

dagger lying across its blade, two flanged axes lying at right angles and two more daggers at right angles. Beside these were three bronze chisels placed in a line. The pot stood on the left side of the male skeleton and the bronze and stone objects on the right beside the leg, knee and foot. Between the heads of the two bodies were placed gold jewellery — two large pins, two hair rings, a massive armlet and a spiral bead. On top of the wooden mortuary stucture a very large cairn of stones was capped by earth. At the time of excavation the barrow was 34 m in diameter and 8.5 m high. Rich and impressive though the Wessex burials were, they do not compare with this.

The burial at Helmsdorf is in many ways similar (Grössler 1907). It was also under a barrow of roughly the same size and had a massive wooden grave chamber. The floor was paved partly with stone slabs and partly with reeds. The crouched body had been placed in a wooden coffin on a wooden bier and was accompanied by a pot within a stone setting, a battle-axe, a bronze flanged axe, a dagger, a chisel and, in gold, two large pins, two hair rings, a massive armlet and a spiral bead.

Two graves in Barrow 1 at Łęki Małe, Kościan, Poland were also within a large barrow and timber mortuary chamber (Kowiańska-Piaszykowa & Kurnatowski 1953). The male burial had with it a flanged axe, a dagger blade, a pin, two bracelets, a metal-shafted halberd, a gold earring and five pottery vessels. The female grave contained a flanged axe, a metal hilted dagger, a chisel, two pins, three gold hair rings, two amber beads and five pottery vessels.

As a result of the exceptional nature of both the burial rite and the contents, these have been called princely graves (Fürstengräber). They make it absolutely clear that there were individuals at particular times who were so powerful that even rich Únětice burial was not enough. The implications have sometimes been reluctantly admitted: 'It seems necessary to see in these rich barrows the proof of social stratification; but it is notable that they are restricted to the latter part of the Early Bronze Age and are by no means typical of the whole' (Coles, J M & Harding 1979, 43). Certainly Helmsdorf and Leubingen are not typical burials or grave assemblages but what they represent is something which should not be surprising. In generalising about Únětice burials, we have passed over the details of the variety, quality and quantity of the grave goods. Whilst there are dangers in directly attributing social status or stratification on the basis of the contents of graves, we shall show that in Britain there is a range from no grave goods at all to very rich ones. These do form a pyramidal structure with the richest graves being the fewest in number.

It is clear that the inclusion of grave goods was always part of Únětice rites. At Helmsdorf, Leubingen and Łęki Małe even greater riches were buried with the dead and, in addition, an impressive and labour intensive monument was built over the burials. A comparison of Leubingen and Helmsdorf shows two barrows of roughly similar size, containing the same type of grave goods — pot within a ring of stones, perforated stone implement, flanged axe, dagger, chisel, gold pins, hair rings, massive armlet and spiral bead. That at Leubingen is even richer, having a halberd and more chisels, daggers and axes than Helmsdorf. At Łęki Małe we again see the same range of objects included in the burials.

It is no coincidence that the radiocarbon dates from Helmsdorf (1663 bc ± 160: Bln-248) and Łęki Małe (1655 bc ± 35: GrN-5037 and 1950 bc ± 150: M-1325) are comparable. It is also reasonable to assume that Leubingen was built at about the same time. This would suggest that the three very rich Únětice barrows were built as reflections of a particular situation at around the same time. It would be easiest to see Leubingen and Helmsdorf which are only c. 50 km (and not 100 km as shown in Gimbutas 1965, 248, fig 161) apart as deliberate competition in burial.

Otto (1955) studied the range of burial types and contents from Únětice graves in central Germany and analysed them in four categories:
1. Chieftains' graves which were very rich in grave goods and in the structure of the grave itself and which are not within a cemetery.
2. Very rich male graves which contained copper or bronze objects as well as gold but were within a cemetery.
3. Rich graves which contained copper or bronze weapons, tools or ornaments, but no gold or halberds.
4. Poor graves which had either pottery or nothing at all.

Otto's explanation of the social structure as a form of stratified military democracy is perhaps inappropriate. Nonetheless, he has shown clearly that differentiation is represented by more than the Fürstengräber — the extreme end of the spectrum.

During the classical Únětice period there were also massive deposits of hoards. Von Brunn (1959) has given details of these from the area under discussion and it is worth examining a number of them — the three hoards from Dieskau, Saalkreis, GDR and that from farther north at Bresinchen, Guben, GDR. Taking the traditional view, Gimbutas (1965,

269) discusses metalwork as the possession of the producer communities and suggests that hoards represent groups of items which were traded and might be buried 'as a precaution'. We have suggested that the deposition of metalwork hoards is better seen as the deliberate 'destruction' of wealth in conspicuous displays and it is interesting to examine the similarities and differences between Únětice hoards and those in Britain. The range of objects placed in the Únětice hoards was very similar to that in graves though the quantities involved are astonishingly greater. This similarity in the range of objects deposited contrasts with the usual practices in Britain.

The three hoards from Dieskau contained: I — a decorated *gold* flanged axe, 2 gold bracelets, a massive gold armring and an electrum ring (von Brunn 1959, 55); II — within a pottery vessel, a necklace of 106 amber beads, 23 bronze spiral beads, 10 neckrings/ingot torcs, 4 annular rings, 2 penannular rings, 7 armrings, 2 spiral armrings, 2 shaft-hole axes, 14 halberds and a flanged axe (illustration 4.24: Förtsch 1905); III — within a pottery vessel 4 massive armrings, 6 spiral armrings, 2 shaft-hole axes, a halberd and 293 flanged axes (von Brunn 1959, 56). The hoard from Bresinchen had, within 2 pottery vessels, 103 flanged axes, 10 neckrings/ingot torcs, a shaft-hole axe, 22 penannular rings, 2 metal-shafted halberds and 8 metal-hilted daggers (illustration 4.23: Breddin 1969).

Certainly, these hoards are large by Únětice standards but they are not exceptionally so. By comparison those in Britain seem poor, but we should not compare British and Únětice practices directly since the nature of the societies and the availability of metal goods within those societies were different. The inclusion in Únětice hoards of objects which are regularly deposited in graves suggests that the disposal of frequently decorated and ceremonial metalwork (eg. the daggers and halberds) as well as personal ornaments in both metal and amber was under the direct control not of the producers of the metalwork as Gimbutas suggested, but those who had authority over the metalworkers and the exchange systems involved after production. The contrast with Britain is primarily that of the scale of deposition, but there are also greater distinctions between what is included in burials and in hoards. We have suggested that rich burials and hoard deposition in Britain should be seen as part of similar social structures, with ideological reasons for the difference between what was buried with the dead and what was put in hoards. There was no great distinction between the contents of Únětice burials and hoards. The wealth of metalwork and amber was in the control of powerful individuals and its deposition as hoards or in graves was part of the same process. Power was seen for what it was without the ideological masking of actual power relations which we have seen in Britain.

It has been suggested that the basis of Únětice wealth was the accessibility of rich sources of copper, gold and tin and the development of a fine metalworking tradition in the area. The Únětice groups were powerful and important and their influence spread over long distances, certainly to Ireland, Britain, Brittany and the Baltic. In the rest of this chapter we shall examine these various connections and the prestige that Únětice-style artefacts had elsewhere. This was not, of course, a one way process and the Únětice people did acquire objects and materials in return.

One area which was the end of a chain of exchanges with central Germany was the Baltic coast and Denmark. The appearance of metal objects here coincides with the expansion of metalworking in central Europe. Since there are no sources of copper or tin in the Baltic area, both finished goods and unworked bronze were brought in. It will be clear that such items would have had a high prestige value in these regions, but since the Baltic peoples were unable to control the production of bronze, how did they attract and control part of its distribution? The main answer is amber. As will be discussed below, amber was considered a special material, was made into necklaces, beads, buttons and cups and access to it was restricted. It was found only in the richer graves and frequently is found in Britain in some form of combination or association with gold, whether it be as composite jewellery, or as beads or necklaces in graves which have other gold items. In Britain, as with the Únětice, amber is one of the components which identify a burial as rich but the difference with Únětice is that amber was also included in rich hoards. The control of goods of amber should be seen as reinforcing the social differentiation which was taking place in Europe (cf. Shennan 1982a). It seems that it was primarily as a result of exchanging bronze for amber that the bronze age of northern Europe developed.

The decision about what to put in graves or hoards was not made at random. The deliberate inclusion at Leubingen and Helmsdorf of polished stone tools, bronze axes, daggers and chisels and the same range of gold objects were all statements about the power of the individuals buried, but also show the prestige of these items. A halberd was also included in the tomb at Leubingen and it is just this range of types which forms the basis of many of the hoards, with the addition of various neckrings/ingot torcs, armrings and bracelets.

Bronze halberds, daggers and axes are found over much of Europe but the contexts in which they have been found imply that they were consistently of high status. Axes and halberds are best known in Britain and Ireland from hoards and daggers from graves. Where axes are found in graves they are usually treated in a special way, for example wrapped in linen (Ridgeway Barrow 7: catalogue number 99.1). The fact that similar forms in bronze were being used over long distances suggests that there were contacts between the groups and we can see in the prestige use of gold and amber, halberds and daggers a view of objects and materials which was 'international'. We are not suggesting that there was major movement from group to group, but a common European understanding of which symbols were symbols of power. These would have been recognised in Ireland or in Germany, in Denmark or in Brittany and beyond.

It is not simply at the general level of materials and tool forms that connections may be seen. In his discussion of the Dieskau II hoard Butler (1963, 34-35) drew attention to an axe which not only has a characteristically Irish shape and decoration but whose metal content is not of central European origin. One of the halberds in the hoard is also better understood as being of Irish rather than continental European

4.81 *Metalwork hoard from Wageningen, Gelderland, Netherlands (177)*

4.82 *Necklace from Exloo, Drenthe, Netherlands (172)*

4.83 *Bronze dagger with horn hilt from Bargeroosterveld, Drenthe, Netherlands (170)*

form (Ó Riordáin 1936, 281-83) although the source of metal used to make it was the same as that of some of the characteristically Únětice forms in the hoard.

There are two important points here. First there are finds of objects of Irish origin in Únětice hoards. Second, some of the metal used in Únětice objects seems also to have originated outside central Europe, though the use of such analyses must be handled with great care. Both would suggest that the powerful Únětice groups acquired these exotic objects and materials as prestige items which confirmed their authority and importance.

In a thorough and detailed analysis already referred to Butler (1963) has made it clear that there were connections between the British Isles and central Europe through the Netherlands and western Germany. Small numbers of objects of recognisable forms and materials are found in these areas, no doubt themselves the prestigious possessions of local leaders. The hoard from Wageningen (illustration 4.81) contained metalwork whose source of material was central Europe but some of whose forms, particularly those of the axe and the rivets are close to British/Irish traditions whereas the dagger has German parallels. The necklace from Exloo (illustration 4.82) combines amber, faience and tin beads in a combination of rare materials which is reminiscent of some of the associations of grave goods in Wessex. The closest parallel for the tin beads is, in fact, from a lost find from Sutton Veny, Wiltshire (Hoare

1812, 103). Metal-hilted daggers are characteristic of Únětice finds and one was included in the burial at Saint-Fiacre, Brittany (illustration 4.76) though it is not a typical Únětice form. The dagger with horn hilt and tin nails from Bargeroosterveld (illustration 4.83) has close central European associations. The unusual bronze cones and tubular beads in the hoard from Migdale (illustration 4.35) have been suggested as 'direct imports' from the Únětice area (Butler 1963, 200). The best British parallels for metal-shafted halberds are the halberd pendants from three Wessex burials: Wilsford G8, Wiltshire (illustration 4.56), Preshute G1(a), Wiltshire, and Hengistbury Head, Hampshire (illustration 4.55: Piggott, S 1938, 84-85).

The examples cited here are small in number and restricted to rich burials and hoards. This is exactly what we should expect for the pattern of long distance exchanges with, at either end of the network, powerful groups who displayed their authority through the control and acquisition of particularly rich symbols.

What we have tried to show here is that when powerful individuals were in authority in Wessex and Brittany, a similar situation existed in central Europe. The basis of power was different as was the absolute wealth of each group. Despite this, the symbols of power were remarkably similar and the way they were controlled and consumed were parallel. As well as the Wessex, Brittany, Únětice contacts, there was exchange of goods involving Ireland, Denmark and the Baltic. It is clear that in the second millennium bc there were important areas where leaders were so powerful that they could call on social debts and personal riches, display their symbols of power and conspicuously dispose of them in burials and hoards. Although the sources of wealth were different the ways they chose to symbolise their power were remarkably similar.

4.84 *Barrows on the skyline in Wiltshire*

Social differentiation in British graves

In Wessex, as we have seen, the extraordinary richness of some graves indicates that power and wealth increasingly came to be held in the hands of individuals in the early to mid-second millennium bc. Recognition of such a series of 'rich' burials inevitably raises questions concerning the nature of the 'poorer' graves in the region or the spectrum of burials to be found elsewhere in the country. In this final section, we survey some aspects of the evidence for social differentiation in Britain during the period from c. 1700-1250 bc. On the basis of the funerary record, on which we are almost entirely dependent, it will be seen that we can discern differences in the treatment of the dead, partly correlating with variations in age and sex, that we can reasonably assume to reflect differences in the status of the deceased in life.

Very broadly speaking, the material available to us for study consists of either inhumation or cremation burials, placed in pits, in wooden coffins or in stone cists and either left as flat graves or else covered by, or incorporated in, an earthen mound or cairn. Solitary graves occur, but often burials were placed in cemeteries of flat graves or mounds (illustration 4.84) or the mound or cairn itself may encapsulate enough burials to warrant description as a cemetery. Various ceramic types tend to be associated with the burials. The earlier part of the period with which we are concerned in this section, from c. 1700-1450 bc, saw the currency of late forms of beakers and the emergence and adoption of new forms of ritual wares. Food vessels occur with inhumations or cremations and are widespread mainly in northern Britain and Ireland where several regional varieties have been recognised. The terms beaker and food vessel were applied by 19th-century antiquaries, but are now used only in a descriptive and not a functional sense. Urns, on the other hand, almost invariably accompanied or held cremations and are found throughout the British Isles in a wide variety of forms (cf. illustration 5.36). During the latter part of the period under discussion, from c. 1450-1250 bc, urns became the principal type of funerary pottery since cremation superseded inhumation as the dominant form of burial rite in most parts of Britain (cf. Megaw & Simpson 1979, 230-41; Burgess 1980, 295-325 for outlines of the variability and complexity of the burial record and the pottery of the period).

In view of the great range of the burial evidence, the scope of this section has deliberately been limited to a consideration of the various stages of burial viewed as an abstract process with the aim of noting, with examples, the possibilities for recognition of social differentiation at each stage. On the basis of analysis of ethnographic data, Binford (1972, 232-33) suggested that the process of burial generally involved three major variables: treatment of the body, preparation of the grave and provision of grave furniture to be placed with the body. These divisions have been adopted here simply for convenience of discussion and to them may perhaps be added the issue of subsequent treatment of the grave.

For each of his stages, Binford suggested that subdivision was possible. For example, under the overall heading of treatment of the body, it was possible to distinguish separate categories of preparation, treatment and disposition. Differentiation at the preparatory stage of the burial process might involve distinctions made in the washing of the corpse or in the exhibition of the body prior to the graveside ritual. It is important to remember that differences in status may be apparent at this stage of the proceedings even though this activity will be archaeologically undetectable. In particular, the body may be displayed with wealth or symbols of rank, which may then be removed or destroyed prior to interment (cf. Ucko 1969, 266-67). In the case of cremations, in particular, artefacts might well be destroyed on the pyre, if left with the body. However, the burnt and twisted bronze axe from Llanddyfnan (illustration 4.85), or the burnt arrowheads from the burial at Clocaenog (illustration 4.86) show that even if prestige artefacts were treated in this way, care was often taken to ensure their recovery. Wells has pointed out that the form of construction of the pyre and the position of the body within it may affect the ease with which the skeletal remains can be recovered after cremation (1960, 34-35): the same would, of course, have applied to artefacts deposited with the corpse.

A further category of treatment of the body is represented by what Binford termed the disposition of the dead, comprising the decisions taken concerning their disposal, that is whether or not the mortuary

4.85 *Grave group from Llanddyfnan, Anglesey (127)*

treatment would entail formal burial, exposure, and so on. In the context of the burial record of the earlier second millennium bc, archaeologically detectable treatment is mainly limited to the evidence of formal burials (in barrows, cairns, cists and pits). It has been suggested that in England and Wales, with due allowance for sites destroyed, the burial monuments of this period could have accounted for the entire population (Atkinson, R J C 1972). However, the estimates, of c. 2000 for the whole of England and Wales have been considered unacceptably low, especially in view of the demands of contemporary agriculture (Bradley 1984, 86), and it is considered more likely that sites such as barrows and cairns accommodated only a proportion of the population at death. If we assume that an unknown sector of the population received less formal burial, then we are in effect recognising at the outset an important element of social differentiation. Access to barrow or cairn, irrespective of additional treatment such as the provision of grave furniture, may reflect a certain level of status on the part of the deceased.

These observations are supported by the results of analysis of the remains of individuals from Scottish short cists (Glenn nd). Out of a sample of 137 burials that could be sexed, 82 were male, 38 female and 17 sub-adult (the term embraces individuals from neo-natal to adolescent). Of these, the males were found to have had a higher life expectancy at 36.7 years in contrast to 28.8 years for females; some fifteen per cent of the males were 45 or older, whereas the oldest female was in her mid-forties. With due allowance for the small sample

4.86 Grave group from Bedd Emlyn, Denbighshire (125)

population at her disposal, Glenn suggested that the age/sex proportions did not conform to those to be expected within a representative cross-section of a population, and that this indicated some special section of a broader population was receiving burial in short cists.

The second major variable considered by Binford in his analysis of mortuary treatment is represented by the preparation of the place of burial and this stage too could be seen to be composed of distinct categories. Firstly, the form of the grave was seen to be of some significance, in that different formal characteristics such as size or building materials might be reserved for individuals of different status. Subsequent studies of mortuary practices have suggested that the effort or energy expended on the interment process may be the most reliable guide to recognition of differences in status between individual burials (cf. Tainter 1978), although we must add the qualification that there can be no universal scale of measurement of effort expended, and comparison of different types of burial construction using different materials will pose particular problems (Brown 1981, 29). Allowing for regional variations, it is possible to cite cases where the form of grave correlates significantly with other features and suggests more elevated status of the deceased.

In Yorkshire barrows, for example, Pierpoint found that the richest beaker graves in terms of the quality of the grave goods were those which could also be differentiated by their greater than average depth, reflecting greater labour in their preparation. Such graves, often in central positions within the barrows concerned, tended to be occupied by adult males (1980, 223). Such patterns of differentiation were not so pronounced among the burials with food vessel associations, but it was noted that wood-lined graves frequently contained the vessels of highest quality and again tended to be occupied by adult and sub-adult males (*ibid*, 227-32).

In northern Britain, where cist burials predominate, there appears to be a significant correlation of size and complexity of construction with the quality of the grave goods (McAdam 1974). Features such as clay luting of the joints between the slabs or the use of prepared flooring in the form of slabs or laid gravel reflect careful preparation of the graves concerned: examples include several dagger burials, such as those found at Ashgrove and Masterton in Fife (catalogue numbers 75 & 114). The slabs utilised in the construction of such cists may be of considerable size and the effort involved ought not to be underestimated. Experimental reconstruction of one of the cists from the burial mound at Dalgety Bay in Fife indicated that the building of such structures would probably have required the participation of extended family groups. Procurement of the stones made the greatest demands on time and manpower, although it was recognised that these demands would be heavily dependent on the location and availability of suitable material. The side-slabs of what was by no means an unusually large cist could have required up to eight persons to bring them to the site (McAdam & Watkins 1974; Watkins 1982, 114-18). The more massive cists, often set in deeper pits and in some cases with double capstones, undoubtedly indicate a considerably greater degree of mobilisation of time and labour.

The final form of differentiation recognised by Binford in discussing the context of the burial was its physical location. Ethnographic evidence indicated that a high degree of participation in the social life of a group or community might be recognised by rites conducted in an obtrusive fashion and in a location in keeping with the scale of community involvement. Without a clear picture of the contemporary environment of many burial sites, for instance in relation to local settlement, the significance of their location may often be unclear. In many cases, however, the prominent siting of cairns and barrows on crests or ridges leaves us in little doubt about their intended visual impact. On the Yorkshire Moors, for example, some important burials were placed in prominent moor-top barrows, which have clearly been deliberately sited so as to be widely visible (Pierpoint 1980, 266-70).

The third aspect of the burial process isolated by Binford was the provision of grave furniture. The exceptional concentration of rich graves in Wessex sets them apart from the vast majority of British graves of the period, which are marked by a relative paucity of grave goods. It has been estimated that the proportion of burials simply accompanied by or contained in a pot varies between 25 and 50% from region to region (Burgess 1980, 98-99). Burial with no more than a finely made, carefully decorated vessel (illustrations 4.87-88) may thus in itself have been a mark of the status of the deceased. Certainly, on the basis of subjective assessment of the quality of beakers and food vessels from Yorkshire, Pierpoint showed that the finer vessels were consistently associated with the richer burials (1980, 222-33). However, the poor quality of the late beaker from the undoubtedly 'rich' dagger grave from Ashgrove, Fife (illustrations 5.39 & 53) indicates the danger of expecting any simple patterns to be seen when comparing the significance of single types of artefact in various regions.

The number of burials with grave goods other than a pottery vessel is proportionately very small, although we ought not to be tempted into making easy equations of richness and poverty simply on the basis of what may be only a narrow surviving range of artefacts. Among food vessel burials the range of associations is limited and rather heterogeneous (cf. Simpson 1968). Several of the types recall symbols more commonly associated with beakers, and include occasional stone battle-axes, bronze rings, daggers and awls, jet buttons and bone toggles. A food vessel from Kinneff, Kincardineshire was found with at least two butt-jointed bronze armlets (illustration 4.89) of the type which we have already seen in association with a beaker from Crawford, Lanarkshire (illustration 4.17), but best represented in the Migdale hoard (illustration 4.33). As we have already noted, hoard deposition could be used as an alternative means of expressing power. At the same time, such cases remind us that the absence of prestige items from graves does not necessarily indicate contemporary poverty.

Other artefacts represent novel forms of the expression of prestige in a funerary context. The most spectacular type found with food vessels are the spacer-plate jet necklaces, often taken to be the northern counterpart of the amber necklaces of Wessex (illustration 4.51). On the basis of analysis of the distinctive motifs on the spacer-plates, Shepherd (see below p 214) offers convincing arguments for seeing the jet necklaces as prestige goods made in Yorkshire and distributed from there to the

4.87 Food vessels from Duncraigaig,
Argyll (left: 123) and Denovan,
Stirlingshire (right: 122)

4.88 Accessory cup from West Skichen
Farm, Angus (141)

4.89 Grave group from Kinneff,
Kincardineshire (118)

4.90 *Jet necklace from Mount Stuart, Bute (120.2)*

4.91 *Grave group from Killicarney, Co Cavan, Ireland (121)*

various regions where they were deposited. Many of the necklaces show considerable signs of wear and refurbishment (eg. Mount Stuart, Bute: illustration 4.90). In the case of the Melfort grave (illustration 5.46), parts of 2 necklaces are represented but even together they are insufficient to make up a single necklace, unless one presupposes the use of wooden or other organic beads or their attachment to a textile backing. On the other hand, we have seen that token deposits are a frequent feature of burials elsewhere. The necklaces also illustrate the variability that is such a marked feature of the burial record of the period. Insofar as they have seen considerable wear, they are unlike many of the prestige objects in the Wessex rich graves, which appear to have been made specifically for burial in pristine condition (Coles & Taylor 1971; although Megaw & Simpson 1979, 227 have expressed some doubts on this point).

One distinctive group of objects with both food vessel and urn associations are bone 'belt-hooks', representing versions in an organic medium of the magnificent gold belt-hook from Wilsford G5 (Bush Barrow) in Wessex (illustration 4.30). Examples in bone are known from Fife, Yorkshire, Wiltshire, and Ireland where one is present in the relatively rich grave group from Killicarney, Co Cavan (illustration 4.91). The richness of Wessex has tended to mean that, even if only subconsciously, items such as these are assumed to derive from that region, but what we may be seeing is a type of artefact that was nationally known, and simply seized on for special treatment by the Wessex master craftsmen in much the same way that conical shale buttons were

4.92 *Grave group from Folkton LXXI, Yorkshire (117)*

4.93 *Grave group from Gourlaw, Midlothian (131): a. cinerary urn; b. bone mount*

4.94 *Grave group from Magdalen Bridge, Midlothian (132) a. cinerary urn; b. bronze razor*

enhanced with gold. The tendency to look to Wessex for datable parallels for objects found elsewhere in the country has perhaps masked our appreciation of the likely capabilities of craftsmen in those regions. The set of decorated cylindrical bone beads from a barrow at Folkton in Yorkshire represents accomplished work in a readily available raw material, using variations on a decorative motif for which no external source need be invoked (illustration 4.92).

Turning to cinerary urns, we can recognise the existence of a similar spectrum of funerary associations, with an urn and a cremation at one end of the scale and rich burials at the other (illustrations 4.93-97). Some of the particular problems of cremation burials may be noted here. In the

4.95 *Grave group from Balneil, Wigtownshire (130)*

first place, the practice of placing objects on the pyre with the body may well have affected their collection after cremation, although the relative frequency of burnt objects such as flint flakes suggests that considerable care was taken to recover such material (eg. Clocaenog: illustration 4.86). More to the point is the likely failure in the recent past to recognise burnt or mis-shapen pieces in the course of recovery or excavation of such vessels. A second major element is that the cremation rite offered the possibility of curation of the burnt bone for formal burial at a later date, according to whatever rules or constraints operated within the community concerned. Multiple cremations within a single urn are known, consequently 'rich' grave groups associated with such deposits may represent amalgamations of artefacts designated for separate, but presumably somehow related, individuals (cf. Petersen, Sheperd, I A G & Tuckwell 1974, 50; Shepherd, I A G & Cowie 1977). A particularly good example is the rich group from Breach Farm, Glamorgan (illustration 4.98) which was associated with three individuals, although this does not of course detract from the fact that the quality of the artefacts must still reflect, jointly or severally, recognition of considerable status on the part of the deceased.

Cremation deposits do, therefore, invite caution and, as Longworth

4.96 *Grave group from Snailwell,
Cambridgeshire (128): a. cinerary urn; b.
bone and flint objects*

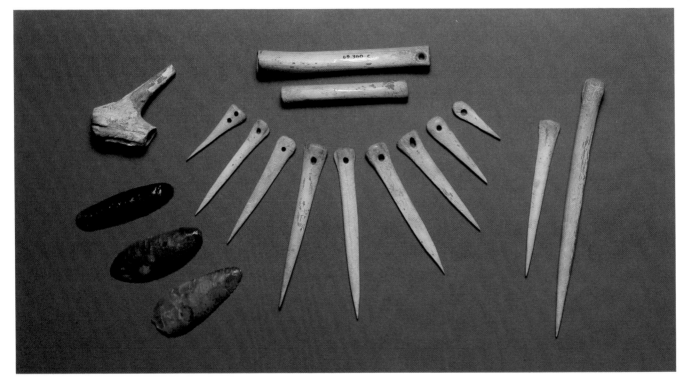

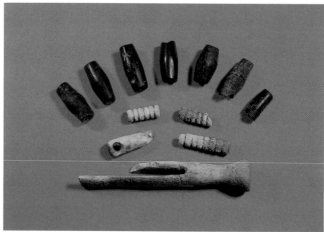

4.97 *Grave group from Bloxworth Down, Dorset (126): a. cinerary urn; b. jet and faience beads; ? ivory pendant and bone 'tweezers'*

4.98 *Grave group from Breach Farm, Glamorgan (138)*

(1984, 48) has pointed out in the case of collared urns, assessment of the significance of grave goods can only be valid for those urns for which there are details of the context, that is around 950 and not the overall surviving total of around 2250. Seen in these terms, the proportion of urns with some form of associated artefact is not significantly different from food vessels. We may suppose, therefore, that formal disposal in an urn reflected some measure of status or recognition not afforded to un-urned burials.

What made Wessex unusual was the exceptional concentration of rich graves. Elsewhere in Britain, the spectrum for 'poor' to 'rich' graves is less pronounced but, as we have seen, there are clear indications that formal burial in a cist, cairn or barrow was restricted to only a proportion of society. The qualification for such burials is uncertain and could in any case have varied, but in several areas the evidence consistently points to the importance of the mature male, accompanied in death by high status items, among the highest ranked burials. As in Wessex, the catalytic event in the second millennium bc clearly seems to have been an ideological change accompanied by the introduction of the beaker and other prestige artefacts. The eventual eclipse of inhumation by cremation as the predominant rite perhaps marks a further ideological change, possibly reflecting a weakening need to maintain individual identity in burial. However, to judge by the range and quality of contemporary metalwork, this is best seen as a reflection of changing approaches to the expression of power and prestige, in favour of their display in the world of the living, rather than the dead.

THE IMPORTANCE OF CRAFTSMEN

SOME OF the materials which have been illustrated in our discussion are familiar to us in 1985 — stone, gold and other metals, pottery, wood — and yet very few people have experience in working these let alone such specific types of materials as flint, copper, jet, amber or faience. Modern techniques of potting and woodworking are very different from those used in the third and second millennia bc. We have argued that there is a range of objects which were prestigious and used as symbols of power but to anyone other than a specialist, illustrations of some of these objects look like scrap metal or something left to rot. Quality of craftsmanship is dependent on several things — the properties of raw materials, techniques of manufacture, the purpose of the object to be made and the skill of the craftsman. We cannot judge the quality of prehistoric objects in late twentieth century terms since natural processes of decay have altered them and dulled their finish but, more importantly, because the craft of each era can only properly be judged in its own terms. This is not to say that tastes do not change, but that quality of craftsmanship is something different from taste.

Each of the following sections deals with a material or range of materials which was important in the third and second millennium bc, some because they were used frequently, others because they were specially produced. In order to provide a measure by which to judge the quality of prehistoric craftsmanship, each section investigates the various stages which were necessary in order to produce finished objects — acquisition of the raw material, processing, manufacture and fine details of working and decoration. Differences in quality are identified in each area and these are discussed in terms of how objects were being used.

The underlying theme is that of craftsmanship and work produced by skilled individuals and groups. At times the hand of a single person can be identified but it is not only in such circumstances that craftsmen, as opposed to craftsmanship, were important. The ability to control high status objects was important, but it was even more prestigious to have at one's call the craftsman who could make these objects. We see similar attitudes in the relationship of patronage by which many medieval (and modern) architects, artists, composers and craftsmen followed their own specialities in the service of powerful groups and individuals whose status was enhanced through such a relationship and by the possession of the products of the craftsman's skill.

Because many materials decay naturally when they are buried or left exposed, some composite objects (axes, arrows, daggers, clothing etc) are only known from those parts which are the most durable. Thus stone axe heads are quite common, whereas wooden axe handles are very rare. As a result we can only discuss in detail those materials which have survived.

STONE
C R Wickham-Jones

A discussion of lithic artefacts should cover everything made of stone, from the impressive monuments at Stonehenge or Cairnholy, to the smallest bead or 'penknife' blade. Only a part of this wide range can be examined here and emphasis will be given to the manufacture and use of stone tools. These objects are at the smaller end of the spectrum of size and comprise those items which were so important in different ways throughout earlier prehistory, eg. arrowheads, scrapers and blades.

Techniques of manufacture

The manufacture of stone tools requires little alteration to the structure of the natural stone. Sometimes heating or soaking in water may improve the quality of a selected piece (Mandeville 1973; Patterson & Sollberger 1979) but the techniques used are generally deductive processes: the removal of specific amounts of stone from a parent nodule, or core, until a desired shape is achieved. Pecking, grinding and flaking are different methods of removing material to produce an artefact. Of these, flaking is considered to be the most efficient.

Flaking

The process of flaking is best illustrated in the use of flint. It has the property that, when struck in a controlled manner, the amount of material to be removed (the size and shape of the flake) can be accurately predicted (Crabtree 1972, 4-7; Shepherd, W 1972, 37-39; Tixier, Inizan & Roche 1980, 37-59). There are many ways of controlling the strike — the use of hammerstones of different weights or hardness (illustration 5.1); variation in the angle of strike or amount of force used (illustration 5.2); or the preparation of an area called the platform, upon which to strike. As the line of fracture within a flint nodule tends to follow any pre-existing surface features, a flint knapper can produce the desired type of flakes by creating a series of ridges or by emphasizing other features on the core (illustration 5.3). The removal of useful flakes from a core always involves much careful preparatory work and invariably produces large quantities of tiny waste flakes where a flint knapper has been at work (Fischer *et al* 1979; Vemming Hansen & Madsen 1983, 47-55).

Both the pieces produced — the flakes and blades — and the surviving core may form useful tools. Although the flakes and blades usually have very sharp edges, further modification may be wanted and this is generally achieved by removing small flakes. This is done through the skilled application of both percussion and pressure, for which an antler tine is particularly suitable (illustration 5.4). Such secondary alteration is known as 'retouching' and may be used either to produce a particular type of edge or to completely change the shape of a tool.

Flint is just one of a large number of stones which may be worked in this fashion. In Britain many other siliceous rocks are available, all of which fracture in a more or less predictable way. Chert, quartz, quartzite,

5.1 *The use of different types of hammers in flaking: a. a stone hammer on a prepared core (compare the grip on the hammer-stone with that in 5.2b); b. an antler hammer on a prepared core; c. a wooden hammer on a roughly flaked nodule*

5.2 *Different ways of striking flakes from a core or nodule: a. indirect percussion on a prepared core, using an antler hammer and punch, with the core gripped firmly between the knees; b. bipolar flaking by direct percussion using a stone hammer with the nodule seated on an anvil stone (compare the grip on the hammer-stone, in this instance to ensure maximum force, with that shown in 5.1a)*

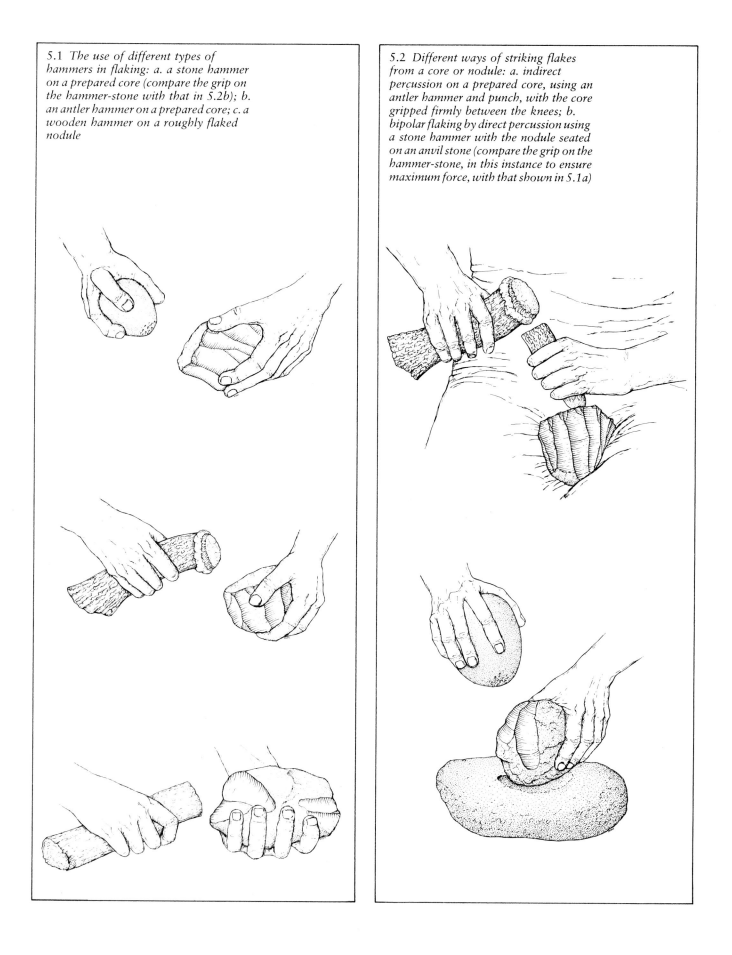

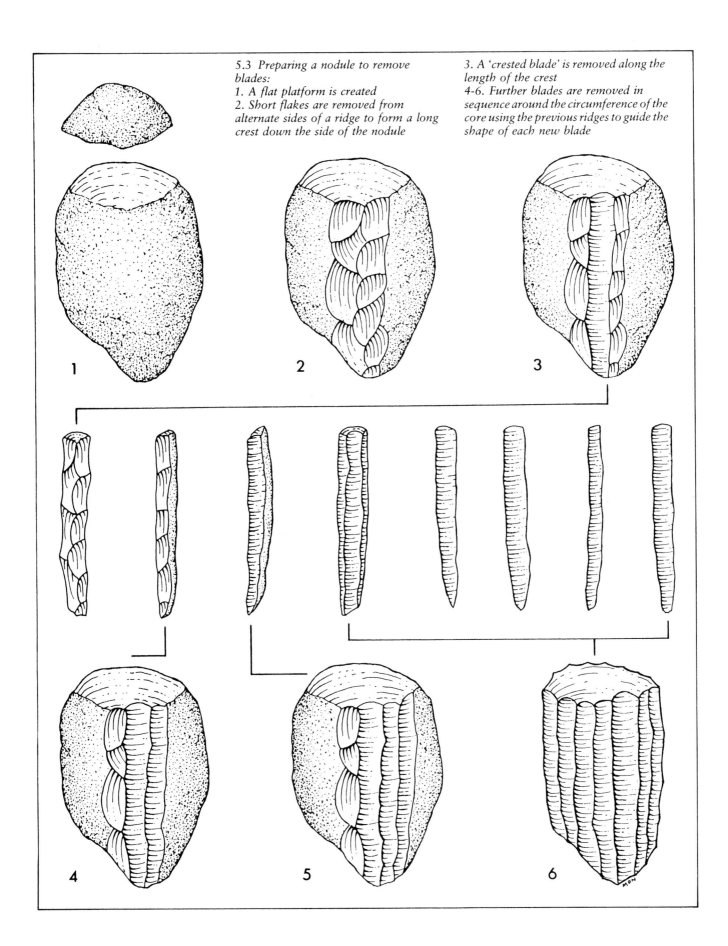

5.3 *Preparing a nodule to remove blades:*
1. *A flat platform is created*
2. *Short flakes are removed from alternate sides of a ridge to form a long crest down the side of the nodule*
3. *A 'crested blade' is removed along the length of the crest*
4-6. *Further blades are removed in sequence around the circumference of the core using the previous ridges to guide the shape of each new blade*

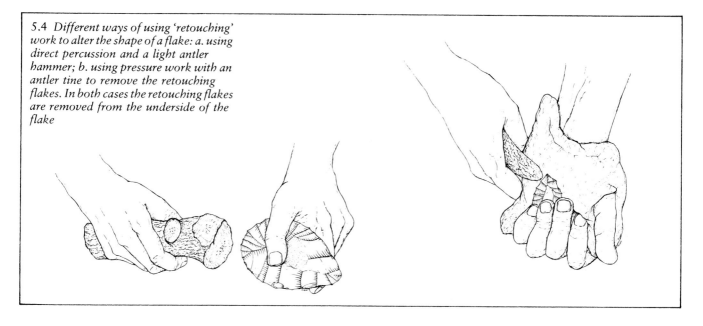

5.4 *Different ways of using 'retouching' work to alter the shape of a flake: a. using direct percussion and a light antler hammer; b. using pressure work with an antler tine to remove the retouching flakes. In both cases the retouching flakes are removed from the underside of the flake*

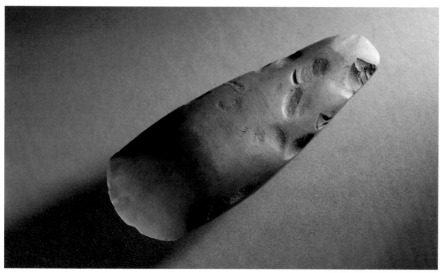

5.5 *Stone axe from Tongland, Kirkcudbrightshire with remnant flake scars still visible where they have not been polished away*

Arran pitchstone, Rhum bloodstone and other stones (Berry, Mason & Dietrich 1983, 395-99, 540-43) were all used in prehistory (Wickham-Jones 1981). Many other rocks can also be worked with a knapping technique. Ground stone axes of fine grained volcanic rocks, such as dolerite or tuff, were first roughly flaked into shape before they were ground (illustration 5.5: Houlder 1979). As the structure and quality of each material varies, so the techniques used in flaking must be changed to suit the properties of the piece of stone being worked.

Flaking is the method by which controlled amounts of material may be removed from the core with minimum expenditure of effort. Pecking and grinding involve more effort to remove less material. The advantages are, however, a smoother, finer finish and in some cases this can be very beneficial. A sharp flaked edge, for example, is very vulnerable to damage during use as the pressures produced are very similar to those applied during manufacture and can cause flaking. A ground edge, however, presents a less vulnerable but still efficient surface (Olausson 1983, 61-65).

Grinding and polishing

Grinding and polishing differ only in the degree of finish achieved (Adkins & Jackson 1978, 12). A polished surface has a finer gloss which generally takes longer to produce than a ground surface and may be finished off by burnishing, for example with soft leather. Artefacts are commonly flaked or pecked into a rough shape before grinding. The latter is achieved by drawing them across a grained surface such as a sandstone boulder. Water may be used to assist the motion, although it reduces the friction, and sometimes an additional medium such as quartz sand may be added (Olausson 1982, 22-33). A reduction in size takes place not only upon the ground artefact, but also upon the grinding stone. The elongated hollows formed by repeated grinding of axes and their blades have been found on several stones subsequently built into large monuments (Piggott, S 1962, 19-21). As the stones chosen are frequently very susceptible to natural erosion, examples are often difficult to find outside known archaeological sites (Evans, J 1897, 261-71). Axes were often ground all over to reduce wear, not only upon the edge, but also on other areas such as those in contact with the haft. Grinding was also used upon isolated edges, frequently in combination with flaking, for example when a flaked flint tool was given a ground edge (illustration 3.35). In some instances, the grinding of small indented areas is recorded and in these cases a hand grinding stone of suitable size must have been employed (cf. illustration 5.7). This would have been a particularly lengthy process (Anderson, J 1909).

Pecking

Pecking differs from grinding since the removal of material is effected not by a rubbing motion, but by percussion. Unlike flaking this is not designed to remove large areas of stone, but rather to remove specific amounts of the grainy matrix of the rock. For this reason fine, homogenous materials such as flint, although susceptible to grinding, are least effective to peck. Ordinary hammerstones, such as beach pebbles, may be used to peck a rock into shape but unless they are harder and of a finer matrix than the nodule to be worked they will abrade more quickly than the artefact in production. Since pecking relies little upon the movement of a fracture through a rock, it may be used like grinding to produce results unobtainable by flaking (illustration 5.6: Dickson, F P 1981, 147-50).

All of these methods of lithic reduction reduce not only the parent nodule, but also the tools with which they are achieved. In addition to the grinding slabs mentioned above, a variety of hammers and anvils are recovered from archaeological sites. Little study, however, has been undertaken on the different types of wear produced on such tools and this has resulted in a general lack of recognition of hammers of any material as valuable archaeological resources. Clearly, the debris resulting from the

5.6 Detail of decorated stone from Pierowall Quarry, Orkney (56)

different processes outlined here varies greatly and by studying it much can be learned about the manufacturing activities taking place on any site. Experimental work may be used not only to test the potential of different methods of production, but also to assess the types and amounts of waste produced and to look at the wear produced by use on tools.

Raw materials

A wide variety of stones may be used to make tools. The selection of a particular stone or source is part of the skill of the stone worker. Several things influence this selection: whether the stone is suitable for the techniques which will be used to make the tool and the way the tool itself will be used; whether the source of the stone is of the right quality and, if so, how easy it is to extract and how much is available. During the third and second millennia bc, many complex mines and quarries were in operation, particularly for flint (Weisberger 1981). Such expenditure of effort shows that the deliberate extraction of particular raw materials was important.

In Scotland, the sources of flint are poor and are usually small pebbles which have eroded from glacial gravels (Gemmell & Kesel 1979; Rankine 1952). This flint was often used but it did influence the range and size of tools which could be made. Large objects, such as axeheads, required a careful search for and selection of large nodules. If these were not available locally then a suitably sized piece of the raw material of a finished or partly finished object could be acquired from those with access to a more suitable raw material. Since Scottish flint was of poor quality, other stone sources — quartzite, bloodstone, pitchstone, etc were sometimes used and even themselves 'traded' (Ritchie, P R 1968; Thorpe, O W & Thorpe, R S 1984). In Britain, detailed studies have shown that stone axes were deposited hundreds of miles from their geological sources (Clough & Cummins 1979). The exact mechanisms of this trade remain unclear. It may have been gift exchange or barter. It may have involved the movement of finished objects over long distances by an individual, or the transfer from group to group of several partly finished pieces. Such pieces would then have the final desired details completed locally (Vemming Hansen & Madsen 1983). Certainly, there are many alternatives to 'trade' as we know it (Clough & Cummins 1979; Earle 1982; Ericson & Purdy 1984).

Deposits and deposition

In an age before the widespread use of metal, lithic artefacts clearly played a most important role. In domestic settlements a wide range of tools were made and these served many tasks. The majority of domestic tools relied upon varying local stone sources and it is likely that the knowledge needed for both the procurement of the raw material and their flaking were widely held throughout a community. Such collections of domestic tools tend, however, to be found only from accidental depositions such as chance loss, or discarded as waste, or as a result of breakage or over-use. An examination of the archaeological record shows the existence of other, more purposeful depositions which highlight a rather different role played by lithic artefacts in prehistory. Although equally 'practical', in its own way, this role has more to do with attitudes and beliefs about life held in the past.

Perhaps the most obvious of such contexts is the deliberate deposition of lithic artefacts in burials. Lithic objects were commonly included in many different types of funerary deposits. The impressive chamber tombs, for example, contain a variety of pieces. Many are readily paralleled from everyday domestic situations, others are known only from funerary contexts or as isolated finds, such as elaborate maceheads like that from Knowth and those forming the Maesmore group (illustration 5.7). The ornamentation upon these and similar pieces must have involved much time consuming work and this separates them from the plainer maceheads recovered from various types of site (Roe 1968). Other stone artefacts also occur in simpler forms upon settlement sites. In some cases surprising features, and not just the fine craftwork, have been observed upon objects from burials. A study of the flint knives from Giants' Graves and Tormore, Arran (illustration 2.6-7), suggested that they were completely fresh and unused and this has been noted on objects from other sites.

Stone tools are not only associated with such communal tombs. They also continued to play an important role in individual burials. Here too they are often distinct from domestic collections. Many pieces show a high quality of finish and a level of craftwork rarely seen on domestic sites. Arrowheads such as the groups from Culduthel, Inverness-shire (illustration 4.16) or Breach Farm, Glamorgan (illustration 5.8), are particularly skilfully flaked as are other artefacts like the flint dagger from Garton Slack, Yorkshire (illustration 4.9), or the knives from Snailwell, Cambridgeshire (illustration 4.97).

5.7 *Stone maceheads: a. from Maesmore, Merionethshire (47); b. from Airdens, Sutherland (49); c. from Quarnford, Staffordshire (right: 48) and Urquhart, Moray (left: 50)*

Burials are not the only non-domestic contexts where lithic artefacts had an important place. Of clear importance in prehistory was the deposition of hoards of tools. Some appear to have had a practical role, the so-called merchant's hoards for example, but this discussion is concerned only with those which suggest a more 'ritual' purpose. In many cases the stone objects are associated with large groups of metal goods, but generally a characteristic fine finish and unusually high quality craftsmanship are present. Hoards composed only of lithic artefacts do, however, occur, as at York (illustration 5.9) and Smerrick (illustration 5.10). Hoards are commonly defined as comprising groups of objects, but it is worth noting those objects that are frequently found singly, some of which rarely occur on settlement sites. Carved stone balls, for example, have few contexted occurrences and may well represent the incorporation into ritual of a carefully made lithic artefact as at Skara Brae (illustration 3.27). The same process may explain many of the apparently unused fine axeheads and maceheads which clearly differ

5.8 *One of the arrowheads from Breach Farm, Glamorgan (138.1)*

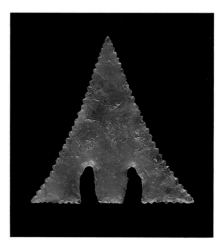

5.9 Stone hoard from York (38)

from other examples which may be broken or damaged and must have been thrown away or even lost after use.

Range of tools

The great range of objects used in everyday life has already been mentioned. When studying objects from non-domestic sites certain points stand out. Generally, the range is somewhat limited, but it does include certain types not found on settlement sites at all. Stone wristguards for example, were commonly incorporated into beaker inhumations (eg. Sewell, Bedfordshire: illustration 4.5) and it is only from such burials or as isolated finds that they are known today. Nor have

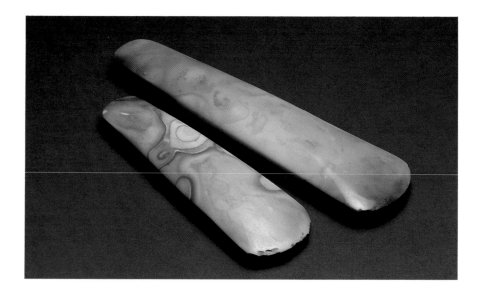

5.10 *Stone hoard from Smerrick, Banffshire (39)*

manufacturing sites been recognised, though these pieces are finely ground and would leave little debris. On occasion they are finished off with the inclusion of gold capped rivets (eg. Driffield, Yorkshire: illustration 4.15) and the ends may be decorated or accentuated (eg. Culduthel, Inverness-shire: illustration 4.16). A wristguard would have protected the wrist in archery. The stone wristguards were themselves attached to a leather wristband and were apparently made and worn for display or burial only, replacing the everyday leather ones, of which none have survived.

Skill, quality and materials

Three areas of quality may be identified in an object: the raw material itself (how easy or difficult it is to work), the skill of the maker (how well or badly made the object is) and the intended role of the finished product (whether it is intended as a ceremonial dagger or for chopping vegetables). Such variation in quality is well illustrated by stone axes.

Olausson (1983, 10-35) has looked at the arguments for assessing the prestige value of an axehead and it is clear that some of those recovered from contexts interpreted as 'ritual' score highly as prestige objects. Those from Greenlawdean, Berwickshire, and Sweet Track, Somerset for example (illustrations 3.30-31), show exceptional beauty of shape, unusual finish and craftwork and are made of a material, jadeite, which particularly lends itself to such fine working and which must have been brought from continental Europe.

Here we see not only the use of a rare stone, but also an investment of time and a degree of skill which is considerably greater than that required for 'practical' axes. Of course, plainer axes, assumed by this argument to be more practical are sometimes also found in 'ritual' contexts, but such elaboration as this is generally typical of a whole range of artefacts including both maceheads and battle-axes. In each case, exceptionally fine pieces (the maceheads from Knowth and Maesmore for instance) head a spectrum of finds at the other end of which are rougher examples.

Elaboration of quality and therefore investment of time and skills is not only observed upon ground and polished artefacts. The flaked flint dagger from Garton Slack, Yorkshire, and some of the flaked knives, for instance those from Giants' Graves and Tormore, Arran, also show a degree of skill and finish rarely observed on artefacts from domestic sites. The manufacture of these objects was only possible with large, good quality nodules of flint. The existence of such objects highlights the work of skilled specialists who were able to reserve or import selected raw material. It has already been noted that specialised manufacture solely for inclusion with a burial, is further supported by the fact that some of these knives are unused.

An examination of other flaked artefacts demonstrates this specialisation of craftwork even more clearly. Barbed and tanged arrowheads, for example, occur commonly in both domestic and other contexts but there are certain interesting differences. As already noted, the very fine flaking and particular attention to the final shape of the piece which may be finely symmetrical or serrated separate certain groups of arrowheads from the frequently rougher examples found on domestic sites. Not only is the level of skill required to make the two groups very different but careful selection of materials is often apparent. Arrowheads found upon domestic sites were frequently made with a minimum of flaking on thin flakes of an average quality raw material. Those from non-domestic contexts were often made of high quality material. The flakes themselves were carefully thinned with pressure work (note the preforms from Breach Farm, Glamorgan: illustration 4.98) and in some cases other features such as colour appear to have been important. It has been argued that the choice of browny-yellow flint for pieces such as those from Culduthel may reflect a desire to suggest the use of copper or bronze (Hamilton 1983, 38-39).

Finally, it should not be forgotten that 'ritual' life is a reflection of everyday life and in many places the two coincide. So, alongside the occurence of elaborate or unusual artefacts as discussed above, many non-domestic contexts also contain a variety of mundane stone tools which would be quite at home in any domestic settlement. Culduthel for instance, with the gold riveted wristguard and eight finely flaked arrowheads, also has a flaked strike-a-light of flint, quickly made with little special skill and apparently heavily used. Here we see that the value of some of these artefacts may be associated with actions or concepts, in this case the making of fire, rather than with the pieces themselves, ie. they are symbols. Other flint strike-a-lights occur in comparable contexts, at Newmill, Perthshire (illustration 4.2) for example. Everyday objects, scrapers and simple flakes, are amongst a range of finds often paralleling those of high quality.

This discussion has tried to explore the deposition of lithic artefacts in non-domestic contexts throughout the third and second millennia bc. The great variety of artefact types, including variation within a type, is immediately apparent as is the wide range of situations in which pieces might be deposited. The medium of stone provided a range of uses expressed in many different ways, from the thoughtless deposition of a worn out scraper to the specific, time-consuming creation of an over-elaborate knife. In some cases actions, such as the making of fire, might be important, in others the use of stone itself to supplant another material, as with the wristguards, suggests a certain inherent value for some types of stone. Here, the existence of antler maceheads, possibly complementary to those of stone, might also be noted. Whatever the case, different types of stone were carefully selected for different purposes. The use of jadeite might enhance the production of a fine axe, the use of copper coloured flint might impart a value new to those normally working with stone.

Today, a single meaning is all too often given to the presence of stone tools throughout prehistory. In the past, a range of terms must have existed to cover the variety inherent in such material. We can understand such variety when discussing the use of fabrics or metals, both still commonly employed. The use of stone in these ways has long passed from western traditions, and only now are we starting to appreciate the many ways in which stone tools could be used to express a number of values throughout all aspects of life. Clearly, a great range of skills and expertise were available both to procure and select materials and to produce the objects required, be it an arrowhead for hunting or a grand ceremonial dagger.

COPPER AND BRONZE

The development of copper and bronze metallurgy was very important in Britain for those higher in the social scale. In the second millennium bc, access to metals was very restricted and they are known almost entirely from burials, hoards and other deliberate deposits. The production of metal tools requires specialised knowledge about sources of raw materials and techniques of manufacture and it is likely that the role of the smiths, as in other societies, was an important one which, because of the mysterious knowledge of how to turn stone into metal, set them apart. Here we shall concentrate on the production of copper and bronze objects in Britain with some reference to Ireland and mention of continental Europe where appropriate.

Origins of metals and metallurgy

There is no evidence for an indigenous development of metallurgy in the British Isles. The earliest associated objects are copper tanged daggers known from beaker burials (eg. Winterslow, Wiltshire: illustration 4.4). These daggers would have been bright, polished ceremonial objects of great prestige and it seems likely that the earliest ones were brought from the Continent. The bronze spiral-headed pin from Sewell, Totternhoe, Bedfordshire (illustration 4.5), the earliest known bronze find in Britain, is certainly not a British object and is thought to have originated in Central Europe. In Ireland much of the early metalwork comes from hoards and the copper axes, awls and knife-dagger from Knocknague (illustration 5.11) is one of the earliest known.

Studies of the origins and development of metallurgy and its products have taken two major directions — scientific analysis of the metals of which the objects are made and typological analysis of the products. The scientific analysis has focused on composition (eg. Coghlan & Case 1957, Junghans, Sangmeister & Schröder 1960, 1968) and involved the relative quantities of elements within a sample taken from the object. The main interests have been the major elements, in order to assess basic sources and alloying, and the trace elements and isotopes, to attempt to specify the ore type and source location. The assumptions made by archaeologists, but not necessarily by the analysts themselves, were that the composition of a sample represented that of the whole object and was not only a direct reflection of the metal used but could also indicate, through various trace elements, particular ores and ore sources. The critique, spurred by theoretical considerations (eg. Tylecote, Ghaznavi & Boydell 1977), a wide range of experimental replication of smelting and casting (eg. Tylecote 1980) and archaeological interpretation of the results, has shown that these assumptions are valid only within limits. Some elements are volatile and will be differentially lost during smelting and casting. The composition of an object is not consistent throughout and is related to manufacturing techniques as well as ore sources and the possibility of recycling of the metal itself. The general results of analysis of composition do, however, still stand and suggest that there was a change through time in the type of copper sources used from native copper (ie. naturally occurring in its metallic state) to oxide ores and more complex ores (Slater 1985, 47-48). The earliest use of sulphide ores occurs after the period discussed here (Tylecote 1980, 5). This sequence was part of an explanation which saw the development as related in some measure to the relative depth of ore sources below ground level and changes in the technology of metallurgy whereby different properties of materials were being deliberately produced. As Slater (1985, 48) notes, this model was constructed in isolation from archaeological interpretations, particularly of the type supported here.

5.11 Metalwork hoard from Knocknague, Co Galway, Ireland (149)

The second area of analysis has been that of typological seriation. This identified similarities and differences of form and technology and classified objects upon this basis, then ordered them in a time sequence, generally from 'simple' to 'complex' (eg. Case 1966, Burgess 1974, *Prähistorische Bronzefunde*).

Both areas of study are important as they enable us to refine our understanding of the developments in materials' use and form. Combined with these, however, have been studies of manufacturing techniques and, more recently, the role of metal objects in society. In the rest of this section we shall examine these various areas. First, however, it is necessary to describe what was involved in the manufacture of items of copper and bronze.

Manufacture

As has already been mentioned, the first metal objects were brought from continental Europe and these would have been very prestigious items. Coming as they did as part of the beaker complex, reactions to them would have varied throughout Britain. Bright, shiny objects which were eminently for display and ceremonial would have been a major challenge to groups who relied on fine stone implements. The mystery of their source — the transformation of stone itself — would have made them all the more potent. If British groups were to be able to control access to such items it was important that they controlled not only distribution in Britain but also acquired the expertise of manufacture and production. It would have become clear that Britain and Ireland had native metal and ore sources and to have no control over such sources or their use would have carried the seeds of exploitation and the undermining of the social order (cf. mineral resources on Australian Aboriginal lands, or North Sea oil exploration). An understanding of prospecting and metallurgy was therefore necessary and no doubt these were carefully restricted, though it is interesting to note that initial metallurgical developments in Britain do coincide with the beaker phenomenon and the collapse in most areas of authority based on access to the gods and control of more 'traditional' resources.

There were sources of native copper in Britain and these would have been exploited first as they would require little transformation: small objects could even have been cold hammered and larger ones made by melting the copper and then casting in open moulds (illustration 5.12). The oxide and complex ores required smelting, ie. heating in a reducing atmosphere to extract the metal from its ore. There is no excavation evidence for the types of furnace used in Britain at this time, but experimental work has shown that the requisite conditions can be achieved in simple bowl furnaces of clay set in the ground surface and by making use of bellows (Slater, E pers comm). It is unlikely that such furnaces would survive for four thousand years.

More complex moulds were developed — closed moulds. Initially these consisted of two joining pieces with the shape of the object to be cast carved or moulded into both faces. The molten metal would then be poured in and left to set. The changes in sources or ores resulted in

5.12 *Stone mould for casting flat bronze axes from Strathconan, Ross-shire*

different compositions of metal with varying properties being produced and this would have been noted and controlled by the metalworker. Before 1700 bc tin-bronze alloys (copper and tin) were being produced in Britain (eg. Auchnacree: illustration 4.26) and thus by this stage the whole sequence from ore extraction to final object was quite complex. It is worth detailing this as it forms an impressive demonstration of what was involved in bronze manufacture. 1. Prospection of ores of copper and tin. 2. Acquisition/quarrying/mining of the ores. 3. Smelting with or without a flux (dependent on the type of ore). 4. Re-smelting to obtain refined metal. 5. Combination of copper and tin to obtain bronze prior to 6. casting. When we consider, in addition, the provision of fluxes and charcoal and the manufacture of moulds it is clear that the sequence was a complex one which relied on careful organisation, timing and skill at each stage. In principle, the number of sequences was not much greater than that of stone axe manufacture, but some of the techniques were more complex and they all required greater co-ordination. The ability of a society to construct massive earthwork and stone monuments is perhaps more impressive in terms of organisation of labour. The difference is in the fact that the production of metals was not a major communal effort but one dependent on individuals and small groups, even if prospection, quarrying and manufacture were themselves specialised tasks performed by different groups. The very development of metal technology echoes the open acknowledgement of personal power represented in individual burials and hoards.

Once objects had been cast there were various stages of finishing and fine working to perform. On those objects which had been cast in two-piece moulds there would be strips of metal to remove where the moulds had joined. Some pieces were decorated with punch marks or other tooling (eg. near Eildon, Roxburghshire: illustration 4.18). Axes and daggers would have had their surfaces and blade edges hammered and polished to make the surface smooth and the edge sharp and the characteristic expanded blade of copper and bronze axes is a result of this working. Alterations to the physical properties of the objects could be made by reheating, annealing and hammering and minor changes to the shape of some objects would then be made eg. the creation of small flanges on the side of flat axes by hammering. Sheet metalworking was also undertaken with the initial piece presumably beginning as a thin ingot which was then hammered out. Thick pieces such as the bracelet from Mill of Laithers (illustration 5.13) were worked from a straight bar to form a penannular ring and then decorated. The armlets from Masterton (illustration 5.14), however, began as bronze hammered into thin sheet which was then curved into a cylinder and then riveted to hold its shape. The surface was then carefully decorated using hammers and punches.

In the graves at Lunteren (illustration 4.3) and Soesterberg (catalogue number 160) were found cushion stones which acted as surfaces upon which hammering took place. Another example is known from the rich burial at Leubingen (catalogue number 169.2). Whetstones were for resharpening blades and have been found in the graves at Hove, Sussex (illustration 4.45) and Wilsford G23, Wiltshire (illustration 4.52) and a number of similar stones were with the cremation at Sandmill, Wigtownshire (catalogue numbers 134.2-4), though these are of a more everyday form. Few other tools for working copper and bronze are known from this period in Britain.

5.13 *Bronze armlet from Mill of Laithers, Aberdeenshire (84)*

5.14 *Bronze dagger and armlets from Masterton, Fife (114.1-3)*

Materials and objects

The early Irish industries were primarily in copper and it has already been said that the earliest objects from Britain were also of copper. The development of stronger copper-arsenic alloys (whether deliberate alloying or, more likely, the result of using arsenic-rich ores) and copper-tin alloys (true tin-bronze) seems to be a general technological development in the second millennium bc. Analysis of axes has shown that the earliest examples are thick-butted flat axes (eg. Knocknague) followed by ones with thinner butts. Hammered flanges became a feature and finally cast flanges were produced. The addition of features such as stop bevels and elaborate, hammered, recurving cutting edges can be seen in the axes from Arreton (illustration 4.27) which are made from tin-bronze (Britton 1963, 293-97; Schmidt & Burgess 1981).

The variation in the form of daggers has been studied by Gerloff (1975) who also traced similar developments in the raw materials and changes in shape. Beginning as simple flat daggers and small knives (eg. Masterton and Knocknague), they tend to increase in size and then have midribs and grooving, both of which strengthen the blades, but are also decorative.

Halberds were ceremonial blades mounted almost at right angles at the top of a wooden shaft. The fact that these were mostly made in copper and yet are associated in some hoards with bronze axes (eg. Sluie: illustration 5.15) suggests that there was deliberate archaism in the choice of copper rather than bronze for these important items of display.

At this period we are only seeing the beginning of the development of spearheads. Most were tanged and were attached to their hafts by rivets. From Arreton however, tanged spearheads, a tanged and collared one

5.15 *Metalwork hoard from Sluie, Moray (148)*

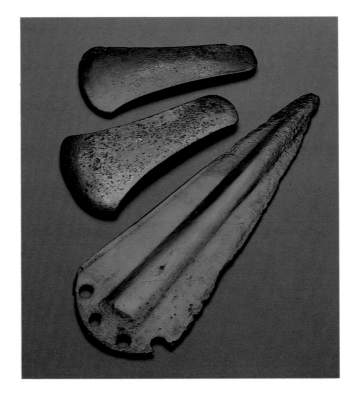

THE IMPORTANCE OF CRAFTSMEN 181

and an early form of socketed spearhead were found. Apart from the different type of mounting which would be necessary for the latter, an important feature to note is the use of a mock rivet design on the socket. This is again an archaising feature since the spearhead was attached by a transverse peg through the shaft.

A number of other finishing details are worth noting. The two axes from Sluie have surfaces which have been tin enriched to such an extent that it almost forms a distinct external layer. This would have given the axes a silvery appearance and made them especially distinctive. A number of other axes from Britain are known to have been treated in a similar way (Kinnes *et al* 1979; Close-Brooks & Coles 1980; Needham & Kinnes 1981).

Most of the daggers from the rich burials in England and the Scottish dagger graves do not, in fact, have sharpened edges (Bradley, R and Henshall, A S pers comm). This would suggest that they were never intended as utilitarian objects and were deliberately made as objects of display. Equally, the massive 'swords' from Beaune (illustration 4.22) and Jutphaas (illustration 7.35) have never had rivet holes made for attachment of a hilt nor have the edges of the blade been other than blunt. Objects of such a size are not fighting weapons but were ceremonial objects as well as a tribute to the metalworker's craft. It is thought that the Jutphaas 'sword' was made by the same craftsman as two identical ones from Ommerschans, Netherlands and Plougrescant, France (Butler & Bakker 1961). The much smaller rapier from Kimberley (illustration 4.22) is likely to belong to the same group (Butler & Sarfatij 1971, 309, fn 2) but as illustration 4.22 shows there is quite a difference in scale between these. The same type of display object is seen in the massive axehead from Lawhead, Lanarkshire (illustration 4.19), never intended for chopping wood or anything other than conspicuous use in ceremony and deposition as a hoard.

It must not be thought, however, that pieces made from copper or bronze were *never* used. The flat axes in the hoard from Dail na Caraidh, Fort William, Scotland (Gourlay & Barrett 1984) have differential wear of the blade edges as does one of those from Sluie. This is a clear sign of usage. These objects were nevertheless deposited as hoards and it is clear from that found at Colleonard, Banffshire (catalogue number 145) that they were not deposited with their hafts still on but as unmounted blades. Daggers are most often found in graves in Britain and some of them had specially decorative handles, sometimes enhanced with gold pommels or bindings or even with tiny gold pins.

Details have already been given of the diverse circumstances in which such objects were found and the different ways in which, for example, axes and daggers were treated. What emerges clearly from these variances in practice, however, is that large metalwork items were prestigious, and that some were deliberately enhanced with extra decoration — fine hilts, grooving, pointillé decoration. Those which we know from hoards and graves played a major part in the reinforcement of the status of the individuals who controlled the objects, who were, no doubt, patrons to the metalworkers and enabled the raw materials to be made available through exchange contacts.

We do not know whether smiths were itinerant or whether production was centralised or small scale and local, but it would seem that in the second millennium bc most final casting and working was locally based even if the preliminary smelting of ores was not. Comparison of the size of hoards from Britain and Ireland with those from the Únětice areas shows that there was quite clearly a major difference in the scale of production. In Central Europe there must have been a large-scale industry in bronze and gold manufacture.

The use of a range of materials makes it clear that deliberate choices were being made on the basis of what the finished product was for. This is exactly as we should expect. The major evidence we have for copper and bronze metallurgy in Britain and the source of our information are the objects themselves which come from graves, hoards and other deliberate deposits. Most can be categorised as prestigious objects and many were made specifically for display.

Mistakes in production and casting were made and miscast pieces are known but unlike those of stone, many of these must have been recycled. Thus we cannot assess the failure rate of smithing, but only judge on the basis of those objects which were removed from circulation and have survived. It is likely that other artefacts which did remain in circulation, including more mundane tools, were themselves recycled.

During the second millennium bc, sources of metals and access to them were restricted. Copper and bronzeworking are, by definition, skilled crafts practised only by the initiated and access to both metals and craftsmen was very important to those who were or wanted to be leaders.

GOLD AND SILVER

Joan Taylor

Goldwork first appeared in western Europe, principally in funerary contexts of high status, in the early second millennium bc. At the same time copper 'trinkets' appeared but both mediums were scarce giving objects made from them a role of special or valued use. Casting of tools such as flat axes in simple moulds, if not coincidental with the introduction of copper, must have followed shortly after with both copper ornaments and cast tools being produced by indigenous smiths.

The natural enrichment of native metal by tin and copper, detected through trace element analysis, suggests alluvial sources for gold at this period. Such sources constituted a supply of easily workable metal available from streams in Brittany, Cornwall, Wales, Scotland, west and north Ireland, as well as the central European area of Transylvania (Taylor 1980, 18, 33, 40). The drift source in the Wicklow Mountains, Ireland was *not* the sole source for the British Isles, as has often been maintained, but insufficient ore analyses prevent the tracing of individual objects to these more varied sources. Source identification will probably become possible for the earlier goldwork but objects of later date, which may have been crafted from re-cycled gold or alloyed with an addition of copper are probably permanently masked from their initial source by the consequent mixing of trace elements (Taylor 1980, 18).

The preference for sheet work in Britain, Ireland, Brittany and other parts of Atlantic Europe, which continued long after its first introduction, rather than cast massive ornaments is not because gold was in short supply or the technology lacking so the explanation must lie in its role in prehistoric society. Judged by the context in which gold objects are found, there is no question that gold played a valued role, principally being associated with elite burials in the second millennium bc. The objects were not simply art or ornamentation but probably designated both the high social rank of a person and their political, religious or occupational status. The ability to cast metal is shown by the presence of copper and later tin-bronze flat axes, and casting was probably part of the initial preparation of gold prior to beating into sheet to judge by the occasional find of cast 'slug-like' gold ingots in Britain. In contrast various styles of wire 'ingots' were preferred for the trading of gold from Czechoslovakia, such as those associated with the gold bowl at Rongères, Allier, France (Taylor 1980, pls 34.h, 62.d).

Why sheetwork was preferred to cast ornaments can only be a matter of conjecture but it cannot be argued that the preparation of sheet is far less difficult for a smith, especially one with the skill that is demonstrated consistently in the beaker earrings, discs and lunulae. Ornamentation of sheetwork conformed to the linear geometric incised art-style typical of the highly evolved beaker art of the period. This art-style follows a sophisticated artistic formula utilizing a range of complex motifs, which are applied according to a general convention. They involve simple mirror imaging and a pattern of negative and positive zones of decoration and impressions compiled from a universal range of motifs (Taylor 1970a, 47-48, 56-62). The motifs, built on a theme from simple to complex, form the basis for design, while the principles of their application established the function of the art on its various shapes and mediums, including pottery, metals, exotic materials (eg. amber and shale) and probably organic mediums (eg. leather, textiles and wood). This art-style enjoys an extensive geographical distribution, from Hungary in the east to the British Isles in the west and from Scandinavia in the north to Gibraltar in the south. This suggests a considerable network of social contacts.

In the application of this geometric style the goldsmith showed a facility in controlling line and layout and followed with careful execution the complexity of beaker art, which made him a skilful worker of gold and a sophisticated artist. The British Isles were the dominant centre for beaker goldwork and although there were links with Brittany, the latter area seems to have lacked the same skills to work gold until a later date. Although the smaller ornaments seem to have an aspect of personal aggrandisement, the large gold collars or lunulae, principally produced in Ireland, appear not to share this aspect of individual possession as they were never committed to the grave (Taylor 1970a, 68-75).

The production of gold sheet to its highly burnished finish in itself commands awesome respect. Despite the apparent ease of working native gold, the quality of sheetworking in its known range and size and thickness argues for considerable skills. Two methods of beating into sheet seem obvious but do not fully explain the outstanding burnished finish of the sheet, especially apparent in the lunulae and Wessex grave groups. Lunulae were probably worked directly but leather must have been employed to ease the depth of hammer marks. Most of the Classical and a number of the linear Provincial lunulae have been worked to give greatest thickness along the inner edge for reinforcement of the area under most strain. Thickening also occurs along the outer edge while the body of the crescent was beaten thinnest. Intentional planishing over burnished surfaces in the central void were employed to alter the texture in some cases, for example those from Southside Farm (Coulter), Peeblesshire. More dramatic are the gold grave goods from Wessex which are the masterpieces of this period. The gold must have been beaten between leathers to achieve the thinness of modern heavy-duty aluminium foil, and then cut to shape; yet the above technique leaves a great gap between its initial stage and the burnished surfaces found, for instance, on the Bush Barrow belt hook and lozenge plate, the Clandon lozenge plate or the Upton Lovell button cover. This high burnish of such thin sheets inspires awe in modern silversmiths who are unable to explain the processes necessary for its production. Cold welding, by hard burnishing down on the thin sheet, was used to fuse permanently the overlapping edges of some of the Wessex gold pieces, for example the Bush Barrow belt hook. On other pieces of this period this technique could be applied to obliterate the joins for the casual observer as, for instance, on the gold rings of the shale beads, for example from Preshute G1(a), Wiltshire (Annable & Simpson 1964, no 196), and other apparently continuously crafted pieces.

The precision of decoration on the most accomplished pieces and the high relief on the surface opposite to that in which the decoration was impressed suggests the use of a medium that held the objects firmly but had sufficient plasticity to support the impression as it was applied. Modern jeweller's pitch would offer such a base and in the fill of the Lannion box we have evidence of just such a material. Analysis showed it to be finely ground glauconitic sand and fir resin mixed proportionately 1:1 (Lanting 1974, 164-67). Lumps of similar material adhere to the back of the collar of the pommel cover from Ridgeway Barrow 7 (Taylor 1974, 152). Once held in the pliable jeweller's pitch the object would be firmly gripped for the most intricate designs whether applied with a stylus or hammer punch. No evidence of scribed guidelines survives on the surface, suggesting that the goldsmith either marked the pattern in an easily removable coating such as bees-wax or else possibly worked free-hand. Whatever the technique, a number of near perfect pieces survive displaying complex linear geometric designs with *no* overrun lines. Examples of this high precision are the Classical lunulae from Ireland (illustration 5.16) and Blessington, Co Wicklow and the belt hook and lozenge plate from Bush Barrow (illustration 4.30). Less accomplished pieces are, of course, known from this period: two examples of mistakes in decoration are the right-hand horn of the Auchentaggart lunula and the Little Cressingham rectangular plate (illustration 4.29) where the awl has torn the sheet during application of the dots.

THE IMPORTANCE OF CRAFTSMEN 185

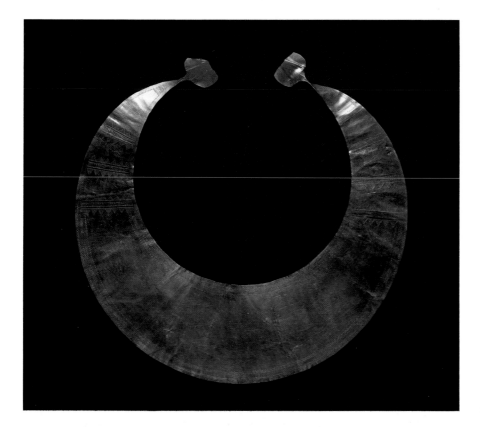

5.16 *Gold lunula from Ireland (65)*

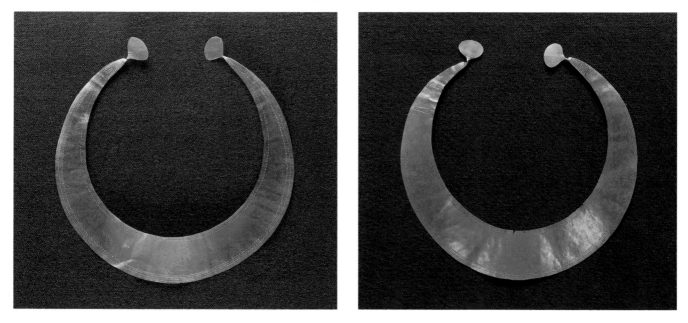

Punches, other than the fine pointed metal awls, seem to be restricted to the decoration of lunulae. The Southside Farm pair (illustration 5.17) show one punch with a slight central hollow being used to dot the lines on both lunulae, thereby leaving the signature of the same smith's hand on both pieces. Again, a lopsided diamond-headed punch was held at two different angles to produce the dot-line effect decorating the

5.17 *Gold lunulae from Southside, Peeblesshire (61)*

Auchentaggart lunula while a chisel-like tool has been hammered along to produce an unintentional, discontinuous staccato line noticeable on the right-hand horn, particularly above where the smith erred.

No true engraving, ie. the excising away of gold to cut a line of decoration, is known from this period. Lines were either hammered using implements such as those just discussed or impressed by a stylus of bone or wood, often of varying sizes and degrees of sharpness, as demonstrated on the Upton Lovell button cover. In some cases, the sharp points of metal awls, probably of bronze, were employed, as in the application of dots in the bottom of rounded grooves initially formed by a stylus with a gentler point, for example on the gold-bound amber discs from Wilsford G8 and the discs from Barnhill, Broughty Ferry, Angus (illustration 4.31).

Finally the use of fine gold pins, a technique common to Britain and Brittany, should be noted. They were primarily employed for decoration, as on the Bush Barrow dagger hilt, but they are functional on the top of the collar of the Ridgeway pommel cover (Taylor 1970b). These pins were no doubt cut from wire, made by first forming a sheet into a tube similar to that of a modern drinking straw and then rolling down, for the technique of drawing wire was not known at this period. Their smallness suggests that a myopic person must have set them into position or a rock crystal magnifier may have been used. The jeweller's pitch would have been an aid since their size prevented them from readily being hammered into place. Apart from one small platelet in Brittany, the pommel is the only example of a solely functional use of pins. It is interesting to note that, apart from the Lannion box, the Ridgeway pommel mount is the only piece of the Wessex phase to display damage consistent with that caused by wear or use.

In Wessex goldwork, there appears the first consistent use of gold combined with other exotic materials, such as shale or amber, to produce composite objects. This practice was common in the Aegean but not known elsewhere in western Europe at this time. It can be seen in some of the work of a master craftsman who produced several gold objects solely for grave use in Wessex and Armorican grave groups. The pristine condition of these extremely delicate sheet objects speaks against their use by the living. This master craftsman wrought the Bush Barrow sheet ornaments, the covers for the shale buttons at Upton Lovell (illustration 4.57), the Clandon lozenge plate (illustration 4.54) and the gold-bound amber discs and button cover from Wilsford G8 (illustration 4.32). These items are linked to his hand, not only through the tooling of the ornament but by the technique employed in working the sheet into its various shapes and the choice of the motifs applied. The large Bush Barrow lozenge plate is so skilfully composed as to accommodate the holes for attachment. This piece shows similarities in the stylus grooves with the belt hook and small lozenge from the same grave group and all are in keeping with the beaker art-style of linear geometric zones interspersed with voids. Both the belt hook's boxed construction and that of the larger plate show the use of a grooved line on the inner lapped edge, seen also on the Clandon plate and the Lannion box (illustration 4.66), a means of finishing off the piece which might help it grip its now missing backing. The decoration of the larger lozenge plate is paralleled on the cone of the

Upton Lovell button cover while the base displays the identical complex double cross comprising the central motif of the Clandon plate. The latter also shows the dot in groove decoration found on the Wilsford G8 button cover and gold-bound amber discs. Neither the Little Cressingham plate nor the Barnhill, Broughty Ferry pair of discs can be attributed to the master craftsman. He could apparently work in the other luxury materials of amber and shale for the Wilsford gold-bound discs are exactly paralleled in the amber discs, this time without gold, in the Kernonen, Plouvorn grave group (Briard 1970). The same Armorican grave group contained an amber parallel for the Lannion box. This type of ornament, perhaps imitating an archer's bracer or wristguard is exclusive to the Armorican graves.

Out of the several hundred graves attributable to the Wessex phase, only 19 contain gold while a similar number in the Armorican tradition contain gold and silver. The necessary gold for all the objects contained in these 40 or so graves could be realised from perhaps four lunulae.

In turning now to consider the range of gold types represented in this period, it is only possible here to comment on the salient aspects of some of them. The earliest group are the basket earrings and discs decorated with the laddered-cross motif. Unlike the latter, the earrings were also made in copper and bronze, for example the fragment in the Migdale hoard and those from a grave at Cowlam, Yorkshire (Greenwell & Rolleston 1877, 52, figure 47, 222-25). The Radley earrings may be the oldest worked gold in Britain (J D van der Waals pers comm: illustration 4.13) but the development of basket earrings continued into an extreme form, not seen among their Continental cousins, which resulted in the examples found at Orbliston Junction, Morayshire, of which only one survives. Unlike the discs, which demonstrate on some a true understanding of repoussé technique, the earrings are only decorated in one direction from behind to raise the sheet on the surface, producing a suggestion of false repoussé. Nevertheless, like the discs, the outline of the sheet is bordered in keeping with the beaker art-style as on the Boltby

5.18 Gold earrings from Boltby Scar, Yorkshire (79)

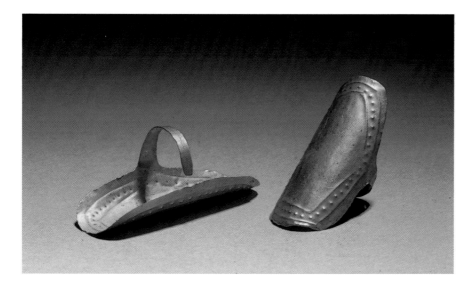

5.19 Gold earring from Orbliston Junction, Moray (81)

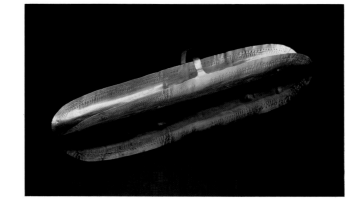

5.20 Gold disc from Castle Treasure, Co Cork, Ireland (83)

Scar, Yorkshire pair (illustration 5.18) and the one from Orbliston Junction (illustration 5.19), while the Radley pair and the one from Kirkhaugh, Northumberland (illustration 4.7) have the tangs bordered as well. Maryon (1936, 212) stressed that the Kirkhaugh earring had tooling by a blunt tracer on the surface to enhance the lines applied to the back which arguably would be tending towards true repoussé.

Sheet goldwork is difficult to produce and the beaker goldwork, which forms consistent groups of personal items within the British Isles, tends to be small in size. Irish craftsmanship can be distinguished even at this early stage by its superior working of the medium but unfortunately few ornaments can be provenanced or associated with other objects. The Castle Treasure disc from Co Cork (illustration 5.20) demonstrates an understanding of true repoussé as a technique for giving a three-dimensional quality to an otherwise two-dimensional object. Decoration has been raised from both the front and back of the disc principally with the lines raised from the back and the dots applied to emphasize elements on the front of the ornament. The two central perforations were not sufficient for attachment so the edge was pierced for the further securement of the disc. This combination of edge stitching and central perforations suggest permanent attachment to some perished material, possibly an article of clothing, while the motif seems to be derived from that found on some racquet-headed pins in Czechoslovakia (Taylor 1978, 237, 240-44). Since there was a general lack of interest in pins of this type in both Britain and Ireland, this is a good example of symbols being more important than the objects they decorate.

The magnificent gold collars (lunulae) contain the greatest volume of gold in use in western Europe at this period. Their distribution is predominantly Irish with eighty-one examples attributed to provenances in that area. Not only can various schools of style be identified among the Classical and Unaccomplished groups but two preferences can be seen for the ornament on the Provincial group. The three groups separate on the basis of width and thickness of sheet as well as techniques and choice of design. The Classical are wider and thinner, giving the greatest expanse of sheet relative to the volume of gold. They are also the most exquisitely and skilfully decorated. This is not so with the Unaccomplished group which usually contain less volume of gold as well as being less competently beaten and poorly ornamented. The execution of the

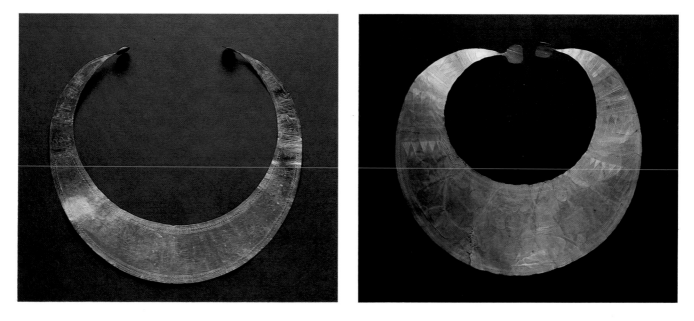

ornament frequently fails to achieve symmetry or to conform to the dictates of the beaker art-style. The Provincial group are frequently more robust and may even contain more gold than the Classical but are the simplest in their choice of ornament (Taylor 1970a; 38, 40-56). Examples of these groups are: Classical — ?Ayrshire (illustration 5.34); Blessington, Co Wicklow; Co Galway (illustration 5.21); one of the Harlyn Bay, Cornwall pair (illustration 5.22) and the unprovenanced

5.21 *Gold lunula from Co Galway, Ireland (64)*

5.22 *Gold lunula from Harlyn Bay, Cornwall (58.2)*

5.23 *Gold lunulae from Rathroeen, Co Mayo, Ireland (66)*

Irish find; Unaccomplished — Rathroeen, Co Mayo; Ballybay, Co Monaghan; and one from near Sligo (illustrations 5.23-25); Provincial — Auchentaggart, Dumfriesshire; the other of the Harlyn Bay pair (illustration number 5.26); and the pair from Southside Farm (Coulter), Peeblesshire. The similarity of the ?Ayrshire and the Co Galway lunulae suggest that they might come from the same Classical workshop whereas the unprovenanced lunulae from Ireland would appear to be that of another workshop. The Blessington, Co Wicklow lunula is from a third workshop and represents the most complex of the Classical group, portraying the fundamentals of the beaker art-style including mirror imaging by both reflecting through the centre of each horn as well as from horn to horn. The Harlyn Bay Classical lunula is likely to have been made in Ireland although found with a Provincial lunula and an early form of flat axe in Cornwall. The Unaccomplished lunulae listed demonstrate many of the features assigned to the group. Rathroeen has been worked in a repoussé technique similar to that used on the dot-line Kerivoa lunula (Taylor 1980, pl 16a-b, d-f, Eluère 1982, 59-63, figs 74a-b, 75) and in keeping with other beaker repoussé ornaments, but not following normal lunula style. The example from near Sligo has the vertical decoration on the horn, typical of a group within the Unaccomplished classification, and is largely included with this type for its lesser use of gold and late and unusual motif styles applied vertically. The third, from Ballybay, is only decorated with a crude border. Of the Provincial group, the example from Harlyn Bay is identical to one from the Kerivoa hoard (Taylor 1980, pl 15a-d; Eluère 1982, fig 72). The Auchentaggart lunula and the two from Southside Farm have dot-line decoration in a manner common to the barbed-wire decoration of the beaker art-style.

The four discs from Knowes of Trotty, Orkney (illustration 4.39) are late in the sequence of discs, a view which is reinforced from several directions. The high tin ore source is likely to be the same as that used for

5.24 Gold lunula from Ballybay, Co Monaghan, Ireland (62)

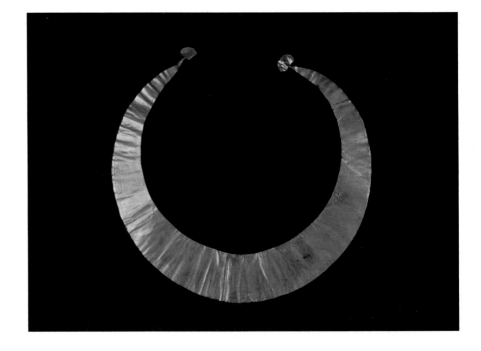

the hiltbands of the Blackwaterfoot, Arran (illustration 4.40) and Collessie, Fife daggers (Taylor 1983, 64) and the decoration of the discs is similar to that represented on the base of a food vessel from Kilmartin, Argyll (Taylor 1978, 244: illustration 5.27). A comparable hiltband accompanied the dagger and food vessel in a burial at Topped Mountain, Co Fermanagh (Plunkett & Coffey 1898) and along with the example from Skateraw, East Lothian (illustration 5.28) this group of eight objects appears to have been made from a Scottish high tin source in a relatively short period of time, probably contemporary with the rich Wessex graves.

The masterpieces of gold sheetwork from the Wessex grave groups have already been commented on as have the close links between that area and Brittany. In Brittany, however, beaten sheet silver was used to make vessels, fragments of which survive from Saint-Fiacre and in the reconstructed Saint-Adrien cup. The Saint-Adrien silver cup (illustration 4.68-69) is constructed in two parts: a rounded base riveted to a waisted collar, with the strap handle extending from the base. The gold waisted collar of a similar vessel was recorded from Ploumilliau, Côtes-du-Nord (Eluère 1982, 102, fig 122). Briard notes that the process of cupellation necessary to extract silver from lead apparently was not known at this period and although silver sources are common in Brittany they all require such a process for their extraction (1984, 94, 136). There is a question, therefore, as to where the source of silver for Saint-Fiacre and Saint-Adrien may be located but the vessels' design strongly suggest that the silver was worked locally. The shale cup from Farway Down, Devon (illustration 4.46) and the amber cup from Clandon, Dorset both carry the pointed base common to that of the Saint-Adrien cup which contrasts with the flatter bases of the Rillaton, Fritzdorf and Eschenz cups (illustration 4.44, 4.47, 4.48).

5.25 Gold lunula from nr Sligo, Ireland (67)

5.26 Gold lunula from Harlyn Bay, Cornwall (58.3)

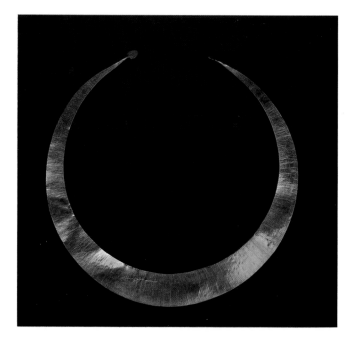

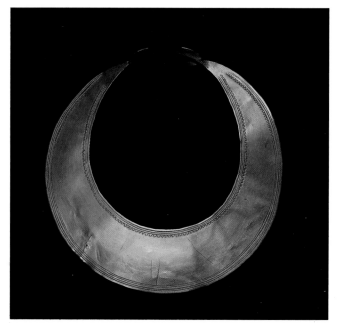

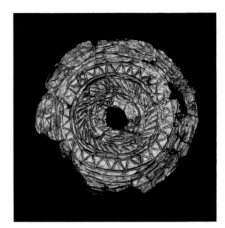

5.27 *Comparison between the decorative motifs on the base of a food vessel from Kilmartin, Argyll (left) and one of the gold discs from Knowes of Trotty, Orkney (right: 104.1)*

5.28 *Grave group from Skateraw, East Lothian (115)*

The manufacture of the Rillaton and Fritzdorf cups suggest that they were both made in the same workshop. Further, both have handles secured with rivets and diamond-shaped washers, suggesting the same craftsman. The Eschenz gold cup, on the other hand, can not be proved to be linked to the Armorican versions or to those found in the British Isles although many of the decorative themes are common to both areas, no doubt because they derive or have evolved from the universal 'traditional beaker' range of motifs. The absence of a handle and the general composition of the cup, involving possible imitation rivets where the slightly waisted collar meets the bowl, may be a clue that it is more an imitation of the Amorican style than of any of the British examples.

Showing both indigenous and Continental influence, the Mold cape from Flintshire (illustration 4.41) parallels not only the early Rongères bowl, drawing itself from central European sources although found in eastern France, but also with the lenticular boss found on the Migdale 'spacer-plate' and the Melfort, Argyll bronze armlets (illustration 4.38). This distinctive boss motif, surrounded by fine dots outlining the lenticular shape, has a long duration in Scotland and obviously survived in the indigenous repertoire of ornament elsewhere to re-appear on this unusual cape. With its fine repoussé work the Mold cape represents the last major piece of second millennium bc sheetwork. Thereafter, the dominant preference for sheetwork in the British Isles is eclipsed and the desire is more for massive goldwork in the form of solid bracelets, twisted bar-flanged torcs and solid rings. Occasionally, as in the case of the small Irish workshop on the Shannon which produced repoussé gorgets, sheet was still used but never again did it enjoy the long popularity demonstrated by its presence in the early grave groups.

POTTERY

Introduction

Containers of one form or another are a universal requirement of human societies. In our own daily lives, we are surrounded by containers of so many shapes, sizes and materials that we probably do not often pause to think about their implications, beyond token environmental concerns. For this reason, some points relevant to the theme of this section may best be made using modern analogies.

The following list of articles may be considered to be containers, familiar to most of us at least in name if not by ownership:
— breakfast coffee mug
— Royal Doulton china tea cup (1985)
— Sèvres porcelain tea cup (1766)
— disposable polystyrene cup
— electric kettle
— tea caddy
— commemorative mug issued on the occasion of the Coronation (1953).

This seemingly unconnected list can be considered in several ways: among some of the objects — for example, the kettle, the tea caddy and the 1985 tea cup — we can observe formal differences imposed by their requirement for, respectively, the functions of preparation, storage and consumption of a beverage. From that viewpoint, the shape and size of the Sèvres piece would suggest comparison with the contemporary fine-quality Royal Doulton cup, but today the former would be more likely to be found in a collector's cabinet, its original function superseded in favour of a new-found role as ornament (or investment) with a value and status unrecognisable at the time of manufacture (cf. Ehrich 1966, 14-16). Unlike the antique piece with its acquired status, however, the Coronation mug, though outwardly of similar function represents an artefact never intended for use, but to have an immediate, and lasting, commemorative value (illustration 5.29).

5.29 *Pottery mug commemorating the Coronation in 1953 AD*

5.30 *Sèvres tea cup and saucer, 1766 AD*

The breakfast mug in daily use — often drawn from an unmatched set that has survived breakages — suggests a different functional connotation from the contemporary fine quality tea cup, that of the distinction between the 'everyday' and the 'special' occasion. The name on the base of the tea cup — if the guest does not already recognise the design — introduces a further element relevant to our theme, that of status and differing qualities of product, not to mention their uses in different social milieux. The disposable cup from the vending machine effectively underlines the point!

Finally of course, we ought to note the importance of the contents of containers: the relevant points can again be made by suggesting familiar contemporary examples. Two wine bottles, for instance, may be identical but the vintage date and labels will carry differing promises of what each holds. Quoting Ehrich slightly out of context, we might add that the contents of the bottles render them 'a status symbol both in respect to the ability to have them, and the implied sophistication necessary to appreciate them properly' (1966, 14).

The above examples have all been associated with beverages, but obviously containers figure much more widely in our lives than solely within the sphere of sustenance or subsistence: the packaging of consumer goods, for example, is an area where particular messages of quality or value may be conveyed by different types of stimuli (cf. Packard 1957; Pierpoint 1980, 117-19).

These random and light-hearted analogies are not inappropriate in the context of this section, for while the tastes and fashions of modern consumer society cannot be applied to the past, they do serve to reiterate one of our recurrent themes, that objects are loaded with symbolic values and meanings (cf. Hodder 1982). In approaching prehistoric artefacts, we need to be aware of this inherent characteristic, even if the nature of the evidence at our disposal inevitably deprives us of access to the details of their original meaning.

Turning to prehistoric Europe at the period with which we are concerned, we must envisage the requirement for containers being fulfilled in a considerable variety of ways, of which pottery will have been only one. The importance of organic materials particularly needs to be acknowledged at the outset. We can safely assume the widespread use of plant and animal products, even if the nature of the survival of the archaeological evidence has left us only a very partial picture of their original range (cf. Clark, J G D 1952; Coles, J M, Heal & Orme 1978, 15-17). Ethnographic studies are illuminating in this respect. For example, an inventory of the contents of an inhabited compound of the Turkana, a pastoral tribe of Northern Kenya, showed that 63% of the objects were perishable (in the archaeological sense), while 48% of the entire material culture of the compound consisted of containers (Robbins 1973, 210-11). Turning to containers made from inorganic materials, some will have been intrinsically valuable and rare at the time of their production, owing to the rarity or fragility of the raw material and the technological prowess needed for their manufacture. Among these we might include silver and gold vessels and the cups made from fossil carbons such as amber and shale.

The raw materials for the manufacture of pottery on the other hand, were available in most regions although really high quality clays have a restricted distribution (Clarke, D L 1976), and the skills required for its manufacture widely known. The plastic nature of the raw material makes it suitable for a wide range of types, and a receptive vehicle for group tastes and traditions in terms of design and decoration. Once processed and fired, most ceramic products are, from an archaeological point of view, extremely resistant to decay and even if in a fragmentary state, the nature of the material often allows accurate reconstruction of the original shape and decoration. This high survival rate and the short 'working life' of pottery make it a relatively sensitive indicator of stylistic change. As such, pottery types have in the past often been taken as indices of different human groups (eg. 'the Beaker people'), an equation which ethnographic evidence and more recent work on ceramics have shown to be unsound. We must, in other words, be careful to make the distinction between 'beaker users' and 'beaker people', a distinction that can be illustrated best by analogy: the introduction of Sèvres porcelain (illustration 5.30) into English tea-drinking circles patently does not reflect an invasion from France, but the introduction of prestigious artefacts into a particular social group. The misconception, that particular pottery types reflect specific ethnic groups, had arisen partly because it had commonly been assumed, explicitly or implicitly, that over much of prehistory Europe the manufacture of pottery was carried out in a domestic context with only domestic needs in mind. Since the 1960's, research has gradually exposed this misconception and we ought to recognise that the production, distribution and use of pottery was often more than just a day-to-day household activity (cf. Clarke, D L 1976, 462).

Production

In the lay mind too, there may be a tendency to equate the unfamiliar or the restored or fragmentary vessels which occupy museum cases with careless or somehow casual manufacture, or there may be a notion that, to the primitive household, such vessels would be of little worth and breakages of little consequence, on the assumption that a new pot could be quickly thrown together to make good the loss. In fact, even where pottery production was geared towards domestic use, ethnographic studies suggest that pottery production was likely to have been far from casual. The manufacture of pottery involves several distinct processes which may be summarised as follows: *procurement* of the raw materials, *preparation* of the clay; *forming* the clay shape; *drying* to a leather-hard stage; and *firing* to the fired or finished shape. *Decoration* may be carried out after forming, drying or firing. While recognising the existence of marked differences in quality of the finished product, it can be seen that each vessel represents an investment of accumulating time and energy and in that respect each pot is a craft product in its own right: the features which may allow us to distinguish craft specialisation will be discussed in due course. As general details of the technology of pottery are readily available (eg. Shepard 1956 with refs), only a few points will be made here relevant to the period and material under discussion.

The environmental prerequisites for the manufacture of pottery are adequate supplies of clays and tempering materials suitable for the types of product required, sufficient renewable fuel resources and favourable enough climatic conditions to allow for the drying of both fuel stocks and clay wares prior to firing (Howard 1981, 6). On the basis of a survey of ethnographic data, Arnold (1981, 36) has shown that the preferred size of territory exploited by communities to obtain ceramic raw materials has a radius of one kilometre, while 82% of the communities obtained their clay from distances of 7 km or less. Clay quarries may be exploited at greater distances if they are directly accessible by suitable forms of transport, such as canoes (cf. Clarke, D L 1976, 469: quoting Lauer).

Unlike today's high quality prepared clays, few freshly dug clays are suitable for forming without considerable preparation to improve their texture. Clays that are too plastic, and therefore prone to excessive shrinkage, require the addition of filler or tempering materials such as crushed stone or flint, shell or chaff. The importance of these to the archaeologist lies in the fact that they may betray non-local wares: for

5.31 *Some features of pottery manufacture: a. use of a simple turntable; b.-c. simplified illustrations of typical building stages of beakers and food vessels*

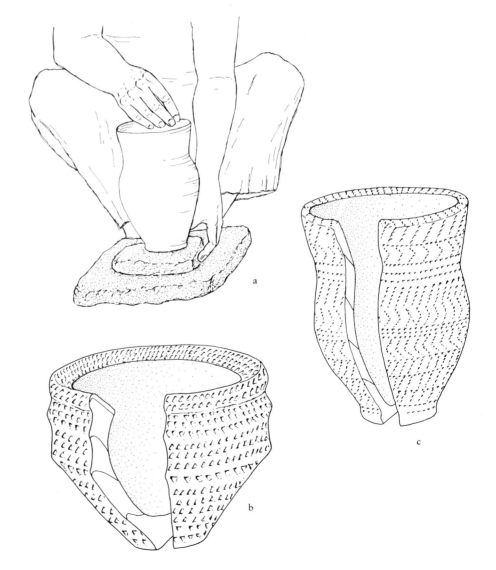

example, shell-filled pottery found at the causewayed enclosure of Windmill Hill, in North Wiltshire must have been imported to the site, probably from the Bath/Frome area, a distance of some 32 km (Smith, I F 1965, 46). As with the clay sources, ethnographic data suggests that the raw materials for tempering are usually locally obtained (within 1 km of the site), with 8 km being the maximum range (Arnold 1981, 36).

Forming or shaping of vessels is carried out using a variety of techniques, all of them involving a considerable degree of skill. Without exception, the vessels referred to in the catalogue are hand-built without the aid of a wheel, although some of the beakers may have been made with the help of a simple hand- or foot-powered support (cf. van der Leeuw 1976, 95, 98-99, figures 9-10). In most cases, it may be assumed that the vessels have been constructed by ring-building, in which the walls are built up of successive rolls of clay, the joints between each being smoothed out as the work progresses (cf. Stevenson 1939, 233-39; 1953: illustration 5.31). Although it might be expected that the plasticity of pottery would allow scope for free expression on the part of the potter, obvious signs of individuality are rare: rather the close similarities of form and decoration of the various insular types reflect the extent to which pottery production was limited by social constraints.

A variety of decorative techniques and designs were employed by prehistoric potters, and together with shape, form the principal means of distinguishing the cultural affiliations of different types of ceramics. The following examples are not intended as any more than illustrations of the repertoire found in the period with which we are concerned. Various forms of grooved decoration are seen to best effect in the distinctive ornament applied to predominantly bucket-shaped vessels excavated from henge monuments, such as the massive ceremonial earthwork at

5.33 *Fragment of pottery decorated with spirals and lozenges from Skara Brae, Orkney*

5.32 *Fragment of pottery with spiral decoration from Durrington Walls, Wiltshire (20.6)*

Durrington Walls (illustration 3.19). The plasticity of pottery provided a suitable medium for displaying important contemporary symbols such as the spiral (illustration 5.32) or the lozenge (eg. a sherd from Skara Brae; Childe 1931b, plate XIV: illustration 5.33). Other late third millennium bc wares are distinguished by the frequent use of impressed techniques of ornament: the decoration of beaker pottery, for example, is chiefly characterised by zonal arrangements of motifs made up of dentated comb-shaped impressions, of which there may be as many as 2000-5000 on some heavily decorated vessels (Clarke, D L 1976, 470). As on certain gold lunulae (illustration 5.34) which carry related motifs (Taylor 1980, 28-31), considerable emphasis may be placed on symmetry and mirror imagery (eg. beakers from Winterslow Hut: illustration 4.4 or Crawford: illustration 4.17).

Among the various insular traditions of food vessels and urns a wide range of decorative techniques and designs is found, but within each type there is often a degree of orthodoxy of design that shows potters were clearly working within socially imposed constraints (for example, the implicit need to symbolise group identity). Techniques include the use of various forms of twisted cord impression, a range of stamped impressions made with the fingernails, toothed combs, the articular ends of small bird or animal bones, points and spatulae of wood or bone and a variety of forms of incised ornament. Some of the more commonly occurring designs include repetitive herringbone or chevron patterns composed of diagonal incisions, cord impressions or comb-stamps (illustration 5.35), incised or corded arrangements or opposed filled triangles (illustration 5.36), lattice patterns (illustration 5.37) or panels of horizontal and vertical lines (illustration 4.87).

Some of the very finest incised decoration is found on the small cups or accessory vessels, which often accompanied cremation burials (illustration 5.38). The incised ornament on the extremely fine vessel from Breach Farm (illustration 4.98) had been augmented by red

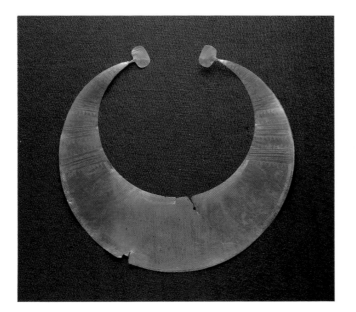

5.34 Gold lunula from ?Ayrshire (60)

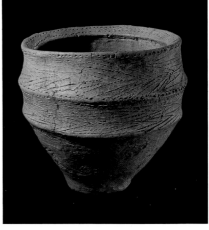

5.35 Food vessel from Mount Stuart, Bute (120.1)

5.36 Cinerary urns from Newton of Montblairy, Banffshire (left: 137), Magdalen Bridge, Midlothian (centre: 135) and Kirkpark, Midlothian (right: 136)

5.37 Cinerary urn from Milngavie, Dunbartonshire (133.6)

5.38 Accessory cups from near Dunbar, East Lothian (left: 139) and North or South Ronaldsay, Orkney (right: 140)

colouring matter: such additional colourings may have been more common on pottery than the limited surviving evidence would suggest (cf. Clarke, D L 1970, 567 with reference to beakers).

For purely domestic consumption on a small scale, firing could often have taken place in or around the domestic hearth, but in the case of communal or specialist pottery production, the process is more likely to have been carried out in bonfire kilns prepared for the purpose. There is unfortunately very little evidence for this stage of the manufacturing process during the period with which we are concerned. On the basis of ethnographic data, pottery production is generally considered to be a seasonal activity and it is possible that it may often have taken place in early Autumn, in the light of impressions of seeds and grains incorporated in the wet clay and burnt out on firing (Howard 1981, 25).

Craftsmanship and its recognition

Earlier in this section, it was suggested that the nature of much surviving prehistoric pottery or our assumptions about its method of production carried connotations of 'cheap' or casual manufacture. Ethnographic data shows that this is a misconception. As we have seen, potting is a process carried out in multiple stages, each of which involves the investment of time and energy, resources which have to be set against a variety of competing demands. In one study of the economics of domestic pottery production in New Guinea, the total manufacturing time *per vessel* was over five hours (Clarke, D L 1976, 469: quoting Lauer). On the basis of results such as these and on empirical grounds, Clarke suggested that contemporary assumptions about the nature of prehistoric pottery production and distribution were anachronistic and misleading. Pointing to the high levels of craftsmanship involved in the manufacture of much beaker pottery (cf. van der Leeuw 1976) and the very considerable investment of time and energy that were bound up in the production process, Clarke argued convincingly that it was inappropriate to view such vessels as somehow worthless and cheap. In his own vivid words, a fine decorated beaker would have been 'an expensive chunk of congealed time and energy', well illustrated by the estimated production time of 4-6 hours continuous work, required for some Dutch beakers (exclusive of collection or preparation of the clay, drying or firing) (Clarke, D L 1976, 470). Such vessels, it was proposed, would be far more likely to have formed elements in networks of reciprocal exchange. Rather than being drawn from an undistinguished mass of domestic pottery, they would have formed the components of an upper tier of 'fine wares', part of a hierarchical range of ceramic products in use within any given community, distinguished by its quality and function from everyday and heavy-duty wares (*ibid,* 462-68).

More recently, attempts have been made to define with greater precision the physical features that we might expect to be correlated with ceramic function (see Howard 1981, 8-10, Table 1.1). Cooking vessels, for example, will tend to have fabrics designed to withstand thermal shock, a high degree of care in their manufacture but a low frequency of decoration. Ritual vessels, on the other hand, may often be of complex shape and, if intended for display, will tend to be well made and frequently elaborately decorated.

Such studies emphasise the fact that ceramic production is geared to demand. In the context of the period with which we are dealing and the themes addressed in this book, the demand for prestige goods may well have stimulated craftsmanship in pottery, although ceramics are also likely to have featured in earlier exchange systems, as the widespread distribution of neolithic pottery from Cornish sources has demonstrated (Peacock 1969). It is interesting to note, however, that in general terms the production of late beakers marks the start of the decline in quality of our prehistoric ceramics, and this may in turn reflect the partial displacement of pottery as a major item of prestige (cf. Bradley 1984, 70-73). Among the rich male graves of Wessex and Brittany, for example, pottery is noticeable by its absence.

Finally, it is worth reiterating the importance of the contents of the vessels. At least some of the interments in Scottish graves appear to have been accompanied by vessels containing fermented drinks, as indicated by the analysis of scrapings taken from a beaker from Methilhill, Ashgrove, Fife (illustration 5.39) or the food vessel from North Mains, Strathallan, Perthshire (Barclay 1983, 178-80, 186: illustration 5.40). The possibility that strong liquor may have formed part of the male status kit in northern Britain will perhaps come as no surprise to some (for the possible implications cf. Burgess 1980, 63).

Conclusion

The wide availability of the raw materials and the necessary skills, and the universal requirements for containers, suggest that a certain level of craftsmanship would have been inherent in most pottery producing communities. It may be noted, for example, that a very high degree of

5.39 Beaker from Ashgrove, Fife (75.3)

care in manufacturing and firing is required for some everyday wares, such as cooking pots, if they are to work successfully (cf. Howard 1981, 9, Table 1.1). However, where there was a consumer demand for prestigious display or ritual wares with high symbolic values, more specialised production for wider circulation may have been stimulated, perhaps associated with specific communities favoured with good quality clay sources or especially skilled potters. In the British Isles, relatively little research has been carried out on the production/distribution aspects of ceramics of this period: however, vessels have occasionally been found that may represent the dispersed products of an individual hand or workshop (cf. Pierpoint 1980, 119-21; Barclay 1983, 255 — figure 29) and it is certainly in the context of virtuoso works of craftsmanship that we ought to view the superb handled beaker from Fordham, Cambridgeshire (illustration 4.50) and other fine beakers and food vessels (illustration 5.41).

5.40 facing page Food vessel from Strathallan, Perthshire and a bunch of meadowsweet. Microscopic traces of this species were found inside the pot

5.41 Finely made food vessel from Duncraigaig, Argyll (left: 123) and beakers from Skateraw, East Lothian (centre) and Chapel of Garioch, Aberdeenshire (right)

JET AND AMBER

Ian A G Shepherd

The third and second millennia bc witnessed a use of jet and amber for personal ornament and display which was more intensive than at any other time in the prehistory of north-western Europe. Resinous and lustrous, they were not simply desired for their beauty but for what these attributes both represented, the property of static electricity. This was noted by the Venerable Bede many centuries later:

'. . . being warmed with rubbing (jet) holds fast whatever is applied to it, like amber' (*in* Scudder 1910, 4-5).

This mysterious property in itself must have been an object of wonder and it is easy to conjecture that the possession of objects crafted in such materials may have been a source, or a symbol, of power and prestige.

Acquisition

The sources of jet and amber are limited in number. Jet occurs only rarely in Britain, in narrow strata amidst the fine-grained cannel coals exposed in cliff falls and exposures along the eastern coast of North Yorkshire (Map *in* Shepherd, I A G 1981, figure 1). Other jet-related substances may have, on occasion, been used, such as cannel coal and lignite, from Brora, Sutherland or shale from Kimmeridge in Dorset (Pollard, Bussell & Baird 1981, 151-53). Another source may have been the black lignitic shales commonly found as glacial erratics in the boulder clays of northern and eastern England (Briggs, *in litt, Curr Archaeol,* 82 (May 1982), 351).

Jet workers during the third and second millennia bc probably relied on recognising raw lumps of jet eroding out of cliff exposures. However, greater skill in prospection and winning could be inferred from a grave such as Garton Slack C53, East Yorkshire, which contained besides the two inhumations, Yorkshire Vase food vessel and two bronze earrings, a ribbed jet object, an ammonite, and some ochre (Mortimer 1905, 218, figures 558-59). This is because in 19th-century AD jet prospection, ammonites were sought as indicators of a fruitful seam while ochre was used as a polishing agent (Shepherd, I A G 1981, 44). Furthermore, the occurrence of fire-making equipment consisting of a flint strike-a-light and a lump of iron pyrites in British beaker graves could have been a by-product of jet prospection as jet shales are richly pyritic (Hemingway, Wilson & Wright 1968, 8).

The fossil resin amber is derived from (in the most part) submarine deposits mainly around the Baltic coast, principally the eastern Baltic and the northern and western coasts of Jutland (Beck, C W, Wilbur & Meret 1964; Beck, C W *et al* 1965) which are still eroded to this day. Amber is still cast up on the Norfolk shores in lumps 'resembling modern building bricks in size' (Taylor 1980a, 45). Such locally available amber could have been spotted readily by beach-combers whose eyes were attuned to searching for the straw-coloured gritty cortex of beach-pebble flint, particularly when, once picked up, amber's light weight would have made it very distinctive. There is, however, some doubt whether the amber used to make objects such as the spacer-plate necklace from Upton Lovell G2(e), Wiltshire, came from gathering on the east coast or from 'directional trade' with south Scandinavia (Shennan 1982a, 40; following Piggott, S 1938, 81, 84).

Leaving the source of amber to one side for the moment, the evidence from objects crafted in jet hints that access to the Yorkshire sources was restricted to specialists. A case can be made (based on motif analysis of beakers and space-plates) for viewing eastern and northern Yorkshire as the main area for the manufacture of jet spacer-plate necklaces, whence they were dispersed to Scotland and four English regions *(infra)*. Eastern Yorkshire was certainly the key area in the production of both main V-bored button series (Shepherd, I A G 1984), while recent X-ray fluorescence analysis of jet and jet-like material from 72 early Bronze Age contexts held by Devizes Museum showed that approximately half the collection was of jet, presumably from the Whitby area of Yorkshire, rather than of the locally available shale (Pollard, Bussell & Baird 1981, 160). All this activity in the area of the one source can be related to the extension of settlement in beaker times into the otherwise less favoured North York Moors area which would have given access to the Whitby area (Bradley 1984, 90).

Processes and organisation

Although both jet and amber are relatively soft materials which can be cut, split or snapped with a certain amount of ease, they do require skilful processing and finishing as jet turns brown and dull when cut or worked, while amber loses its translucence if drilled or sawn. Four main processes can be identified in the manufacture of an object such as an amber spacer-plate or a jet button: shaping, drilling, final detailing, polishing. Tools and materials to cut, grind, drill and polish were therefore required. (Although jet splits conchoidally, like flint, the working of jet and amber is essentially different from lithic tool technology: flaking, by whatever means, would have been a wasteful process on such plastic substances).

The preliminary roughing-out of a jet or amber lump could be accomplished by cutting with a flint saw, or by abrasion. The degree of control or choice exercised by these craftsmen obviously varied from type to type and from object to object. McInnes has suggested, for example, that the shape of jet sliders was controlled to a large extent by the shape of the jet lump available (1968, 137), and angular beads, such as that from Cairnholy I (illustration 5.42), certainly still preserve the look of a simple jet pebble. However, this is not to deny that a great deal of conversion could not take place, when desired, as for a jet pulley ring such as that from Harehope or an amber cup, for example Hove (illustration 4.45).

Experiments have shown that jet can be cut readily by short sharp strokes of a flint saw in one direction (towards the operator) as long as a slice is first removed to free the movement of the saw. A cut 1 mm deep and 15 mm long could be made in 4 minutes (Greaves 1872, 284, illustration; Shepherd, I A G 1981, 44-46). Abrasion against coarse sandstone or quartz sand could remove spar, the stony inclusions found

5.42 *Jet bead from Cairnholy, Kirkcudbrightshire (14)*

5.43 *Rough-out for a jet terminal plate from Skirling, Peeblesshire*

on the surface of jet lumps; alternatively, it could be chipped off with the point of a flint or bronze knife.

The manufacture of jet rings, whether simple such as that from Upton Lovell G2(a) (Annable & Simpson 1964, number 243), or complex, such as the pulley ring from Harehope (catalogue number 93.1), would have involved either the drilling out of the centre, or, more likely, its cutting out either with a flint point and a template or with a flint 'compass', a flint with a sharp point at each end of a concave face, used trephine-like (Shepherd, I A G 1981, 45). It is likely that, once a cut of a certain depth had been made in a jet or amber blank, the piece was simply snapped in two, rather than subjected to more, time-consuming, sawing. Two examples of roughed-out jet necklace plates were noted by I A G Shepherd (1981, 46) to which should be added the jet lump in the National Museum of Antiquities of Scotland from Skirling, Peeblesshire (illustration 5.43) which is shaped and grooved as for a necklace terminal plate.

More complex techniques may have, on occasion, been used. The shale and amber cups (eg. Farway Down illustration 4.46, or Clandon), are generally thought to have been produced on a pole-lathe (Newall 1929). It is not impossible that the unusually tall, hipped Wessex buttons which were covered in gold (eg. Upton Lovell G2(e) and Wilsford, Wiltshire: illustration 4.32) began life as wasters from turning shale cups. This suggestion is perhaps reinforced by the decoration of deeply incised (horizontal) concentric circles executed on the shale button and used as a former for the decoration on the gold sheet — which is unparalleled on other British V-bored buttons, but which is similar to the grooved decoration on the cups themselves (eg. Farway Down). These sites are already closely linked: Taylor has suggested that one master goldsmith made the Upton Lovell, Clandon and Wilsford G8 goldwork (1980a, 46).

Drilling the holes, whether in a V, as in a jet button (Migdale: illustration 4.37) or an amber pendant (eg. Kernonen, Plouvorn: Briard 1970, 32-35), or in a Y as in some necklace spacer-plates (eg. the amber ones from Knowes of Trotty: illustration 5.44, or the jet examples from Pitkennedy: illustration 5.45) was probably the operation that required the greatest skill from the craftsman. The sequence of operations followed by the Victorian jet workers of rough-out, drilling, decoration/polishing (Greaves 1872, 283), would most likely have also been followed by craftsmen at this earlier period as it is at the drilling stage that a jet or amber object is at its most vulnerable, and a breakage early in the process would have been less costly than a later one (Shepherd, I A G 1981, 48). While a triangular flint point, possibly similar to that found with the Harehope buttons (Jobey 1980, 109, figure 17, 1) and a swivelling action of the wrist were probably sufficient to create the cone-shaped borings on such jet buttons as that from Crawford Moor, Lanarkshire (*Proc Soc Antiq Scot*, 2 (1854-57), 306-07; Shepherd, I A G 1981, figure 2,4) or on those from Migdale (Shepherd, I A G 1981, figure 2,3), the long narrow holes, *c*. 2 mm in diameter, on slim spacer-plates such as those in jet from Pen Y Bonc, Anglesey (Lynch 1970, 121, figure 40) or in amber from Knowes of Trotty, Orkney, were

5.44 *Amber pieces from the Knowes of Trotty, Orkney (104.5-11)*

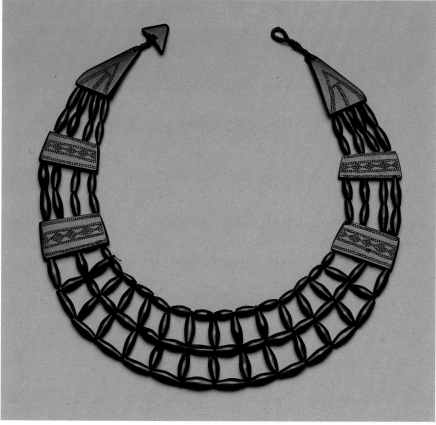

5.45 *Jet necklace from Pitkennedy, Angus (124)*

probably done by a hollow cylindrical awl, possibly of bronze, and an abrasive such as fine quartz sand. The tubular bronze beads in the Migdale hoard (illustration 4.35) show that the appropriate technology was in existence, if required.) In this connection the recent XRF analyses of the Devizes jet and shale objects are of interest. High values for copper were found in 11 objects which may be best explained as residues from being worked with a bronze awl (Pollard, Bussell & Baird 1981, 158-9). One should not underestimate the time, skill and care needed to produce even straight borings, although the 19th-century AD estimate that a flint point would take 6 hours to drill a hole 25 mm long in jet (Greaves 1872, 283) must be seen as an overestimate. Recent experiments by the writer with a simple, hand-held, solid bronze awl suggest that such a boring could be completed in 40 minutes.

Some of the borings carried out at this time were virtuoso accomplishments: for example, the V-borings in the small amber pieces from Knowes of Trotty, Orkney, which are traditionally interpreted as pieces of a chopped-up spacer-plate (Piggott, S & Stewart 1958, number 33) are less than half the diameter of the borings in the surviving necklace plates which themselves are carefully executed and between 2 and 3 mm in diameter. This difference and their regular, gabled shape suggest that they should be reinterpreted as prismatic buttons, characteristic of late beaker times in western Europe (eg. Treinen 1970, 286) and paralleled in the Winterslow, Wiltshire, amber buttons (Stevens & Stone, 1939, 176-80).

The striations which can often be seen on the bases of jet buttons (such as on the majority of the decorated buttons from Harehope) or on the side of spacer-plates (eg. Pitkennedy) are the result of the final shaping of the piece.

The punctulated decoration on spacer and terminal plates of crescentic necklaces (found on 60% of plates: Shepherd, I A G 1973, 66, after Coutts) was probably done after the plates had been drilled for the necklace string. Most such decoration was executed with a pointed tool and a swivelling wrist action. On the other hand, the decoration on the important group of jet buttons from Harehope (19 out of whose 33 are decorated, which 19 increase by 150% the number of decorated buttons known from Britain) was done by cuts with a flint or bronze point (illustration 5.46).

Another technique can be seen on the Law Hill button (illustration 5.47) where gently convex surfaces and line decoration mimic the Bush Barrow gold belt hook (Taylor 1980, 45). Here the decoration has been picked and then ground out after narrow guidelines had first been incised (Shepherd, I A G 1981, figure 2,5).

Finally the decoration on jet buttons demonstrates that considerable skill was required for even simple motifs. On the Marshalmark Hill, New Cumnock, Ayrshire button (Munro 1902, 468; Ritchie, J N G & Shepherd, I A G 1975, 30 figure 5: NMAS FN 144) and on the largest of the Harehope buttons the decoration was probably done some considerable time after the buttons had left the hands of their craftsmen. On the former button, crude punctulations were chipped out of the surface, while on the latter, an irregular, unpolished ladder pattern was

executed on the highly polished surface of one of the largest buttons in Europe. The flaking and over-running of the lines, caused by over-heavy pressure and a crude point, can be seen clearly; the decoration of this button contrasts strongly with the highly accomplished (angled) decoration on another button (part of catalogue number 93.4) from Harehope which was done by the same hand as was responsible for the Harehope pulley ring. An intriguing sequence of use/manufacture/ redecoration can be seen in these Harehope buttons, which form the second biggest button find in Britain (second only to the 39 in the Grindlow, Over Haddon, Derbyshire, grave: Bateman 1861, 46-48). The great majority of the 19 decorated buttons have unworn bases and very slightly worn, well executed, ladder patterns, whereas the largest button has a very worn base and a secondarily cut design. The 14 plain buttons divide almost equally into worn and unworn. It can therefore be suggested that there was a gap between the acquisition of the plain buttons and the large button (initially undecorated) and the coming of the decorated examples. It may be that their decoration caused the owner to attempt to alter his largest and most splendid specimen: shortly after, however, all the buttons were deposited in the grave. A similar instance of secondary and inexpert decoration, presumably done at some considerable remove from the original hand, can be seen on spacer-plate B from South Mound, Houston, Renfrew, on which an additional line of dots has been quite crudely executed (Morrison, A 1979, 32, plate 8).

Finally in this section, the surprisingly high levels of calcium found in the archaeological jet material analysed by X-ray fluorescence and neutron activation analysis must be noted (Pollard, Bussell & Baird 1981, 156-7); these may be explained as residues of the polishing process, using

5.46 Jet buttons and pulley-ring from Harehope, Peeblesshire (93)

5.47 Jet plate from Law Hill, Angus (107)

rottenstone (decomposed siliceous limestone: Shepherd, L A G 1981, 49).

Evidence of how the production of jet and amber objects was organised must be largely inferred from the objects themselves. The only definite sites of prehistoric jet working (in Derbyshire) are late in our period and domestic, being concerned with shale bracelet production (Machin 1971; Radley 1969).

However, with regard to jet, the occurrence of a high grade source (near Whitby), the similarity of the techniques used, and used well (eg. V-boring; Y-boring on spacer-plates; punctulated rather than incised decoration on spacer-plates) and the evidence of secondary decoration, done badly on buttons at considerable distances from their source, all suggest a limited number of craftsmen working near to the source of the raw material.

The evidence for amber working is more difficult to assess. Early finds such as Greenbrae (illustration 3.38) show the minimum of conversion and could easily represent local working of beach amber, were it not for their association with a widely dispersed type of jet bead (Smith, I F 1974, 40). The Kellythorpe, Driffield amber buttons were surely fashioned in Yorkshire in the prestigious amber (illustration 4.15). The later, Wessex, amber objects can be interpreted as having been worked in Britain by a very limited number of craftsmen using material imported from Jutland/south Scandinavia (Shennan 1982a, 40), or beach amber from Norfolk, acquired along the Icknield Way (Taylor 1980, 45). Although one of the chief characteristics of the Wessex phenomenon was its wide continental links (Burgess 1980, 104) into which an amber exchange network could fit quite readily, it does not seem impossible that both sources could have been utilised when necessary.

Craftsmanship

A wide range of personal ornaments and other objects was made from jet and amber during the third and second millennia bc some pieces were relatively simple to make, others consumed many man-hours. Some slight diachronic trends can be seen in the objects under discussion; in general the products which require the most complex craftsmanship, such as spacer-plate necklaces with Y-boring (eg. Melfort: illustration 5.48), amber dagger pommels, shale and amber cups, occur towards the end of our period. On the other hand, collared beads such as those from Greenbrae, Aberdeenshire (illustration 3.38) are relatively difficult pieces of craftsmanship which date towards the beginning of the period. However, the comparatively large size of both collared beads and belt sliders may have made their manipulation during manufacture rather easier than some of the smaller and later objects.

Certainly they are among the simpler types to make, involving either boring a relatively large diameter hole or cutting a sizeable section of the piece. An analysis of the various stages of manufacture can give some indication of the complexity of craftsmanship involved in an object. The items of jet and amber illustrated in this volume can be divided into three groups. The first group required two or three principal operations

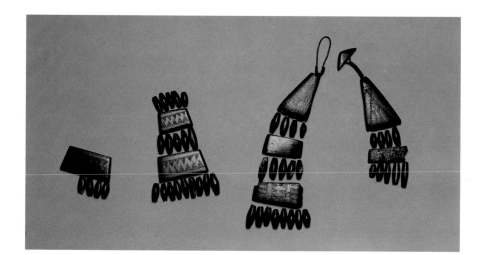

5.48 Parts of two jet necklaces from Melfort, Argyll (119.2)

5.49 Shale and gold macehead from Clandon, Dorset (94.3): a. with gold caps removed; b. with the gold caps in position

(roughing out, drilling or cutting out a perforation or aperture and final detailing) and comprises (belt) sliders, large biconical beads, disc beads, simple fusiform beads, simple pendants and bracelets. (The basic preparation of some of the Wessex gold-bound pieces could also fit in here — in particular the amber discs). The second group, those objects requiring approximately four operations (roughing out, drilling, final shaping, final decoration and polishing) includes collared jet beads, plain V-bored buttons, the Clandon macehead (illustration 5.49), amber plaques and pendants, elaborated biconical beads and faceted fusiform beads such as those from Masterton (illustration 5.50). The third group contains those objects requiring the most complex treatments, in some cases up to seven separate operations. These are decorated V-bored buttons, reflexly concave buttons (cf. Migdale), pulley rings, necklace spacer-plates, dagger pommels and cups.

Using the figures given in the preceding section, approximate calculations of the time necessary to manufacture some of these objects can be made. Simple forms, such as the jet bead from Cairnholy I, may have taken as little as 3 hours to make, perhaps broken down thus:

roughing out	1	hour
drilling perforation	½	hour
final shaping and polishing	1½	hours
	3	hours

(The amber bead from Culduthel (illustration 4.16) probably took an even shorter time to make, in the region of 1½ hours.) On the other hand, the estimate for the drilling alone of 8 elbow, 8 straight and 8 Y-borings on the terminal and spacer-plates of the Pitkennedy necklace is 11 hours, that is one rather busy and wrist-tiring day, or, perhaps more likely, spaced over two or more days.

Even if these estimates are out by, say 25% (allowing for the greater skill of Bronze Age craftsmen, the possible use of a bow drill, etc), they should give some idea of the amount of time and degree of skill involved in working jet or amber. The production of the most complex items, such as amber pommels or cups must therefore have been a most exacting and lengthy process.

The concept of high quality in the context of jet and amber objects has two aspects, which often intersect in the same object. First, there are objects which are clearly the product of highly skilled craftsmen and second there are objects whose use (and deposition) reflect a high perceived value in the eyes of their owners or of contemporary society. Space permits only a few examples of each aspect.

The largest of the Harehope buttons (in its original undecorated state) and the others mentioned, including the pulley ring, must represent the

5.50 *Jet necklace from Masterton, Fife (114.5)*

very many jet buttons whose manufacture was the product of high skill. The Harehope disc beads are also worthy of note, being exceptionally regularly cut and bored. The Knowes of Trotty amber buttons, hooked objects and spacer-plates, the Upton Lovell G2(e) complex-bored spacer-plate and the Clandon cup are all work of master craftsmen. The Wessex gold does also, of course, represent work of the highest quality: Taylor stresses how rare it must have been for craftsmen to work in two different media (1980, 47).

The second aspect of quality is represented by the efforts made by the owners to repair and keep serviceable their possessions. The crescentic jet necklaces provide many examples of replacement or refurbishment: the toggle on the otherwise heavily worn Mount Stuart necklace (illustration 4.90) is clearly a replacement, while several of the fusiform beads on the Masterton necklace have been re-made from larger pieces, possibly spacer-plates, given the evidence of old borings on their sides. There are several V-bored buttons with replacement borings, eg. the one from Cairn Riv, Banffshire (Shepherd, I A G 1981, 49, figure 2, 6) or the Garton Slack C52, Yorkshire, button that was rebored at least twice (Mortimer 1905, 216-18, figure 556). Whether these operations reflect fluctuations in the supply of jet must remain an open question.

Finally, there may be evidence to suggest that some types of bead were perceived to be of higher value or status than others. How else can one account for the observation made at Almondbank, Perthshire, where a short cist was found to contain a disc-bead necklace in which the discs had been arranged in groups of differing sizes which simulated the profiles of individual fusiform beads (Dr Margaret Stewart pers comm)?

Distributions in time and space

Three groups of jet and amber objects, determined on broadly functional, but in some respects intersecting, criteria, can be discerned.
1. *Jewellery:* collared beads, spacer-plate and other necklaces, bracelets, Wessex gold-covered beads and buttons.
2. *Clothing accessories:* (Belt) sliders, pulley rings, buttons (for cloaks, leggings, tunics or pouches: Shepherd, I A G 1984).
3. *Ostentatious artefacts:* cups, maceheads, dagger pommels, plaques, wristguards.

Certain interesting trends and differences in the distribution of these classes of object can be observed which permit further inferences about the organisation of their production.

Amongst the jet objects in group 1, the type with perhaps the most intriguing distribution is also the earliest, the collared bead. These are concentrated in south-west England (Gloucester, Devon, Dorset, Wiltshire), with a relatively small number in what may be taken to be their source area, Yorkshire (Smith, I F 1974, 40). They contrast to a certain extent with another early jet type, the probably more functional belt slider (illustration 3.36), whose distribution clusters in Yorkshire, with one smaller grouping in central southern England (McInnes 1968, 138, figure 28). However, these apparent differences may be accounted for by the suggestion that sliders were produced for only a short period *(ibid)* and by the association of such collared beads as those from Greenbrae, Aberdeenshire, with other objects of high status such as amber beads and a type of edge-polished flint axe (Seamer) generally found in non-domestic or 'ritual' contexts (Kenworthy 1977, 85). It is thus possible to see the initial use of jet as being very tightly controlled as perhaps an exclusive 'export commodity', for use only in certain prestigious exchanges and political or social contacts.

The Greenbrae group can be seen as a precursor of the late beaker links between Yorkshire and eastern Scotland which are exemplified by the distribution of spacer-plate necklaces and V-bored jet buttons. Spacer-plate necklaces are found in three main areas of Scotland — south Argyll and Bute, Angus and Moray (Morrison, A 1979, figure 4, after Coutts) — and in four discrete clusters in England — east Yorkshire, Derbyshire, Norfolk and Wessex. An analysis of the thirteen motif groups found on spacer-plates showed that ten correspond closely to ten of the motif groups found on beaker pottery as defined by D L Clarke (1970, 16-23, 424-8). Five fall into Clarke's 'Southern British Motif Group 4', while the other five are paralleled in his 'Panels and Metopes Motif Group 5'. These similarities are generally very close: for example the distinctive Clarke motifs numbers 35 iii and 35 vi (1970, 428) appear on 15% of decorated spacer-plates (Shepherd, I A G 1973, 72). The distribution of decorated spacer-plates (*c.* 60% of the total) follows the basic pattern outlined above, with the majority in Scotland. However, the distribution of late beakers (in Lanting and van der Waals' steps 5 and 6: 1972) sharing motifs with spacer-plates reverses this pattern, showing a preponderance in England, principally Yorkshire, and the central, southern and eastern counties and three small groupings in Scotland (Shepherd, I A G 1973, 72, Map 2-4).

The most economical hypothesis to explain this contrast postulates that necklaces were manufactured and decorated in the south, notably in the jet-bearing area of east Yorkshire and then traded north to eastern Scotland, possibly as a response to, or part of, the first regular bronze-working, the Migdale — Killaha stage (Burgess's Stage IV: 1980, 75-79).

Yorkshire is also a fulcrum area in the distribution of the various types of V-bored button, possibly for similar reasons to its role in spacer-plate necklace production. The jet buttons in the Migdale hoard belong to the 'reflexly concave' series, characterised by the button from Balbirnie, Fife (Shepherd, I A G 1974). This series, and the large conical button type, as seen in the larger of the Harehope buttons, have a Yorkshire/Scottish distribution which is similar to the pattern already described for spacer-plate necklaces. In contrast, the small conical buttons are scarcely present in the north at all but are concentrated in Yorkshire, Derbyshire and Wessex (Shepherd, I A G 1984). The Yorkshire/Wessex connections have recently been emphasised by the identification of a high proportion of jet, rather than shale, amongst the Devizes collection (Pollard, Bussell & Baird 1981, 160).

There is some evidence of sexual differentiation between these button series: of the 19 sexed skeletons with large conical and reflexly concave buttons, 15 are male, 2 are female and 2 are children. Conversely, of 10 small conical button graves, 6 were female, 3 were male and 1 was with several skeletons of both sexes. (However, in this group there is quite a high proportion of unsexed skeletons: Shepherd, I A G 1973, 52).

Certainly several of the large buttons seem to have been used as cloak fasteners, eg. Kellythorpe, while several of the multiple finds of small conical buttons were clearly strung as necklaces, being recorded as 'round her neck' (Bateman 1861, 25) and exhibiting string wear on the *outer* rather than inner, edges of their borings. However, buttons in both series were also used for buttoning shirts, tunics or leggings in a variety of thicknesses of fabric and also (often when associated with pulley rings) as pouch fasteners. In fact, one can speculate that the multiple Harehope find combines many of these functions and envisage a chieftain or grandee clad in a loosely buttoned tunic that was gathered at the waist with a belt, fastened with the pulley ring and on to which was buttoned a pouch, itself adorned with other jet buttons; the whole ensemble being finished off with an imposing cloak, fastened at the neck by an enormous shiny cone of jet.

It should be stressed that V-bored buttons, of all the amber and jet objects currently under discussion, have the widest distribution, both in time and space. They can be found right across Europe, from Co Sligo in the west to the Caucasus in the east and from Malta to the Gulf of Finland (Klejn 1968). Such a geographical range is reflected in a considerable chronological span, from the second half of the fourth millennium down to the early second millennium bc. The 'international' nature of such buttons has recently been stressed (Bradley 1984, 87) and, while it is possible to distinguish a common, generalised type, the small conical or slightly domical button, it must be emphasised that in different areas it appears in differing proportions to other types — and in a variety of material (jet, amber, stone, tin, bone, shell). The enormously wide spatial and chronological distribution of these objects, their usually small size (in general smaller than the British examples) and their location, in bell beaker graves in Central Europe, in quantities on or in front of the upper part of the skeleton (Hajek 1957, 422), all suggest that they functioned as necklace elements or general trinkets, rather than as clothing fasteners (cf. Gimbutas 1956, plate 27.2; Arnal 1954, 256).

Turning, finally, to the remaining object-types, the Wessex gold-enhanced jewellery and the ostentatious artefacts, their continental links are too well known for further reiteration (Gerloff 1975). However, complex and enigmatic relationships can be inferred from the distributions within Britain of classic types such as amber and shale cups (Newall 1929; Piggott, S 1938, 82-83; Burgess 1984). Most commentators imply that amber, and by analogy jet or shale, was imported to Wessex in a raw state (by whatever route), for conversion into luxury items by the Wessex mastercraftsmen (Piggott, S 1938, 81; Taylor 1980a, 45; Shennan 1982a, 43). Their products need not have had a purely southern English distribution if the possible cup from the East Riding of Yorkshire (Newall 1929) and the two probable fragments from Northumberland (Newbigin 1941, 109, plate VIII.7; Jobey 1966, 37, 41, figure 15) are taken into account. With these a more complicated and far-reaching pattern of exchanges emerges, perhaps involving the networks that were responsible for disseminating the necklaces. The three Wessex-type amber pestle beads found in a tumulus in Lanarkshire (Sim Collection, NMAS EQ 108-10) along with six jet beads suggest similar connections.

In conclusion, the contexts in which these jet and amber objects have been found are almost invariably funerary. That is to say they have been disposed of as part of elaborate ceremonials in which individual wealth was consumed — whether as expressions of grief and mourning or as a means of confirming the status of the deceased (and, by deposition, restricting access to the objects). The objects were the products of highly proficient craftsmen, working with simple but effective tools on two materials whose supply was possibly restricted in some periods. The distribution of these products bear witness to large scale exchange networks whose operation and *raison d'être* are still imperfectly understood. What is clear is how great was the effort expended during the third and second millennia bc to win, convert, display and ultimately to dispose of, these resinous, magical, substances.

FAIENCE

Faience occurs in contexts dating to the second millennium bc in Britain and Ireland only in the form of beads or, more rarely, closely related forms of pendants. The pioneering studies of H C Beck and Stone (1935; Stone & Thomas 1956), which first drew attention to these important finds, remain the primary sources for this area although knowledge of discoveries elsewhere in Europe has been augmented by several studies (Gimbutas 1956; Moucha 1958; Harding 1971; Harding & Warren 1973; Barfield 1978; Foster 1979 — the latter work contains a wide-ranging survey on pp 22-55). Stone felt that 'the invention and development of the product can well be claimed as man's first conscious essay in the production of a synthetic material' (Stone & Thomas 1956, 37-38). He further believed, following Lucas, that, although the circumstances surrounding its invention, probably in Western Asia, were unknown, it was 'extremely unlikely that such an extraordinary complex material as faience can possibly have been invented at more than one place'. In this proposal lies much of the explanation of why these small items were initially accorded such importance and how they became the subject of considerable controversy when diffusionist explanations of British prehistory began to be seriously questioned. Many of the beads found in Britain are of the segmented type which it was claimed has particularly close parallels in Egypt, a major centre of faience manufacture in the second millennium bc as indeed at other times. Since Stone subscribed to the idea of a single invention of the process and the subsequent limited diffusion of the techniques involved, the similarities between Egyptian and British beads were to be explained as contact between the Eastern Mediterranean, although not necessarily Egypt, and Britain. The most favoured source of supply was Mycenaean Greece. The virtual absence of faience beads in northern and western Europe other

than Britain, from where some 250 beads are known, suggested direct contact between the two regions and Stone even postulated that it took the form of 'two sea-borne expeditions at least' in order to account for the distribution of the various types of bead within Britain (Stone & Thomas 1956, 61). If this view had remained unchallenged there would, of course, have been little justification for including faience in a section devoted to craftsmanship for the inhabitants of Britain in the second millennium bc would have known the material only in its finished form.

Faience beads (illustration 5.51) form the vast majority of the earliest finds involving a glass-like substance in Britain although the true glass beads from Gilchorn, Angus, apparently associated with a collared urn and accessory cups (illustration 5.52: Hutcheson 1891, 455-56) and the altogether more remarkable example in a dagger grave group from Wilsford G42, Wiltshire (Guido *et al* 1984) show that a variety of materials and processes were available in the second millennium bc. Faience in this context denotes a composite material consisting of a core of fine quartz grains and a separate glaze applied to the surface. The quartz grains of the core are fused together through the admixture of small amounts of lime or alkali or both, and normally colourless. The distinctive blue or green colour of the beads is provided by traces of copper compounds added to the glaze which consists of a soda-lime-quartz isotropic glass applied in powdered form to the previously moulded core. The processes of manufacture involved in

5.51 *Faience beads from Culbin Sands, Morayshire (front: 108) and Glenluce Sands, Wigtownshire (back: 109)*

5.52 *Glass bead from Gilchorn, Angus*

producing Egyptian faience have been considered in some detail by Lucas (1962, 156-67) and Noble (1969). It has generally been assumed that the beads in question would have required two firings, one for the core and one for the application of the glaze. Recent observations by the Wulffs in Iran provide a more vivid picture of the possible processes and incidentally suggest that items such as beads may only have required one firing (Wulff, Wulff & Koch 1968).

Their studies were undertaken in the holy city of Qom where several craftsmen still made donkey beads and other items with a bright turquoise glaze highly reminiscent in their general appearance of the faience objects found in the Near East and Eastern Mediterranean. With some reluctance one of the craftsmen, Ustad Reza Kashipaz, allowed them to inspect his workshop where he employed three adult labourers and six boys. One of the adults was an experienced collector of quartzite pebbles, a second crushed the pebbles and then ground the crushed pieces to a fine powder on a small hand-mill while the third mixed this powder with gum tragacanth dissolved in water to achieve a consistency whereby it could be moulded into the required shape. Once moulded the objects were dried in the sun and, when hard, holes were drilled in the beads. The craftsman himself was responsible for preparing the glazing powder, the basic constituent of which was plant ash. The particular plants were collected from the salt marshes and burnt in large pits where the ashes coalesced into hard blocks. The principal chemical component of the ash was sodium oxide. In the workshop this ash was finely ground and mixed with hydrated lime and powdered quartz to which was added smaller quantities of charcoal and copper oxide. The latter Reza got from a coppersmith who collected it in the form of hammerscale. The three major chemicals forming the glazing powder were silicon dioxide (43%), sodium oxide and magnesium oxide (both 20%).

The boys were responsible for preparing the objects for firing, which was done in unglazed pots in a kiln. Glazing powder was sprinkled on the bottom of the pot, itself some 300 mm in diameter, and a layer of beads placed onto the powder. The beads were close together but did not touch one another. They were completely covered with glazing powder and the process repeated until the pot was nearly full. The final layer was powder which was compressed. The pots were then stacked in a specially designed down-draft kiln and firing took twelve hours with a further twelve hours for cooling. The optimal firing temperature was around 1000°C. The pots were then removed from the kiln and turned upside down to empty the contents. When correctly fired the glazing powder was very friable so that it crumbled when stepped on and the glazed objects appeared bright and glossy all over without any adhering powder.

This process was used to produce some forty thousand beads in a single firing and its very scale may be considered an inappropriate analogy for the production of the relatively small number of British beads if they were indigenously produced. Nevertheless the Wulffs showed in laboratory experiments that the process can be scaled down even to the level of making a single bead without reducing its effectiveness. Equally, the description emphasises that the procedures involved are not in themselves complicated and would not have been beyond the competence of second millennium bc craftsmen in Britain providing they had the technical knowledge. Noble (1969, 438-39, fn 12) suggests that the vapour process was not used in ancient times and to that extent does not find the Wulffs' description to be a close analogy. But the evidence he adduces in favour of his view all derives from the more complex objects such as vases, not seen in Britain, which are perhaps the product of specialist techniques.

From the outset of serious study attempts have been made to demonstrate the Eastern Mediterranean origin of the British beads through scientific analysis (Beck, H C & Stone 1935, 252). The initial hopes were not, however, confirmed and Thomas was forced to conclude that 'the spectrographic analysis of faience beads does not provide any unequivocal indication of their source or date of origin' (Stone & Thomas 1956, 77). Notwithstanding these difficulties a Mediterranean source still appeared the most plausible explanation with the consequence that the beads became the major evidence for a link between Wessex and Mycenae. Other elements supporting such a connection between the two areas were altogether more tenuous and problematic (the issue is discussed in more detail above pp ??). Subsequent considerations, although ostensibly concerned with faience beads, appear to have been motivated by desires to resolve the broader issue of the existence of contact between the two regions. Newton and Renfrew (1970) applied new statistical techniques to Thomas's original data and found the case for local manufacture in Britain to be the most reasonable explanation of the results. This view was disputed by some (McKerrell 1972) but supported by new analyses using the more powerful technique of neutron activation (Aspinall *et al* 1972). There the matter rather inconclusively rests.

In the absence of firm scientific evidence the question of British manufacture is still largely an archaeological problem. We have seen that the techniques involved would not necessarily have been beyond the capabilities of the craftsmen of the period. On the other hand, as Foster has pointed out, the presence of only beads and not more elaborate pieces is surprising (1979, 171). Certainly, beads were a major item in the production of the earliest Aegean and Near Eastern faience industries but vessels, inlaid pieces and ornaments were also made. Although this need be no more than a reflection of different patterns of taste, the close similarities between the segmented type of bead (the only type found in Wessex) from Britain and the Mediterranean is less readily explained. The importance of these similarities has been questioned by Harding (1971, 190) who would see it as no more than a 'multiple annular bead', an idea not dissimilar to the use of graded disc jet beads to imitate fusiform examples in the necklace from Almondbank, Perthshire noted above (p 213). There are, moreover, bead shapes from Britain unrepresented in the Mediterranean material, which, as negative evidence, have not figured as prominently in the arguments. What is certain is that contacts between northern Europe and the Aegean are attested by the confirmed presence of Baltic amber in Mycenaean contexts (Beck, C W 1974). Although there is no clear archaeological evidence to support the idea that amber, tin and faience were involved in complex reciprocal exchange networks, as has often been argued (eg.

Becker 1954, 251-52; Lamberg-Karlovsky 1963; Piggott, S 1965, 136-37), the contact that is reflected by the amber may well have resulted in the transfer of knowledge of the techniques for producing faience beads into more northerly areas of Europe. This information may well have been sufficient to stimulate centres of faience production in Central Europe and Britain (Foster 1979, 171-72).

ORGANIC MATERIALS

The use of organic materials — wood, plant and animal products — was widespread in the third and second millennia bc. Because of their very nature, however, they decay far more easily than any of the other materials previously discussed and it is only in exceptional circumstances that they survive complete. If exposed to the air or buried in soil which is freely draining, acidic or even neutral, natural decomposition takes place and the most that may be left is a staining of the soil. This also applies to bronze and to a lesser extent, jet and amber, but the process of decay is slower with these materials. If, however, the soil is alkaline (because of chalk sub-soil or shell sand) bone will be preserved. If a deposit is waterlogged or objects are buried in a cist which is completely sealed with clay then the movement of air and water is prevented and organic materials may reach a stable condition. Once exposed again to the air, they will begin to decay rapidly unless they are quickly conserved else hide, textiles and wood soon turn to a pulpy mass and bone may fragment and crumble. Hence, a number of items made of leather, textile and bone referred to in the catalogue were seen during excavation, but no longer exist. Even if parts survive they will not be as impressive as the originals: compare the reconstruction of the Ashgrove, Methilhill dagger which is far more attractive than the original (illustrations 5.53-54). How great a part was played by organic materials can only be surmised from these exceptional finds, traces of objects which have accidentally survived and by reference to other, more recent, societies whose use of organic materials has been documented and may be used as an analogue.

Plants and animals

Two types of approach were taken in the acquisition of the raw materials. Either they were deliberately sought eg. wood for building, making bowls or hafts for tools, or else they came as by-products from other activities eg. the killing of animals for food allows access to bone, hide, sinew, gut etc. Some materials may have been gained by either strategy since red deer antler, for example, is grown annually by the male deer and then shed in April/May. Thus, antler can be acquired either by taking it from a stag which has been killed or, more often, collected by following the deer herd during the shedding season.

Since plants and animals were made use of in many ways other than for toolmaking (eg. as foodstuffs) they were familiar in the environment and the initial acquisition of them had more to do with selection and timing rather than the more complex procedures seen in flint mining or the

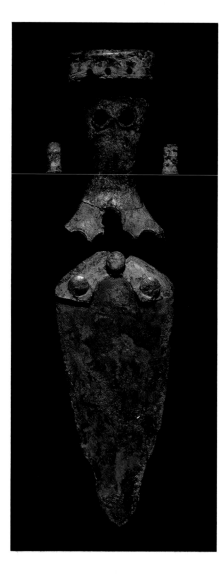

5.53 Bronze dagger with horn hilt and ivory pommel from Ashgrove, Fife (75.1)

5.54 Reconstruction of the Ashgrove dagger (75.2)

production of metalwork. A wide variety of woods was available and used but the prime building timber was oak (Coles, J M, Heal & Orme 1978). Finds of linen imply that flax was being deliberately grown and harvested. The choices made in the use of bone depended upon which animals were available and how useful they were considered to be. Cattle and sheep bones, for example, were regularly used, red deer bone less so but red deer antler was important. Some of the implements from coastal sites are made from whale and other cetacean bone but it would be very surprising if such a material were available to groups living inland. Hide, skin or leather can be obtained from virtually any animal but only rarely has it been possible to use modern techniques to identify the species from which it came.

While wood and bone as materials have physical properties which are common to all woods and all sources of bone, the actual properties of different woods do vary as does the size and shape of bone. The tools available to work organic materials changed through the third and second millennia bc and all these factors constrained the techniques used in manufacture and the type of end product achieved. Substantial amounts of wood were used in building and such excavations as those in the Somerset Levels, where wood has survived in waterlogged peat deposits, have enabled detailed study of constructional techniques to be undertaken (Coles J M, Hibbert & Orme 1973; *Somerset Levels Papers*). In areas where large timbers were scarce eg. Orkney, easily available building stone of high quality was used for walling and whale bone may have formed part of the roof supports which elsewhere were built with wood. The quantity of plant material which must have been used in fires for cooking and heating should not be underestimated.

Techniques of manufacture

We shall now concentrate on the ways in which organic materials were used in the third to second millennium bc to make tools and other items. The techniques of manufacture varied according to the type of product required. Wood was initially chopped down and then split using wedges. It could then be roughly shaped using an axe or adze to take small flake-like pieces from it (illustration 5.55). Finer work was achieved by whittling and then abrading either with sandstone, pumice or some gritty

5.55 Iain Lawson, cabinet maker in the National Museum of Antiquities, using an adze during the creation of a reconstruction of the wooden structure at Bargeroosterveld, Drenthe, Netherlands

5.56 Antler macehead from Watnall, Nottinghamshire (46)

medium and water. A polish could be produced by rubbing with leather. Some bone tools required virtually no shaping at all (eg. shovels made from scapulae or levering picks made from antler). Otherwise, a fracture technique akin to flint-knapping was used to rough-out the desired shape which was then finished off by trimming with either a lithic tool or, later, a more resilient metal blade, or else more commonly by grinding (eg. the bone points from Snailwell A: illustration 4.96). Drilling was used on bone where natural holes were not suitable as is shown in the case of the bracelet of beads from Skara Brae (illustration 3.29) and the much larger perforations in antler maceheads (eg. Watnall: illustration 5.56). Polishing of bone can be achieved by using leather or simply by rubbing with the hands, provided the surface has been sufficiently smoothed in advance.

Horn can be shaped by cutting it and then steaming or boiling it. At this stage it becomes malleable and can either be flattened and then trimmed to shape or else moulded. The hilt plates on the Ashgrove, Methilhill dagger were made by flattening and a horn spoon or ladle found with a beaker at Broomend of Crichie, Aberdeenshire (Miles & Miles 1971, 19: illustration 5.57) shows that moulding was a known technique. Plant fibres, and presumably animal fibres, were woven to make textiles from at least c. 1800 bc (based on typological dating of the Kellythorpe,

5.58 *Detail of the bronze axe from Ridgeway Barrow 7, Dorset, showing traces of linen (99.1)*

5.57 *Horn ladle or spoon from Broomend of Crichie, Aberdeenshire*

Driffield burial: illustration 4.15). Textile is most clearly seen on the axehead from Ridgeway Barrow 7 (illustration 5.58). Hide, leather and skins were being used throughout the third and second millennia bc and cutting, shaping and sewing were all easily within the technology of these times.

The range of uses

The choice of material and the techniques of manufacture employed were very much dependent upon the quality of product to be achieved. Few of the surviving objects are virtuoso pieces of craftsmanship. The distinctions more often seen are in the choice of materials used and the skill of manufacture. Whilst the beads from Skara Brae and West Kennet (illustration 2.9) are simple to make, they require a lot of time and manual dexterity, particularly those made of ivory which are very small and required perforation. The tusk pendants from Skara Brae (illustration 3.29) show particular skill in perforating a very brittle material. The bone points from Snailwell A, which are themselves perhaps part of a necklace, required only a basic knowledge of physical properties and techniques of manufacture as did the fine bone pins from Skara Brae (illustration 5.59) and Quoyness (illustration 5.60) but the latter are products of a completely different quality and in them we can see the imaginative and skilful use of raw materials pushed towards the limits of what could be achieved with a non-metal technology. The decorated pins from Carrowkeel E and Carrowmore 3 (illustration 5.61) are also skilled examples of antler working.

When metal tools became available, there seems to have been a reduction in the quantity of decorative boneworking, though this should not be seen as cause and effect, as many of the pieces made were small beads (eg. Milngavie: illustration 5.62) or toggles (eg. Sewell: illustration 4.5). Nevertheless, intricate pieces could still be made, such as the belt toggle from Culduthel (illustration 4.16) or the simpler belt hook from Killicarney (illustration 4.91).

In some areas of Britain eg. Orkney, the traditions of boneworking were strong and a wide range of objects were made for everyday use as piercing tools, digging tools, for pottery decoration, flint working, burnishing etc. In other areas, such as southern England there seems to have been a more restricted range of domestic equipment made from bone, again covering similar areas of activity but with a far smaller number of forms. The extent to which there was variation in the use of plant materials is as yet impossible to tell because so little has survived.

There were three ways in which organic materials were used: 1. as tools themselves, 2. as part of composite pieces and 3. as objects with which to decorate other materials. Beads and pins have already been mentioned and toggles were probably used as fastenings or mountings on leather or cloth. Amber and jet buttons fulfilled the same function. The perforated phalanges (eg. Skara Brae: illustration 5.63) are enigmatic, though those with a single perforation have been interpreted as whistles. Into this group we must also place clothing made from skins and cloth (eg. that originally attached to the Mold Cape: catalogue number 98), and the

5.59 Bone pins from Skara Brae, Orkney

5.60 Bone pin from Quoyness, Orkney (8.3)

5.61 Antler pins and boar's tusk from Carrowkeel E, Co Sligo, Ireland (16) and Carrowmore 3, Co Sligo, Ireland (bottom right: 17)

5.62 Flint arrowheads and bone beads from Milngavie, Dunbartonshire (133.1-5; 133.7)

5.63 *Perforated phalanges from Skara Brae, Orkney (26.15-16)*

5.64 *The dagger from Bargeroosterveld, Drenthe, Netherlands: a. the pommel; b. the hilt (170)*

records of cloth and hides placed with bodies at burial (eg. linen under the Kellythorpe, Driffield body: catalogue number 68, and the probable aurochs hide under the bodies at Masterton: catalogue number 114).

In the contexts of burials and hoards, organic materials are most frequently known as parts of composite tools. Whilst axeheads needed a haft, usually of wood (cf. Ehenside Tarn: Darbishire 1874), in order to use them, those axeheads deposited in hoards seem to have been unhafted eg. those in the Colleonard hoard (catalogue number 145) were all within a pottery vessel and if a haft had been attached to the Sweet Track jadeite axehead (illustration 3.31), it would have been preserved. In graves, however, complete objects were deposited. At Leubingen pieces of the wooden halberd haft survived (catalogue number 169.11) and numerous copper and bronze daggers have traces of original hilts of wood or horn often preserved by corrosion products from the blade (eg. the daggers from Kellythorpe, Driffield: catalogue number 68.2 and from Hove: catalogue number 97.2). Remains of dagger sheaths of wood or leather have also been found (eg. Winterbourne Stoke G4: illustration 4.43). Where there have been good conditions of preservation, some idea can be gained of the quality of workmanship achieved in these composite pieces. The dagger from Bargeroosterveld (illustration 5.64) with its horn handle decorated with tin nails is impressive. More complex is that from Ashgrove, Methilhill (illustrations 5.53-54) which combined a bronze blade, horn hilt plates over a wooden core and a pommel of ivory (probably from a sperm whale tooth) all placed with a skin sheath. Wood was used to make the hilt plates on the Wilsford G5 daggers (Annable & Simpson 1964, 45). Bone provided the base for a piece of decorated sheet gold from Wilsford G8 (illustration 4.32) and wood is the most likely material over which were formed the sheet gold belt hook and large lozenge plate from Bush Barrow (illustration 4.30). A bronze buckle and traces of leather were found with the Kellythorpe, Driffield wristguard (catalogue number 68.1) and the positioning of various buttons, daggers, axeheads and sliders on or by bodies in the grave implies the existence of straps and bindings.

Organic materials were also used to decorate other materials. The most obvious of these is pottery where lengths of twisted cord, bone or antler combs and unworked pieces of bone have all been used to form designs. In addition it has been suggested that a bone or wooden stylus was used to produce the initial design on the gold button cover from Upton Lovell G2(e) (illustration 4.57) and the large lozenge plate from Bush Barrow (illustration 4.30: Taylor *supra*).

During the third and second millennia bc, organic materials were important and were used to make tools, clothing, decorative objects, handles and hafts and parts of composite pieces. The technology involved was not particularly complex and the range of variation in items made was dependent primarily on the quality of finish required. The most skilled and impressive pieces are, not surprisingly, those intended as items of display and ceremonial.

In their discussion of these quite different materials, the authors have shown that a wide range of techniques, skills and strategies were used to make both the objects used from day to day and those which were prestigious. Differences in quality are identifiable on the basis of several criteria and what was important for leaders in the third and second millennia bc was to be able to control either the production or the distribution (and preferably both) of the objects of high quality in particular. In some cases the relationship of production is thought to have been one of patronage, in others it may have been the leader's social contacts which enabled important raw materials to be acquired. Since gift exchange is likely to have been the means of distribution, prestige items could be controlled through these same contacts. If one were of high status, then the contacts and gifts involved in social relationships were likely to have been equally prestigious. Having symbols of power was about creating and controlling them but, above all, showing how their quality was a reflection of their owner's status.

CONCLUSION

ALL DISCUSSION of prehistoric material, where it goes beyond the mere descriptive, ventures into the unknown and the unverifiable. Our interpretations can be no more than the product of contemporary experience broadened by some awareness of ethnographic data so that the sole test of our conclusions, assuming no basic distortion of what passes for archaeological fact, must be their plausibility for the reader. Some will undoubtedly feel that we have behaved as though the path was lit by searchlights whereas, in reality, it was only a flickering candle while perhaps others will believe something close to the opposite. We have, however, continually applied this test of plausibility and tried as far as possible to be guided by it in forming our judgements, to propose and support ideas that appeared to be a reasonable interpretation of the evidence. Equally, we have sought to avoid 'blocks to falsifiability' created by wide-ranging excursions among arguments intended to explore the considerable variety of views made possible by the ambiguities inherent in the evidence. Such ambiguities can be turned to advantage if they encourage a vigorous series of attempts to interpret the available information or they can, as so often in the past, provide the justification for avoiding explanation altogether.

We have tried in this volume to offer an essentially narrative account of events during nearly two millennia of Britain's past, viewed from the standpoint of power, prestige and status. In so doing, we have probably given emphasis to occurrences that at the time appeared commonplace and ignored what once seemed momentous. Our concern with power and prestige reflects the belief that understanding these aspects is, as Bradley (1984) implies, central to our knowledge of 'the social foundations of prehistoric Britain'. In a broader sense we share his views that social questions are open to investigation through archaeological techniques and are a prerequisite for a 'more rounded approach to prehistory'. Indeed, without the adoption of these concerns the study of prehistory will remain largely the preserve of the specialist with the public domain dominated by unconnected announcements of spectacular discoveries. It is no coincidence that our attitudes have been honed by the demands of creating an exhibition which will, hopefully, appeal to others beside fellow archaeologists. The cultural-historical framework used by most prehistorians is so much a part of our conditioning that it is easy to forget that the Three-Age system and its subsequent refinements often have little meaning for those not active in the discipline. We have eschewed the use of such terminology as far as possible while recognising the risk of suggesting that the chronology is better understood than is actually the case.

In exploring our theme we have tried to show the development of ideologies which permitted the more overt reflection of individual power. Such changes were closely related to expanding areas of political control combined with increasing networks of relations between regions. As the individual regions grew larger the leaders would have become more isolated from the majority of the population. In these circumstances, the need for symbols would have been greater and the maintenance of power in the hands of an elite would have been ensured by control of specialised knowledge and practices. The resulting social systems would have acquired a degree of rigidity, in terms of the ruling elite, with considerable dependence on the wider networks. In such a situation the opportunities for gradual change would have been limited and successful challenges to the system, perhaps prompted by events in other areas, would have occasioned dramatic transformations. This appears to have been the situation, for at the end of the second millennium bc the archaeological record is characterised by a marked absence of formal burials in most areas and the appearance of fortified settlements.

CONCORDANCE
relating catalogue numbers and illustrations

Catalogue number	Illustration number	Catalogue number	Illustration number	Catalogue number	Illustration number
1	7.1	42	3.16	85	7.24
2	2.9	43	3.26	86	7.25
3	7.2	44	7.18	87	4.10
4	7.3	45	3.15	88	7.26
5	2.5-6	46	5.56	89	4.10
6	2.3-4	47	5.7	90	4.10
7	2.8; 3.32	48	5.7	91	7.26
8	3.21; 5.60	49	5.7	92	7.26
9	2.7; 3.32	50	5.7	93	5.46
10	7.4	51	7.19	94	4.54; 5.49
11	7.4	52	7.19	95	4.29; 7.27
12	3.36	53	3.48	96	4.55
13	3.36	54	7.20	97	4.45
14	5.42	55	3.14	98	4.41
15	7.5	56	5.6; 7.21	99	4.58-59; 5.58
16	5.61	57	7.22	100	4.51; 4.53; 4.57
17	5.61	58	5.22; 5.26; 7.23	101	4.30; 4.42
18	7.6	59	4.12	102	4.32; 4.56
19	7.6	60	5.34	103	4.31
20	3.19; 5.32; 7.7	61	5.17	104	4.39; 5.27; 5.44
21	7.8-10	62	5.24	105	4.46
22	3.49	63	4.11	106	4.49
23	4.8	64	5.21	107	5.47
24	7.11	65	5.16	108	5.51
25	7.12	66	5.23	109	5.51
26	3.18; 3.20; 3.22; 3.27-29; 5.59; 5.63; 7.13	67	5.25	110	4.52
		68	4.15	111	4.43
		69	4.9	112	4.40
27	7.14	70	4.13	113	7.28
28	3.33; 7.15-16	71	4.5	114	5.14; 5.50
29	3.37	72	4.4	115	5.28
30	3.34; 7.17	73	4.17	116	7.29
31	3.35	74	4.16	117	4.92
32	3.38	75	5.39; 5.53-54	118	4.89
33	3.24	76	4.2	119	4.38; 5.48
34	3.31	77	4.50	120	4.90; 5.35
35	3.30	78	4.1	121	4.91
36	3.25	79	5.18	122	4.87
37	3.30	80	4.7	123	4.87; 5.41
38	5.9	81	5.19	124	5.45
39	5.10	82	4.14	125	4.86
40	3.26	83	5.20	126	4.97
41	3.26	84	5.13	127	4.85

Catalogue number	Illustration number
128	4.96
129	7.30
130	4.95
131	4.93
132	4.94
133	5.37; 5.62
134	7.31
135	5.36
136	5.36
137	5.36
138	4.98; 5.8
139	5.38
140	5.38
141	4.88
142	4.27
143	4.28
144	4.26
145	4.25
146	7.32
147	4.33-37
148	5.15
149	5.11
150	4.22
151	4.18
152	4.18
153	4.18
154	4.19
155	4.21
156	4.21
157	4.20
158	4.20
159	4.3
160	Not illustrated
161	Not illustrated
162	7.33
163	4.66; 4.76
164	4.74
165	4.68; 4.70-71
166	4.65; 4.77
167	4.73
168	Not illustrated
169	4.78-79
170	4.83; 5.64
171	4.48
172	4.82
173	4.47
174	7.34
175	4.23
176	4.24
177	4.81
178	4.22
179	7.35

List of abbreviations used in the catalogue

L	length
B	breadth
Ht	height
Diam	diameter
mm	millimetres
m	metres
km	kilometres
N	north
S	south
E	east
W	west
horiz	horizontal
vert	vertical
int	interior/internal/internally
ext	exterior/external
max	maximum
min	minimum
unreg	unregistered
bc	radiocarbon date
BC	calibrated (or calendrical) date
cat	catalogue

7

CATALOGUE

CHAMBER TOMBS

1. Chamber tomb assemblage
Ty-isaf, Brecknockshire, Wales

1.1 Flint axe. Partly ground and polished axe of light grey flint, with sides diverging gradually from squared butt to meet ground cutting edge which is in fresh condition. Deep flaking scars on both faces. Asymmetrical lozenge-shaped profile, with noticeably thinner butt. L 104 mm. 39.210.22.

1.2 Bead or pendant consisting of an approximately circular disc of green sandstone with an eccentric hour-glass perforation. Diam 25 mm. 39.210.77.

Associations: Despite considerable earlier disturbance, the floor deposits were intact and produced, as well as the axe, the incomplete remains of 17 individuals, mostly arranged in groups, 2 leaf-shaped arrowheads, a bone pin and sherds of a lugged neolithic bowl. The bead has no certain associations.

Circumstances of Discovery: Found during excavation of a multi-period Cotswold-Severn type chamber tomb. The axe was in the western compartment of the lateral chamber on the W side of the cairn (Chamber I) and the bead in the entrance passage to the lateral chamber on the E side (Chamber II).

References:
Grimes 1939, 130, 131, fig 4.1 & .7, 132

Collection:
National Museum of Wales 39.210.22; 39.210.77

2. Chamber tomb assemblage
West Kennet, near Avebury, Wiltshire, England

2.1 - 2.16 Beads of bone, shale, jet and shell.

2.1 Bone bead of irregularly cylindrical form. L 11 mm. DM 1312.

7.1 *Flint axe and stone bead or pendant from Ty-isaf, Brecknockshire (1)*

2.2 Bone bead of barrel form, utilising natural perforation of the bone. L 11 mm. DM 1200.

2.3 Bone bead, with perforation bored from the solid. L 8 mm. DM 1312.

2.4 Highly polished bone bead with perforation bored from the solid. L 6 mm. DM 1201.

2.5 Bone bead, with perforation bored from the solid. L 7 mm. DM 1178.

2.6 Bead possibly made from the root of a tooth. L 6 mm.

2.7 Barrel-shaped bead of shale or lignite; matt surface; longitudinal perforation. L 15 mm. DM 1202.

2.8 Flattened globular bead of shale or lignite, lightly polished. L 11 mm. DM 1201.

2.9 Broken cylindrical bead of high quality jet or shale; polished surfaces. L 8.5 mm.

2.10 Flattened globular bead of shale or lignite. L 6 mm. DM 1202.

2.11 Cylindrical bead of high quality jet or shale with oblique ends. L 8 mm.

2.12 Flattened globular bead of shale or lignite. L 5 mm. DM 1174.

2.13 - 2.16 Beads made by perforating marine shells. The nearest points of the S coast to W Kennet are about 64 km distant, as the crow flies.

2.13 Perforated shell of *Nucella (purpura) lapillis* (L). The hole has been made by abrading the shell until the surface has broken through. L 32 mm. DM 1200.

2.14 Bead made from whorl of *Littorina littorea* (L). Worn, abraded surface. Diam 17 mm. DM 1200.

2.15 Perforated shell of *Nassarius (Nassa) reticulatus* (L). L 21 mm. DM 1200.

2.16 Perforated shell of *Cypraea* sp. L 10 mm (not illustrated).

2.17 Chalk macehead fragment. Macehead carved from chalk, of uncertain original shape owing to breakage across perforation in antiquity. Fresh striations visible in the perforation suggest breakage prior to or immediately after completion. Subsequently re-bored diagonally from the surface through to broken shaft-hole, possibly for use as a rough pendant as the broken edges are smoothed as if by wear. Ht 54 mm. DM 1226.8/60.

2.18 Perforated ox phalanx. L 62 mm. DM 1187.

2.19 Perforated ox phalanx, with areas of polish on surface. L 68 mm. DM 1190.

Associations: All of the objects described here were recovered from layers forming part of the deliberate secondary blocking-up of the burial chambers, after the final burials had been made on the chamber floors. The blocking material consisted mainly of clean chalk rubble but interspersed through it were discoloured layers and patches containing fine ash, charcoal and burnt chalk. Throughout the filling, but particularly in these 'dirty' layers, there was a scatter of animal bones, worked flints, sherds of pottery, bone tool and beads, and other miscellaneous artefacts. The pottery types recovered included Peterborough and Fengate ware, grooved ware, and beaker. Summary of contexts: 2.1, 2.3, 2.6, 2.9, 2.11, 2.18 from SE chamber; 2.7, 2.10 from NW chamber; remainder from NE chamber.

7.2 Shale bead from Eyford, Gloucestershire (3)

Circumstances of Discovery: Excavation in 1955-56 of the West Kennet long barrow, largest of its type in S England and related architecturally to the Cotswold-Severn group. At the E end of the trapezoidal mound, there are 5 burial chambers opening onto a passage leading in from a semi-circular forecourt and facade of monumental proportions.

References:
Piggott, S 1962, 26-30, 48-53, figs 16.1, 17.4-5, 18.2-13 & 17-19

Collection:
Devizes Museum DM 1174, 1178, 1187, 1190, 1200-02, 1226.8/60, 1312

3. Shale bead
Eyford, Gloucestershire, England

Shale bead. Polished surface. Circular bead with flattened upper and lower surfaces, rounded edges and a cylindrical perforation running through it. At the ends of the perforation, the edges are slightly worn. L 25 mm.

Associations: With male or female burial in Chamber E.

Circumstances of Discovery: Excavated by Rolleston and Royce in 1874. A Cotswold-Severn chambered cairn with 4 side chambers, containing human remains, a dog and pottery. It is uncertain whether the bodies were whole when deposited.

References:
Rolleston 1876
Greenwell & Rolleston 1877, 514-20
Piggott, S 1954, 143, fig 22.9, 146
O'Neil & Grinsell 1960, Upper Slaughter I

Collection:
British Museum 79.12-9.1599

7.3 Shale bead from Notgrove, Gloucestershire (4)

4. Shale bead
Notgrove, Gloucestershire, England

Shale bead. Bead, possibly of Kimmeridge shale, of oblate form with flattened elliptical cross-section, and cylindrical boring expanding at each end into a concave mouth with signs of wear. Surface now laminating. L 38 mm.

Associations: Parts of 2 contracted human inhumations were found in chamber D, accompanied, in addition to the bead, by 2 teeth and the pelvis of an ox, a dog's tooth, a fine leaf-shaped arrowhead and sherds of neolithic pottery.

Circumstances of Discovery: Found in 1881 during the investigation by Witts of a previously undisturbed chamber (Clifford's chamber D) in a multi-period Cotswold-Severn type chambered cairn, re-examined fully in 1934-35.

References:
Witts 1883, 82-83
Clifford 1936, 119-20, 146, fig 6
Piggott, S 1954, 143, fig 22.8, 146

Collection:
Cheltenham Art Gallery & Museum 1978:706:5

5. Chamber tomb assemblage
Giants' Graves, Arran, Scotland

5.1 Flint arrowhead. Leaf-shaped, damaged at tip. L 39 mm. EO 256.

5.2 Flint arrowhead. Leaf-shaped. L 34 mm. EO 257.

5.3 Flint arrowhead. Leaf-shaped, damaged at tip. L 33 mm. EO 258.

5.4 Flint arrowhead. Leaf-shaped, damaged at tip. L 25 mm. EO 259.

5.5 Flint knife, plano-convex, one edge curved, the other quite straight. Fine surface flaking and fine retouch along the edges. L 96 mm. EO 261.

5.6 Flint knife, tip snapped off. Gently curving cutting edge with fine surface flaking and retouch on the edge. Steep retouch on the other edge. Original blade shape would have been oval. L 102 mm. EO 262.

5.7 Flint knife. Curving cutting edge with fine retouch. Steep retouch on the other edge. The butt is very thick. L 86 mm. EO 263.

Associations: Also from the N compartment came a flint flake and various sherds of pottery including beaker, food vessel and collared urn. Large quantities of burnt bone were also found.

Circumstances of Discovery: Excavated in 1902 by Bryce. A long cairn with facade. The chamber is of the Clyde type and has 2 compartments at the N end of the cairn. The catalogued finds were recovered from the N compartment by sieving the soil from the chamber.

References:
Bryce 1903, 44-52
Henshall 1972, 384-85, (ARN 11), nos 14-20

Collection:
National Museum of Antiquities of Scotland EO 256-68, 271

6. Chamber tomb assemblage
Midhowe, Rousay, Orkney, Scotland

6.1 Flint knife with rounded tip and slightly curving sides with steep retouch. Thinned butt. Lower surface has transverse flakes. L 50 mm. EO 459.

6.2 Part of rim and base of decorated, carinated, round-based bowl. Fine hard fabric. Rounded rim with 3 deep horiz incisions below and thinner, shallower vert incisions underneath them. Int surface burnished. Estimated diam 229 mm. EO 461.

6.3 Part of rim and wall of decorated, carinated, probably round-based bowl. Quite thick, vesicular fabric. Rounded rim with expanding neck, decorated above the carination with nail impressions. Int surface burnished. Estimated diam 229 mm. EO 462. (Not illustrated).

6.4 Single sherd from wall of decorated, carinated,

probably round-based bowl. Quite thick, vesicular fabric. 2 sets of oblique, parallel, incised lines on neck set at right angles to each other and forming reversed triangles. L 38 mm. EO 463. (Not illustrated).

6.5 2 rim sherds from decorated, carinated, probably round-based bowl. Thin, hard, porous fabric with black, burnished int. Rounded rim with 2 rows of parallel vert incisions separated by 2 horiz lines, one above, the other between the rows. Max L 82 mm. EO 465-66. (Not illustrated).

6.6 Rim and body sherd from carinated, possibly round-based bowl. Coarse fabric with black surface on int and upper ext. Rounded rim with nail impressions, ext carination. Max L 90 mm. EO 460, 467. (Not illustrated).

6.7 Rim sherd from decorated, probably carinated, round-based bowl. Thickish hard fabric. Rounded rim with incised herring-bone decoration. Max L 42 mm. EO 464. (Not illustrated).

6.8 4 pieces of whale bone and antler.
a. 3 pieces of whale bone split with smoothed ext surfaces. One piece chopped at one end. Max L 87 mm. EO 469-71. (Not illustrated).
b. 1 piece antler. Burr and part of outer surface of shed antler. Split, some modern breakage. Max L 80 mm. EO 473. (Not illustrated).

Associations: 6.1-6.5 and 6.7 found together in SW of compartment 7; 6.6 found in centre of E side compartment 8 with human bone. Other sherds found near the N end of the cairn were opposite the contracted skeletons of a young male, a young individual and an adult skull, vertebrae and other bones which were in the N of compartment 7. The remains of at least 25 individual humans were found in the tomb as well as a range of animal, bird and fish bones and limpet shells.

Circumstances of Discovery: Excavated by Craw, Grant and Callander in 1932-33. A long, stalled, roughly rectangular cairn with horns on one side. The chamber has 12 compartments and had been filled with stony debris before excavation. Some compartments had low 'benches' set within them, on or under which deposits had been placed. The passage to the chamber had been blocked.

References:
Callander & Grant 1934
Henshall 1963, 222-25, (ORK 37), nos 1-7,9

Collection:
National Museum of Antiquities of Scotland EO 459-73

7. Chamber tomb assemblage
Ormiegill I, Caithness, Scotland

7.1 Flint arrowhead, leaf-shaped, quite thick. L 21 mm. EO 126. May come from the cairn at Garrywhin and not from Ormiegill I.

7.2 Flint 'arrowhead', triangular. L 42 mm. EO 124. May be a transverse arrowhead or even a small knife.

7.3 Flint arrowhead, transverse. L 32 mm. EO 125.

7.4 Flint arrowhead, triangular with hollow base. L 26 mm. EO 128. May be a barb for a composite projectile point.

7.5 Flint scraper, circular, steep retouch. L 27 mm. EO 129.

7.6 Stone macehead. Polished surfaces. The head and butt have slightly curving facets. The sides are rounded. L 103 mm. Roe's Ovoid C type. EO 131.

Associations: Anderson's various accounts are contradictory regarding the location of the finds and it is consequently impossible to be certain of associations.

Circumstances of Discovery: Excavated by Anderson and Shearer in 1865. A short, horned cairn with a tripartite chamber. The floor was partially paved and had funerary deposits both above and below it. Most of the bones and the finds were found in this deposit.

References:
Anderson, J 1866, 241-45
Anderson, J 1868, 499-500, 511-12
Anderson, J 1886, 244-48
Henshall 1963, 284-85, (CAT 42), nos 2-6, 8
Roe 1968, 154, 150, fig 32.24

Collection:
National Museum of Antiquities of Scotland EO 124-31

8. Chamber tomb assemblage
Quoyness, Sanday, Orkney, Scotland

8.1 Ground stone object. Roughly cylindrical but ground to 2 tapering points at one end and 2 curving ridges at the other. Lower surface slightly flattened, the upper surface rounded. L 122 mm. EO 133.

8.2 Ground stone object. T-shaped with each projection ground to a cone. 3 oblique ridges run across the top of the junction of the T. Damaged on 2 tips and on part of one of the ridges. B 147 mm. EO 134.

8.3 Bone pin. Polished surface. It has a rounded head and top and a projecting knob on one side. L 180 mm. EO 135.

Circumstances of Discovery: Excavated by Farrer and Petrie in 1867 and Childe in 1951-52. These finds come from the 1867 excavation. The site is a Maeshowe type cairn with a concentric drum-like appearance. A long entrance passage leads to a central chamber with 6 side cells off it. The passage entrance had been blocked. 8.1 came from one of the cells and the other 2 objects from the chamber or one of the cells. Many human and some animal remains were found in the passage, chamber and cells in the first excavation. The second excavation recovered some small sherds of pottery and 2 pieces of worked stone from the chamber and passage. Outside the passage and chamber were found more small fragments of pottery, worked stone, bone and pumice.

References:
Farrer 1868
Childe 1952
Henshall 1963, 228-32, (ORK 44), nos 11-12, 23

Collection:
National Museum of Antiquities of Scotland EO 133-35

9. Chamber tomb assemblage
Tormore 1, Arran, Scotland

9.1 Flint knife, plano-convex. Fine flaking on surface. Rounded tip, slightly ground on one edge and minor retouch on the other. Both edges straight. Remains of resin on butt. L 67 mm. EO 242.

9.2 Flint knife. Steep retouch on both edges, one slightly convex, the other slightly concave. L 65 mm. EO 243.

9.3 Flint knife, plano-convex. Fine flaking on lower surface has left it flat. Upper surface has steep retouch on one edge and polishing on the other. Both edges almost straight. Tip blunt. Butt snapped. L 55 mm. EO 244.

9.4 Stone macehead. Surfaces well polished. The head is a slightly curving facet and the butt is rounded. The sides are rounded. L 87 mm. Roe's Ovoid C type. EO 241.

Associations: Sherds from a grooved ware bowl and other vessels together with a retouched flint blade were found with 9.1, 9.3-9.4.

Circumstances of Discovery: Excavated in 1900 by Bryce. A long cairn with Clyde type chamber and facade. The original number of compartments is unknown. Only 3 survived in 1900 and the excavation consisted of clearing out the contents of these. At the bottom was a charcoal-rich

layer of soil. 9.1, 9.3-9.4 were recovered in the N compartment and 9.2 in the S compartment. Finds from other areas in the cairn and chamber included retouched flint and pitchstone pieces, flint and pitchstone flakes and a few fragments of bone.

References:
Bryce 1902, 95-102
Roe 1968 154, 150, fig 32.20
Henshall 1972, 371-73, (ARN 4), nos 5-8

Collection:
National Museum of Antiquities of Scotland EO 241-44

10. Pumice pendant
Taversoe Tuick, Rousay, Orkney, Scotland

Pumice pendant. Ground to a rectangular shape with rounded corners. Perforation at one end. L 18 mm.

Associations: 35 disc beads of shale.

Circumstances of Discovery: Chamber tomb excavated by Traill Burroughs in 1898 and Grant in 1937. The cairn contains 2 chambers, one on top of the other, entered by separate passages and from opposite directions. The lower passage leads into a chamber with 2 side compartments and 2 smaller compartments on the wall facing the passage. Outside the cairn the line of the passage leads to a separate miniature chamber. The upper passage leads to 2 unequal-sized compartments and a small recess. The inner end of the upper chamber had been blocked with stone. The pendant was found in 1937 under the blocking at the inner end of the upper passage. Many sherds from round-based bowls, several of them carinated and decorated were found throughout the cairn and its passages. There were also fragments of a flat-based vessel, retouched flint objects, a macehead and worked stone. Inside the chambers and passages were found unburnt and cremated human bone.

References:
Turner 1903
Grant 1939
Henshall 1963, 234-38, (ORK 49), no 31

Collection:
National Museum of Antiquities of Scotland EO 752

11. Pumice pendant
Unival, North Uist, Scotland

Pumice pendant, ground to trapezoidal shape with perforation in the narrower end. Broken across the perforation. L 38 mm.

7.4 Pumice pendants from Taversoe Tuick, Orkney (right: 10) and Unival, North Uist (left: 11)

Associations: The detailed associations given by Scott are confused but they appear to be human bones, charred but not cremated, and possibly a beaker or another decorated, ? flat-based vessel.

Circumstances of Discovery: The site, excavated by Scott, in a squarish cairn with a facade. A passage leads from this facade to an oval chamber. Both passage and facade contained funerary deposits including much pottery — mainly open, round-based bowls but also including a beaker and small grooved ware bowl. The pendant came 'from a higher level in the chamber' (Henshall 1972, 533).

References:
Scott, W L 1948
Henshall 1972, 529-34, (UST 34), no 24

Collection:
National Museum of Antiquities of Scotland EO 870

12. Jet slider
Beacharra, Argyll, Scotland

Jet slider, polished surface. L 83 mm.

Circumstances of Discovery: Excavated in 1892 by the Kintyre Scientific Association and later in 1959 and 1961 by Scott. A long cairn with shallow forecourt and Clyde type chamber comprising 4 compartments. 3 compartments contained at their base 2 Beacharra bowls each and one a flint flake. The compartments were deliberately infilled and the slider was included in this infill in the third compartment from the entrance.

References:
Bryce 1902, 102-09
Scott, J G 1964
McInnes 1968, 143, 140, fig 29.10
Henshall 1972, 344-46, (ARG 27), no 8

Collection:
Public Library & Museum, Campbeltown

13. Jet slider
Skye, Scotland

Highly polished. L 76 mm.

Circumstances of Discovery: Isolated find. Early accession records do not confirm Skye as the place of discovery.

References:
Wilson 1863, I, 441, fig 82
McInnes 1968, 144, 140, fig 29.13

Collection:
National Museum of Antiquities of Scotland FN 43

14. Jet bead
Cairnholy I, Kirkcudbrightshire, Scotland

Jet bead, roughly spherical, well polished. Diam 19 mm.

Associations: Other material in the forecourt blocking included pottery sherds, amongst which were those of a carinated bowl, a stone disc and shells.

Circumstances of Discovery: From the forecourt blocking of a long cairn excavated by Piggott and Powell in 1949. The cairn has a facade of upright stones separated by dry-stone walling and a Clyde type chamber with 2 compartments. There was a blocking stone for the entrance and the forecourt had been deliberately infilled with stone.

References:
Piggott, S & Powell 1949, 113-16, 123, 122, fig 9.2
Henshall 1972, 438-41, (KRK 2), no 25

Collection:
National Museum of Antiquities of Scotland EO 829

15. Perforated phalanx
Lower Dounreay, Caithness, Scotland

Perforated phalanx of small ox. Some modern breakage. L 64 mm.

7.5 Perforated phalanx from Lower Dounreay, Caithness (15)

Associations: Contracted skeleton of young man, stone axehead, 2 beakers and sherds of other vessels.

Circumstances of Discovery: Excavated in 1928 by Edwards, revealing a short, horned cairn containing an elongated chamber with rounded end and upright slabs set radially into the wall. The phalanx, skeleton and associated finds were found between 2 uprights on the SW side. Other pottery, human and animals remains were found during the excavation.

References:
Edwards 1929
Henshall 1963, 280-81, (CAT 38), no 5

Collection:
National Museum of Antiquities of Scotland EO 359

16. Chamber tomb assemblage
Carrowkeel E, Co Sligo, Ireland

16.1 Antler pin, mushroom-headed. Heavily burnt. L 90 mm. X 1959.

16.2 Antler pin, poppy-headed with triangular section. Burnt. L 36 mm. X 1958.

16.3 Boar's tusk with unworked facet. L (of chord) 71 mm. X 1960.

Associations: Fragments of bone, fragment of pottery.

Circumstances of Discovery: A trapezoidal cairn with porch-like facade at the S end and a cruciform chamber at the N end excavated by Macalister *et al* in 1911. The main part of the chamber was divided into 4 compartments and these finds came from the outermost one. Fragments of bone were found elsewhere in the chamber.

References:
Macalister, Armstrong & Praeger 1912, 323-24, 332-33, 338
Herity 1974, 274 (Sl 106), nos 1-3

Collection:
National Museum of Ireland X 1958-60

17. Poppy-headed pin
Carrowmore 3, Co Sligo, Ireland

Antler pin, poppy-headed, very heavily burnt. In 2 pieces; the decorated head and piece of shaft. Min L 87 mm. (Shaft not illustrated).

Associations: 3 steatite beads, a quartz pendant, several pieces of other bone/antler pins and 28 lbs of cremated bone including pig.

Circumstances of Discovery: A figure-of-eight boulder cairn excavated in or before 1887, though it had been dug into before. There were secondary inhumation(s) and bones of animals, birds and fish.

References:
Wood-Martin 1888, 21-31
Herity 1974, 264-65 (Sl 11), no 29

Collection:
National Museum of Ireland X 1957

18. Ironstone ball
Loughcrew F, Co Meath, Ireland

Ironstone ball, spherical with smooth polished surface. Diam 78 mm.

Associations: Fragments of bone.

Circumstances of Discovery: A chambered cairn excavated by Conwell in 1865. The mound is kerbed and has a cruciform chamber containing 8 decorated stones. The ironstone ball came from the S chamber and was embedded in a stone and clay deposit which filled up the chamber. From elsewhere in the cairn came a bone pin and a flint flake.

References:
Conwell 1866, 361-62
Conwell 1873, 50
Herity 1974, 234 (Me 8)

Collection:
National Museum of Ireland X 1955

19. Marble ball
Loughcrew L, Co Meath, Ireland

Marble ball, spherical with highly polished surface. Diam 67 mm.

Associations: Many fragments of bone, human teeth, charcoal, 2 bone points, 2 small stone balls, 8 chalk balls and a lentoid piece of jet.

Circumstances of Discovery: A chambered cairn excavated by Conwell in 1865. The mound is kerbed and has a chamber with 7 compartments and 18 decorated stones in it. The ball came from the second compartment. Elsewhere in the cairn were found more burnt human remains and some pottery.

References:
Conwell 1866, 366-69
Conwell 1873, 59-65
Herity 1974, 237-39 (Me 14), no 5

Collection:
National Museum of Ireland X 1956

7.6 Stone balls from Loughcrew F (back: 18) and Loughcrew L, Co Meath, Ireland (front: 19)

COMMUNAL MONUMENTS

20. Communal monument assemblage
Durrington Walls, Amesbury, Wiltshire, England

20.1 Flint arrowhead. Fine bifacially retouched transverse arrowhead, with symmetrical basal concavity. Extreme tip and one apex of base broken. L 44 mm. Clark's class G. DW 258 (=Wainwright & Longworth's cat no F 37).

20.2 Flint arrowhead. Very finely worked transverse arrowhead with asymmetrical basal concavity. The retouch on the upper surface ('ripple flaking') has been very skilfully executed. Tips and barbs broken. L 45 mm. Clark's class H. DW 265-1 (= F46).

20.3 Flint arrowhead. Very fine bifacially retouched arrowhead, with asymmetrical basal concavity: of very similar workmanship to 20.2. Tip and one barb broken. L 44 mm. Clark's class H. DW 265-2 (= F47).

20.4 Flint arrowhead. Very finely worked transverse arrowhead, with markedly asymmetrical basal concavity. Broken at tip. L 40 mm. Clark's class H. DW 264 (= F49).

20.5 Flint arrowhead. Finely worked transverse arrowhead with very markedly asymmetrical basal concavity. One face with edge and side retouch only, the other face with deep invasive retouch over most of its area. L 37 mm. Clark's class H. DW 266 (= F58).

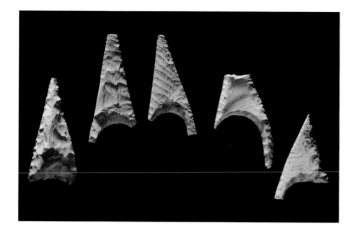

7.7 Flint arrowheads from Durrington Walls, Wiltshire (20.1-5)

20.6 Rim sherd of a large grooved ware vessel, c. 345 mm in diam, of compact fabric. The top of the rim has been decorated with a row of diagonal grooved strokes, the int with 4 irregular horiz grooves, and the ext with a series of horiz grooves enclosing a spiral pattern probably drawn with a finger tip. The probable edge of a further spiral is visible on the left of the sherd. Ht (of sherd) 117 mm. DW 70 217/1971 (= P471).

20.7 Bucket shaped vessel with convex upper body and broad flat base, restored from fragments. Around the slightly thickened and moulded int of the rim there are 5 horiz grooves. Ext profusely decorated from rim to base: around the outside of rim, 3 horiz grooves, with a line of vert incisions between the lower pair; running down from the lowest of these grooves to the base are pairs of approximately vert lines, each pair c. 40 mm apart; these divide the body into a series of panels filled with interlocking, opposed, filled triangles. Where necessary, particularly around the base, awkward gaps have been filled with oblique lines. Ht 142 mm. 40/1952.

Circumstances of Discovery: Material recovered (with the exception of 20.7) during excavations in 1966-67 on the E side of the massive oval ceremonial earthwork enclosure at Durrington Walls. The earthworks were constructed about the beginning of the 2nd millennium bc and consisted of a ditch up to 6 m deep with an external bank some 30 m across. Within the area investigated, were two large circular timber structures. The arrowheads 20.1-20.5 and the decorated rim sherd 20.6 were recovered from the fills of post-holes forming part of the Phase 2 timber structure of the larger, Southern Circle, consisting of 6 nearly concentric circles of massive timber uprights and 39 m in overall diam. 3 radiocarbon dates are available for phase 2: 1950 bc ± 90 from antler; 2000 bc ± 90 from charcoal, and 1900 bc ± 90 from animal bones (BM 395-397 respectively). 2 of the arrowheads (20.2-20.3) formed part

of a group of 4 particularly fine specimens which appear to have been deliberately deposited at the foot of one of the posts (Circle 2A, post hole 24). The Southern Circle produced a majority of both the flint artefacts and the pottery from the site as a whole. The sherds of the restored vessel (20.7) were found in a pit in the course of small-scale excavations on the site in 1951-52.

References:
Wainwright & Longworth 1971, 141, 171, 173, 140 fig 59, 170, fig 73, 172, fig 74

Collection:
Salisbury and South Wiltshire Museum DW 258; DW 264; DW 265-1, 2; DW 266; DW 70 217/1971; 40/1952

21. Communal monument assemblage
Mount Pleasant, Dorchester, Dorset, England

21.1 Chalk balls. Examples of carved chalk balls made by pecking and scraping a lump of chalk to the required shape:
a. Irregular, with profuse striations over its surface. Max dimension 97 mm. (= Wainwright's cat no C12).
b. Carefully shaped ball with few traces of original preparation apart from one large flake scar. Diam 65 mm. (C14).
c. Carefully shaped ball, complete apart from one large flake scar. Diam 64 mm. (C9).

21.2 Chalk phallus. Carefully worked phallus carved from chalk, the head defined by a groove and with longitudinal striations along its length. L 110 mm. (C2).

21.3 Chalk object, possibly phallic. Tapering and apparently complete carved chalk object with an irregularly circular cross-section; prepared by scraping an elongated block to shape. Around its girth, there are 3 deeply incised grooves, while the broader end bears a crudely drawn oval line. L 80 mm. (C15).

21.4 Bronze axe. Faceted sides diverge from the narrow arched butt, gradually at first and then more markedly to meet the expanded cutting edge. Across each face is a horiz bevel, more distinct on one surface than on the other. Very slight flanges run the length of the margins of both faces, which are covered with profuse 'rain pattern' decoration. The ornament extends from near the butt to terminate along the curving line of a bevel set c. 10 mm back from the cutting edge. L 122 mm. (BR 2).

21.5 Antler spatula. 2 fragments of a spatulate implement made of antler. Bevelled at both ends, one of which is worn

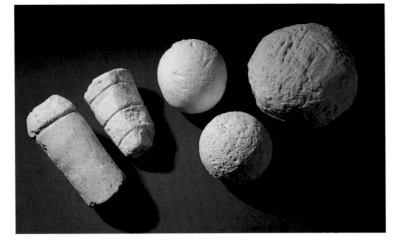

7.8 *Chalk objects from Mount Pleasant, Dorset (21.1-3)*

7.10 *Bone and antler objects from Mount Pleasant (21.5-7)*

7.9 *Bronze axe from Mount Pleasant (21.4)*

as if by use. L 118 mm. (A8). Possibly a tool used for the softening or burnishing of leather.

21.6 Bone bead. Elongated barrel-shaped bead of bone, with oval cross-section and an oval longitudinal perforation. Surfaces decorated with incised patterns separated by a deeply incised line encircling the middle. One half is divided into alternating panels of horiz and vert lines, the other into panels composed of horiz and vert lines and a coarse chevron. L 22 mm. (B2).

21.7 Bone toggle. Segmented bone toggle of oval cross-section with oval longitudinal and transverse perforations; surface decorated with 6 deeply incised grooves. L 24 mm. (B4).

Circumstances of Discovery: Excavation in 1970-71 of large ceremonial earthworks at Mount Pleasant, near Dorchester. The main features investigated included:

1. Massive henge or ceremonial enclosure consisting of a bank and internal ditch surrounding about 11 acres, with 4 entrance causeways. A large circular timber structure was constructed within the enclosure around the same time, *c.* 2000 bc.

2. Major changes took place around 1700 bc when the timber structure in the interior was replaced by a stone setting, and the hilltop was surrounded by a massive timber palisade enclosing about 10 acres. This phase is associated with the appearance of beaker pottery on the site. Occupation and activity on the hilltop continued for much of the bronze age, down to about 1000 bc. The detailed find circumstances of the objects are:

21.1 Chalk balls were the most numerous type of artefact recovered from the palisade trench, where they were mainly found in what had been the packing material around the timber posts.

21.2 Found with a chalk ball on the floor of the enclosure ditch at its terminal on the S side of the W entrance. A radiocarbon date of 1784 bc ± 41 (BM-645) was obtained from an antler pick recovered from the same ditch floor.

21.3 Found in the 'pipe' or 'core' left after the decay or destruction of the timber posts in the palisade trench on its W periphery.

21.4 Found in the sediments of the main enclosure ditch at its terminal on the N side of the W entrance causeway. The axe lay on the surface of a lens of chalk scree. Dateable episodes within the overall silting sequence of the ditch provide bracket dates of 1800 and 1500 bc for the deposition of the axe, 'with the strong probability that it occurred in the century prior to 1500 bc' (Wainwright 1979, 40).

21.5-21.7 From the terminal of the enclosure ditch to the E side of the N entrance. The spatula was found at the junction of 2 layers of secondary silts containing considerable quantities of occupation debris including animal bones. Other bone and antler artefacts in these layers included awls and pins, the decorated bone bead (21.6) and the segmented toggle (21.7). Sherds of beaker and bronze age pottery were present, and large quantities of flint artefacts were recovered. Radiocarbon dates of 1509 bc ± 53 (BM-789) and 1556 bc ± 55 (BM-788) were obtained from charcoal samples from the 2 layers concerned (Cutting XXVIII, Layers 7 and 6 respectively).

References:
Wainwright 1979, esp 34-47, 58, 128-38, 167-71, 175, 177-78, figs 56, 75-76, 78, 80

Collection:
Dorset County Museum, Dorchester

22. Chalk axes
Woodhenge, near Amesbury, Wiltshire, England

22.1 Model triangular axe of carved chalk with straight 'cutting-edge', defective at one apex: proportionately thick, rectangular cross-section. L 88 mm.

22.2 Model axe of carved chalk with sides tapering from sharply pointed butt to curving 'cutting-edge'; flattened oval cross-section. L 79 mm.

Circumstances of Discovery: Investigation in 1926-28 of the site of a complex timber structure set within a circular bank and ditch with single entrance gap and lying immediately S of Durrington Walls. Excavation revealed 6 concentric oval rings of post-holes which had held posts of varying sizes. Near the centre was a grave containing the body of a 3-year old child, possibly a dedicatory burial. The axes were found buried in post-holes of the two outer rings (22.1: 0.61 m deep in B21; 22.2: 0.46 m deep in centre of A16).

References:
Cunnington 1929, 112, 113, pl 22.1-2
Annable & Simpson 1964, no 18 [= 22.1 only]

Collection:
Devizes Museum DM 1355

23. Handled beaker
Balfarg, Fife, Scotland

Handled beaker of 'tankard'-like form. The thickened strap handle springs from a moulded cordon 30 mm below the rim, returning to the wall 15 mm from the base. Ext decorated with incised lines applied with a pointed tool. Between rim and cordon, a zone composed of horiz lines crossed by oblique lines, with a similar but narrower zone around the base. Between these, a metopic arrangement of alternating rectangular and diamond-shaped panels executed in a similar cross-hatched technique. Capacity: 1.54 litres (2.9 pints). Ht 136 mm.

Associations: Small knife of black flint and the vestigial remains of a crouched adolescent, probably male.

Circumstances of Discovery: Found in 1978 during the excavation of a henge monument. The beaker lay on the floor of a deep, slab-covered pit dug into the subsoil near the centre of the monument. It was, although damaged, in an upright position in front of the face and chest of the deceased, probably with the handle close to the hands. The mouth of the pot had been covered, perhaps only partially, by a thin slab of stone. 2 major phases of ceremonial activity involved the construction of concentric circles of timber uprights followed by 1 or 2 stone circles. The relationship of the beaker grave to this sequence was not established stratigraphically.

References:
Mercer 1981b, 72-79, 85, fig 15, 133-36, fig 45

Collection:
National Museum of Antiquities of Scotland (unreg)

24. Fragments of imported stone axes
Cairnpapple Hill, West Lothian, Scotland

24.1 Greater part of the cutting edge of a polished stone axe. Nature of fracture suggests that the fragment has been detached as a result of a blow to the blade perhaps during use or as a result of deliberate breakage. Source of rock shown by geological thin-sectioning to be the Langdale area of the Lake District (Group VI). B (of the cutting edge) 54 mm. EP 166.

24.2 Flake struck from the blade end of a polished stone axe. Part of the cutting edge survives, and as in the case of 24.1, the type of fracture suggests detachment during use or as a result of deliberate breakage. Source of rock shown to be the 'axe-factory' sites around Graig Llwyd in the Penmaenmawr area of N Wales (Group VII). B 50 mm. EP 167.

Circumstances of Discovery: The rounded summit of Cairnpapple Hill is occupied by a complex site excavated in 1947-48. 5 distinct periods of activity were recognised and may be summarised as follows:

1. Group of pits arranged in a rough arc containing or associated with cremation deposits.

2. Henge monument, consisting of a sub-circular bank with an internal quarry ditch and 2 opposed entrances. An oval setting of 24 standing stones (or possibly timbers) was set up within the enclosure and 2 burials were deposited, each associated with beakers.

3. Following dismantling of the stone circle, a cairn was built to one side of the former henge enclosure. The cairn was enclosed by a kerb of large stones and covered 2 cists, one of them containing a food vessel.

4. Enlargement of the cairn to incorporate cremation burials deposited under inverted cinerary urns.

5. 4 extended inhumations in dug graves, probably of Iron Age or later date.

Both fragments of axes were isolated finds on the old ground surface under the burial cairns of periods 3-4, which

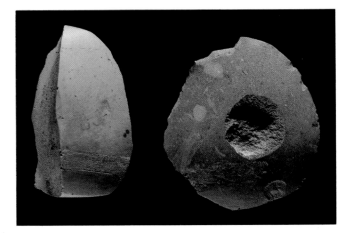

7.11 Fragments of stone axes from Cairnpapple Hill, West Lothian (24)

succeeded the ceremonial use of the hilltop (the henge monument: period 2). The excavator suggested that these flakes might represent axes broken during the initial clearance of vegetation from the hilltop *prior to* its use for religious and funerary purposes, but there are no stratigraphical grounds for ruling out deposition as part of the activities during periods 1 and 2.

References:
Piggott, S 1948, 102-04, fig 16.1-2

Collection:
National Museum of Antiquities of Scotland EP 166-67

SETTLEMENTS

25. Decorated stone plaque
Ronaldsway, Isle of Man, England

Schist plaque. Decorated plaque made from a piece of schist carefully ground into a flat oval shape and ornamented on both faces with lightly incised geometric patterns in the form of rows of chevrons and lozenges. On one face, differences in the degree of wear suggest the decoration may have been applied on more than one occasion. One end is now broken. L 77 mm.

7.12 Decorated stone plaque from Ronaldsway, Isle of Man (25)

Associations: Found with 4 other plaques, 3 of them oval and one axe-shaped, at the E end of the house floor. The associated occupation deposits contained a rich assemblage of finds (typifying the so-called 'Ronaldsway culture') and included pottery, stone and flint artifacts and faunal remains.

Circumstances of Discovery: Rescue excavation in 1943 of the site of a roughly rectangular house, *c*. 7.3 by 4 m, slightly sunk into the ground. The structure had been supported by timbers, set in post-holes arranged along the edges and in the int on either side of a central hearth area.

References:
Bruce, Megaw & Megaw 1947, 150-51, pl XX.e & fig
Piggott 1954, 350-51, fig 61.9

Collection:
Manx Museum, Douglas

26. Settlement assemblage
Skara Brae, Orkney, Scotland

26.1 Stone ball, incised. Spherical ground ball with incised linear, geometric decoration on one half, consisting of rectangle and lozenge pattern within larger, less well defined shapes. Diam 62 mm. Found in Cell 1 of House 2, 1913. Marshall Type 9c. HA 169.

26.2 Stone knife. Sub-oval with ground surfaces. The cutting-edge has been sharpened and the butt flattened. The upper face has a lightly incised geometric pattern of triangles infilled with lozenges. B 76 mm. Found just outside House 10, at floor level, 1930. HA 612.

26.3 Stone ball, ground. Spherical ball with 67 ground

7.13 Decorated stone knife from Skara Brae, Orkney (26.2)

pyramidal knobs forming 5 rows, with 2 groups of 4 knobs at the top and bottom. The knobs and rows are separated by deep grooves. Diam 77 mm. From near a limpet box in House 3, 1861-67. Marshall's type 7. HA 657.

26.4 Stone object, ground. Ovoid with 4 ground pyramidal knobs at each end. 4 panels on side, each of 5 ground parallel ridges, alternately horiz and vert on a raised section round the middle. L 92 mm. Found in the fill of the passage which leads W from the 'market place' by the entrance porch to House 8, 1929. HA 663.

26.5 Stone object, ground and incised. T-shaped with each projection ground to a cone. The T-junction is delineated by single and double grooves, and decorated with 2 panels of incised cross-hatching, one on each side, and between them an incised panel of geometric design consisting of a rectangle filled with lozenges, triangles and irregular quadrilaterals. B 189 mm. Found among stones in the corner of walls 'c' and 'd' on the W of the site, 1930. HA 666.

26.6 Decorated slab. Flagstone with incised large lozenge pattern, some subdivided into 4 smaller lozenges and then decorated further with horiz lines or triangles. Other lines join the apices or middles of the lozenges. L 715 mm. Found in midden material, 1972-73. Unreg.

26.7 Pottery. Single sherd decorated with large flattened applied pellet with incised spiral, part missing. L 69 mm. Found in midden material, 1972-73. Unreg.

26.8 Necklace of bone and ivory beads and tusks. 13 beads of ivory, 13 of bone and 2 tusk pendants. The ivory beads and pendants are ground and perforated, the bone beads only ground. The shapes vary from small discs to large tubes. Beads diam 11-28 mm. Pendants max L 70 mm. Found 1861-67, not necessarily together as a necklace. KD 1.

26.9 Bracelet of ivory beads. 74 small disc beads, all perforated and with polished surfaces. Diam 7-11 mm. Probably from Childe's excavations but not necessarily found together as a bracelet. KD 1.

26.10 Bone pendant. Roughly rectangular, thin polished piece of bone, perforated at the top, linear incised decoration, consisting of an 'asterisk' of 3 crossing lines and one half line, as well as 5 other lines forming triangles and lozenges. L 62 mm. Found in midden material, 1972-73. Unreg.

26.11 Ivory pendant. Elongated rectangle with slightly curving sides and highly polished surface. Perforated at the top, 3 shallow pits drilled in a line on the surface. L 31 mm. Found in midden material, 1972-73. Unreg.

26.12 Whale bone pin. Large, well polished. Square head. with further expansion and perforation below. Partially burnt around the head. Slightly tapering shaft with rounded tip. L 251 mm. Found around entrance to House 3/Passage A, 1861-67. HA 424.

26.13 Whale bone pin. Large, well polished. Domed head with 3 hollowed bands, separated by 3 circular ridges. Further down the shaft is a protruding, perforated knob. Slightly tapering shaft. A large piece of the tip has broken off. L 209 mm. Probably from S side of House 2, 1927. HA 430.

26.14 Bone pin. Very highly polished. Rounded head and tip, with tapering shaft. Band of burning around the shaft. L 134 mm. Found in midden material, 1972-73. Unreg.

26.15 Perforated phalanx. 1st phalanx of *Bos* sp. Perforated on one surface only. L 66 mm. Found in midden material, 1972-73. Method of use unknown, possibly a whistle. Unreg.

26.16 Perforated phalanx. 1st phalanx of *Bos* sp. Perforated on two opposite surfaces. Some polishing on a small area of the bone. L 55 mm. Found in midden material, 1972-73. Method of use unknown. Unreg.

Circumstances of Discovery: The site was covered with sand dunes which began to shift and expose the area prior to 1851, after which occasional objects were recovered. Several periods of excavation took place: 1861-67; 1913; 1927-30; 1972-73 and an excavation adjacent to the settlement in 1977. The site consists of a village of at least 6 contemporary houses and one workshop, with connecting passages, all built of stone. Radiocarbon dates range from 2480 bc± 120 (Birm-637) to 1830 bc± 110 (Birm-437) (roughly 3215-2280 BC).

References:
Petrie 1868
Stewart 1914
Childe & Paterson 1929
Childe 1930
Childe 1931a
Childe 1931b
Clarke, D V 1976a
Clarke, D V 1976b
Marshall 1977

Collection:
National Museum of Antiquities of Scotland HA 1-711, unreg

EARLY INDIVIDUAL BURIALS

27. Early individual burial
Dorchester, Oxfordshire, England

27.1 Flint fabricator. Retouched rod-shaped implement or fabricator of white patinated flint, split and broken by the action of fire; one end completely wanting, the other missing the tip. Unevenly lozenge-shaped in cross-section. L 51 mm. 1947-391.

27.2 Flake of opaque grey flint with small scars where surface affected by action of heat. No retouch but condition of edges suggests this piece has been utilised. L 45 mm. 1947-392.

27.3 Macehead of banded greenish-grey sandy rock: sub-rectangular in plan, expanding slightly towards one end, with flattened elliptical cross-sections. Cylindrical perforation set nearer the narrower end. One corner has been detached perhaps due to burning, which may also have altered the appearance of the surfaces, now matt and rough in places but probably originally polished. L 73 mm. Roe's 'Proto-cushion macehead'. 1947-393.

27.4 Long bone pin of skewer type, of circular section. Although partially burnt, complete apart from the extreme point. L 200 mm. 1947-390.

Associations: Heavily cremated bones of an adult.

Circumstances of Discovery: Excavation in 1946 of a ditched enclosure (Site II) known from aerial photographs. In its third and final structural phase, the site consisted of a causewayed ditch dug to provide material for an int bank in which were deposited 19 cremations, with a further 2 cremations in pits at the centre. The burial was found in a shallow oval pit (B), *c.* 1 m by 0.7 m, near the centre of the Phase 3 enclosure. The cremation deposit lay in a compact mass towards one side of the rounded bottom of the pit, suggesting deposition in an organic container such as a leather or cloth bag.

References:
Atkinson, R J C, Piggott, C M & Sandars 1951, 24, 114, fig 31, 115-16 (nos 146-49)
Roe 1968, 158
Roe 1979, 30, 33, fig 9.i

Collection:
Ashmolean Museum 1947-390-93

28. Early individual burials
Duggleby Howe, Yorkshire, England

Burial 5
28.1 Flint adze. Polished curved cutting edge. Curved butt, blunted and finely flaked. Slightly concave sides. Flattened lower surface and upper surface with central ridge giving triangular cross-section. Both surfaces polished for ⅓ of the length. L 236 mm. Seamer type. 145.42.

28.2 Crown antler macehead. From shed antler. Brow and bez tines and beam removed and surfaces polished. Head rounded and polished. Transverse perforation in beam. L 83 mm. 143.42.

Burial 6
28.3 Flint knife, polished. Very thin, finely ground and polished. Rectangular and slightly curving ends. 3 edges rounded, one long edge bevelled. L 60 mm. 142.42.

Burial 7
28.4 Flint arrowhead, transverse, triangular, spurred. L 32 mm. 139a.42.

28.5 Flint arrowhead, transverse, triangular, spurred. L 35 mm. 139b.42.

28.6 Flint arrowhead, transverse, bell-shaped, spurred. L 34 mm. 139c.42.

28.7 Flint arrowhead, transverse, rectangular, spurred, damaged. L 26 mm. 139d.42.

28.8 Flint arrowhead, oblique, triangular. L 39 mm. 139e.42.

28.9 Flint arrowhead, oblique, triangular, broken. L 38 mm. 148.42.

28.10 Bone pin, polished. Rounded tip, slightly domed head. Eroded surface. L 237 mm. 138.42.

28.11 Beaver incisor ?chisel, broken. L (of chord) 55 mm. 141a.42.

28.12 Beaver incisor chisel. Polished facet. L (of chord) 72 mm. 141b.42.

28.13 Boar's tusk implement. Large area of concave side carved out and ground to thin stem with spatulate end. L (of chord) 100 mm. 140a.42.

7.14 Early individual burial from Dorchester, Oxfordshire (27)

7.15 Flint knife from Burial 6, Duggleby Howe, Yorkshire (28.3)

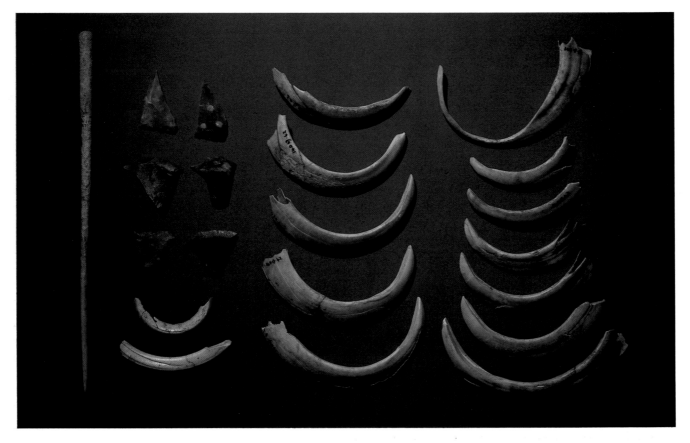

7.16 Grave group from Burial 7, Duggleby Howe (28.4-14)

28.14 11 boars' tusks, some with ground, smoothed or polished facets. L (of chord) from 70-122 mm. 140b.42-140l.42.

Associations: Burial 5: Adult male inhumation; lozenge flint arrowhead. Objects grouped at the chest. Burial 6: Adult inhumation. Knife in front of the face. Burial 7: Adult inhumation. 13 flint flakes. Objects placed by the back.

Circumstances of Discovery: Excavated in 1890 by Mortimer. Central shaft grave followed by other inhumations. Primary barrow constructed with at least 53 cremation deposits. Massive final mound. Burials 5 and 6 respectively in cavity left by settling of the shaft fill and over-lying one edge of the shaft. Burial 7 placed in new hollow close to shaft.

References:
Mortimer 1905, 23-42
Kinnes *et al* 1983

Collection:
Kingston upon Hull City Museums and Art Galleries: Mortimer Collection 70.42, 138-43.42, 145-51.42, 153-55.42.

29. Early individual burial
Folkton CCXLV, Yorkshire, England.

29.1 Chalk cylinder with central boss on top, drum-shaped. Boss has incised line around and inside 2 raised circles with 3 grooves around. These have a figure-of-eight grooving around, covering the whole boss. Between 2 incised lines at the top and bottom are 2 broad panels separated by 2 narrow panels. One narrow panel has a large chevron pattern with solid chevrons separated by ones infilled with very small lines of running chevrons, the whole bounded by vert small running chevron. The other narrow panel has a vert pattern with a complete central lozenge with half lozenges on either side. The lozenges are filled with smaller lozenges and very small running chevrons. Outer edge of panel and space between chevrons has running chevron decoration. One of the broad panels has 2 obtuse-angled chevrons, infilled with vert lines, one pointing down, the other up so that they almost touch. The upper triangle bounded by the chevron is eroded. The 2 triangles at the side have lozenge and triangle decoration, some areas plain, others with vert lozenges. The base triangle has a single lozenge with the centre infilled with oblique cross-hatching, 2 plain areas either side, and in the corners 2 areas of oblique cross-hatching. The second broad panel is divided obliquely into 4 triangles by 3 grooves joining at the centre. The upper triangle has an incised eye with joined eyebrow motif. The left-hand eyebrow has fine vert lines in it. The left hand panel has herring-bone pattern and the right one has chevrons. The lower triangle has 4 complete lozenges, 3 in a row with another above the central one, and 2 partial lozenges at each end. The lower ones are infilled with a smaller lozenge which has vert incised line decoration. Upper lozenge infilled with smaller lozenges. Diam 103 mm. 93.12-28.15.

29.2 Chalk cylinder with central boss on top, drum-shaped. 2 ridges round outside edge of top. Boss has single groove around it. Surface decorated with 4 circles, each with 2 grooves around, placed to form a square. The side has 2 broad panels separated by 2 narrow panels. One narrow panel separated by 2 grooves on one side and 3 grooves on the other. Central area decorated with a lozenge pattern with a central lozenge with smaller one inside. 4 other lozenges, each divided by a line up the centre, are joined to the larger one at its edges. The remaining space is filled with triangles. The other narrow panel is defined by 3 grooves on each side. It is divided into 3 zones by 2 sets of double grooves. The upper zone has 2 chevrons in it, the middle one 2 chevrons with 2 parallel chevrons above, and the lower one a single triangle with a triangular groove above. One of the large panels is divided roughly diagonally by 2 wide-based triangles, one at the top, the other at the bottom. They are defined by 4 grooves which leave 3 raised areas, the central one wider than the other 2. The upper triangle has 6 vert bands of either 3 or 4 lines of small running chevrons. The left and right triangles have a broadly similar pattern of lozenges. In the right hand one, some lozenges are raised and others lowered. In the left one, the lozenges are split along their longest axis, one side being lowered, the other raised. The lower triangle is filled with rectangles, alternately raised and lowered. The second large panel has 2 skewed triangles on each side, infilled with lozenges which are sectioned along their longest axis, one side raised and the other lowered. The apices of the triangles are joined by a vert lozenge infilled with a smaller one and a vert line, surmounted by 2 spirals, one curving to the left, the other to the right, joined by a single line which touches the top of the lozenge. These are reminiscent of horns or eyebrows. At the bottom of the panel are 2 horiz grooves. Diam 124 mm. 93.12-28.16.

29.3 Chalk cylinder with central boss on top, drum-shaped. 3 ridges around outside edge of top. The boss is decorated with 5 concentric grooves leaving a central flat dot with 4 ridges round it. This forms the centre of a 4-pointed star, the tips of which touch the outside of the boss. The remaining areas are filled with cross-hatching. The side is decorated with 2 narrow panels, a very broad panel and a slightly narrower one. One narrow panel is divided from the 2 broad ones by 3 vert grooves. The rectangle is divided diagonally by a band of 3 grooves which link up at the centre. A double groove runs horiz and a single one vert. 8 triangular panels are thus formed which are

alternately plain or have oblique cross-hatching. The other narrow panel is divided and decorated in a similar way although the diagonal dividers do not link at the centre, but simply have their apices touching. The very broad panel is divided diagonally by 2 broad bands which link at the centre and have a lozenge there infilled with smaller lozenges. This forms a saltire. The upper and lower triangles formed, are bounded by 3 grooves and have a central lozenge infilled with oblique cross-hatching and delineated with 4 grooves. The remaining area is infilled with oblique cross-hatching. The side triangles are bounded by 4 grooves and are divided by a double horiz groove with a plain area below and an obliquely cross-hatched area above. The smaller broad panel has 2 triangles at either side whose apices are linked by a lozenge. The triangles are delineated by 3 grooves and then split by a horiz groove, one side left plain, the other obliquely cross-hatched. The central lozenge is infilled with smaller lozenges. Below this area is a double chevron formed by 3 grooves. Above the triangle and lozenge pattern is a raised eyebrow and eye motif, the eyebrows joined to a single vert line between the eyes, which are simply raised dots. With the position of this pattern, the lozenge between the triangles appears as a mouth. Diam 142 mm. 93.12-28.17.

Associations: Crouched inhumation of a child, *c.* 5 years old, and a broken bone pin.

Circumstances of Discovery: Excavated between 1877 and 1889 by Greenwell. The round barrow covered a cairn of flint, stone and chalk which contained 2 adult bodies, one with a beaker. Two ditches ran round the barrow. The burial of the child with chalk drums was in an oval grave which touched the inner edge of the outer ditch. 5 other burials were found all within the inner ditch. 29.1 was placed behind the head while the other 2 were behind the hips.

References:
Greenwell 1890, 14-16

Collection:
British Museum 93.12-28.15-17

30. Early individual burial
Liff's Lowe, Derbyshire, England

30.1 Flint axe, edge-polished. Curved asymmetrical cutting edge, the butt rounded and thin. Edges blunted. Surface finely flaked and edge then ground. L 145 mm. J.93.54.

30.2 Flint axe, edge-polished. Elongated chisel-shape with curved asymmetrical cutting edge, the butt slightly curved and thinned. Edges blunted. Surface finely flaked and edge then ground. L 188 mm. J.93.55.

30.3   Flint arrowhead. Lozenge-shaped. Very thin. L 45 mm. Bateman Collection.

30.4   Flint knife, elongated. One edge serrated, the other polished to a sharp edge. Butt and tip rounded. Lower surface ground. L 99 mm. Bateman Collection.

30.5   Flint scraper/knife/spearhead blank. 'Cutting edge' forms a gentle curve and has been retouched on both surfaces and subsequently snapped. The 'back' is blunted and is formed by 2 straight edges which meet at an obtuse angle. L 87 mm. Bateman Collection.

30.6   Red ochre, 2 irregular pieces, both with small ground areas. L 22 mm and 26 mm. J.93.550.

30.7   Pottery cup. Round based, originally circular section. Rounded rim, straight neck, expanded surface below followed by deep groove and expansion which forms the round base. Neck decorated with 3 rows of incised herring-bone, the lower one cut by 3 horiz lines. Expanded area has 2 rows of herring-bone. The groove has 8 rows of twisted cord decoration. The rounded base has a single row of oblique incisions with *c.* 13 rows of twisted cord impression below. Ht 103 mm. J.93.757A.

30.8   Antler macehead, from base of shed antler. Brow tine removed to make a curving polished area where it joins the burr. This area forms the head. The butt is formed by a section of the beam and is decorated round the edge with a sawn lozenge and square faceting. Large transverse perforation. L 80 mm. J.93.569.

30.9   Boar's tusk blade. Segment from tusk. Lower surface and one edge ground. L 81 mm. J.93.550.

Associations: Another lozenge arrowhead, 2 'spearheads', another piece of ochre, another boar's tusk blade and an inhumation.

Circumstances of Discovery: Round barrow excavated in 1843 by Bateman. The crouched body was in an octagonal cist filled with clay. All the objects, except the macehead (30.8) which was behind the knees, were found behind the shoulders. Higher in the barrow were pieces of human bone, horse teeth, animal bones and 2 pieces of urn. In the 1930's a beaker burial was found in the mound.

References:
Bateman 1848, 41-43

Collection:
Sheffield Museum J.93.54-55, 550, 569, 757A
British Museum: Bateman Collection

7.17 Flint objects from Liff's Lowe, Derbyshire (30.3-5)

31.   Early individual burial
Whitegrounds Barrow, Burythorpe, Yorkshire, England

31.1   Jet slider. Highly polished. L 73 mm. P117.5.

31.2   Flint axe. Expanded, polished cutting edge, gently curving. The butt finely flaked and curving. Concave sides. Flattish lower surface, slight central ridge on upper surface. Both polished for *c.* ⅓ of length. Small area of tiny pits on upper surface. L 114 mm. Seamer/Duggleby type. P117.1.

Associations: Male inhumation, calf's jaw and pig humerus.

Circumstances of Discovery: Excavated in 1968 by Brewster. An original oval cairn with entrance grave was dug into, making a pit for the burial. Pit and earlier cairn covered with enlarged kerbed cairn. Radiocarbon date for this inhumation is 2570 bc ± 90 (Har-5587). Both objects had originally been placed against the small of the back.

References:
Brewster 1984

Collection:
Malton Museum P117.1&5

32.   ?Early individual burial
Greenbrae, Cruden, Aberdeenshire, Scotland

32.1   Edge-polished axe/adze of variegated light to dark grey flint. Narrow butt, slightly concave sides, diverging to meet the curving blade; both faces polished towards the blade only; triangular cross-section and asymmetrical side-view suggest this was an adze or axe/adze (rather than an axe). L 163 mm. Seamer/Duggleby type.

32.2   4 irregularly shaped beads of yellowish-brown amber, with biconical perforations. B (of largest) 32 mm.

32.3-32.6   12 elongated jet beads of varying form but all bored from each end and all retaining a well polished surface. Some have deteriorated in condition since discovery. For descriptive purposes the beads may be subdivided as follows (after Kenworthy):

32.3   Simple flattened, irregularly elliptical bead, with oval cross-section; one end wider than the other, and both showing signs of wear. L 29 mm.

32.4   Simple bead with oval cross-section. L 52.5 mm.

32.5   6 collared beads of 'prolate spheroid' shape, with oval cross-sections; where they survive, the collars are defined by slight grooves. L (of largest) 72.5 mm.

32.6   Very large fusiform/elliptical bead with pointed oval cross-section; collar at one end, defined by slight groove; possibly a large version of group 32.5. L 124 mm.

32.7   3 collared beads of flattened elliptical form with elongation of the ends; flattened oval cross-sections. L (of largest) 82.5 mm.

Circumstances of Discovery: Uncertain. Found *c.* 1812, possibly in an artificial mound.

References:
Smith, I F 1974, 40-42
Kenworthy 1977

Collection:
Arbuthnot Museum, Peterhead [= North-East of Scotland Museum Service] 71.5.1 & .17

STONE AXES

33.   Jadeite axe
Cornwall, England

Jadeite axe. Very highly polished surface. Curved, cutting edge, rounded with some blunting and damage in the centre. The butt was pointed but is now damaged. The sides are flattened. On one surface there is an area of pitting which highlights the polish on the edge and lowers the surface towards the butt. L 293 mm. Smith's type IIa. This is the largest jadeite axe from Britain.

Circumstances of Discovery: Isolated find.

References:
Proc Soc Antiq Scot, 4 (1860-62), 52
Smith, W C 1963, 157, no 8

Collection:
National Museum of Antiquities of Scotland AG 1

34.   Jadeite axe
Sweet Track, Somerset, England

Jadeite axe. Well polished surface, curving, slightly rounded cutting edge. Pointed butt. Straight, round sides. Completely undamaged. L 203 mm. Smith's type Ia.

Circumstances of Discovery: Excavated in 1973 by Coles and Orme. Found under a stray board lying beside the wooden track. The track has radiocarbon dates between 3160 bc ± 90 (Har-1476) and 2600 bc ± 70 (Har-1379).

References:
Coles, J M *et al* 1974, fig 1, pl XXIV.b
Morgan, R 1979
Morgan, R 1984

Collection:
University Museum of Archaeology and Anthropology, Cambridge 1980.1098

35.   Jadeite axes
Cunzierton, Roxburghshire, Scotland

35.1   Jadeite axe. Very highly polished surface. Curved

cutting edge, bevelled on one side. The butt is pointed and the edges form a rounded ridge. The axehead is very thin. L 190 mm. Smith's type Ia. AF 589.

35.2 Jadeite axe. Well ground and slightly polished surface. Curved cutting edge, quite sharp. Pointed, but slightly damaged butt. The edges form a sharp ridge. The surface is flatter on one side. L 174 mm. Smith's type Ia. Perhaps an adze blade. L.1951.3.

Circumstances of Discovery: Found on separate occasions apparently on the land of the same farm. 35.1 was ploughed up in 1882 while 35.2 was found sometime before 1894. There is some confusion in the literature about these axes. It is possible that 35.2 is not from Cunzierton.

References:
Proc Soc Antiq Scot, 17 (1882-83), 320-21
Black 1894, 329, fig 6
Smith, W C 1963, 168, nos 58-59

Collection:
National Museum of Antiquities of Scotland AF 589 & L.1951.3

36.   Flint axe
     Gilmerton, East Lothian, Scotland

Flint axe-head with orange surfaces, mottled grey and brown in places; however, a flake scar at butt indicates an original grey colour. Narrow curving butt from which sides gradually diverge to meet gently splaying blade. Narrow

facets run the full length of each side. Clearly unused and in mint condition, the visible flake scars being the result of minor damage since its deposition or discovery. L 235 mm.

Circumstances of Discovery: Isolated find: turned up by the plough in a field near Gilmerton, in the late 18th century.

References:
Smellie 1782, part I, 91-92, no 220
Moore 1979, 86

Collection:
National Museum of Antiquities of Scotland AF 60

37.   Jadeite axe
     Greenlawdean, Berwickshire, Scotland

Jadeite axe. Very highly polished surfaces. The cutting edge is curved and deliberately rounded and blunt. The butt is pointed and thin and the sides are flattened. The surfaces of the axe are almost completely flat. L 249 mm. Smith's type Ia.

Circumstances of Discovery: Isolated find. Details unknown, but found *c.* 1840.

References:
Proc Soc Antiq Scot, 26 (1891-92), 174-76, fig 2
Smith, W C 1963, 165, no 45

Collection:
National Museum of Antiquities of Scotland L.1951.2

STONE HOARDS

38.   Stone hoard
     York, Yorkshire, England

38.1   Flint axe, edge-polished. Curved cutting edge, butt snapped off. Sides blunted. Surface flaked, then ground. L 77 mm. FW 100.15.

38.2   Flint axe, edge-polished, curved expanded cutting edge, one surface with a larger polished area. Butt curved, rounded and thinned. Sides slightly waisted. Surface flaked

then ground. L 166 mm. Seamer/Duggleby type. FW 100.16.

38.3   Flint axe, edge-polished, curved cutting edge. Butt a rounded area of natural flint cortex. Sides blunted. Surface flaked, then ground. L 91 mm. FW 100.17.

38.4   Flint axe, edge-polished, curved cutting edge, rounded butt. Sides blunted. Surface flaked, then ground. L 129 mm. 446.1948. Not illustrated.

38.5 Stone adze. Ground all over. Curved cutting edge, curving butt. Slightly concave lower surface. L 126 mm. 447.1948. Not illustrated.

38.6 Flint blade with finely serrated cutting edge. L 69 mm. FW 100.10.

38.7 Flint blade with finely serrated cutting edge. L 77 mm. FW 100.11.

38.8 Flint blade with finely serrated cutting edge. L 65 mm. FW 100.12.

38.9 Flint blade with fine serrations on both long edges. L 79 mm. FW 100.13.

38.10 Flint flake, trapezoidal. L 54 mm. FW 100.14.

38.11 Flint knife. Cutting edge finely serrated. Back curved and serrated in places. Thin butt. L 97 mm. FW 100.8.

38.12 Flint scraper/'spearhead' blank. Ovoid with 2 gently curving edges, retouched to acute angle with areas of steep retouch. Thick 'butt'. 'Tip' of cortex. L 86 mm. FW 100.3.

38.13 Flint scraper/'spearhead' blank. Laurel leaf-shaped with 2 gently curving edges, with acute angled retouch on both faces. 'Tip' and 'butt' both curved and blunt. L 87 mm. FW 100.4.

38.14 Flint scraper/'spearhead' blank. Ovoid with 2 curving edges. 'Cutting edge' has steep retouch on both faces, 'back' thick and flat. 'Tip' thick and flat. L 62 mm. FW 100.5.

38.15 Flint scraper/'spearhead' blank. Leaf-shaped with 2 curving edges, both quite thick with occasional retouch. 'Tip' blunt and slightly pointed. 'Butt' curved and blunt. L 51 mm. FW 100.6.

38.16 Flint scraper/'spearhead' blank. Laurel leaf-shaped with 2 gently curving edges with localised retouch. 'Butt' thinned, 'tip' curved and blunt. L 82 mm. FW 100.1.

38.17 Flint scraper/'spearhead' blank. Leaf-shaped with 2 gently curving edges. 'Cutting edge' with acute-angled retouch, 'back' with steep flakes and occasional retouch. 'Butt' thinned, 'tip' curved and blunt. L 80 mm. FW 100.2.

38.18 Flint scraper/'spearhead' blank. 'Cutting edge' has retouch on both faces. 'Back' retouched and blunted. 'Butt' thinned and 'tip' curving. L 70 mm. FW 100.18.

38.19 Flint scraper/'spearhead' blank. Oval laurel leaf-shaped with 2 gently curving edges. 'Cutting edge' has acute retouch on both faces. 'Back' with occasional retouch. Flattish 'butt' and 'tip'. L 87 mm. FW 143.

38.20 Flint scraper/'spearhead' blank. Laurel leaf-shaped with 2 gently curving edges. 'Cutting edge' has acute angled retouch on both faces. The 'back' has retouched areas on alternate faces. 'Butt' broken, 'tip' blunted. L 94 mm. FW 144.

38.21 Flint scraper, oval. Curved scraping edge with steep retouch. L 47 mm. FW 100.7.

38.22 Flint scraper. End scraper with round scraping edge, steeply retouched. One side also has a steep retouch, the other has fine serrations. L 49 mm. FW 100.9.

Associations: The original contents of the hoard are uncertain. There is mention of 14-20 axes, many 'spearheads' and a bushel of flakes. Radley summarises the recorded pieces as: 7 axes, 3 arrowheads (2 leaf, 1 barbed and tanged), 9 'spearheads', 3 scrapers, 11 blades and flakes and 2 worked points.

Circumstances of Discovery: Discovered in 1868 during construction work, some 1.5-1.8 m deep in a bed of sand, beneath 0.3 m of topsoil. The hoard was in a narrow pit sealed by gravel.

References:
Monkman 1869, 47-51
Benson, G 1905
Radley 1970
Manby 1979, 81

Collection:
Yorkshire Museum FW 100.1-.18; FW 143-44; 446-47.1948

39. Stone hoard
Smerrick, Enzie, Banffshire, Scotland

39.1 Axe of marbled grey flint, completely polished. From the narrow butt the sides diverge gradually to meet the gently curving blade. Flattened oval cross-section. Mint condition: the few flake scars are due to damage sustained since deposition or discovery. L 251 mm. AF 61.

39.2 Axe of marbled grey flint, completely polished. From the narrow butt, the sides diverge gradually to meet the blade, which has a slightly asymmetrical curve. Slightly convex facets run the length of the sides. Both butt and blade have sustained some damage but as in 39.1, the nature of the flake scars suggests this has occurred following deposition or discovery. L 183 mm. AF 62.

Associations: A third axe of stone (NMAS: AF 74) may have been found at the same time.

Circumstances of Discovery: Found during the digging of a farm drain in or before 1881.

References:
Proc Soc Antiq Scot, 16 (1881-82), 407-08, figs 1-2

Collection:
National Museum of Antiquities of Scotland AF 61-62

STONE BALLS

40. Stone ball
Balallan, Lewis, Scotland

Stone ball, ground. 6 prominent cylindrical bosses. Diam 76 mm. Marshall's type 4b.

Circumstances of Discovery: Isolated find.

References:
Marshall 1977, 44, 68

Collection:
National Museum of Antiquities of Scotland (unreg)

41. Stone ball
Fyvie, Aberdeenshire, Scotland

Stone ball. Pecked and then ground. 53 small projecting knobs, most with their tops rounded. Max diam 74 mm. Marshall's type 7.

Circumstances of Discovery: Isolated find.

References:
Proc Soc Antiq Scot, 24 (1889-90), 8
Marshall 1977, 70

Collection:
National Museum of Antiquities of Scotland AS 80

42. Stone ball
Towie, Aberdeenshire, Scotland

Stone ball. Ground then incised. 4 protruding discs; one undecorated; one with 4 interlinking spirals and concentric lines to fill in the space left on the disc; one with 3 dots, each surrounded by a ring, and placed as a triangle surrounded by a 'concentric' trilobate pattern following the shape of the 3 rings and dots; one with a central spiral surrounded by curving parallel ornament and occasional chevrons joined by a zone of herring-bone. 2 of the triangular areas between

the discs are decorated, one with 'stab and drag' decoration, the other with 3 shallow pits. Max diam 76 mm. Marshall's type 9a.

Circumstances of Discovery: Isolated find. Recovered when digging a drain *c.* 1 m below the surface.

References:
Proc Soc Antiq Scot, 3 (1857-60), 439
Smith, J A 1876, 43-45.
Marshall 1977, 54, 70

Collection:
National Museum of Antiquities of Scotland AS 10

43. Stone ball
Turriff, Aberdeenshire, Scotland

Stone ball. Ground surface. 6 prominent hemispherical bosses. Max diam 78 mm. Marshall's type 4b.

Circumstances of Discovery: Isolated find.

References:
Proc Soc Antiq Scot, 21 (1886-87), 286
Marshall 1977, 67

Collection:
National Museum of Antiquities of Scotland AS 68

44. Stone ball
Urlar, Perthshire, Scotland

Stone ball. Ground surface. 6 thin discs; one undecorated; one with 1 small pit; one with 8 small pits; one with 20 small pits; one with *c.* 38 very shallow small pits; and one divided into quadrants by 2 grooves; in opposing quadrants a simple cross formed by 2 lines at right angles, and in the other 2 quadrants, incised chevrons which gradually get smaller within each quadrant. Max diam 68 mm. Marshall's type 9c.

Circumstances of Discovery: Isolated find.

References:
Proc Soc Antiq Scot, 31 (1896-97), 31
Marshall 1977, 43, 62, 71

Collection:
National Museum of Antiquities of Scotland AS 122

7.18 *Stone ball from Urlar, Perthshire* (44)

MACEHEADS

45. Antler macehead
Garboldisham, Norfolk, England

Antler macehead. Highly polished surface. Head rounded, butt flattened with one end of the perforation in it. Decorated with an incised double spiral, one on each side, and a single spiral partly on one side and partly on the top. L 102 mm.

Associations: Animal bones (no further details).

Circumstances of Discovery: Found in 1964, 1.5 m below the bed of the River Little Ouse during bridge repairs.

References:
Edwardson 1965

Collection:
Moyses Hall Museum, Bury St Edmunds, Suffolk 1977-846(05)

46. Antler macehead
Watnall, Nottinghamshire, England

Antler macehead. Made from the base of a red-deer antler, from which the main beam and two tines have been removed. The resultant bosses have been polished smooth, together with the remains of the burr. The shaft-hole is irregular in profile, polished smooth at the oval openings where it has cut through the hard exterior of the antler, but uneven and pitted where it has met the softer, central, cancellous tissue. L 95 mm. 'Crown antler' type.

Circumstances of Discovery: Isolated find: said to have been discovered 'in the sandstone rock'.

References:
Proc Soc Antiq Scot, 81 (1946-47), 190, no 13
Manby 1974, 93, 94, fig 39.1, 124

Collection:
National Museum of Antiquities of Scotland AI 13

47. Stone macehead
Maesmore, Corwen, Merionethshire, Wales

Stone macehead. Light cream coloured flint with highly polished surfaces. The shaft-hole is set towards the narrower end, and has been very accurately bored from both faces. The decoration is arranged almost symmetrically and consists of a lattice design of over 190 lozenge-shaped facets. At each end of the upper and lower surfaces, the lozenges are attenuated into a series of converging grooves. L 77 mm. Roe's Ovoid type (Maesmore group).

Circumstances of Discovery: Isolated find: discovered *c.* 1840 by a labourer while grubbing up a wood on the Maesmore Estate.

References:
Barnwell 1860
Proc Soc Antiq Scot, 6 (1864-66), 42
Anderson, J 1909, 377-79, fig 1
Roe 1968, 165, fig 37

Collection:
National Museum of Antiquities of Scotland AI 1
(Currently on loan to National Museum of Wales 82.19H)

48.   Flint macehead
Quarnford, Staffordshire, England

Flint macehead. Mottled grey and light-brown flint with highly polished surfaces. Ornament, almost certainly part of a scheme which was never completed, is confined to the broader end, which is covered with a lattice arrangement of 18 lozenge- or pear-shaped facets. L 83 mm. Roe's Ovoid type (Maesmore group).

Circumstances of Discovery: Isolated find: found before 1901.

References:
Anon 1901, 99
Anderson, J 1909, 383-84, fig 4
Roe 1968, 167, fig 38

Collection:
Hunterian Museum B.1914.245

49.   Stone macehead
Airdens, Sutherland, Scotland

Stone macehead. Highly polished surfaces. The top and bottom have close-set, roughly parallel lines whereas the sides are covered with lozenge-shaped facets. L 60 mm. Roe's Ovoid type (Maesmore group).

Circumstances of Discovery: Isolated find. Discovered during the cleaning out of a ditch.

References:
Anderson, J 1909, 379-81
Roe 1968, 160, fig 35a

Collection:
National Museum of Antiquities of Scotland AH 139

50.   Flint macehead
Urquhart, Moray, Scotland

Flint macehead. Light coloured flint with prominent mottled dark brown patches; the butt-end is highly polished and covered with a lattice pattern of 17 shallow lozenge-shaped facets. However, the overall scheme of ornament has never been completed, for on one side the decoration is limited to a series of incomplete facets along the upper and lower edges, while on the other side only a series of 17 narrow nicks have been marked out. The sides themselves retain a matt texture and traces of the original preparatory flaking scars. L 73 mm. Roe's Ovoid type (Maesmore group).

Circumstances of Discovery: Isolated find: found near Kenny's Cairn (or Hillock) in or before 1871.

References:
Morrison, J 1872, 258-59, pl XXI, fig 1
Anderson, J 1909, 381-83, fig 3
Roe 1968, 149, 160, fig 35b

Collection:
National Museum of Antiquities of Scotland AH 37

51.   Stone macehead
Bloody Quoy, Deerness, Orkney, Scotland

Stone macehead. The upper and lower surface and sides have been polished, highlighting the veined structure of the granitic stone, but the ends have been left matt and rough. Flattened oval cross-section, with near cylindrical shaft-hole. L 119 mm. Cushion type.

Circumstances of Discovery: Isolated find: part of a collection of stone implements from Orkney purchased in 1888.

7.19 *Stone maceheads from Egilsay, Orkney (left: 52) and Bloody Quoy, Orkney (right: 51)*

References:
Proc Soc Antiq Scot, 23 (1888-89), 16, no 22
Callander 1931, 95

Collection:
National Museum of Antiquities of Scotland AH 89

52.   Stone macehead
Egilsay, Orkney, Scotland

Stone macehead. Veined and speckled stone, polished all over. Oval cross-section with carefully smoothed shaft-hole bored from each face. L 110 mm. Roe's 'Thames' pestle type.

Circumstances of Discovery: Isolated find: part of a collection of Orcadian material donated by W G Grant, 1930.

References:
Proc Soc Antiq Scot, 65 (1930-31), 14, no 26
Callander 1931, 95
Roe 1968, 148-49

Collection:
National Museum of Antiquities of Scotland AH 186

DECORATED ITEMS

53.   Decorated chalk plaques
Near Stonehenge Bottom, Wiltshire, England

53.1 Chalk plaque. Piece of chalk carved into an approximately square shape with a slightly concave upper surface and a smoothed but uneven lower face. The upper surface is decorated with a complex incised rectilinear design which may best be described as an opposed key pattern or stepped motif, composed of multiple lines forming right-angled ziz-zags. The pattern on one half of the face is larger than the other. Pricked dots, oblique incisions and cross-hatching fill the spaces between pairs of lines so as to emphasise parts of the overall pattern. On the reverse side, there are 2 rather haphazardly executed lozenges made up of finely incised lines. L 78 mm.

53.2 Chalk plaque. Piece of chalk carved into an approximately square shape, with scraping marks visible around the edges. One surface is virtually flat, but the other is uneven and convex, and bears shallow grooves, which may be a result of the process of preparation of the block of chalk. The flat upper surface has been ornamented with incised designs. A pair of lines approximately parallel to the margin contains a triple-lined zig-zag or chevron and frames a central squared area filled with a lozenge design set between 2 rows of chevrons. Part of one corner has flaked off and there has been some damage to the edges, but the decoration and intact edges appear to be unweathered. L 58 mm.
Associations: Animal bones, many sherds of grooved ware and a number of small chalk lumps marked with grooves were recovered from the same layer as the plaques.

Circumstances of Discovery: The remains of a small pit were exposed in the chalk of the verge of the A303 during road alterations between King Barrow Wood and Stonehenge Bottom. About two-thirds of the pit survived: it had been oval, with a diam of 1.07 m to 1.22 m and a depth of 0.61 m. After deposition of the layer containing the plaques, the upper part of the pit appears to have been deliberately backfilled.

References:
Vatcher 1969
RCHME 1979, 20

Collection:
Salisbury and South Wiltshire Museum (unreg)

54.   Decorated stone
Brodgar, Orkney, Scotland

Decorated stone slab with flat, narrow surface which has 8 vert bands of incised decoration, each defined by a vert line on either side. These bands are: oblique lines; chevrons; 4 lines of herringbone; 1 whole and 2 half lozenges, the central whole one divided into 4 smaller lozenges; double pendant triangles at top and bottom infilled with smaller triangles, with a lozenge in the centre divided into 4 smaller lozenges; single lozenge and half lozenge both infilled with smaller lozenges; 3 lines of herringbone; 2 crossing zig-zag lines forming a central square with triangles on the sides. L 752 mm.

*7.20 Decorated stone from Brodgar,
Orkney (54)*

55. Decorated stone
Eday Manse, Orkney, Scotland

Decorated stone slab with pecked decoration consisting of a double spiral with additional concentric lines; 2 ring marks, each with a central pit and 3 rings around it, one with an additional segment of a circle; 3 concentric arcs. At one end a single ring with central pit and 2 rings around it. L 1.12 m. Possibly a lintel slab.

Circumstances of Discovery: From a chambered cairn, destroyed *c.*1821 and the site excavated in 1860 by Hebden. The tomb was almost certainly of Maeshowe type. The decorated stone was found lying face downwards at the entrance to one of the cells.

References:
Proc Soc Antiq Scot, 4 (1860-62), 185-86
Henshall 1963, 198 (ORK 16), pl 24B

Collection:
National Museum of Antiquities of Scotland IA 2

56. Decorated stone
Pierowall Quarry, Westray, Orkney, Scotland

Stone slab, decorated with pecked designs. These comprise 2 double spirals linked back to back, one with extra concentric grooves and the other with a straight line joining 2 of the spirals. On the right side of the motifs are 4 roughly concentric grooves. Running from this are 4 straight grooves. To the left of the double spirals are 2 semi-circular patterns centred on the upper and lower edges of the stone, their outer arcs linking in the centre. Both have central circular pits. One has 9 grooves around it and the other 10. Between this and the double spiral is a lozenge with concave sides centred on a pit. There are 3 grooves around the central lozenge, all of which run off at an angle on to the upper edge of the stone. An additional groove has been added to the pattern. To the left of the semi-circles is a double spiral with 2 oval grooves around it, one linking the outer edge of the spiral and the other outside this. In the lower left hand corner is another semi-circle of 3 grooves with a central circular pit. Other grooves and pits form infilling between the motifs. L 1.34 m.

Circumstances of Discovery: Found 1981. One half of the stone was discovered during quarrying, the other was recovered during excavation. The slab was probably associated with a passage of a ?Maeshowe type chambered cairn which had been slighted. It is interpreted as a lintel. Other, smaller decorated stones were also found.

References:
Sharples forthcoming

Circumstances of Discovery: Found in 1925 during ploughing. 4 cists were found parallel to each other, 3 large and one small. The 3 large cists contained unburnt bone. The decorated slab was outside and overlapping the end of 2 of the large cists. The decorated edge was uppermost. At the base of the slab and under the middle was another cist containing burnt bone.

References:
Marwick, H 1925
Marwick, J G 1926

Collection:
National Museum of Antiquities of Scotland IA 44

Collection:
Tankerness House Museum, Kirkwall, Orkney 1981/1. The object displayed is a cast.

57. Decorated stone
Wester Yardhouses, Carnwath, Lanarkshire, Scotland

A sub-oval slab of red sandstone, ornamented on one face only with curvilinear and triangular designs in the 'Passage-Grave' art style, and all executed in the pecking technique. In its original position covering the cist, the decoration occupied what was the underside of the slab. The curvilinear designs comprise several multiple-ringed motifs and concentric arcs, but the original pattern is incomplete owing to flaking of the stone and the fracture of the edge of the slab in antiquity prior to its use as a capstone. The principal triangular patterns consist of a pair of roughly equilateral triangles subdivided into smaller pecked triangles, leaving a trapezoidal area in false relief. 2 small opposed triangles occupy a space between elements of the curvilinear ornament. It is likely that the slab was originally prepared for another purpose, and was re-used by the builders of the beaker cist: this is suggested by the fact that portions of the designs have been destroyed by the fracture

7.21 *Decorated stone from Pierowall Quarry, Orkney (56)*

7.22 *Decorated stone from Wester Yardhouses, Lanarkshire (57)*

of the edge, implying loss of an originally more extensive scheme of decoration. Some differential weathering of the ornament is also apparent, again suggesting that the markings on the slab were made prior to its incorporation to the cist. L 1.2 m.

Associations: No bones were discovered in the cist, but a beaker stood upright in one corner, filled with black earth.

Circumstances of Discovery: During clearance of a small cairn a short distance N of Wester Yardhouses farm a cist

was discovered, aligned N-S. The slab formed the capstone, and lay decorated face downwards.

References:
Rankin 1874, 61-63
MacLaren 1970, 137-38, pl IX
Simpson & Thawley 1972, no 17
RCAMS 1978, no 113 (3), fig 22 & pl 7B

Collection:
National Museum of Antiquities of Scotland EQ 166

GOLD LUNULAE

58. Metalwork hoard
Harlyn Bay, Merryn, Cornwall, England

58.1 Flat axe of bronze with sides diverging from gently curving butt to meet expanded cutting edge, one tip of which is broken. Flattened elliptical longitudinal section. Surfaces pitted and corroded. L 111 mm.

58.2 Gold lunula of thin sheet gold beaten out into a flexible crescentic collar with small, moderately expanded oval terminals set almost perpendicular to the plane of the crescent. The decoration of the lunula is concentrated towards the horns and is arranged in such a way that the overall ornament is very nearly symmetrical about 2 major axes, viz. the midline not only of the whole lunula but also of each horn. The zoned decoration of each horn consists of transverse panels made up of multiple horiz lines with fringes either of finely incised vert strokes or of short diagonal strokes making up zig-zag lines of dentition. There are also 2 major zones of opposed triangles, filled with diagonal lines and creating central diamond-shaped voids. Similar filled pendant triangles protrude into the central collar area. This complex arrangement is bordered by 2 sets of 3 concentric incised lines which run around the margins of the crescent to converge at the terminals. Around the central area of the collar, both margins are occupied by matching symmetrical arrangements of short vert fringes enclosing 2 sets of triple concentric lines and a pair of zig-zag lines of dentition. The edges of the collar have been beaten out slightly unevenly. There are some modern repairs to tears in the gold, the most serious one running in from the edge for c. 35 mm. Max diam 222 mm. Classical group.

58.3 Gold lunula composed of a crescentic collar of heavy sheet gold with expanded 'spade-shaped' terminals at right angles to the plane of the crescent. The terminals have tapering 'midribs'. The inner margin of the crescent is decorated with 3 deeply incised concentric lines, the

7.23 Flat bronze axe from Harlyn Bay, Cornwall (58.1)

innermost of which is fringed by a zig-zag line of short diagonal strokes or dentition. The outer margin is, for the most part, ornamented simply with 4 concentric lines, but towards each of the horns the innermost of these is replaced by a further line of dentition. The lunula is complete apart from one tear 20 mm long on the outer edge of the crescent; on the back there are some minor areas of foliation of the gold, possibly due to the hammering, during manufacture, of a dirty or roughened surface. Max diam 210 mm. Provincial group.

Associations: What may have been a further piece of associated metalwork was discarded at the time of discovery: it was described by the finder as being 'something like a bit of a buckle'.

Circumstances of Discovery: Found in 1864 on the W side of Harlyn Bay, near Padstow, by a labourer digging a pond. The objects lay at a depth of about 1.83 m from the surface among earth and stones said to be of an 'artificial character', in Smirke's account, or 'in a square stone cist' according to Crawford's informant.

References:
Smirke 1865, 275-77 & figs
Crawford 1921, 294
Taylor 1970a, 73 (cat no Co 6-7)
Taylor 1980, 25, 34, 35, pl 15.b,d (cat no Co 6-7)

Collection:
Royal Institution of Cornwall: County Museum & Art Gallery, Truro

59. Gold lunula
Auchentaggart, Dumfriesshire, Scotland

Gold lunula composed of a crescentic sheet with expanded terminals. Part of the right-hand terminal has been broken in antiquity and an attempt has been made to repair it by preparing a line of 9 perforations for securing the detached portion, but this was either not present or not recovered at the time of discovery. The repair visible on the left-hand horn is modern for it is known that the lunula sustained damage at the hands of its finder. The decoration is concentrated near to the horns and consists of 3 asymmetrical sets of cross-panelling in each. A similar range of motifs has been used throughout, those on the left horn being the more neatly executed: they include horiz lines, some overlaid with punched dots or transverse nicks, and fringes and filled zones of dentition. On the right hand horn one of the cross-panels has been set out inaccurately and the craftsman has attempted to make good his error by 'fudging' the ornament to fill the space. Concentric with the inner edge of the lunula are 4-5 deeply incised lines drawn freehand, of which the inner and outer have punched impressions at intervals, the so-called dot-line motif characteristic of this style of lunula. Bordering the outer edge, are 5-6 deeply incised lines, the intervening ridges being partially filled with zig-zag dentition or transverse nicks. Max diam 224 mm. Provincial group.

Circumstances of Discovery: Isolated find: discovered in the winter of 1872-73 in the course of ploughing. When found, the lunula was folded together and rolled up almost like a ball.

References:
Clark, J G 1880, 222-23, pl 1
Taylor 1970a, 52, 73, pl VIII (cat no Df 1)
Taylor 1980, 34, pl 17 (cat no Df 1)

Collection:
National Museum of Antiquities of Scotland FE 3

60. Gold lunula
?Ayrshire, Scotland

Gold lunula composed of thin, flexible crescentic sheet with oval terminals lying flat in the plane of the collar. The main decorative panels occupy the horns and have been precisely applied with a fine point achieving near symmetry about several planes. The ornament consists of repetitive patterns of cross-hatching and pendant triangles to form a series of filled zones and voids. The centre of the collar is bordered by cross-hatching enclosed within finely incised concentric lines. Max diameter 243 mm. Classical group.

Circumstances of Discovery: Unknown: the lunula was purchased in 1898 at the sale of the contents of Lanfine House, Ayrshire, on the basis of which Coles has suggested a possible Ayrshire provenance, but there is *no* documented evidence for this.

References:
Proc Soc Antiq Scot, 32 (1897-98), 240, fig 2
Coles, J M 1969, 92
Taylor 1970a, 74 (cat no NLS 9)
Taylor 1980, 28, 34, pl 7 (cat no NLS 9)

Collection:
National Museum of Antiquities of Scotland FE 63

61. Gold lunulae
Southside Farm (Coulter), Peeblesshire, Scotland

61.1 Gold lunula with oval twisted terminals. Central crescent-shaped undecorated area, bounded by curving parallel lines. The upper edge has 3 lines, the outermost 2 embellished with punched dots. The lower edge has 4 lines, the uppermost and third uppermost with punched dots on them. The plain panel within the lines has been hammered and roughened. Diam 178 mm. Provincial group. FE 1.

61.2 Gold lunula closely comparable to 61.1. Diam 178 mm. Provincial group. FE 74.

Circumstances of Discovery: Found in 1859/60 when digging a field recently brought into cultivation. Traditionally a hoard, although it is not clear whether they were found together at the same time. Taylor believes them to be the work of the same craftsman.

References:
Proc Soc Antiq Scot, 4 (1860-62), 291-92

Stuart 1866, 161
Proc Soc Antiq Scot, 50 (1915-16), 16
Taylor 1970a, 74 (cat no Pb 2-3)
Taylor 1980, 34, 35, 74, pl 18.a-e (cat no Pb 2-3)

Collection:
National Museum of Antiquities of Scotland FE 1; FE 74

62.   Gold lunula
Ballybay, Co Monaghan, Ireland

Gold lunula, sheet gold with oval, twisted terminals. Central undecorated area which extends towards the terminals, bounded above and below by repoussé decoration comprising an inner and outer line with rising triangles between the lines. In some areas up to 4 more lines run over the triangles. Crumpled surface. Diam 250 mm. Unaccomplished group. Decoration believed to be incomplete.

Circumstances of Discovery: Details unknown.

References:
Fraser 1897, 65
Taylor 1970a, 70 (cat no Co Mo 2)
Taylor 1980, 34, 35 (cat no Co Mo 2)

Collection:
Ulster Museum 200:1913

63.   Gold lunula
Blessington, Co Wicklow, Ireland

Gold lunula of sheet gold. 2 twisted rectangular terminals. The central area is undecorated and has above and below it 10 parallel lines at the top and 12 at the bottom, both sets of lines enclosed above and below by a running chevron. At each end of the central area are 4 triangles infilled with smaller triangles. On both horns is a decorated triangular area. At the base of the triangle are 5 horiz bands, the first, third and fifth plain, the second with running chevron and the fourth with short vert strokes. The next panel has 2 groups of 4 triangles set with their apices touching and leaving a lozenge pattern between them. Each triangle is infilled with horiz lines and a single smaller triangle. Above is a horiz band of oblique cross-hatching with a thin plain band above and below. The next panel has a central lozenge with 2 half lozenges, one on either side. These are infilled with oblique cross-hatching. Above is a repeat of the 5 alternately plain and decorated bands followed by the opposed infilled triangles. A short band of oblique cross-hatching is then separated by 2 thin plain bands. Above are 2 triangles with triangular infilling. Finally, the apex of the triangular panel is filled with horiz lines. Diam 221 mm. Classical group.

Circumstances of Discovery: Unknown.

References:
Taylor 1970a, 46, pl III (cat no Co Wk 1)
Taylor 1980, 28, pl 8.b-d (cat no Co Wk 1)

Collection:
British Museum WG 31

64.   Gold lunula
Co Galway, Ireland

Gold lunula. Sheet gold with oval terminals at right angles to the plane of the lunula. Central plain area bounded above and below by 2 bands of running chevrons with 2 incised lines above and below. At the edge of the plain area on both sides, are 2 pendant triangles infilled with smaller triangles. On both horns are 2 triangular panels bounded by 2 incised lines all round. Each has 6 zones of decoration consisting of 2 groups of motifs which are alternated 3 times. At the base of the panel are 3 narrow decorated bands, the first and third obliquely cross-hatched and the central one with vert lines. Each band is bounded above and below by a horiz line with a single horiz line between. The next zone has 3 pendant and 3 rising triangles, opposed, infilled with smaller triangles. This is followed by a reversed version of the first panel with 2 bands of vert lines enclosing a band of cross-hatching. Above is a zone with 2 pendant and 2 rising infilled triangles. The fifth zone repeats the decoration of the first, and the sixth zone has a single rising infilled triangle. All the decoration is incised. Part of the surface of the undecorated area has been hammered and roughened. Diam 196 mm. Classical group.

Circumstances of Discovery: Isolated find. From Mr French's Estate (? near Ballinasloe).

References:
Wilde 1862, 18-19, no 10
Taylor, 1970a, 69 (cat no Co Gw 10)
Taylor 1980, 105 (cat no Co Gw 10)

Collection:
National Museum of Ireland W 10

65.   Gold lunula
Ireland

Gold lunula of thin sheet with 2 twisted rectangular terminals, the left hand one cut at the top. The central area is undecorated and has above and below it a band of panels alternately plain, hatched, plain, chevroned. To either side of this band are 2 incised lines and a running chevron pattern. At each end of the central area is a line of infilled triangles. On both horns there is a decorated triangular area. This consists of 4 zones each beginning with a band of alternate vert lines and chevron decoration followed by a panel with infilled triangles at the top and bottom. Only the fourth zone (that closest to the terminals) is different, the outer edges having short horiz lines and the upper and lower a running chevron adjacent. Above the fourth zone are 4 thin bands of enclosed running chevron. The whole area of this decoration is enclosed by the 3 incised lines continuing from the central area. Diam 211 mm. Classical group.

Circumstances of Discovery: Unknown.

References:
Catalogue Nat Mus Antiq Scot, 1892, 214
Taylor 1970a, 72 (cat no NLI 29)
Taylor 1980, 115 (cat no NLI 29)

Collection:
National Museum of Antiquities of Scotland FF 1

66. Gold lunulae
Rathroeen, Co Mayo, Ireland

66.1 Gold lunula, sheet gold with oval terminals at right angles to the plane of the lunula. Undecorated. Narrow front panel. Oval in shape. B 157 mm. Plain. Believed to be unfinished. 1965:30.

66.2 Gold lunula, sheet gold with circular terminals at right angles to the plane of the lunula and with a ring of repoussé dots on the outer edge. The central undecorated area is bounded above and below by a line of impressed dots which has an incised guideline for the decoration on the lower surface of the lunula. On both the left and right horns towards the terminals, is a panel of decoration bounded by repoussé dots to the left and right and consisting of an incised rectangular panel with incised opposed triangles with a line of horiz repoussé dots between. On the left side are 8 panels, 4 with 4 triangles, 3 with 3 triangles and one with 2½ triangles. On the right side are 7 panels: 2 with one line of 4 triangles and the other of 5 triangles, one with 4 opposed triangles, 2 with 3 triangles, one with one line of 3 triangles and the other of 2½ triangles and one with a line of

3 triangles and the other with one triangle and an oblique line. Both panels are surmounted by a linear repoussé triangle with impressed dots. The repoussé lines on the inner and outer edges of the lunula continue towards the terminals. Oval in shape. B 152 mm. Unaccomplished group. 1965:31.

Circumstances of Discovery: Found together in ?1965 *c.* 0.65 m down in a field.

References:
J Roy Soc Antiq Ireland, 98 (1968), 118-19, fig 15
Taylor 1970a, 70 (cat no Co Ma 15-16)
Taylor 1980, 35, 109 (cat no Co Ma 15-16)

Collection:
National Museum of Ireland 1965:30-31

67. Gold lunula
Near Sligo, Co Sligo, Ireland

Sheet gold lunula. Semi-circular terminals, untwisted. The central area is undecorated and has above, 2-3 parallel lines and below, 2 parallel lines with a running chevron above them. On left and right horns is a central line of 6 lozenges linked end to end with 2 lines running through the centre. The lozenges are infilled with an indistinct design. The running chevron on the lower edge stops opposite the lozenges, but both sets of parallel lines continue. Above the lozenges there is a running chevron. All the decoration is worn. Diam 179 mm. Unaccomplished group.

Associations:
A second Unaccomplished group gold lunula.

Circumstances of Discovery: Found in a bog in 1847.

References:
Taylor 1970a, 71 (cat no Co Sl 6)
Taylor 1980, 111 (cat no Co Sl 6)
Windele nd, 205-06, 453-54

Collection:
British Museum 49.3-1.21

BEAKER GRAVES AND RELATED MATERIAL

68. Beaker grave group
Kellythorpe, Driffield, Yorkshire, England

68.1 Stone wristguard with gold-capped bronze rivets. Wristguard has the shape of part of a hollowed cylinder with convex upper surface and concave lower one.

Flattened ends. Ground, polished surface with 4 perforations. Decayed copper or bronze rivets with conical gold caps. L 127 mm. 84.5-20.1.

68.2 Copper knife-dagger. Tip broken. Sharpened edges. Single rivet in hilt plate with remains of possibly 2 more rivet holes. Curving raised ridge at junction of blade and hilt plate with part of wooden hilt surviving. L 87 mm. 79.12-9.1981.

68.3 Beaker, burnished ext surface decorated in 2 zones. Upper zone with 4 horiz cordons, each with a panel of oblique comb stamping above. These impressions run alternately to right and left. The uppermost panel has additional short strokes at right angles. Below the neck and the fourth cordon is a panel of oblique comb stamping angled to the right with 3 horiz lines below and a further band of oblique impressions below that. The motif is repeated twice below, each panel separated by an undecorated area. In the second panel the lines angle to the left with 4 horiz lines between. The third panel has oblique lines to the right with 5 horiz lines between. Ht 183 mm. Clarke's N2(L) group. 79.12-9.1984.

68.4 Amber button, V-bored, oval, boss-shaped. In poor condition. L 29 mm. 79.12-9.1982.

68.5 Amber button, V-bored, only part surviving. Boss-shaped. L 23 mm. 79.12-9.1983.

Associations: Male crouched inhumation, bronze buckle for wristguard, wooden sheath for dagger, a third amber button and the head and beak of a hawk.

Circumstances of Discovery: Excavated in 1851 by Londesborough. A round barrow with the beaker burial central in a cist. The body appeared to be wrapped in linen from head to foot. At least 9 other skeletons were found in the barrow, 2 with a food vessel and other implements. The wristguard was found on the right forearm; the knife-dagger behind the back; the beaker between the feet and thighs; and the 2 buttons around the neck.

References:
Londesborough 1852, 252-56
Clarke, D L 1970, no 1265, fig 553
Gerloff 1975, no 237, pl 23

Collection:
British Museum 79.12–9.1981–84; 84.5–20.1

69. Beaker grave group
Garton Slack 37, Yorkshire, England

69.1 Flint dagger. Leaf-shaped, sharp tip, rounded butt. Blade broadest near the butt. Fine flaking all over with edge retouch to sharpen around the tip and blunt the edge of the butt. One surface and edges of the other heavily patinated. Possible remains of organic material on the hilt surface. L 170 mm. 267:162a.

69.2 Stone battle axe. Polished surface. Rounded, blunt cutting edge. Flat rectangular butt. The upper and lower surfaces are flat and the sides slightly rounded, expanding by the perforation. L 132 mm. Roe's Woodhenge group. 267.426.

69.3 Beaker. Burnished red ext surface decorated in 3 zones. First zone from rim to neck. Below rim 4 horiz bands, first and third with vert strokes, second and fourth plain. Bands separated by horiz lines. Below is a panel of horiz lozenges linked at corners. Each has 2 outer lines of ?comb stamping with the strokes at right angles to the lozenges. 4 lozenges, gradually getting smaller, lie within the space defined. Separated by a plain band, there are 2 horiz bands below this, each carrying pendant triangles with elongated bases. Each triangle infilled with vert strokes. Remainder plain. Second zone below narrow plain horiz band. It begins with 4 thin horiz bands, the first, third and fourth have short vert ?comb stamping, the second is plain. The main panel is of linked lozenges with their longer dimension vert. Outer band of each lozenge is an oblique band of comb stamping at right angles to the lozenge edge, sometimes with a plain band and 2 lines of comb stamping below, sometimes with simply a comb stamped line. Below the panel is a horiz band with short vert strokes. Third zone below a narrow plain horiz band. At its top is a horiz band with short vert strokes, below which is a pattern of plain pendant triangles. The space below them, also triangular, is defined with 2 lines, 2 bands with short strokes at right angles to the triangles, sometimes a further line and finally a plain triangle below. A horiz line separates the triangles from obliquely impressed lines which decorate the slightly protruding foot. Ht 157 mm. Clarke's S1 group. 200.42.

69.4 Jet button, conical, V-bored, polished upper surface. Lower surface ground. Diam 40 mm. 267.42c.

Associations: Adult inhumation, flint strike-a-light and iron ore nodule, possible traces of wood.

Circumstances of Discovery: Barrow excavated by Mortimer in 1865 and 1871. The beaker burial is primary being in a grave over which the mound was built. The objects were found behind the skull. In the mound were a further 14 inhumations, one with a food vessel, as well as a cremation deposit and a second food vessel. Recent work by Brewster has shown that the mound is superimposed on a long barrow.

References:
Mortimer 1905, 209-11
Roe 1966, 239
Clarke, D L 1970, no 1296, fig 778
Brewster 1980

Collection:
Kingston upon Hull City Museums and Art Galleries: Mortimer Collection 200.42; 267.42c; 267.162a; 267.426

70. Beaker grave group
Radley, Berkshire, England

70.1 Flint arrowhead. Barbed and tanged arrowhead of white patinated flint, slightly asymmetrical curved barbs with rounded tips, and tapering tang. Centrally thickened cross-section. L 21 mm. 1944.123.c.

70.2 Flint arrowhead. Barbed and tanged arrowhead of white patinated flint, straight sided, barbs with curved tips, and tapering tang. Centrally thickened cross-section. L 27 mm. 1944.123.a.

70.3 Flint arrowhead. Barbed and tanged arrowhead of white patinated flint with slightly curved sides, slightly asymmetrical barbs, the surviving one with a curved tip, and a tapering tang. L 26 mm. 1944.123.b.

70.4-70.5 Gold earrings, basket-shaped. 2 virtually identical gold earrings, each composed of a thin oval sheet of gold folded into the form of an elongated basket or open-ended tube of semi-circular profile, with a thin tapering tongue emerging from the centre of one long side and curling around the ext to form a hook for suspension. The decoration consists of repoussé lines hammered up from what was to become the int surface. 2 lines run around the margin of the oval sheet with gaps at the middle of each side; 2 sets of 6 lines run slightly obliquely across the sheet on either side of the tongue, which itself has a single repoussé line running down its centre. Both earrings are intact apart from some very minor buckling of the edges. L 47 mm. 1944.122.a-b.

70.6 Beaker. Collared beaker of a fine smooth reddish fabric, with a hollow base. Apart from a reserved band around the foot, the ext is decorated with repetitive zones of horiz lines and split herring-bone patterns, all applied with a rectangular toothed comb-stamp. Vessel restored in places. Ht 205 mm. Clarke's European Bell Beaker group. 1944.121.

Associations: Crouched skeleton of a young male.

Circumstances of Discovery: Excavation of Barrow 4A, the smaller of a pair enclosed by a single continuous ditch, and forming part of the extensive barrow cemetery at Barrow Hills Field, Radley. The objects accompanied the primary inhumation burial in a rectangular pit, 2.29 by 1.37 m, encircled by a trench 8.5 m in diam and subsequently covered by an earthen barrow capped with gravel. The skeleton was lying on its back but with legs drawn up at an acute angle to the body. One earring lay beneath the left ear, as worn, the other had slipped onto the right shoulder. The beaker lay on its side near the sole of the left foot. The arrowheads were discovered, separately but at the same level, in the gravel immediately above the skeleton and had presumably been deposited deliberately during the infilling of the grave.

References:
Williams 1948, 5-6
Inventaria Archaeologica, GB 2
Clarke, D L 1970, no 33, fig 63
Taylor 1980, 22, 33, 47, pl 3 (cat nos Be 2-3)

Collection:
Ashmolean Museum 1944.121-123

71. Beaker grave group
Sewell, Bedfordshire, England

71.1 Stone wristguard, rectangular, flat. Polished surfaces with 4 perforations, 2 at each end. Ends bevelled, sides rounded. L 101 mm. P1976.4-1.3.

71.2 Bronze spiral-headed pin. Square-sectioned shaft. At the head a single square-sectioned spiral curves down, twisted 4½ times, to touch the shaft. Originally there was a second matching spiral, now broken off. L 72 mm. P1976.4-1.1.

71.3 Beaker. Red burnished ext surface decorated in 4 zones, all comb stamped. Below the rim is a panel of 3 horiz lines with below it a series of oblique lines cut at right angles by short oblique lines. Below are 4 horiz lines. The second panel has a small running chevron with 4 horiz lines below followed by a further running chevron with triangular infilling of each triangle. Below are 4 horiz lines with small running chevron at the bottom. The third panel has 4 horiz lines with oblique lines below, again cut by short lines at right angles. Below this are 4 horiz lines with running chevron below. Just above the base are 5 horiz lines. Ht 179 mm. Clarke's Wessex/Middle Rhine group. P1976.4-1.4.

71.4 Bone 'belt toggle'. Cylindrical piece of bone, natural longitudinal perforation. The upper surface has a circular perforation. L 28 mm. P1976.4-1.2.

Associations: Male crouched inhumation; traces of fibrous material.

Circumstances of Discovery: Uncovered during quarrying in 1968. The burial was in a pit cut 0.76 m into the chalk. A second burial was cut into the fill of this burial. The wristguard was found on the left forearm; the pin by the left arm; the beaker at the feet and the 'belt toggle' on the sternum.

References:
Matthews 1976, 19-24
Clarke, D L 1970, pl 3

Collection:
British Museum P1976.4–1.1-4

72. Beaker grave group
Winterslow Hut, Winterslow, Wiltshire, England

72.1 Flint arrowhead. Barbed and tanged arrowhead of flint with elongated tang; one barb broken. L 66 mm. Green's Ballyclare type. NC 207.

72.2 Stone wristguard consisting of a thin rectangular plate of fine-grained grey-green slatey stone, with 6 tapering or countersunk perforations drilled from one side only and set, 3 to each end, in flattened triangular arrangements. One surface is highly polished, but the other, while smoothed, lacks the lustrous finish and instead has profuse fine striations (suggesting its secondary use as a ?whetstone). L 122 mm. NC 461.

72.3 Tanged copper dagger with dark green patina. The sides of the tang have been hammered into very slight flanges; at the base of the blade there is a flat curving mark left by the decayed organic hilt. The blade is tongue-shaped with bevelled edges and a broad shallow groove lining each side. L 134 mm. Gerloff's Roundway group. NC 428.

72.4 Beaker. Tall slender beaker in fine red fabric with carefully smoothed surface. Decoration is confined to the ext and consists of zoned ornament in 2 groups, one around the upper body, the other extending downwards from the shoulder to just above the narrow foot. The decoration has been applied throughout with rectangular-toothed comb stamping, but in places the stamp has been applied and then drawn along the clay, smearing the impressions of the individual teeth and giving an incised effect. The upper zone is composed of a repetitive arrangment of horiz lines, narrow bands of criss-cross impressions and 2 broader bands of diagonally filled triangles. The arrangement has been designed symmetrically, the zones above and below the criss-cross band encircling the middle of the neck being mirror-images of each other. Below the shoulder, further horiz lines enclose a narrow criss-cross band and encircle the body above a series of large pendant triangles consisting of double stamped outlines with obliquely drawn infill. Their spacing has been miscalculated, however, and an awkward gap has had to be filled by inserting an extra, smaller triangle. Ht 218 mm. Clarke's Wessex/Middle Rhine group. NC 507.

Associations: A skeleton described as 'of an immense size, the skull very large and the teeth all perfect'. A second barbed and tangled arrowhead, now lost.

Circumstances of Discovery: Exploration by Rev A B Hutchins in 1814 of a bell barrow, about 25 m in diam, one of a large group of barrows near Winterslow Hut, NE of Salisbury. The grave group accompanied the primary inhumation, said to be in a 'cist' about 0.9 to 1.2 m deep in

the chalk beneath the old ground surface. The body had been placed with the head to the N and the feet to the S, in what appears to have been a contracted position. The dagger was found near one arm, the accounts varying as to which; the bracer was said to have been under the right arm, the beaker was found between the knees and the feet, and inside it, were 2 flint barbed and tanged arrowheads, one black and one white. The arrowheads, one of which is now lost, are not mentioned in one of the early accounts, but there is no reason to doubt their association with the grave, and both are shown in an oil painting of the group made at the time of discovery by a Mr Guest of Salisbury. The painting is now in the Salisbury and South Wiltshire Museum.

References:
Hutchins 1845, 156-57
Thurnam 1971, 322, fig 10, 429, fig 121, pl XXXI. fig 2, pl XXXII. fig 2
Stevens & Stone 1939
Clarke, D L 1970, no 1204, fig 134
Gerloff 1975, no 4, pl 1 & 41.D
Green 1980, 353, corpus no 254

Collection:
Ashmolean Museum NC 207, 428, 461, 507

73. Beaker grave group
Crawford, Lanarkshire, Scotland

73.1 Bronze ring. D-sectioned. Max diam 75 mm. EQ 139.

73.2 Beaker. Ext surface completely decorated in 3 zones. From rim to neck horiz incised lines. From neck to base 2 zones of triangles, filled with horiz lines, form mirror images of one another separated by 2 horiz lines enclosing a poorly executed running herring-bone motif. All decoration in these 2 lower zones appears to be executed in comb stamping. On the inside of the rim, comb stamped decoration, partly running herring-bone, partly oblique lines. Ht 152 mm. Clarke's N3 group. EQ 138.

Associations: Cremated bones and ashes sufficient to half fill the beaker.

Circumstances of Discovery: Found in 1850 when quarrying removed a small cairn covering two cists, in one of which were the beaker and bronze ring.

References:
Irving 1855, 7-8
Anderson, J 1886, 58-59, figs 64-65
Clarke, D L 1970, no 1702, fig 674
RCAMS 1978, no 35

74. Beaker grave group
Culduthel Mains, Inverness-shire, Scotland

74.1 Barbed and tanged arrowhead of greyish-brown flint; one barb broken. L 25 mm. EQ 848.

74.2 Barbed and tanged arrowhead of translucent light brown flint; pointed barbs, serrated edges. L 28 mm. EQ 849.

74.3 Barbed and tanged arrowhead of grey-white chert or flint; drooping squared barbs, serrated edges. L 26 mm. EQ 850.

74.4 Barbed and tanged arrowhead in translucent light-brown flint; drooping squared barbs, serrated edges. L 23 mm. EQ 851.

74.5 Barbed and tanged arrowhead in light brown flint; drooping squared barbs, serrated edges. L 32 mm. EQ 852.

74.6 Barbed and tanged arrowhead in grey flint; drooping squared barbs. L 26 mm. EQ 853.

74.7 Barbed and tanged arrowhead in pale brown flint; drooping squared barbs, tang broken. L 26 mm. EQ 854.

74.8 Barbed and tanged arrowhead in pale orange-brown flint; drooping squared barbs, serrated edges. L 28 mm. EQ 855.

74.9 Flint implement made on a thick flake of mottled grey cherty flint, iron stained from contact with gravel in the grave. Roughly chipped along the edges and broader end, worn smooth at the thinner end. L 47 mm. Heavily used, probably as a strike-a-light held in the hand. EQ 847.

74.10 Wristguard of mottled green and grey stone, highly polished with convex upper and concave lower surface; the ends are slightly expanded and emphasised by a slightly raised moulding. Four rivet-holes have been bored from the back of the bracer and each holds a bronze or copper rivet with a solid conical head and a decorative cap of sheet gold. L 116 mm. EQ 844.

74.11 Beaker restored from numerous fragments. Ext decorated in two major zones from the rim to the neck and in a lower register from shoulder towards the base. Ornament consists of bands of horiz comb stamped lines alternating with vert or oblique stamps applied with a stouter comb. The impression of a grain of barley is present on the base. Ht 226 mm. Clarke's N2(L) group. EQ 843.

74.12 Bead made from irregularly shaped piece of amber, with hour-glass perforation set towards one edge. L 14 mm. EQ 846.

74.13 Bone toggle or belt-ring of 'napkin-ring' shape originally with flanges at each end, and a pair of central ribs spanned by two or more loops of which only one survives intact. Around the exterior of the surviving flange, and in the concave zones between the ribs are rows of decorative dots, c. 5 mm apart. Max diam 29.5 mm. EQ 845.

Associations: Crouched skeleton.

Circumstances of Discovery: Found in a cist excavated in 1976.

References:
Harrison 1980, 92-93, illus 65

Collection:
National Museum of Antiquities of Scotland EQ 843-55

75. Beaker grave group
Ashgrove, Methilhill, Fife, Scotland

75.1 Flat bronze dagger with remains of composite hilt and pommel. The arched heel of the blade contains 3 plug rivets, the central one set in a notch. The lower edge of the hilt is slightly convex and has a semi-circular recess, but fine cut-marks on the blade below it show that the hilt was trimmed back or replaced on at least 2 occasions. The sides of the blade are slightly convex in outline, with bevelled edges, and taper to a rounded point. On the surface of the blade, when excavated, were the last vestiges of the sheath, identified as some kind of animal skin, with traces of sewn ribs running lengthwise. The dagger was found with the remains of the hilt still attached: it had been made of 2 plates of cattle horn, and most probably had a wooden core. The plates and core were held in position by the rivets at the heel of the blade and by a further 2 (now loose) near the pommel. The trough-like pommel would have been slotted over a tang projecting from the core of the hilt, and was fastened by 3 pegs, probably made of wood. The pommel itself is made of ivory, almost certainly from the tooth of a sperm whale, and would originally have been highly polished. L (blade) 134 mm; (with hilt and pommel) 210 mm. Gerloff's Butterwick type. 1964.4.1.

75.2 Reconstruction of the complete dagger (made by Mr I A R Davidson, Edinburgh College of Art). L 210 mm.

75.3 Beaker. A coarse reddish-buff biconical vessel, with deeply but roughly incised decoration on the ext: there are 3 horiz lines made up of a series of short strokes around the uppermost part; a lattice of criss-cross diagonal lines encircling the neck; a further 7 horiz lines around the middle; and a second, broader zone of lattice ornament extending to the base. Ht 160 mm. Clarke's S4 group. 1964.4.2.

Associations: On the gravel floor lay the remains of a crouched skeleton laid on its left side, with the head at the N end. The body had been that of an adult, aged about 55 and probably male. The careful sealing of the cist with clay had created conditions that had helped to preserve more organic remains than usual. Over the skeleton and the cist floor was a thin deposit of black crumbly matter, particularly concentrated in the area of the chest. The dagger was embedded in this deposit in a position suggesting that it had been placed in the hand, with the tip pointing towards the chest. The beaker lay on its side against the E side-slab. Analysis showed the black organic deposit to be composed of plant remains, mostly leaf fragments, amongst which were identifiable macro-fossils of birch, cross-leaved heath, rush, bog moss and fairly abundant sphagnum moss. A fern rhizome also lay across the upper part of the body which would thus appear to have been covered with leaves and other vegetation. In addition, pollens of 23 species were identified, including unusually high proportions of lime and meadowsweet. It was formerly thought that these high proportions might indicate deposition of a flowering bunch of these two fragrant plants; however, as a result of recent re-analysis, it has been suggested that these pollens are more likely to have derived from the spilled contents of the beaker, which may have contained mead (or mead-sweetened ale or honey), for lime is a very common constituent of honey, and meadowsweet (= *medesweete*) a traditional flavouring for fermented drinks. Finally some short, straight bovine hairs, possibly from the now extinct aurochs (*Bos primigenius*) were found on the outer surface of the dagger hilt, and may represent the last vestiges of an ox-hide.

Circumstances of Discovery: One of 3 or 4 short cists found in 1963 during construction of a housing estate. The cist had been very carefully made and consisted of 4 sandstone blocks neatly fitted together with internal dimensions of 1.22 m by *c.* 0.7-0.8 m. It had been very effectively sealed by applying clay to all the joints between the stones including the gap between the sides and the massive cover-slab. As a result, the interior was dry and free of soil at the time of discovery.

References:
Henshall 1964a
Henshall 1968, 184 (no 7), 182, fig 41
Clarke, D L 1970, no 1662.1, fig 1016
Gerloff 1975, no 27, pls 3 & 41.G
Dickson, J H 1978

Collection:
Kirkcaldy Museum & Art Gallery 1964.4.1-2
National Museum of Antiquities of Scotland (reconstruction)

76. Beaker grave group
Newmill, Perthshire, Scotland

76.1 Flint fabricator. Keeled rod of light grey flint with whitish mottling and irregular retouch along the sides; broader end worn and rounded smooth. Microscopic analysis of the edge damage sustained by the implement suggests that it was used as a strike-a-light. L 60 mm.

76.2 Flint knife. Triangular flake of grey-brown flint, with bifacial retouch along the longest edge. Microscopic analysis has shown that the flake was set in a haft and had been used as a knife to cut soft material. L 34 mm.

76.3 Beaker with flaring rim and low belly giving distinctive S-profile. Ext crisply decorated from neck to base with 12 rows of chevrons executed by inserting a pointed tool or spatula into the clay at an angle to form narrow diagonal impressions. Ht 134 mm. Lanting & van der Waals' All-Over-Ornamented group (Step 1).

Circumstances of Discovery: The beaker and the 2 flint implements were found in a grave set within a penannular ring ditch discovered in the course of excavation of a later settlement. The burial, presumably an inhumation, although no trace had survived, had been placed in a coffin or container or organic material set in a bath-shaped grave pit prepared for its reception. The beaker lay towards one end and the 2 flints were placed roughly centrally on the base of the grave.

References:
Lanting & van der Waals 1972
Watkins & Shepherd 1980

Collection:
National Museum of Antiquities of Scotland (unreg)

77. Beaker
Fordham, Cambridgeshire, England

Handled beaker. Red-buff, burnished ext decorated in 3 zones. Below the rim, a panel with a single horiz comb stamped line above and an incised groove and cordon below. Panel decorated with incised lozenges with horiz lines inside. At the top of the panel are infilled pendant triangles and on part of the lower line, infilled triangles rise from it. The lozenges are placed to form an oblique pattern. Below the cordon is a horiz band of finger-nail impressions with 2 incised lines below. These lines, and 2 others lower down, define a panel interrupted by the handle. The panel is decorated with a pattern of vert linked lozenges, each line of which is separated from the next by an undecorated zig-zag area. The lines have alternately 3 complete lozenges and 2 complete lozenges with a half lozenge above and below.

Each lozenge is infilled with horiz lines. The third zone has 2 horiz bands of finger-nail impressions separated by 2 horiz lines and with a final horiz line below the lower band. The handle makes an oval finger hold. At the top is a horiz comb stamped line. Under the handle, 2 vert lines of comb stamping form the ends of the central panel. Ext surface of the handle is decorated with 3 complete and one half lozenges vert linked. Each has a smaller lozenge within, infilled with horiz lines. To the left and right of the line of lozenges is a pattern of horiz lines, bounded by a vert comb stamped line. On either side of the handle is a pattern of finger-nail impressions. The base is decorated with a circle of finger-nail impressions bounded by a comb stamped line. Within this is a comb stamped circle enclosing at its centre a square surrounded by a pentagon. Running radially from the centre are 22 small bands alternately plain and with horiz/curved comb stamping. Some of the decorated bands are segments of the circle, others more rectangular. Ht 128 mm. Clarke's SH3(B) group.

Associations: Inhumation although only a skull survives. Association is uncertain.

Circumstances of Discovery: Found *c.*1900 by poachers in a gravel pit.

References:
Mss Cat Univ Cambridge Mus Archaeol Anthrop
Fox 1923, 66, pl II, 1
Clarke, D L 1970, no 71, fig 1061 & pl 7

Collection:
University Museum of Archaeology & Anthropology, Cambridge 1903.204

78. Beaker
Bathgate, West Lothian, Scotland

Beaker with flaring rim and low angular belly; apart from 2 narrow reserved bands immediately below the rim and around the carination, the ext is completely ornamented with the impressions of lengths of twisted cord, spirally wound around the body. Comb stamping is used in a small area of smudged corded decoration. There are a further 3 lines of corded impressions on the int of the rim. Ht 140-146 mm. Clarke's All-Over-Cord group.

Circumstances of Discovery: Found in 1906 in a sand-pit 1.6 km E of Bathgate in circumstances which suggest displacement took place before discovery.

References:
Mann 1906, 369-71
Clarke, D L 1970, no 1788, fig 2

Collection:
National Museum of Antiquities of Scotland EG 47

79. Gold earrings
Boltby Scar, Yorkshire, England

79.1 Gold earring, basket-shaped, sheet gold. Formed from an oval with a tang coming from it which has then been curled. The oval area is decorated at the edge with 2 roughly parallel lines enclosing a ring of dots. Repoussé decoration. L 33 mm. 1940.4-4.1.

79.2 Gold earring, basket-shaped, sheet gold. As 79.1. L 31 mm. 1940.4-4.2.

Circumstances of Discovery: Found under the rampart of Boltby Scar Camp.

References:
Brailsford 1953, 34
Taylor 1980, 22, 34, pl 3.e (cat no Yk 1-2)

Collection:
British Museum 1940.4–1.1-2

80. Gold earring
Kirkhaugh 1, Northumberland, England

Gold earring, basket-shaped. Tanged oval of sheet gold curled into a cylinder with the tang on the outside. Oval decorated with 2 rows of repoussé dots around the edge and a tongue-shaped impression in the centre. Tang decorated with single row of dots on each edge. Gap on tang decoration for ear lobe. L 34 mm.

Associations: No unequivocal associations although other broadly contemporary material, including a barbed and tanged flint arrow head and an AOC beaker, together with later material was found within *c.* 1 m.

Circumstances of Discovery: From the central area of a ring cairn excavated by Maryon in 1935.

References:
Maryon 1936, 207-16
Clarke, D L 1970, no 651 (where wrongly associated with AOC beaker)
Taylor 1980, 22, 23, 84 (cat no Nb 9)

Collection:
Museum of Antiquities of the University and the Society of Antiquaries of Newcastle upon Tyne 1936.13

81. Gold earring
Orbliston Junction, Moray, Scotland

Gold earring, basket-shaped, consisting of an elongated oval sheet of beaten gold folded into a semi-tubular shape, from one long edge of which springs a slightly thicker tongue-like tang for attachment. The edges of the earring have been decorated with repoussé relief, applied prior to folding from what was to become the inside surface. The motifs include raised dots set at intervals within 2 parallel lines close to the margin, with a fringe of short vert or slightly oblique strokes. L 135 mm.

Associations: One of a pair: the second, lost by about 1870, was said to have been 'identical in form and material'.

Circumstances of Discovery: Found in 1863 in the remains of a cist in a gravelly mound, being quarried for use in the construction of the railway line from Elgin to Keith. The earrings lay about ⅓ of the way from one end of the cist on either side of what may have been very decayed skeletal remains.

References:
Paton 1870
Coles, J M 1969, 52, 100, pl 1a
Taylor 1980, 22, pls 3.f & 16.c (cat no Mr 3)

Collection:
National Museum of Antiquities of Scotland EQ 117

82. Gold disc
Kirk Andrews, Isle of Man, England

Gold disc with 2 perforations near one edge and decorated with 3 concentric rings of repoussé dots near the edge. Finely scratched guidelines for this decoration are visible. Diam 50 mm.

Circumstances of Discovery: Found 1782. Details unknown.

References:
Gage 1836, 430
Taylor 1980, 23 (cat no IOM 1)

Collection:
British Museum: Townley Collection

83. Gold disc
Castle Treasure, Co Cork, Ireland

Gold disc. Sheet gold, decorated and perforated. Outer ring of repoussé dots with 4 lightly incised lines within. Inside this circular area is a cross forming quadrants, each of which has an arc of repoussé dots at its outer edge. The cross has an incised outer line enclosing a repoussé line and a ladder pattern with an incised outer line and repoussé rungs. 2 central perforations, a single large one by the edge as well as *c.* 22 smaller ones. Diam 44 mm.

Circumstances of Discovery: Thought to have been found *c.* 1816 during cultivation of farmland.

References:
Taylor 1980, 23 & pl 4.b (cat no Co Ck 20)
Smith, C R nd, 222-23

Collection:
British Museum 54.12–27.2

84. Bronze Armlet
Mill of Laithers, Turriff, Aberdeenshire, Scotland

Bronze penannular armlet made from a narrow flat band bent so that the ends almost meet. Traced decoration, now very worn, runs around the hoop in a pattern composed of criss-cross lines forming lozenges and opposed triangles, set within marginal lines. At least one of the rows of triangles may have been emphasised by filled lines. At each of the terminals, 4 narrow transverse panels are ornamented with alternating chevrons and nicks. Diam 53-58 mm.

Associations: Said to have been found with the butt end of a bronze flat axe, now lost.

Circumstances of Discovery: Possibly found in a grave.

References:
Henshall 1964b, 428-29
Coles, J M 1969, 102
Schmidt & Burgess 1981, 51, no 293, pl 134.B

Collection:
National Museum of Antiquities of Scotland L.1962.139

85. Copper neck-ring or diadem
Yarnton, Oxfordshire, England

Neck-ring of almost pure copper composed of a rod of circular section, varying from 5-6 mm in diam along its length, and tapering at each end into slightly overlapping spade-shaped expanded terminals, *c.* 2 mm thick. The upper surface of each terminal is ornamented with a hammered 'stepped' design: the line of the main hoop is continued as a slightly raised flattened band bearing short transverse grooves, and these are set perpendicular to a

7.24 Copper neck-ring or diadem from Yarnton, Oxfordshire (85)

7.25 Copper neck-rings or diadems from Lumphanan, Aberdeenshire (86)

series of longer grooves worked on the expansion beaten out on either side. Diam 168 by 163 mm.

Circumstances of Discovery: Found in or before 1875 in a grave 'near the head of a contracted skeleton' at a site which seems, according to Evans' remarks, to have been a prehistoric cemetery.

References:
Evans, J 1881, 379, fig 470, 380
Butler 1956, 59-60
Butler 1963, 188
Taylor 1968, 260-61, pl XVII.B

Collection:
Ashmolean Museum 1927.2696

86. Copper neck-rings or diadems
Lumphanan, Aberdeenshire, Scotland

86.1 Neck-ring or diadem of almost pure copper, composed of an oval-sectioned rod 9-10 mm in diam tapering at each end into spade-shaped expanded terminals only 1.5 mm thick. The ends of the rod overlap giving the ring overall dimensions of 156 by 163 mm, but unfolded the length would amount to *c.* 330 mm. FA 33.

86.2 Neck-ring or diadem of almost pure copper composed of an oval-sectioned rod 9-11 mm in diam tapering at each end into spade-shaped terminals 1.5-2 mm thick. The ends of the rod overlap giving the ring overall dimensions of 158 by 172 mm but unfolded the length would amount to *c.* 330 mm. FA 34.

Circumstances of Discovery: Unknown: 'found in the parish of Lumphanan' before 1832.

References:
Archaeol Scot, 5 (1890), 13
Butler 1956, 59-60
Taylor 1968, 259-61, pl XVI.D
Coles, J M 1969, 53, 91

Collection:
National Museum of Antiquities of Scotland FA 33-34

87. Stone battle axe
Broomend of Crichie, Aberdeenshire, Scotland

Stone battle axe. Ground and smoothed surfaces. The cutting edge is a rounded ridge. The butt is rounded. On the upper and lower surfaces it has been waisted where the shaft was drilled. 3 incised grooves run round the outside of each of the waistings. L 102 mm. Roe's Crichie group, decorated. Fenton's Northern Variant with incised grooving.

Circumstances of Discovery: The site, excavated *c.* 1856, consists of a henge enclosing a stone circle. The battle axe was found *c.* 0.45 m from one of the stones, inside the circle. Adjacent to it were 3 cremation deposits, one is a stone-lined pit, one in an inverted cinerary urn and one unenclosed.

References:
Dalrymple 1884, 321-22, fig 2
Roe 1966, 221, 241, no 350
Fenton 1983, Appendix I

Collection:
National Museum of Antiquities of Scotland EP 2

88. Stone battle axe
Burnside Mill, Angus, Scotland

Stone battle axe. Polished surfaces. The cutting edge is a blunt ridge and the butt is rounded. The upper, lower and side surfaces are flat. A thin bevel joins the upper and lower surfaces to the side. L 115 mm. Roe's Herd Howe group. Fenton's Early type.

Circumstances of Discovery: Found in a cist.

References:
Proc Soc Antiq Scot, 48 (1913-14), 16
Roe 1966, 241, no 357
Fenton 1983, Appendix I

Collection:
National Museum of Antiquities of Scotland AH 142

89. Stone battle axe
Chapelton, Ayrshire, Scotland

Stone battle axe. Ground surfaces. The cutting edge is blunt and flattened and the butt is a flattened facet. The battle axe has been waisted on the upper and lower surfaces leaving 2 polished concave facets around the shaft-hole. 3 incised grooves run round the outside of the waistings, though they are very worn in places. L 106 mm. Roe's Scotsburn group. Fenton's Northern Variant with incised grooves.

Associations: In a cinerary urn with cremated bones.

Circumstances of Discovery: Found 1865 during the deep ploughing of a field. The inverted urn was struck by the plough.

References:
Proc Soc Antiq Scot, 9 (1870-72), 383
Roe 1966, 241, no 366
Fenton 1983, Appendix I

Collection:
National Museum of Antiquities of Scotland EQ 65

90. Stone battle axe
Longniddry, East Lothian, Scotland

Stone battle axe. Polished surface with expanded cutting edge formed by a rounded ridge, now slightly damaged. The butt is a circular flat facet. The upper and lower surfaces are flat apart from where they join the cutting edge or butt. The left and right sides are rounded and gently curving with a broad groove running all the way round below the upper surface and above the lower one, following the shape of the elongated upper and lower surfaces. L 177 mm. Roe's Loose Howe group. Fenton's Intermediate — Developed type.

Circumstances of Discovery: Isolated find. Discovered on a farm *c.* 1800.

References:
Proc Soc Antiq Scot, 28 (1893-94), 239-42
Roe 1966, 242, no 387
Fenton 1983, Appendix I

Collection:
National Museum of Antiquities of Scotland AH 108

91.   Stone battle axe
Pentland, Midlothian, Scotland

Stone battle axe. Ground and partly polished surface. The cutting edge is a blunted ridge at the top and a flattened polished facet at the bottom. The butt is a protruding flattened circular facet. The upper and lower surfaces are flattened and the sides are rounded. L 115 mm. Roe and Fenton regard this as an import from the European mainland.

Circumstances of Discovery: Found in a cist.

References:
Proc Soc Antiq Scot, 5 (1862-64), 127
Roe 1966, 242, no 399
Fenton 1983, Appendix I

Collection:
National Museum of Antiquities of Scotland EQ 64

92.   Stone battle axe
Portpatrick, Wigtownshire, Scotland

Stone battle axe. Polished surfaces. The cutting edge is a blunt ridge and the butt slightly rounded. The upper and lower surfaces are oval in shape and slightly dished towards the shaft-hole. The left and right surfaces are rounded and curved. L 121 mm. Roe's Herd Howe group (dished). Fenton's Early type.

Circumstances of Discovery: ?Isolated find.

References:
Proc Soc Antiq Scot, 12 (1876-78), 567
Roe 1966, 243, no 451
Fenton 1983, Appendix I

Collection:
National Museum of Antiquities of Scotland AH 45

93.   Shale belt ring and buttons
Harehope Cairn, Peeblesshire, Scotland

93.1   Circular belt-ring of shale with double V-borings on one edge; incised ladder decoration on both faces and around the edge except in the area of the perforations. Diam 24 mm.

93.2-93.10   32 V-bored, round conical buttons and one button of semi-ovoid form all of shale. For descriptive purposes, the round buttons may be divided into 8 groups by size, the presence or absence of ornament and by assessment of the apparent degree of wear. Large buttons are here defined as those with a diam of 25 mm or greater. The majority are *c.* 8 mm in ht.

93.2   2 large decorated conical buttons with worn bases. This group is composed of the 2 largest buttons in the assemblage (one of them of exceptional size), ornamented with a ladder-pattern cruciform design. A single peripheral groove runs between the 4 arms of the cross in each. Diam 63 mm & 34 mm.

93.3   2 large plain conical buttons with worn bases, one

7.26 Stone battle axes from Pentland, Midlothian (left: 91), Burnside Mill, Angus (centre: 88) and Portpatrick, Wigtownshire (right: 92)

with a marked 'pimple' on the apex. Diam 28 mm & 27 mm.

93.4 3 small decorated conical buttons with worn bases, ornamented with a ladder-pattern cruciform design. In one case, a single peripheral groove runs between the 4 arms of the cross, and in another, the margin is decorated with a ladder band. Diam 22-23 mm.

93.5 4 small, plain conical buttons with worn bases. Diam 18-24 mm.

93.6 Large decorated conical button with fresh striations: upper surface ornamented with ladder-pattern cruciform design. Diam 25 mm.

93.7 3 large plain conical buttons with fresh striations. Diam 27-31 mm.

93.8 12 small decorated conical buttons with fresh striations; 7 ornamented with ladder-pattern cruciform design, 5 with variation in which only three arms run from

apex to circumference. In one of the former, a single peripheral groove runs between the 4 arms of the cross. Diam 19-25 mm.

93.9 4 small plain conical buttons with fresh striations, including one example with a chamfered edge possibly due to reshaping. Diam 18-24 mm.

93.10 Semi-ovoid button with V-perforation in line with its long axis. L 36 mm.

Associations: A flint knife.

Circumstances of Discovery: The belt-ring and the buttons were found in a rectangular grave pit under the cairn.

References:
Jobey 1980, 96-113, figs 15-16

Collection:
National Museum of Antiquities of Scotland (unreg)

RICH INDIVIDUAL GRAVES AND RELATED MATERIAL

94. Accessory cup grave group
Clandon Barrow, Martinstown, Dorset, England

94.1 Bronze dagger. Very fragmentary bronze dagger blade missing both hilt-plate and tip. The surviving pieces indicate a blade with strongly defined midrib bounded by 2 or 3 lateral grooves. Found in remains of a wooden sheath, traces of which adhere to the blade. L 175 mm. Gerloff's Armorico-British B (Cressingham) type. 1884.9.26. (Not illustrated).

94.2 Gold lozenge-shaped plate. Lozenge-shaped sheet of gold, 0.3 mm thick, folded over irregularly at the edges into a narrow flange up to 2 mm deep, the only visible means by which the plate was attached to a core possibly of organic material which has left no trace. The surface of the plate is decorated with a series of 6 deeply incised lozenges of diminishing size composed of groups of 4 lines all of which conform to its outline shape. The outermost and innermost sets of lines have dots punched at approximately 1.6 mm intervals along the grooves. The innermost lozenge is ornamented with a series of incised chevrons composed of groups of 3 lines, arranged so that their apices meet at the centre of the plate. The sheet has one long tear running in from one side and several smaller holes, probably as a result

of its compression against the flints of the cairn (see below); the decoration itself is very 'crisp' and fresh. L 155 mm. 1884.9.36.

94.3 Shale macehead with decorative gold caps mounted on shale insets. An ovoid polished block of shale has been elaborately decorated by hollowing out a series of 5 holes or sockets c. 20 mm in diam to a depth of c. 5 mm; into these have been re-inserted plugs of shale with slightly conical tops covered with caps of thin gold foil held in place by narrow flanges around their circumferences. Of the original 5 decorative insets, one is empty, 2 retain only their shale plugs, and 2 retain their gold caps. A third gold cap survives only as detached fragments (not shown in catalogue illustration). On the underside of the macehead there is an irregular sub-triangular hole for the reception of a shaft. L 77 mm. 1884.8.34.

94.4 Accessory cup. Bipartite cup with upper body tapering in sharply to an int bevelled mouth decorated with a row of punctulations. Upper part of ext ornamented with incised horiz lines enclosing diagonal strokes. Lower body heavily restored: as restored, the decoration consists of a series of panels formed by pairs of vert incised lines enclosing a vert row of punctulations. Between the panels are horiz incised lines and, just above the flat base, a row of perforations jabbed through the wall at an angle. There is a possibility, however, that the lower body has in parts been wrongly restored, for the breakage pattern of the original sherds suggests that the perforations may have been rather more elongated openings in the wall, implying an original form of vessel related to the so-called perforated wall cups. Ht 50 mm. 1884.9.40.

94.5 Amber cup. Handled cup now in fragmentary condition: carved from a single block of amber, it has originally had a flaring rim, concave neck and conical base. The lower end of the single strap-like handle is visible as a stub where it springs from the wall just below the shoulder carination. It is known from earlier records that the upper end of the handle lay just below the ext lip of the rim. Ht 99 mm. 1884.9.37.

Circumstances of Discovery: Barrow (Grinsell's Winterborne St Martin 31) excavated in 1882 by Edward Cunnington: a prominent conical mound nearly 21 m in diam and 5.6 m in ht, composed of layers of sands, clay and gravel. Investigated by digging a central shaft which for reasons of safety was abandoned without reaching the original ground surface. About 2.13 m from the surface of the barrow a low cairn of flints (*c.* 2.45 m in diam) was found. The dagger (94.1) lay on the S edge of the cairn in the remains of its wooden sheath, to which adhered a small bronze ring subsequently lost. The gold plate (94.2) lay on top of the cairn, compressed against a flint; and near it lay the macehead (94.3). Scattered among the flints over an area about 0.6 m across were the fragments of the amber cup (94.5). The accessory cup (94.4) lay broken below the cairn, its pieces scattered on the underlying bed of fine white clay. The combined group of objects is customarily assumed to represent the scattered grave goods of a disturbed secondary burial in the barrow. A collared urn was also found, about 1.8 m from the barrow's centre and 0.3 m from the cairn, crushed on a layer of ashes and flints: this is now believed to represent a separate and possibly subsequent interment.

References:
Acland 1916, 40
Drew & Piggott, S 1936b, 18-20, 22-24, pl I-III.A
Piggott, S 1938, 102
Grinsell 1959, 152
Gerloff 1975, 74, no 127, pl 12 & 46.D
Taylor 1980, 45-48, pl 25.a & b (cat nos Do 9-10)
Longworth 1984, no 508, pl 23.d

Collection:
Dorset County Museum 1884.9.26, 36-37, 39-40

95. Dagger grave group
   Little Cressingham, Norfolk, England

7.27 *Watercolour drawings by Frederick Sandys of the grave group from Little Cressingham, Norfolk (95)*

95.1 Bronze dagger with damaged hilt-plate and triangular blade, missing tip. The heel has had a gently curving line of 6 rivet-holes for peg-rivets, of which 2 remain in position and 2 survive loose. Differential corrosion has left an omega-shaped mark indicating the line of the lower edge of the decayed organic hilt. The blade has a well-defined flat midrib, flanked in turn by narrow outlining grooves, broad tapering furrows, and lateral ribs which expand and merge towards the tip. L 205 mm. Gerloff's Armorico-British B (Cressingham) type. 178.950(1).

95.2 Bronze knife-dagger. Fragmentary flat, riveted knife-dagger with badly damaged hilt-plate and blade missing tip. Traces of 4 rivet-holes survive as notches in the heel, where an omega-shaped hilt-mark is visible. The blade, now broken into 3 pieces, has a flat cross-section. Present L 54 mm. 178.950(2).

95.3 Gold rectangular plate. Rectangular plate of sheet gold folded over at the edges in order originally to lap over some core, presumably of organic material, which has decayed leaving no trace. Additional means of attachment have been provided by 3 small holes, *c.* 1 mm in diam, set out along each short side. The plate has been decorated with a series of concentric rectangular grooves, arranged in groups of 3 parallel lines, except for the marginal group, which is composed of 4 lines where it runs along the long sides of the plate but splits into triple and single lines along the short sides. The central rectangle is bisected longitudinally by a further set of 3 lines. Punched marks occur at intervals along the grooves in 2 different but symmetrical arrangements: in the case of the short sides of the various concentric rectangles, the punch marks occur only along the inner and outer grooves of each set of 3 lines; along the long sides, however, the punch marks have been applied to complete alternating sets of lines. L 92 mm. 178.950(3).

95.4 Gold 'box': incomplete cylindrical 'box' of corrugated sheet gold with slightly convex polished base/top and sides ornamented with impressed grooves; int surface matt, with a reddish tinge. Ht (surviving) 5 mm; diam 17 mm. 178.950(4).

95.5 Gold 'box': base/top and part of the side of fragmentary cylindrical 'box' of similar form to 95.4. Diam 18 mm. 178.950(5).

95.6 Gold 'box': flat circular sheet of gold representing the base/top of a cylindrical 'box' of similar form to 95.4. Diam 17 mm. 178.950(6).

95.7 Corrugated band of sheet gold, with slightly everted upper and lower edges, and ornamented with 13 horiz impressed grooves. Both ends broken, but possibly originally an oval band with max dimension of *c.* 25 mm. B 18 mm. Possibly a pommel mount associated with the dagger. 178.950(7).

95.8 Amber beads: the best preserved examples have been conjecturally restrung as a necklace. The beads can be grouped as follows:

a. 28 small disc beads. Max diam 9 mm.

b. annular beads. Max diam 16 mm.

c. 2 fusiform beads. Max L 12.5 mm.

d. 2 oblate beads. Max L 10 mm.

e. 7 large pestle-shaped beads or pendants of graduated sizes, with transverse perforations through their narrower ends. L 21.5 mm - 35 mm.

Among fragmentary material, not illustrated, are a further 2 pestle-shaped beads and part of another annular bead. 178.950(8).

Associations: Skeleton of adult male: according to Barton (*in litt*): '. . . he had passed the meridian of life and made good use of his masticating organs. I should question his being much of an anchorite or one of those who was "for abolishing black-pudding and eating nothing with blood in" '!

Circumstances of Discovery: A skeleton was found by a labourer at a depth of *c.* 0.36 m from the surface, on what proved to be the site of a ploughed-out barrow in a field formerly called the 'Hills Field'. The skeleton lay with its head to the S and its legs drawn up. The dagger (95.1) lay by the side of the body, with the position of its wooden hilt marked by 'black dust'. Near the dagger lay the knife-dagger (95.2), thought at the time to be a 'javelin-head'. The rectangular gold plate (95.3) lay upon the breast of the skeleton, while the amber beads were found scattered around the neck. A portion of a gold 'armilla' — the possible pommel mount (95.7) — was found lying on one side of the skeleton, but the location of the 3 gold cylindrical boxes (95.5 - 95.7) was not specified. When found some ot the objects were in better condition than now: contemporary watercolours by Frederick Sandys (1829-1904) show that the dagger retained all 6 of its rivets and provide a clearer idea of the original form of the gold 'boxes'.

References:
Barton 1849
Barton 1852
Thurnam 1871, 454, fig 158, 502, 526-28, fig 219
Piggott, S 1938, 92, 93, fig 22
Norwich Castle Museum 1977, 32, figs 6-10
Gerloff 1975, 75, no 132, 166, no 298, pl 12, pl 25, pl 46.F
Taylor 1980, 45-47, pl 26.a-c (cat nos Nf 12-16)
Lawson, Martin & Priddy 1981, 45, 46, fig 11

Collection:
Norwich Castle Museum 178.950(1)-(8); Sandys' watercolours: 1223.B58.235.951 & 1223.B114.235.951

96. Urn grave group
Hengistbury Head, Hampshire, England

96.1 Halberd pendant. A miniature triangular blade of copper or bronze has been set in a club-shaped haft of amber, and had originally been secured by small pins or rivets set in 2 perforations. At the base of the 'haft', there are a further 2 perforations in the same plane as the blade, for suspension of the pendant. L 18 mm.

96.2 Gold cone. Circular button cover or decorative cap of very thin gold foil, made from a single rounded sheet and decorated with 3 concentric grooves around the margin. The edge has been folded over so as to grip some material since decayed. Some damage by buckling. Diam 22 mm.

96.3 Gold cone. Virtually identical to 96.2. Some distortion and damage by buckling but originally circular; tear in one edge. Diam 22 by 20 mm.

96.4 Collared urn. Ext of collar decorated with 3 lines of horiz twisted cord impressions; at the base of the neck 2 rows of short impressions have probably been made by applying a loop of the same cord twisted back on itself. Ht 330 mm. Longworth's Secondary Series, South-Eastern Style.

96.5 Accessory cup. Restored perforated wall accessory cup with convex profile and concave base. There are 10 oblong openings in the body; on the wall between each of these, are groups of 3 vert twisted cord impressions, made with 2 different cords. The remainder of the body and the int edge of the rim are ornamented with incised herring-bone patterns and horiz lines of twisted cord impressions, again applied using 2 different cords. Ht 68 mm.

96.6 Amber beads. 2 amber beads of flattened spherical shape, with a central perforation. A third bead can no longer be traced. Diam 10 mm.

Associations: Cremated remains of a young adult. The tooth of an animal, tentatively identified as badger, was also found with the burial.

Circumstances of Discovery: Primary burial in bowl barrow (I), one of three excavated in 1911-12. The urn was inverted.

References:
Bushe-Fox 1915, 14-17, figs 9-11, pl II-III
Piggott, S 1938, 103, no 23a
Taylor 1980, 81 (cat nos Ha 3-4)
Longworth 1983, 73, fig 22, 76 (cat no B1)
Longworth 1984, no 375, pl 139.a

Collection:
Private collection

97. Dagger grave group
Hove, Sussex, England

97.1 Stone battle axe. Highly polished surface. Expanded cutting edge formed on rounded ridge. Butt also expanded, having a central flattened oval facet with a rounded ridge above and below. Upper and lower surfaces flattened, rising towards cutting edge and butt. Sides rounded, expanded near the perforation. L 126 mm. Roe's Snowshill Group. R 5643.2.

97.2 Whetstone-pendant. Rectangular with polished, flattened surfaces, perforated at one end. On one surface and 2 sides there are remains of ?fabric. L 68 mm. R 5643.3.

97.3 Bronze dagger. Short bronze blade, lentoid section. Surface decorated with one deep and 2 shallow grooves. Rounded tip, ogival edge with signs of sharpening. Hilt-plate retaining one rivet and remains of possibly 2 more rivet-holes, and separated from blade by omega-shaped ridge. Remains of wooden sheath on blade and of wooden hilt on hilt-plate. L 141 mm. Gerloff's Camerton type. R 5643.4.

97.4 Amber cup. Highly polished, round base. Flattened rim with shallow groove below and a horiz band of 5 incised lines interrupted by the handle. The ribbon handle gives an almost circular finger hold and is expanded at top and bottom where it joins the cup. 2 incised horiz lines across top of handle and 2 curving bands of 5 roughly vert incised lines on either side of the outer surface. Diam 90 mm (with handle 112 mm). R 5643.1.

Associations: Inhumation in tree trunk coffin of oak within round barrow. All the finds were in centre of coffin 'as if . . . on breast of the body'. Some burnt bone was also found in the coffin.

Circumstances of Discovery: In 1856 the levelling of a round barrow, already partially removed by an earlier road development, uncovered the coffin in the original centre of the mound at a depth of c. 2.75 m. A radio-carbon date of 1239 bc ± 46 (BM-682) has been obtained for the coffin.

References:
Phillips 1857
Roe 1966, 221, 237, no 207
Gerloff 1975, 105, no 183, pl 18

Collection:
Brighton Art Gallery and Museum R 5643

98. Gold cape
Mold, Flintshire, Wales

Oval sheet gold cape which covers the shoulders, upper arms and upper chest, higher at the back and lower round the front. Round the neck and base are a line of perforations. 3 zones of decoration — a band running round the base, a curving panel which dips at the neck and rises over the shoulders and 2 matching panels to fill in the upper arms. Above the perforations at the base are 2 high ridges and a deep groove with above it a line of conical bosses which runs round the whole cape but bifurcates at the front to rise up over the triangular panels at the upper arm. The bosses at the front are enlarged. At the *front* the sequence of decoration above the bosses is, from bottom to top: ridge, 3 rows of small domed bosses, ridge, row of square-based pyramids, ridge, row of small domed bosses, ridge, row of lentoid bosses, ridge, 3 rows of small domed bosses, ridge, row of rectangular bosses, ridge, row of small domed bosses, ridge, row of lentoid bosses, ridge, 3 rows of small domed bosses, ridge, row of conical bosses and finally 3 ridges. The *back* has the same sequence with the addition, from bottom to top, of ridge, row of lentoid bosses, ridge, 3 rows of small domed bosses, ridge and a row of lentoid bosses. The 2 triangular areas on the upper arm are bounded at the front by a ridge, row of lentoid bosses and a ridge. At front and back it is then bounded by 3 rows of small domed bosses. Inside this is a ridge, row of conical bosses and 2 ridges with a groove. The central area is filled with small domed bosses. At base of each ridge and the large bosses are fine punched indentations (pointillé). In places the perforations at the base are double. In areas where parts of the cape are missing there are perforations (? from a previous repair). Now mounted on cloth. B 458 mm.

Associations: Male inhumation. Upon the cape were possibly 200-300 amber beads in rows. There were remains of coarse cloth and 16 fragments of sheet bronze which seem to have been a backing for the gold. In places the gold was riveted on to the bronze with bronze rivets. There were also two gold 'straps'.

Circumstances of Discovery: Found in 1833 during the filling of a gravel pit. The body was in a rough cist within a cairn. The cape was found over the upper body of the skeleton. 0.6-0.9 m from the grave was an urn with large quantities of burnt bone and ash.

References:
Gage 1836
Powell 1953
Taylor 1980, 51-52, 55, 59, pl 29 (cat no Ft 3)

Collection:
British Museum 36.9-2.1; 56.10-14.1; 57.12-16.1; 77.5-7.1; 81.5-14.1; 81.5-16.1-2; 83.12-7.1; 1927.4-6.1; P 1972.6-1.1-4

99. Dagger grave group
Ridgeway Barrow 7, Weymouth, Dorset, England

99.1 Bronze axe. Badly damaged, wanting both butt and cutting edge, but surviving surfaces in good condition, with smooth dark green patina. The butt portion of the axe is straight-sided but from about midway the sides diverge markedly to meet the tips of an expanded cutting edge. Low flanges run the length of each side. At approximately the middle of each face there is a slight horiz bevel; adhering to one face near the cutting edge there is an area of textile remains which have been identified as linen. L 90 mm. 1884.9.20.

99.2 Flat riveted dagger of bronze. Curving heel with central notch, rounded shoulders and triangular blade with straight sides converging towards the broken tip. 6 rivet-holes are set in a gentle curve across the base of the blade, and apart from one torn outer hole 5 of them still contain complete or fragmentary peg-rivets. An omega-shaped mark is visible where the lower edge of the hilt has decayed. On each face, there are 2 sets of 3 lateral grooves, following the straight outline of the bevelled edges. L 146 mm. Gerloff's Armorico-British A (Winterbourne Stoke) type. 1884.9.16.

99.3 Gold pommel mount made from sheet gold in 2 separate pieces which have originally been fixed in place partly by means of tiny gold pins set into a pitch-like substance applied to the pommel, perhaps partly by the adhesion of the pitch itself, and partly by the turned-in flanged lower edge of the mount. The *cap* of the pommel mount is composed of a single oval sheet of gold which has been folded over around the edges so as nearly to meet the upper edge of the separate *collar*. This has probably been made from a single piece of gold by splitting the centre and hammering it into an oval band. About 1 mm from its upper edge is a row of tiny holes which would originally have held the gold pins used for its fixture. The decoration of the collar consists of 4 grooves running around its lower edge. The upper surface of the cap has been decorated with outer and inner oval arrangements of 3 and 5 grooves respectively, while its edge is ornamented with a row of horiz chevrons enclosed by a further 2 grooves. It has been suggested that all the decoration has been applied with a bone or fine wooden stylus that has left a tapering rounded groove profile. Diam of cap 58 by 38 mm. 1884.9.17.

Associations: Cremated bones, Armorico-British A type dagger and fragments of a small bronze knife-dagger.

Circumstances of Discovery: Found during the opening of Ridgeway Barrow 7 (Grinsell's Weymouth 8) by Edward Cunnington in 1885: the mound was *c.* 34 m in diam and still measured almost 4 m in ht, despite reduction by ploughing. These objects formed part of the grave group which accompanied a secondary burial (interment no 3) found only about 0.5 m from the top of the barrow. A pit, c. 2.4 by 1.2 m, had been cut into the upper surface of the chalk of the existing mound and in it had been placed a small deposit of cremated bones on top of which were placed the 2 riveted bronze daggers of Armorico-British A type, each found with traces of their decayed wooden sheaths; fragments of a bronze knife-dagger; the flanged axe; and the gold pommel mounting, which was discovered in 2 separate pieces.

References:
Drew & Piggott, S 1936b, 20-21, 24-25, pl III.B-V
Piggott, S 1938, 103
Grinsell 1959, 141
Taylor 1970b
Gerloff 1975, 71-72, nos 114-16, pl 11
Taylor 1980, 46-49, pl 27.a-e (cat no Do 15)

Collection:
Dorset County Museum 1884.9.16-17, 20

100. Urn grave group
Upton Lovell G2(e), Wiltshire, England

100.1 Gold beads, 11, cylindrical. Made from sheet gold using a hollow cylinder and 2 end caps. Each bead has 2 small perforations side by side and is decorated with 2 grooves at each end and tiny indentations at the base of each groove. L 9-11 mm. DM 903.

100.2 Gold cone, sheet gold. Upper surface conical, lower surface flat with a waisted area between, decorated with 12 horiz grooves. Made in 2 pieces which join at the waist. Ht 20 mm. DM 898.

100.3 Gold cone, sheet gold. As 100.2 but the upper surface also has 3 grooves round the edge. 11 horiz grooves. Very small triangular perforation on one side (? modern). Ht 20 mm. DM 898.

100.4 Rectangular plate of sheet gold, the edges slightly curved and folded over underneath. There are 4 perforations, one in each corner. Round the edge of the plate are thin oblique lines with 4 grooves within, surrounding a central panel with 3 zones of decoration. The 2 outer zones are separated from the central one by 4 linear grooves and are decorated with a cross-hatch pattern. The central zone has bands of decoration alternately a plain band with 3 separate groups of 3 chevrons, the outer ones pointing in the same direction, and 4 linear grooves. There are 10 bands of chevron decoration and 9 bands of grooving. L 156 mm. DM 897.

100.5 Gold button cover, sheet gold, consisting of cone and base-plate, both with incised decoration. The cone has at its base 3 grooves with a running chevron above, surmounted by a further 3 grooves. Above is a plain band and a further 3 grooves. The base-plate is dished and has 2 perforations in it. It is decorated with a circle divided into quadrants by 3 linear grooves. Each quadrant has 3 grooved triangles following the shape of the quadrant. The 2 larger ones have been made with 3 grooves and the smaller one with 2 grooves. Covered a shale button with the same decoration. Ht 33 mm. DM 899.

Associations: The excavation in 1803 revealed a small deposit of burnt bones only c. 0.6 m below the surface of the mound in a shallow basin-like cist. About 0.3 m away from the cist, was a considerable quantity of ashes intermixed with burnt bones and c. 0.6 m away from this deposit were discovered the gold objects 100.1-100.5 described above (and a further 2 cylindrical gold beads which were subsequently lost), together with an accessory cup, several amber spacer-plates and 'over 1000' amber beads of various sizes (either an exaggeration or many now lost).

The barrow was opened again in 1807, as Hoare was not satisfied that the interest of the site had been exhausted, and he still hoped to locate primary interment. 'At the same level and within a few inches of the very spot where the golden trinkets and the amber beads had been found', the renewed work revealed 2 urns, one inside the other, of which the larger and more ornate was broken to pieces at the time, and also a small knife-dagger, a bronze awl and further amber beads possibly from a second necklace. It has customarily been assumed that the 2 groups of material derive from the same secondary cremation burial, but the contemporary methods of excavation and the interval of several years between discoveries leave this association uncertain.

Summary of surviving objects in Devizes Museum not included in catalogue:
From the 1803 excavation
— accessory cup of the type known as grape cups, with cord decoration around rim. Ht 49 mm.
— multi-strand amber spacer-plate necklace presently made up of 8 plates with complex pattern borings and some 350 beads.
From the 1807 excavation
— bronze awl. L 78 mm.
— flat riveted knife-dagger, with damaged heel. L 69 mm.
— collared urn of Longworth's Secondary series, with finger-drawn grooves encircling collar and neck, and transverse slashes on int rim bevel. Ht 154 mm.
— further amber beads (illustrated by Hoare as a single-strand necklace: 1812, pl XI).

Circumstances of Discovery: Exploration of a now destroyed bowl barrow, usually referred to as the 'Golden Barrow' or Upton Lovell G2(e). It was opened by Hoare and Cunnington on 2 occasions, in 1803 and 1807. The primary interment was a simple unaccompanied cremation deposit in a 'cist'.

References:
Hoare 1812, 98-101, pl X, XI
Piggott, S 1938, 106, no 81, pl VII
Grinsell 1957, 193 (Upton Lovell G2e)
Annable & Simpson 1964, 48, nos 225-33
Coles, J M & Taylor 1971, 11-12, pl VIa
Gerloff 1975, 164 no 272, pl 24 & 53.A
Taylor 1980, 39, 46-47, 50, pls 23.d & g, 24.b & d (cat nos Wt 23-27)
Longworth 1984, no 1710, pl 223.e

Collection:
(for catalogued pieces) Devizes Museum on loan to British Museum

101. Dagger grave group
Wilsford G5 (Bush Barrow), Wiltshire, England

101.1 Large lozenge-shaped plate of sheet gold with flattened edges decorated with a single groove and folded over. The upper surface is perforated at each end of the lozenge and has incised decoration consisting of bands of 4 grooves. The first of these runs round the outer edge of the lozenge, the other 3 gradually reducing in size and placed inside the outer one. The innermost lozenge has a cross-hatched decoration of 4 crossing lines. The outermost 2 have a running chevron pattern down each side which does not join at the perforated ends, but does at the other 2. L 185 mm. DM 752.

101.2 Small lozenge-shaped plate of sheet gold with flattened edges decorated with a single groove and folded over. The upper surface has 3 incised lozenges, following the shape of the outer edge and placed one inside the other. L 32 mm. DM 753.

101.3 Belt hook, sheet gold, made in two parts — a base plate and a hook. The base plate is a quadrilateral with 2 edges slightly concave and the other 2 slightly convex. The edges are flanged and on these are small perforations at each corner underneath. There is a single groove on the back. The upper surface has incised decoration following the shape of the outer edge. This consists of 4 bands of 3 grooves set one inside the other. The 2 middle ones are linked at a perforation made for the hook. The hook extends from the back of the plate and curves out and down over the plate. It is of sheet gold and has a rectangular hollow interior. The upper surface is plain but the sides and end are grooved with 4-9 grooves. L 72 mm. DM 754. It must originally have covered a belt hook of organic material, now decayed, probably of wood.

Associations: Found with the primary inhumation burial on the floor of the barrow. The skeleton was that of 'a stout and tall man' lying, unusually, with the head to the S, the opposite direction being the norm. It has been assumed that the body was laid out in an extended posture but this is not explicitly stated in Hoare's account. The accompanying grave group was exceptionally rich and its disposition and contents may be summarised as follows:

— about 18 inches (0.46 m) to the S of the head lay an area *c.* 0.3 m across in which bronze rivets were intermixed with wood and some thin bits of decomposed bronze. This deposit has tentatively been interpreted as the remains of a composite helmet or, less likely, a shield. A small hook-like object of bronze and 33 rivets survive.

— near the shoulders, a small bronze flanged axe, with traces of cloth impressions on the corrosion adhering to the blade. L 159 mm. Thomas claims that it had been buried in its wooden knee-shaft handle but the evidence is far from conclusive.

— near the right arm: (a) a dagger (of copper with high arsenical content) of Armorico-British A (Winterbourne Stoke) type. L 270 mm. Found with the remains of its wooden hilt which had been ornately inlaid with thousands of minute gold nails. (b) a large bronze dagger of Armorico British B (Cressingham) type. L 330 mm. (c) the gold belt-hook (101.3) or, more likely, the smaller lozenge-shaped gold plate (101.2) — the early accounts are ambiguous.

— beneath the fingers of the right hand, a 'lance head', almost certainly a third dagger, which corroded and broke to pieces on discovery.

— immediately over the breast of the skeleton, was the large lozenge-shaped gold plate (101.1).

— on the right side of the skeleton: (a) polished macehead with cylindrical perforation made from a fossil Stromatoporoid (*Amphipora ramosa*). (b) 5 cylindrical bone mounts with their edges carved into zig-zags. Although restored and displayed on a modern wooden shaft in conjunction with the macehead, it is now thought that the macehead would have been hafted separately. (c) 'many small rings of bone' that no longer survive: (d) the smaller lozenge-shaped gold plate (101.2) or the gold belt hook (101.3).

Circumstances of Discovery: Investigation by Hoare and Cunnington in 1808 of the large bowl barrow usually known as Bush Barrow (Wilsford G5), which forms part of the large linear barrow cemetery on Normanton Down, *c.* 800 m to the S of Stonehenge.

References:
Hoare 1812, 202-05, pl XXVI, XXVII
Piggott, S 1938, 105, no 53, 63, fig 3, pl X
Grinsell 1957, 196-97 (Wilsford G5)
Ashbee 1960, 76-78, fig 24
Annable & Simpson 1964, 22-23, nos 168-78
Oakley 1965, 119
Thomas 1966, 2-3, fig 2, 7-8
Coles, J M & Taylor 1971, 10-13, pl IV.b-d
Gerloff 1975, 71, no 113, 74, no 124, pls 11, 12 & 45.B
Taylor 1980, 45-9, pl 25.c, d-e & g (cat nos Wt 3-6)

Collection:
(for catalogued pieces) Devizes Museum on loan to British Museum

102. Grave group
Wilsford G8, Wiltshire, England

102.1 Gold and bronze ring, pennular with upturned horn-like ends. Sheet gold has been folded over a bronze core and there are lines of tiny indentations on both sides of the fold. At the top of the middle of the ring are 2 perforations. Diam 33 mm. DM 1062.

102.2 Gold-bound amber disc. The central amber disc is surrounded by 2 pieces of sheet gold, each with a circular hole in the centre and 2 bands of incised decoration surrounding it. The inner band has 3 lines and the outer one 4. The grooved lines have tiny indentations. The edge of the disc is decorated with 3 grooves (no indentations) and has 2 perforations. Diam 27 mm. DM 1061.

102.3 Gold-bound amber disc. As 102.2 but probably with 3 perforations on the edge. Diam 27 mm. DM 1061.

102.4 Gold button cover, sheet gold, consisting of cone and base plate which overlaps the cone at its edge. Both have incised decoration. The cone has 4 groups of 4 horiz lines on it. The base-plate has 2 perforations and has 3 concentric rings, each of 4 lines. All the lines have tiny indentations. Covered a shale button with the same decoration. Ht 29 mm. DM 1059.

102.5 Bone pendant with sheet gold cover on one face. Sub-circular pendant with a circular notch at the top and 2 tiny perforations running from the back and into the notch. The bone base of the pendant has been ground smooth and is stained green (? from contact with bronze). The upper face is covered with gold decorated with a square cross-hatching formed by 7 vert and horiz lines. The gold runs onto the side of the bone and is decorated with a single groove. L 17 mm. DM 1060. Thomas has suggested that it is to be regarded as a model lunula.

Associations: Found on the floor of the barrow with the primary cremation deposit consisting of 'a quantity of burned bones'. Besides the items of gold 102.1-102.5 described above, the following objects were recovered:
— accessory cup of perforated wall type, with twisted cord decoration. Ht 44 mm.
— halberd pendant, consisting of a bronze or copper blade slotted into a 'haft' bound with 4 ribbed strips of sheet gold. L 25 mm.
　— 4 pestle-shaped amber pendants. L (of largest) 24 mm.
　— bottle-shaped amber pendant. L 18 mm.
　— 3 flat amber pendants, with faint corrugations on one

surface. L (of largest) 18 mm.
— another amber pendant: subsequently lost.

Circumstances of Discovery: Excavation by Hoare and Cunnington of 'a fine bell-shaped barrow' about 28 m in diam and 3.3 m high, forming part of the well-known linear barrow cemetery on Normanton Down, to the S of Stonehenge. According to Hoare no other barrow opened by him produced 'such a variety of singular and elegant articles'.

References:
Hoare 1812, 201-02, pl XXV
Piggott, S 1938, 105, no 71, pl IX
Grinsell 1957, 211 (Wilsford G8)
Annable & Simpson 1964, 46, nos 179-92
Thomas 1966, 7
Coles, J M & Taylor 1971, 11-12, pl III
Gerloff 1975, 260, Appendix 7, no 26
Taylor 1980, 45-47, pls 23.e & h, 24.a & e (cat nos Wt 30-35)
Longworth 1983, 84 (cat no E9)

Collection:
(for catalogued pieces) Devizes Museum on loan to British Museum

103. Knife-dagger grave group
Barnhill, Broughty Ferry, Angus, Scotland

103.1 Bronze flat riveted knife-dagger, with butt missing; much corroded, but faint trace of broad omega-shaped hilt-mark. L 85 mm. EQ 198.

103.2 Gold disc or 'button cover' consisting of gently domed circular sheet of gold folded over at the edge and originally gripping some internal support no longer surviving. Around the margin there are 2 repoussé grooves the bottoms of which are filled with tiny dots at intervals of 1 mm or less, while fainter dots run around the inner lip of the inner groove. Transverse nicks have been neatly applied around the circumference of the disc, the upper surface of which has been highly burnished. Diam 33 mm. EQ 199.

103.3 Gold disc. As 103.2. Diam 33 mm. EQ 200.

Circumstances of Discovery: One of a number of cists found in 1875-76 during the construction of a road near Broughty Ferry. The objects were in a large cist orientated NW-SE with a prepared floor, partly slabs and partly gravel. The cist was clay luted.

References:
Hutcheson 1887
Coles, J M 1969, 52-53, 99, pl 3b
Gerloff 1975, 165, no 285, pl 24
Taylor 1980, 45, 49, pl 28.k (cat nos An 8-9)

Collection:
National Museum of Antiquities of Scotland EQ 198-200

104. Grave group
Knowes of Trotty, Huntiscarth, Orkney, Scotland

104.1-104.4 Circular discs of very thin gold foil, ornamented with concentric ribs with one band of zig-zag lines and one band of vert or oblique lines enclosed between pairs of ribs. The decoration has been executed by indenting the foil from the under-side. Function uncertain — possibly covers for shallow conical buttons. Diam (of most complete disc) 76 mm. EQ 126-29.

104.5-104.11 Beads, plates, pendants and fragments all of amber, possibly representing a necklace composed of the surviving pieces or reworked fragments of a more elaborate spacer-plate necklace. EQ 130.

104.5 2 roughly hemispherical beads. Diam 11.5 mm; 12.5 mm.

104.6 2 pendants in the form of hooks, with diagonal perforations running from their bevelled upper edge through to the side. Overall L 30 mm.

104.7 Pointed fragment perhaps part of an object similar to the hook-shaped pendants. L 18 mm.

104.8 Fragmentary spacer-plate with 'complex' pattern of borings. B 35 mm.

104.9 Fragment of terminal plate of spacer-plate necklace with converging pattern of borings. Max B 19 mm.

104.10 12 fragments of thin plate, mostly of approximately triangular shape, perforated either with V-borings or simple transverse holes; in some the borings have broken through to the edge. Made from reworked spacer-plates, or possibly originally designed as prismatic beads. L (of largest) 15 mm (at base of triangle).

104.11 One small fragment of thin plate, without trace of perforations. L 7 mm.

Associations: Cremated bones according to the farmer who excavated the site. Further amber beads may have been lost in the course of clearance of the debris from the grave.

Circumstances of Discovery: Found together on a flat stone in one corner of a cist, about 0.75 m long, during the exploration in 1857 of the largest barrow in a barrow cemetery known as the Knowes of Trotty.

References:
Petrie 1860, 195, pl XXII
RCAMS 1946, vol I, 22, pl 6; vol II, Inv no 73
Inventaria Archaeologica, GB 33
Coles, J M 1969, 53, 100, pl 2.a
Taylor 1980, 23, 49, pls 4, 5 & 28 (cat nos Ok 1-4)
Taylor 1983

Collection:
National Museum of Antiquities of Scotland EQ 126-30

105. Shale cup
Farway Broad Down 53, Devon, England

Lathe-turned single-handled cup of Kimmeridge shale with flaring rim, concave neck and conical lower body. Although almost intact, the upper part in particular is badly distorted and has been compressed into an oval shape. Ext ornamented with 4 sets of concentric grooves: around the rim, midway down the lower body and around the base these sets consist of 3 grooves, but around the shoulder there are 4, and all appear to have been turned. The single carved ribbon handle springs from just below the ext lip of the rim and contracts in width slightly before expanding again at the point where it meets the shoulder. The decoration of the handle has been contrived so that the uppermost groove of the set encircling the rim has been continued by hand down the side of the handle to merge gracefully with one of the grooves of the set around the shoulder. The face of the handle is ornamented with 2 pairs of curving marginal grooves conforming to its outline. In the int of the mouth, there is a single horiz groove running around the lip, below which there is a pendant zig-zag design composed of paired V-shaped incisions. Ht 91 mm.

Circumstances of Discovery: Found in 1869 during exploration of Barrow 53 on Farway Broad Down. The mound appears to have been erected over the site of a funeral pyre. At the centre of the barrow a deposit of calcined bones rested on a bed of charcoal which in turn lay on a levelled pavement of flints with signs of burning. The cup lay slightly above but immediately contiguous to the cremation deposit.

References:
Kirwan 1868, 624-27, figs 1-2
Worth 1880, 131-32 & figs
Newall 1929, 115, fig 4, 116
Gerloff 1975, 258, pl 57.O

Collection:
Rougemont House Museum, Exeter Ant 290

106. Handled vessel
Balmuick, Perthshire, Scotland

Handled vessel with flaring rim and pronounced shoulder. From a moulded cordon around the neck springs a broad strap handle, which meets the wall again at the shoulder carination. Apart from a narrow band near the rim, the whole ext is decorated with multiple horiz lines apparently applied by impressing a blunt comb or length of whipped cord repeatedly around the surface. 2 lines of similar ornament encircle the flat top of the rim, with a third emphasising the inner edge of the lip. 3 worn concentric lines are present on the base. Ht 145 mm.

Associations: When found, a few fragments of bone lay in the bottom of the pot.

Circumstances of Discovery: The vessel was found, lying on its side, at the W end of a small cist which lay eccentrically within the southernmost of 3 burial mounds excavated in 1884.

References:
Boston 1884, 306-08
Clarke, D L 1970, 417, fig 1081

Collection:
National Museum of Antiquities of Scotland EH 8

107. Jet plate
Law Hill, Dundee, Angus, Scotland

Trapezoid jet plate or button, ornamented around the margin of its upper surface with sets of 3 deeply cut grooves. These had initially been marked out by inscribing fine parallel guide-lines still visible in 2 places. On the back is a large V-perforation, the hole being in line with the axis of symmetry of the plate. L 43 mm.

Circumstances of Discovery: Found in a cist at Law Hill, Dundee before 1880.

References:
Sturrock 1880, 266, figs 8-9
Taylor 1980, 45
Shepherd, I A G 1981, 47, fig 2.5, 49

Collection:
National Museum of Antiquities of Scotland EQ 210

108. Faience beads
Culbin Sands, Morayshire, Scotland

108.1 'Segmented' bead. Square sectioned with one surface undecorated and the other 3 with alternate oblique grooves and ridges. The decoration on each surface is slightly offset from that on the next and gives the appearance of spiral decoration. L 19 mm.

108.2 'Segmented' bead. Circular sectioned with a single incised groove spiralling the length of the bead. L 19 mm.

Circumstances of Discovery: Isolated finds.

References:
Beck, H C & Stone 1935, 245, fig 1

Collection:
National Museum of Antiquities of Scotland B IB 4

109. Faience beads
Glenluce Sands, Wigtownshire, Scotland

109.1 Star-shaped bead with 9 points and central perforation with raised edges. Bluish surface. Max diam 23 mm. BHB 1.

109.2 As 109.1 but with greenish-blue surface. Max diam 23 mm. BHB 2.

Circumstances of Discovery: Isolated finds.

References:
Beck, H C & Stone 1935, 247, fig 1

Collection:
National Museum of Antiquities of Scotland BHB 1-2

DAGGER GRAVES

110. Dagger grave group
Wilsford G23, Normanton Down, Wiltshire, England

110.1 Whetstone-pendant of dark grey fine-grained stone, oblong in shape with a rounded projection at one end with an hour-glass perforation for suspension. Fine striations, resulting from use, on the slightly concave sides and in various places on the surfaces. L 72 mm. DM 1043.

110.2 Bronze dagger with a triangular-concave outline to the blade. The slightly curved heel has 6 small rivet-holes. The holes nearest to each shoulder have been torn but the remainder retain at least parts of their original peg-rivets. On both faces, an omega-shaped hilt-mark is visible at the base of the blade, which has a prominent rounded midrib with pointillé decoration on its upper part. 3 straight grooves run on either side of the midrib to converge where it tapers out near the point. Traces of organic material on the hilt-plate and blade represent the remains of a wooden hilt and possibly a composite sheath. The upper part of the sheath appears to have been strengthened by a cross-bar of wood just below the hilt. L 200 mm. Gerloff's Armorico-British B (Cressingham) type. DM 1042.

110.3 Bronze knife-dagger. The rounded heel has 2 rivet holes at the shoulder, one of them torn, and a possible central rivet-notch. An omega-shaped mark indicates the lower edge of the hilt. The blade is straight-sided with a faint midrib bordered by broad shallow grooves, all tapering towards the rounded tip of the blade. There are some traces of wood on the hilt-plate. L 106 mm. DM 1044.

110.4 Bronze crutch-headed pin. The head consists of a hollow tube of oval cross-section and open at the ends, decorated with 3 sets of traced horiz lines with opposed filled triangles in the intervening spaces. L 114 mm. DM 1045.

110.5 Fragments of a bone tube, now partially restored, made from part of the hollow long bone of a swan *(Cygnus cygnus)* or similar large bird: one end is original and has been smoothly finished, but it is known that when found it was 175-95 mm long, with a rough perforation at the centre. There may also have been a second hole about a third from the narrower end. L 188 mm. Possibly a bone flute. DM 1046.

Associations: Found with a pile of burnt bones in a ?central chalk-cut pit under the barrow.

Circumstances of Discovery: Exploration, under the auspices of Hoare, of a bowl barrow in the linear cemetery on the crest of Normanton Down 800 m to the S of Stonehenge. The barrow was composed entirely of earth.

References:
Hoare 1812, 199, pl XXIV
Megaw 1960, 9, pl II.6
Annable & Simpson 1964, 44-45, nos 163-67
Gerloff 1975, 76, no 135, 170, no 321, pls 13, 26 & 47.A

Collection:
Devizes Museum DM 1042-46

111. Dagger grave group
Winterbourne Stoke G4, Wiltshire, England

111.1 Ogival dagger of bronze with arched heel and 3 rivet-holes with all 3 plug-rivets still in place. Traces of the wooden hilt are present on the base of the blade, where there is a clear omega-shaped mark indicating its lower edge, and running down the full length of the blade from this is a prominent midrib. From the shoulders, the bevelled edges of

the blade taper in an ogival curve to the tip: on each face 4 finely drawn grooves follow the outline of the blade to converge at a point c. 30 mm from the tip, and the area they enclose is profusely decorated with fine lines of pointillé decoration. L 217 mm. Gerloff's Snowshill type. DM 1027.

111.2 Flat riveted knife-dagger of bronze with triangular blade. The damaged heel has a 2 rivet-holes for peg-rivets, one of them intact, the other hole being torn and its rivet missing. Linking the shoulders is a very gently curving hilt-mark, while there are traces of a wooden sheath on the blade, which also has 2 wide shallow grooves running parallel to the edges. L 74 mm. DM 1026.

111.3 Bone tweezers, made from a length of hollow bone; the shaped head has a transverse perforation. Their function is generally assumed to have been depilatory but Thomas (1966, 6-7) advances cogent arguments against such an interpretation. L 52 mm. DM 1024.

Associations: Found with the primary cremation deposit in a wooden box on the old ground surface under the barrow. The box was about 1.07 m long and 0.61 m wide, placed N-S, and had been covered with bluish clay. The wood appeared to be elm, although some pieces were deemed to be oak. Other surviving associated finds include 2 polished bone mounts with bronze rivets, almost certainly the fittings for a composite pommel for the dagger, and 2 fragments of sheet bronze which may have been parts of attachments for the box. A bone pin disintegrated on discovery and several bronze rivets were lost subsequently.

Circumstances of Discovery: Exploration in the early 19th century by Cunnington and Crocker of a bell barrow in the well-known linear cemetery at Winterbourne Stoke Crossroads, about 2 km WSW of Stonehenge.

References:
Hoare 1812, 122, pl XIV
Annable & Simpson 1964, 48, cat nos 219-24
Thomas 1966, 4-6
Hardaker 1974, no 23
Gerloff 1975, 101, no 154, 161, no 244, pls 15, 23 & 47.C

Collection:
Devizes Museum DM 1024, 1026-27

112. Dagger grave
Blackwaterfoot, Arran, Bute, Scotland

112.1 Dagger blade of bronze, surfaces badly corroded and edges damaged, particularly around break. On each face, there are 3 fine ribs tapering slightly towards the point, each rib outlined by very fine dots spaced at intervals of 1-1.3 mm. 2 rivets, 9 mm long, are set in the angular heel, which is of unusual form with deep notches on either side of a fish-tail-shaped central tang. The W-shaped outline of the base of the hilt is delineated by differential corrosion, and also by a row of tiny dots. L 228 mm. Gerloff's Sproughton type. EQ 268.

112.2 Pommel mount made of a ribbed band of sheet gold, possibly from a Scottish source. The band is now broken into 2 pieces and heavily distorted, but originally would have had a tapering profile, with flanges for attachment at the upper and lower edges. Ornamented by 5 horiz impressed grooves. L of each piece 44 mm. EQ 268.

Circumstances of Discovery: A very large cairn formerly stood in low-lying agricultural land near the shore of Blackwaterfoot: when noted by Pennant in the later 18th century it was said to be 'a stupendous cairn . . . of a vast height'. By 1900 it had been thoroughly robbed for building stone and only the base survived. Many 'stone coffins' were said to have been found in it previously but were all destroyed unrecorded. The dagger and pommel mount were the only objects found in a large cist exposed in 1900. The cist, possibly the central burial, was very well made, using dressed slabs, and measured 1.3 by 0.7 m.

References:
Bryce 1902, 117-19
Bryce 1910, 109-11, text figs 52-54
Henshall 1968, 183, no 5, 185, fig 42
Gerloff 1975, 134, no 227, pl 21
Taylor 1980, 23, 49, pl 28.a (cat no Bt 2)
Taylor 1983

Collection:
National Museum of Antiquities of Scotland EQ 268

113. Dagger grave
Collessie, Fife, Scotland

113.1 Dagger blade of bronze, now very badly decayed; edges damaged mainly since discovery, but much of the original glossy surface intact. At the heel, parts of 2 broad rivet-holes, and remains of a central notch (or third rivet-hole). The position of the lower edge of the hilt is clearly visible as an omega-shaped outline delineated now partly by differential corrosion, partly by original very fine cut marks in the metal. L 153 mm. Related to Gerloff's Masterton type. EQ 52.

113.2 Pommel mount made of a ribbed band of sheet gold now greatly distorted as a result of damage sustained since discovery. The gold is possibly from a Scottish source. When found, it was oblong with rounded ends and a slightly tapering profile. There are flanges for attachment around the upper and lower edges, and 5 ornamental horiz

impressed grooves. L 38 mm (originally 40 mm). EQ 53. (originally 40 mm). EQ 53.

Associations: Cremated bones of ? adult.

Circumstances of Discovery: Investigation of the Gask Hill at Collessie, a very large cairn about 36 m in diam and 4.25 m in ht. The items were found in a cremation deposit *c.* 1.22 m below ground level in the SE quadrant of the cairn. The dagger appears to have been deposited in a sheath made with an outer covering of ox hide on a wooden foundation.

References:
Anderson, J 1878, 439-40, figs 1-2, 451-53
Henshall 1968, 185, fig 42, 186, no 8
Gerloff 1975, 60, no 84, pl 8
Taylor 1980, 19, 23, 49, pls 28.a & c (cat no Fi 1)
Taylor 1983

Collection:
National Museum of Antiquities of Scotland EQ 52-53

7.28 *Grave group from Collessie, Fife (113)*

114. Dagger grave group
Masterton, Fife, Scotland

114.1 Bronze armlet. Pieces and fragments of sheet bronze, curled into a cylinder with a slight waist and fastened with 3 small rivets. Upper and lower edges folded over. Decorated central panel with 2 raised bands with occasional swellings and pointillé decoration at base. Upper and lower edges have a groove with short vert line decoration and a thin raised edge on the side towards the centre. Diam *c*. 75 mm. EQ 639.

114.2 Bronze armlet. Exactly comparable to 114.1. EQ 639.

114.3 Bronze dagger. Corroded with damaged surface and edges. Flat surface, with broken tip, and remains of 2 rivet-holes in the hilt-plate and one surviving rivet. Edge of hilt-plate defined by W-shaped line. Remains of horn hilt were also found. L 134 mm. Gerloff's Masterton type. EQ 640.

114.4 Small bronze blade. Broken. Oval blade with sharp but badly eroded edges. May have had small wood/horn handle with knob at the end. L 38 mm. EQ 641.

114.5 Jet necklace. 68 fusiform beads, 88 small disc beads, one perforated triangular toggle. Strung as 5 rows of fusiform beads with discs on the end of each string. Fusiform beads L 12-28 mm; disc beads diam 5 mm; toggle L 35 mm. EQ 642.

Associations: Very fragmentary remains of ? 2 skeletons thought by excavators to be male and female side by side, on the basis of the grave goods and their location in the cist. The hide of a bison or aurochs was laid on the floor of the cist.

Circumstances of Discovery: Excavated in 1961 by Henshall and Wallace. The cist was exposed by work on an approach road for the Forth Road Bridge in undulating agricultural land. Large cist with clay-luted joints and 2 post holes, covered up in the NW and SW corners. Built in pit over 1.5 m deep from surface.

References:
Henshall & Wallace 1963
Henshall 1968, 189, no 10, 191, fig 44
Gerloff 1975, 58, no 70, pl 7

Collection:
National Museum of Antiquities of Scotland EQ 639-42

115. Dagger grave group
Skateraw, East Lothian, Scotland

115.1 Bronze dagger. Highly corroded surface. Broken in 2 pieces and repaired. Central tang with notches below and 2 rivets still in place. Hilt-plate has W-shaped lower edge. L 148 mm. Gerloff's Masterton type. EQ 237.

115.2 Pommel mount of gold possibly from a Scottish source. Oval piece of ribbed sheet gold, tapering. Single sheet with overlap, decorated with 4 ridges and 3 grooves. Flanged at top and bottom. L 32 mm. EQ 238.

Associations: Human skeleton and pieces 'resembling fragments of a blue glass bottle' (?faience).

Circumstances of Discovery: Found in a cist within a cairn some time between 1806-14 during clearance of cairn for agriculture. The dagger was on the right-hand side of the body.

References:
Proc Soc Antiq Scot, 27 (1892-93), 7-8
Henshall 1968, 183-84, no 6, 185, fig 42
Gerloff 1975, 60, no 83, pl 8
Taylor 1980, 23, 49, pl 28.a & b (cat no El 2)
Taylor 1983

Collection:
National Museum of Antiquities of Scotland EQ 237-38

DECORATED SLAB

116. Decorated cist slab
Badden Farm, Kilmichael Glassary, Argyll, Scotland

Decorated cist slab. Roughly oblong slab of greenish-grey phyllite rock of local origin with pecked geometric decoration on what has been the internal face of the side-slab of a grooved-and-rebated cist. The decoration consists principally of a pattern of interlocking concentric lozenges, which fall into 2 groups covering the upper part: a series of 7, with carefully executed double or triple outlines about a central point, is set out in a tight composition on the right-hand half, while a further series of 7 less regular lozenges with double outlines is arranged in a less accomplished fashion to their left. A modern plough scar obscures the junction between the 2 groups. Near each end,

7.29 Decorated cist slab from Badden, Argyll (116)

and partly truncating the carvings there is a vert groove into which would have been fitted the end-slabs of the cist. At their lower ends, the grooves run into the rebated area of the slab, where the face has been thinned to a tapering section by dressing away the stone (both features reflecting what are essentially woodworking techniques). Beyond the right-hand groove, there are traces of further decoration, apparently 2 incomplete lozenges. Despite the truncation of the lozenge patterns by the vert grooves and the consequent separation of the ornament at the end, it is generally considered that the designs have been executed after selection of the stone to form part of a cist. L 1.53 m.

Circumstances of Discovery: Found during ploughing in

1960. Excavations failed to reveal any sign of a cist, although a setting of rounded boulders 5.2 m by 2.4 m in area, and up to 0.6 m deep, was found sunk into the natural gravel.

References:
Campbell, Scott & Piggott 1961
Campbell & Sandeman 1962, 36, no 258, 38, no 272
Simpson & Thawley 1972, no 11
Morris 1977, 51 (ARG 13)
Twohig 1981, 123

Collection:
Glasgow Art Gallery & Museum A6045

FOOD VESSEL GRAVES

117. Food vessel grave group
Folkton LXXI, Yorkshire, England

117.1 Food vessel (Yorkshire vase). Ext surface with slip. The rim is decorated with 2 rows of ? bird bone impressions. The neck has a single row of ? bird bone impressions at the top with below it a panel with 6 vert expansions each of which has a horiz perforation. Each expansion has ? bird bone impressions and the zones between have 6/7 horiz rows of twisted cord impressions. Below the neck is a single row of ? bird bone impressions with 6 horiz rows of twisted

cord impressions. Below this and running to the base are vert twisted cord impressions. Ht 123 mm. 79.12-9.1130.

117.2-117.5 4 bone beads, probably made from the same bone.

117.2 Tubular, polished bead. The upper surface has a St George cross painted in a dark pigment. The lower surface has 4 triangles painted one in each corner leaving a plain lozenge in the centre. L 14 mm. 79.12-9.1141.

117.3 Tubular, polished bead. The upper surface has a single line down the centre and a flattened triangle at either side painted in a dark pigment. The lower surface has been painted with 4 triangles, one at each edge, leaving a saltire unpainted. L 15 mm. 79.12-9.1142.

117.4 Tubular, polished bead. The upper surface has a straight line down the centre with a triangle at each side painted in dark pigment. The lower surface is eroded but appears to have 2 triangles, one at each side. L 15 mm. 79.12-9.1143.

117.5 Tubular, polished bead, undecorated but stained green in places (? from contact with the bronze awl). L 14 mm. 79.12-9.1144.

Associations: Female inhumation, flint scraper, bronze awl, leg and ribs of young pig, astragalus of sheep/goat.

Circumstances of Discovery: Round barrow excavated before 1877 by Greenwell. The mound of the barrow, which had slipped, contained 14 other burials, both inhumations and cremations, one with a food vessel and one with a miniature collared urn. The crouched body was found in an oval grave, then 2.7 m from the centre, with pieces of chalk set round it. There was a male inhumation 0.3 m below in the same grave and parts of an adult and child within the grave filling. The food vessel was in front of the face, one of the beads (117.5) was below the hips, and the other 3 by the right elbow.

References:
Greenwell & Rolleston 1877, 274-79
Simpson 1968, 197, 199, fig 45.5, 200

Collection:
British Museum 79.12–9.1130, 1141-44

118. Food vessel ?grave group
Kinneff, Kincardineshire, Scotland

118.1 Bronze bar armlet made from a rod of nearly circular cross-section, bent so that the ends fit tightly against each other in a butt-joint. Corroded in places. Diam 82 mm. EQ 148.

118.2 Bronze bar armlet very similar in construction and condition to 118.1, but with a more D-shaped cross-section. Diam *c.* 76 mm EQ 149.

118.3 Tripartite bowl food vessel, one side largely restored. Ext divided into zones by horiz lines executed by applying a whipped cord into the clay and there may originally have been 2 such lines on the int bevel of the rim. Short vert strokes, also applied with a whipped cord,

emphasise the slight moulded ridges which give the vessel its tripartite form. Around the outer edge of the rim, and on the neck, there are single lines of impressions made with a flat triangular point, but around the middle, 2 bands of opposed triangular impressions form zig-zag patterns in 'false-relief'. Ht 126 mm. EQ 147.

Associations: The fragmentary rings mentioned in the original notice of donation were subsequently lost. Although unrecorded in that notice, Anderson later stated that the objects were found in association with an unburnt burial, but this may have been inferential.

Circumstances of Discovery: Uncertain: 'a vase with a number of bronze rings of various sizes two of them entire, the rest in fragments' were found in 1831 'in trenching a field on top of a cliff near the site of the Old Castle of Kinneff, Kincardineshire'.

References:
Anderson, J 1886, 59, fig 66-67
Archaeol Scotica, 5 (1890), Appendix: 27
Young 1951, 44, 45, fig 3.22, 49
Inventaria Archaeologica, GB 34

Collection:
National Museum of Antiquities of Scotland EQ 147-49

119. Grave group
Melfort, Argyll, Scotland

119.1 Bronze armlet. Sheet bronze, only two-thirds surviving. Cylindrical with waisted sides. There are 5 horiz panels of decoration, the first, third and fifth comprising 3 grooves, the second and fourth composed of lentoid basses, with 2 bosses, one on top of the other, followed by a single boss, then 2 more, etc. Diam 69 mm. DO 51.

119.2 Jet necklaces. 49 fusiform beads, 6 trapezoidal spacer-plates, 2 triangular end-plates. 1 toggle: reconstructed as 2 necklaces.

Necklace A (26 fusiform beads, 3 trapezoidal spacer-plates, 2 triangular end-plates, toggle). 3 spacer-plates, one large and 2 small, all with pointillé decoration forming vert bands of opposed triangles with an undecorated area between. The smaller plates have 2 bands of 3 opposed triangles and the larger one 2 bands of 4 opposed triangles and a third band of 5 opposed triangles. The smaller plates have 4 perforations at the top and 5 at the bottom, the larger plate 5 perforations at the top and 8 at the bottom. One triangular end-plate is decorated with a large triangle with a smaller opposed one above. Inside the large triangle are 5 smaller triangles set out as 2 opposed triangles and a fifth one above. The other end-plate is probably decorated in the same way but it is difficult to identify clearly.

Necklace B (23 fusiform beads, 3 trapezoidal spacer-plates). 3 spacer-plates (2 large, one small). The larger plates have at the top and bottom a row of double pointillé decoration with 2 rows of opposed triangles offset to leave the zig-zag area between undecorated. The upper row has 6½ triangles and the lower one 7 triangles. The small plate is decorated in a similar way but both rows have 5 triangles. The larger plates have 5 perforations at the top and 9 below, the smaller one 5 above and 5 below. Beads L 13-25 mm; spacer-plates B 34-51 mm. 90.4-10.1.

Associations: Adult inhumation and matching bronze armlet (not surviving). 2 more fusiform beads were found.

Circumstances of Discovery: Found c. 1878 in a cist during road alterations. 2 other cists were found nearby, one containing a partly cremated burial and a flint scraper.

References:
Proc Soc Antiq Scot, 19 (1884-85), 134-36
Inventaria Archaeologica, GB 25

Collection:
National Museum of Antiquities of Scotland DO 51
British Museum 90.4–10.1

120. Food vessel grave group
Mount Stuart, Bute, Scotland

120.1 Tripartite vase food vessel. Upper part of ext principally decorated with chevron patterns executed with a rectangular toothed comb which has also been used to form an irregular zig-zag line below the shoulder. The upper of the 2 moulded ridges and the ext of the rim are further emphasised by lines of impressions made with a flat triangular point, the same technique having also been employed to ornament the int of the rim. Ht 175 mm. EQ 100.

120.2 Jet spacer-plate necklace represented by 100 complete and fragmentary fusiform beads, 4 trapezoidal spacer-plates, 2 triangular end-plates, one of which is perforated, and an ?unworn triangular toggle, also perforated. The beads vary in their degree of wear, with surfaces ranging from matt to highly polished, and are in variable condition. The spacer-plates are decorated with designs consisting of multiple pointillé lines. On the larger pair of trapezoidal plates, with 4 and 8 holes in their longer sides, the pattern consists of 2 diamonds with central voids, linked with a W-shaped design at either end, the whole being set within horiz borders. The smaller pair of trapezoidal plates, with an arrangement of 4 holes in each side, are similarly decorated. The broad end of the int triangular end-plate is ornamented with a design based on

opposed filled triangles meeting point to point to create a central diamond-shaped void while a triangle is set close to the apex. L (of beads) 10-27 mm. Max B (of spacer-plates) 54 mm. EQ 101.

Associations: Skeleton of young woman with ? trepanned skull (accepted as such by Munro but dismissed as 'allegedly trepanned skull', by Piggott (1940, 114) without further explanation, though Bryce (1904, 67-68) was of the same opinion), small fragment of bronze, and fragments of 2 'pins or skewers' which do not survive.

Circumstances of Discovery: Found in a cist in 1887. It is uncertain whether the cist was covered by a barrow or set in a natural mound. The inhumation was crouched with the food vessel at the feet, the jet beads around the neck, the bronze in the hands and one each of the 'pins' at head and feet.

References:
Munro 1892, 5-8
Hewison 1893, 68-72
Bryce 1904, 63-69
Piggott, S 1940, 114

Collection:
National Museum of Antiquities of Scotland EQ 100-01

121. Food vessel grave group
Killicarney, Co Cavan, Ireland

121.1 Stone axe. Small with polished surfaces. Slightly curving, blunt cutting edge and oblique roughened butt. Thick rounded sides. L 70.5 mm. 1880:68.

121.2 Ribbed bowl food vessel. Stepped int rim with short vert strokes of comb stamping on the inner edge and top of rim. 4 zones of decoration on the ext surface. Below the rim is a band of short vert strokes with a horiz line running through their middle. The lower half of the strokes is on a cordon. The second zone consists of a band of horiz linked lozenges with their apices touching. Each has an outer lozenge with up to 4 smaller ones inside and the smallest filled with horiz lines. All this in comb stamping. Below this is a panel of 4 horiz cordons with 3 grooves between, all decorated with horiz comb stamped lines. As the angle changes towards the foot of the vessel, inverted roughly triangular panels of sometimes horiz, sometimes oblique comb stamped lines are formed, each separated from the other by 2 opposed vert lines of ?finger-nail impressions making a zig-zag pattern. At the base is a band of very short vert comb stamped lines. Ht 131 mm. 1880:66.

121.3 Bone belt hook. Flat, square, ground plate with bevelled edges. On one side, 2 polished 'prongs' extending out and curving underneath, partly broken. The opposite side has 5 slight cut marks/notches regularly spaced. B 36 mm. 1880:71.

Associations: The axe and belt hook may have been associated with a vessel now lost, and not the one illustrated here. Both vessels held cremated bone.

Circumstances of Discovery: Found by workmen in a cist divided into 2 by cross-slab some time in or before 1879. The cist was set into natural mound which had been augmented. 2 other cists, one with an encrusted urn, were found in the mound.

References:
Wakeman 1882, 190-94, fig 5, 6.1 & 4
Simpson 1968, 206, fig 49.3

Collection:
National Museum of Ireland 1880: 66, 68, 71

122. Food vessel
Denovan, Dunipace, Stirlingshire, Scotland

Tripartite vase food vessel. Apart from 3 narrow reserved bands, the whole of the ext is decorated with horiz rows of impressions neatly applied with a flat triangular point. The rather flat int bevel of the rim is similarly ornamented. Most of the rows run in unison, but around the rim and the 2 moulded ridges, the triangular impressions have been applied apex to apex to form zig-zag bands of 'false-relief'. Ht 145 mm.

Circumstances of Discovery: Found in a short cist discovered during sand/gravel quarrying in 1967.

References:
Hunter 1971

Collection:
National Museum of Antiquities of Scotland EE 167

123. Food vessel
Duncraigaig, Argyll, Scotland

Bowl food vessel of bipartite form with constricted waist, which acts as a plane of near symmetry for much of the zoned decoration on the upper and lower parts of the vessel. The ornament mainly consists of horiz and vert rectangular-toothed comb stamped lines integrated with impressions

made with a blunt triangular point. Around the foot, the triangular impressions are opposed to form a near 'false-relief' zig-zag emphasised by oblique comb stamping. The base is decorated with a saltire composed of, and encircled by, triangular impressions, the resultant fields of the cross being filled with combed chevrons. Ht 97 mm.

Circumstances of Discovery: Discovered during exploration by Greenwell, in 1864, of a large cairn some 30 m in diam at Duncraigaig in the Kilmartin valley, Argyll. The bowl was found in a small cist about 6.7 m from the centre of the cairn: it lay on the gravel which partly filled the cist, and amongst the gravel were burnt bones and a few flint chips.

References:
Greenwell, 1866, 347
Anderson, J 1905, 237-39, figs 5-6
Craw 1930, 134-35, fig 11

Collection:
National Museum of Antiquities of Scotland HPO 11

124. Jet necklace
Pitkennedy, Angus, Scotland

Jet necklace with 100 fusiform beads, 4 spacer-plates, 2 triangular end-plates and 1 toggle. Highly polished. The spacer-plates have pointillé decoration, 2 lines at the top and bottom with a panel in the centre bounded above and below by 2 lines with linked lozenge pattern between, comprising 3 complete and 2 half lozenges. The triangular end-plates are decorated with a triangle which has a T-shape within. The upper part consists of 2 lines of dots and the lower of 3 lines of dots. 2 spacer-plates have 4 perforations running through. The other two have 4 perforations at the top and 8 at the bottom. The end-plates have 4 perforations each and the toggle a single perforation. L (of beads) 9-19 mm. Max B (of spacer-plates) 45 mm.

Associations: Found within an urn (details unknown). There were originally 104 beads.

Circumstances of Discovery: Found in a cist in a 'natural' mound in 1857 during gravel extraction. The cist was near the middle of the mound, *c.* 0.65 m below the surface.

References:
Jervise 1860

Collection:
National Museum of Antiquities of Scotland EQ 384

CINERARY URN GRAVES

125. Urn grave group
Bedd Emlyn, Clocaenog, Denbighshire, Wales

125.1 11 barbed and tanged flint arrowheads; several broken, all burnt and calcined. They fall into 2 main groups: 3 or 4 appear to have had straight sides terminating in squared off, drooping barbs; the remainder have slightly convex or ogival sides, all but one terminating in squared off barbs, and have slightly broader tangs. L (of longest) 27 mm. 10 of Green's Conygar Hill type, 1 of his Sutton b type. 60.522.5-15.

125.2 Plano-convex flint knife. Calcined; retouch on straight sides and irregularly rounded distal end. L 35 mm. 60.522.16.

125.3 Enlarged food vessel urn. Bipartite vessel, with lower body much restored. Ext bevel of rim ornamented with 2 horiz lines of twisted cord impressions; below the rim, 6 undecorated pendant loops of applied clay are spaced at roughly equal intervals around the upper part of the neck, which is divided into 2 by a slight horiz moulding. The spaces between the loops are filled with horiz cord impressions. The lower part of the neck is filled with groups of horiz and vert cord impressions arranged in panels, while a row of short looped cord impressions runs around the shoulder. All the corded ornament on the ext appears to have been made with a cord looped and twisted back on itself. On the steep int bevel of the rim, there are 5 horiz lines of the more usual twisted cord impressions. Ht 278 mm. 60.522.4.

Associations: Cremated bone.

Circumstances of Discovery: Found in 1960 on the site of a round barrow or cairn previously destroyed by afforestation. The urn was found inverted in a small pit cut into the upper filling of an earlier inhumation grave pit. A small slab had protected the base of the vessel.

References:
Savory 1961, 11-12, 16-21, figs 5-6
Savory 1980, 144 (cat no 399), figs 50 & 59
Green 1980, 315 (corpus no 111)

Collection:
National Museum of Wales 60.522.4-16

126. Urn grave group
Bloxworth Down 4a, Dorset, England

126.1 Collared urn. Decorated on collar with a lattice pattern of twisted cord, on int of rim with 2 circles of twisted cord. Collar expands at its base with a shallow neck below. Blackened on the inside. Ht 426 mm. Longworth's Secondary Series, Form Ic. 92.9-1.257.

126.2 Jet beads. 7 fusiform, polished. L 13-16 mm. 92.9-1.258.

126.3 Faience beads. 4 (one fragmentary) segmented, one with 8 segments, 2 with 6 segments. L 11-17 mm. 92.9-1.258.

126.4 ? Ivory pendant, broken. Flattened head with circular perforation. Broken shaft. L 16 mm. 92.9-1.260.

126.5 Bone 'tweezers', broken. Flattened nail-shaped head. The shaft is cut into 2 parallel strips. L 55 mm. 92.9-1.261.

Associations: Burnt bones and ashes, another jet bead and 2-4 additional faience beads.

Circumstances of Discovery: A disc barrow excavated in 1854 by Shipp and Durden. It contained 4 other burials, probably all inhumations. The cremation and finds were in a cist in the centre of the barrow which had been filled and then covered with chalk. The urn was inverted and contained the bones, ashes and other objects.

References:
Warne 1866, II, 12-13
Grinsell 1959, 168
Longworth 1984, no 372, pl 204a

Collection:
British Museum 92.9–1.257-61

127. Urn grave group
Llanddyfnan, Anglesey, Wales

127.1 Small bronze axe badly distorted by action of fire. From a narrow, gently curved butt the sides run straight before diverging to meet an expanded cutting edge, one tip of which is broken. L 76 mm. 42.395.4/5.

127.2 Bronze chisel, with very narrow elongated body. From the sharpened, curved butt the sides run approximately parallel as far as the midpoint, beyond which they gradually diverge before expanding to meet the splayed cutting edge. L 110 mm. 42.395.4/2.

127.3 Bronze dagger. Ogival dagger blade of bronze, largely intact apart from damaged tip. There are 3 rivet-holes in the curved heel, 2 of them undamaged and still containing peg-rivets. An omega-shaped hilt-mark is visible as a result of differential corrosion around the base of the blade. Double shallow grooves along the edges of the blade outline an area of 'rain pattern' decoration applied with a tracer. L 100 mm. Gerloff's Aylesford type. 42.395.4/1.

127.4 Food vessel. Bipartite vessel with slack shoulder. On the ext, the rim bevel and the line of the shoulder bear rows of diagonal 'maggot' impressions made with a whipped cord; the remainder of the upper portion of the vessel is ornamented with horiz lines of twisted cord impressions. The deep int bevel is decorated with 7 such lines. Ht 192 mm. 42.395.4/13.

Associations: Cremated bones, large food vessel urn and a piece of antler, now lost.

Circumstances of Discovery: Excavation in 1908 of a large round barrow, nearly 30 m in diam, consisting of a mound of gravel and sand in which had been deposited at least 7 urn burials. The barrow is one of 5 forming a linear cemetery near the village of Pentraeth. The objects were found with a cremation burial inside a large cinerary urn of the food vessel tradition. The urn had been inverted and deposited in a protective cist of stones in the make-up of the mound only 0.25 m below the surface, and about 3 m from the centre of the barrow. It appears that the axe, which is badly twisted by fire, must have been on or with the body when it was cremated: it and the bones were subsequently placed in the urn. Before the urn was turned over for burial, the dagger and chisel — both unburnt — were pushed down into the bones point first, and a piece of antler, 130 mm long and rubbed smooth at each end, was placed on top of the bones. The antler was lost after discovery and its original function is unknown. The relationship of the food vessel (127.4) to the burial is uncertain: it was found lying on its side with its mouth facing away from the urn, which it was said to be touching. It may therefore have been deposited as an accessory vessel, within the cist. However, it has also been suggested that it represents broken pottery derived from an earlier interment disturbed by insertion of the urn burial.

References:
Baynes 1909, 320-23, figs 7-9
Lynch 1970, 140-45, fig 48
Gerloff 1975, 69, no 107, pl 10
Savory 1980, 131-32 (cat no 334), figs 51 & 58

Collection:
National Museum of Wales 42.395.4/1-2, 5, 13

128. Urn grave group
Snailwell A, Cambridgeshire, England

128.1 Flint knife. Elongated with 2 straight edges and one curving end. Fine surface flaking with very fine retouch on both edges and one end. L 63 mm. 49.300B.

128.2 Flint knife. Elongated but broad. 2 gently curving edges, one rounded end. Fine surface flaking. The 2 edges have been serrated by retouching. L 62 mm. 49.300B.

128.3 Flint knife. Roughly triangular. 2 straight edges with a rounded tip. Fine surface flaking and fine retouch on edges and tip to make a serrated blade. L 63 mm. 49.300B.

128.4 Collared urn. Red burnished ext, grey int. Rim bevel decorated with 2 rows of opposed, touching triangles (one pendant the other rising) formed with short lengths of twisted cord impressions. Collar decorated with twisted cord running chevrons. The neck has twisted cord herringbone decoration with 3 rows of angled oblique lines on the neck and a fourth below the shoulder. The shoulder has finger impressions. Ht 416-427 mm. Longworth's Primary series, form Ib. 49.300A.

128.5 Perforated antler. Segment of beam and tine of roe deer antler, ends flat, centre drilled out. L 51 mm. 49.300C.

128.6 Perforated bone point. Flat head. L 105 mm. 49.300C.

128.7 Perforated bone point. Flattened head. L 103 mm. 49.300C.

128.8 Perforated bone point. Flattened head. L 90 mm. 49.300C.

128.9 Perforated bone point. Rounded head. L 76 mm. 49.300C.

128.10 Perforated bone point. Flat head. L 75 mm. 49.300C.

128.11 Perforated bone point. Flat head. L 72 mm. 49.300C.

128.12 Perforated bone point. Rounded head. L 52 mm. 49.300C.

128.13 Double-perforated bone point. Flat head. L 46 mm. 49.300C.

128.14 Perforated bone point. Rounded head. L 36 mm. 49.300C.

128.15 Bone point, no perforation. Rounded head with

7.30 Grave group from Westerdale, Yorkshire (129)

localised green stain (? contact with bronze). L 159 mm. 49.300C.

128.16 Bone point, no perforation. Flat head. L 96 mm. 49.300C.

128.17 Bone tube, perforated at one end. L 106 mm. 49.300C.

128.18 Bone tube, no perforation. L 77 mm. 49.300C.

Associations: Cremated bone.

Circumstances of Discovery: Excavated by Lethbridge in ? 1940 after Snailwell barrow cemetery had been levelled. Barrow A contained 3 other cremations in collared urns. Cremation II which these finds accompanied was roughly central in a pit. The flint, antler and bone objects were placed beside the urn, which was mouth down. Further details about the barrow are unclear, and confused by inconsistencies in the excavation report.

References:
Lethbridge 1950, especially 33-34, fig 2
Longworth 1984, no 104, pl 46c

Collection:
University Museum of Archaeology and Anthropology, Cambridge 49.300

129. Urn grave group
Westerdale, Yorkshire, England

129.1 Stone battle axe. Surface polished in places. Expanded, rounded cutting edge. The butt is a circular flattened facet. The upper and lower surfaces are flattened but rise a little towards the cutting edge and butt. The sides are expanded by the perforation to form a ridge on both sides. Running round the upper and lower flattened surfaces is a shallow groove. L 114 mm. Roe's Loose Howe Group, decorated. 76.4-10.34.

129.2 Accessory cup. Flat base, biconical shape with irregular rounded rim. The outer surface is broken in places. Ht 43 mm. 76.4-10.33.

129.3 Collared urn, flattened rim, slipped surface. The collar is decorated with an incised running chevron pattern. Each triangle formed by the lines has a smaller triangle below. Unburnt int. Ht 336 mm. Longworth's Secondary series, North Western Style, form II. 76.4-10.31.

129.4 Collared urn. The collar is decorated with impressed twisted cord decoration. At the top and bottom are 2 horiz lines with between them a running chevron design which has within each triangle one or 2 oblique lines. Burnished ext. Burnt int. Ht 306 mm. Longworth's Secondary Series, South Eastern Style, form IIb. 76.4-10.32.

129.5 Bone toggle. Roughly cylindrical with natural longitudinal perforation, flattened ends. Outer surface is decorated with a single ridge formed by incising a groove which runs the length of the piece in a spiral. At each end the ridge runs into a circular ridge running round. This gives it the appearance of being segmented. There is an oval perforation in the middle of one side. L 41 mm. 76.4-10.35.

Associations: 129.3 contained cremated bone and 2 burnt pins. 129.4 contained cremated bone, all the other small objects and 4 bone pins. All 6 pins are now lost.

Circumstances of Discovery: Excavated in 1863 by Atkinson. The urns were under a round barrow, at the edge of a central cairn. 129.4 was upright and covered by a stone.

References:
Atkinson, J C 1863, 549-50
Roe 1966, 240, no 315
Longworth 1984, nos 1301-02, pl 103a-b

Collection:
British Museum 76.4–10.31-35

130. Urn grave group
Balneil, Wigtownshire, Scotland

130.1 Bronze lugged chisel. Tang of trapezoidal cross-section swelling into slightly rounded shoulders, from which straight sides extend to meet the curved cutting edge; surfaces corroded. L 110 mm. EQ 342.

130.2 Cordoned urn. Plain apart from two cordons which have been worked up from the surface of pot; rim moulded to form a slightly concave int bevel. Ht 377 mm. EQ 341.

130.3 Quoit-shaped faience bead, greenish grey in colour. Diam 20 mm. EQ 343.

130.4 Crutch-headed bone pin, with the end of the shank fashioned into a phallus; partially distorted by heat. L 55 mm. EQ 344.

Associations: Cremated bones of two adults: sex not determined.

Circumstances of Discovery: Found during ploughing, by the edge of a low rocky knoll in a field NE of Balneil Farm. The urn was inverted.

References:
Curle 1916, 302-05, figs 1-2
Burgess & Cowen 1972, 174, fig 5

Collection:
National Museum of Antiquities of Scotland EQ 341-44

131. Urn grave group
Gourlaw, Lasswade, Midlothian, Scotland

131.1 Collared urn profusely decorated with a spatulate implement jabbed into the clay at an angle to form chevron patterns around the collar and neck. The same technique has been used to apply transverse lines across the rim, and below that a further series of chevrons on the deep concave int moulding, ending in a double line of horiz twisted cord impressions. Ht 360-75 mm. Longworth's Primary Series, form 1a. EA 164.

131.2 Burnt bone object, possibly a handle-plate, consisting of a rectangular piece of bone with a curved cross-section, pierced by 4 perforations. L 26 mm. EA 166.

Associations: Cremated bones.

Circumstances of Discovery: From a cairn on the slopes of Gourlaw, a prominent sandy hillock. The urn was inverted.

References:
Coles, F R 1905, 415-17, figs 3-4
Longworth 1984, no 1926, pl 33g

Collection:
National Museum of Antiquities of Scotland EA 164 & 166

132. Urn grave group
Magdalen Bridge, Joppa, Midlothian, Scotland

132.1 Broken oval blade of tanged bronze razor. Finely ornamented with incised lattice decoration set within a pointed ellipse. Edges of the grooves forming the ellipse are decorated with close-set, tiny punch marks. Central lattice consists of cross-hatched lines forming rows of diamonds, the alternate rows filled with oblique lines. L 74 mm. Class I razor. DI 4.

132.2 Tripartite cordoned urn with low mouldings or cordons worked up from the surface of the clay. The upper register thus formed is elaborately decorated with whipped cord, applied in a series of metopes or panels. 2 groups of 3 horiz lines encircle the vessel below the rim and above the upper cordon. These act as borders to panelled ornament consisting of lattice, filled and partially filled triangles, and diamond designs framed by vert lines. The steep int bevel of the rim is also ornamented, with oblique lines applied using the same whipped cord technique. Ht 295 mm. EA 41.

Associations: Cremated bones and ashes.

Circumstances of Discovery: From a flat cemetery of urns protected by stone cists discovered in 1882 at Magdalen Bridge, Joppa, near Edinburgh during the removal of sand for building purposes.

References:
Lowson 1882, 422-24, figs 2-3
Piggott, C M 1946, 130, fig 4.7, 135, no 7

Collection:
National Museum of Antiquities of Scotland D I 4 & EA 41

133. Urn grave group
Milngavie, New Kilpatrick, Dunbartonshire, Scotland

133.1 Flint arrowhead, barbed and tanged, burnt. L 39 mm. EQ 303.

133.2 Flint arrowhead, barbed and tanged, burnt. L 36 mm. EQ 304.

133.3 Flint arrowhead, barbed and tanged, burnt. L 31 mm. EQ 305.

133.4 Flint arrowhead, barbed and tanged, burnt, broken. L 25 mm. EQ 306.

133.5 Flint ? arrowhead roughout, burnt, broken. L 34 mm. EQ 307.

133.6 Collared urn. Ext of collar decorated with diamond or lattice pattern formed by applying lengths of twisted cord in intersecting lines; on int bevel of rim, 3 lines of twisted cord impressions. Ht 350 mm. Longworth's Secondary Series. 5-50.

133.7 Bone beads
a. segmented bead, 3 segments, 2 grooves, burnt. L 24 mm. EQ 299.
b. segmented bead, 3 segments, 2 grooves, burnt. L 24 mm. EQ 300.
c. toggle bead, transverse perforation on both sides, burnt. L 19 mm. EQ 301.
d. toggle bead, broken transverse performation, burnt. L 16 mm. EQ 302.

7.31 Grave group from Sandmill, Wigtownshire (134)

Associations: Cremated human bone which nearly filled the urn.

Circumstances of Discovery: Found 'some years before' 1908 in a mound during levelling for a golf course. 2 urns were found: one inverted and containing the flint and bone objects while the second (NMAS: EQ 298) was broken by the workmen.

References:
Callander 1908, 218-19
Scott, J G 1948
Piggott, S 1958, 227-29
Green 1980, 297, corpus no 41
Longworth 1984, no 1973, pl 202g

Collection:
National Museum of Antiquities of Scotland EQ 298-307
Glasgow Art Gallery & Museum 5-50

134.   Urn grave group
Sandmill, Wigtownshire, Scotland

134.1   Stone battle axe. Polished surfaces. Expanded cutting edge with blunted ridge. Rounded butt with flat central facet. The upper and lower surfaces are concave, rising towards the cutting edge and butt. The sides expand beside the perforation and are decorated with 3 incised grooves on the upper and lower edges. L 119 mm. Roe's Loose Howe group, decorated. Fenton's Intermediate-Developed (with incised grooves) group. EQ 486.

134.2   ?Cushion stone/whetstone. Rectangular large pebble with artificially smoothed and flattened surfaces. L 109 mm. EQ 489.

134.3   ? Cushion stone/whetstone. Rectangular large pebble with 2 artificially smoothed, flattened surfaces, almost polished in places. L 84 mm. EQ 490.

134.4   Whetstone. Irregular flattish pebble with rounded area and a groove, both of which have smoothed surfaces. L 94 mm. EQ 491.

134.5   Blade of bronze razor. Leaf-shaped, straightish edges leading to rounded tip. Snapped at the heel and bent just above it. Sharpened edge bevel on blade, one side with damaged edge. L 71 mm. Class I razor. EQ 487.

134.6   Collared urn. Rim and collar decorated with impressed pitting (? finger nails) in roughly vert lines. Neck decorated with an oblique lattice pattern. Ht 397 mm. Longworth's Secondary series, North Western style, form Ia. EQ 485.

134.7   Bone pin, broken. Part of the shaft with a single line of zig-zag decoration. Burnt. L 22 mm. EQ 488.

Associations: Cremated bones of an adult and ashes.

Circumstances of Discovery: Found during ploughing in or before 1941. The urn was inverted in a pit and contained the bones, ashes and other objects.

References:
Anderson, R S G 1942
Piggott, C M 1946, 131, fig 5.13, 136, no 13
Roe 1966, 221, 243, no 452
Fenton 1983, Appendix I
Longworth 1984, no 1806, pl 91c

Collection:
National Museum of Antiquities of Scotland EQ 485-91

135.   Cordoned urn
Magdalen Bridge, Joppa, Midlothian, Scotland

Tripartite cordoned urn, with 2 moulded cordons encircling the upper body. The upper register thus formed is ornamented with multiple incised lines. 2 horiz lines border, and form the baselines for, an arrangement of opposed interlocking triangles. These have been rather haphazardly set out, and oblique lines have had to be inserted to fill an awkward gap at the end. Ht 342-350 mm.

Associations: Cremated bones and ashes.

Circumstances of Discovery: From a flat cemetery of urns protected by stone cists discovered in 1882 at Magdalen Bridge, Joppa, near Edinburgh during the removal of sand for building purposes.

References:
Lowson 1882, 421-22, fig 1

Collection:
National Museum of Antiquities of Scotland EA 40

136.   Collared urn
Kirkpark, Musselburgh, Midlothian, Scotland

Collared urn, decorated throughout with patterns composed of twisted cord impressions: on ext of the deep collar, a design of interlocking, opposed filled triangles bordered above and below by pairs of horiz lines; on the neck, a lattice pattern with a single horiz line around the shoulder, below which there is a fringe motif of short diagonal lines. On the steep int bevel, there are 3 horiz lines. Ht 360 mm. Longworth's Secondary series, North Western style.

Associations: Burnt bones; many of them were stained green, possibly by contact with bronze, although no metalwork was found.

Circumstances of Discovery: Following the discovery of urns in a sandpit, investigations in 1893 revealed a cemetery of at least 12 inurned and 8 unaccompanied cremation deposits. The urn was inverted in a pit.

References:
Lowe & Anderson, J 1894, 65, 75-76, fig 12
Longworth 1984, no 1932, pl 96d

Collection:
National Museum of Antiquities of Scotland EA 146

137. Food vessel urn
Newton of Montblairy, Alvah, Banffshire, Scotland

Enlarged food vessel urn. Rim everted, with a broad int bevel decorated with a deeply incised herring-bone pattern, and vert or slightly oblique incisions on the ext lip. A horiz moulding divides the upper part of the vessel into 2 concave zones, the upper of which has originally been spanned by 5 applied bars embellished with incised strokes. In the neck zone there is a single row of oblique incisions between the applied bars, but from the moulding to below the shoulder the ornament is set out as a series of chevrons. Ht 340 mm.

Circumstances of Discovery: Found on the farm of Newton of Montblairy, Alvah, Banffshire in the mid-19th century.

References:
Proc Soc Antiq Scot, 2 (1854-57), 346-47, 371
Anderson, J 1886, 115-16
Walker 1966, no 32, pl XVII.1
Cowie 1978, 113 (Ban 4), fig 15

Collection:
National Museum of Antiquities of Scotland EA 13

ACCESSORY CUP GRAVES

138. Accessory cup grave group
Breach Farm, Llanbeddian, Glamorgan, Wales

138.1 13 flint barbed and tanged arrowheads falling into 3 groups while possessing considerable differences in detail.
a. 3 arrowheads of grey flint with convex sides and flat-based barbs.
b. 4 arrowheads of grey flint with slightly convex sides and squared drooping barbs.
c. 6 arrowheads of honey coloured flint with squared barbs and tangs, and finely serrated, slightly concave or convex edges. These are, as yet, unsurpassed for quality of workmanship within the British Isles.
L (of longest) 37 mm. 11 of Green's Conygar Hill type, 2 of his Green Low type. 38.37.5-17

138.2 Roughouts for arrowheads. 3 flakes of grey or grey-brown flint bifacially worked into discoidal shape, with some secondary working around the edges. L (of longest) 45 mm. 38.37.23-25.

138.3 Roughouts for arrowheads. 3 flakes of grey flint bifacially worked into triangular points with convex sides. L (of longest) 44 mm. 38.37.20-22.

138.4 Flint ?knife. Pointed oval with finely retouched edges and sides; plano-convex cross-section. L 54 mm. 38.37.19.

138.5 Primary flake of black flint with prominent boss of chalky white cortex on one end. The other end has been retouched to form a convex scraping edge, which appears to be unused. L 52 mm. 38.37.18.

138.6 Stone arrowshaft smoothers. 2 oblong pieces of sandstone, each with a longitudinal groove *c.* 11 mm across, running down the middle of their flatter surfaces. L 55 and 56.5 mm. 38.37.3-4.

138.7 Bronze axe. From the narrow, damaged butt, the sides, which have weak ?cast flanges, diverge gradually before expanding to meet the splayed cutting edge. There is a prominent bevel at about the midpoint of both faces. Very corroded. L 84 mm. 38.37.1.

138.8 Accessory cup. Biconical cup with contracted mouth and sharply tapering lower body with slightly convex base. Decoration, all incised, is as follows: on the int lip of the rim, a row of vert or slightly oblique strokes; on the upper half of the ext, 3 equidistant horiz lines enclose 2 rows of filled triangles, arranged so that the triangles in the 2 registers are out of step; on the lower body, 2 horiz lines enclose 2 rows of opposed filled triangles, their apices offset so as to form a reserved zig-zag pattern; on the base, 4 incised lines form a saltire: 2 of its fields are filled with straight lines, the other 2 with multiple chevrons. There are traces of red colouring in the incisions. 2 small perforations, 50 mm apart, are present in the shoulder carination. Ht 51 mm. 38.37.2.

Associations: Cremated bones of 3 individuals, 2 unworked flints and 3 bronze objects too decayed to be recovered. One was identified as a tanged chisel and another as a small flat dagger.

Circumstances of Discovery: From the excavation of a round barrow: the central burial has been covered by a mound of clay, enclosed within a stone ring 24.7 m in diam. No other burials were found within the portions of the barrow that were excavated. The grave group accompanied the burial in a central oval pit *c.* 0.75 m across and the same in depth below the old ground surface. At the bottom of the pit lay a deposit of burnt bones, about 0.25-0.30 m thick. The grave goods lay on top of the bones, the accessory cup to one side, the remainder in a compact mass against the other wall of the pit. A quantity of wood, mostly identified as willow, was also present in the pit but it had been reduced to a pulp-like consistency and its significance is uncertain; however, in view of its position in the grave, one specimen, identified as ash, appears to have been part of the dagger hilt.

References:
Grimes 1938, 109-11, 113-17, figs 4-7
Savory 1980, 132-33 (cat no 338), figs 18, 49, pl I
Green 1980, 334 (corpus no 186)

Collection:
National Museum of Wales 38.37.1-25

139. Accessory Cup
Near Dunbar, East Lothian, Scotland

Accessory cup. Bipartite, with convex upper body and tapering sharply inwards from the shoulder to a proportionately narrow dished or omphalos base. The shoulder is perforated by 2 neat holes 30 mm apart. Ext ornamented with incised patterns bordered by single or paired horiz lines: on the upper portion, filled diamonds and herring-bone motifs; on the underside 2 bands of filled and reserved triangles, and on the omphalos base a single filled diamond. Ht 60-65 mm.

Circumstances of Discovery: Unknown.

References:
Smith, J A 1872, 195-96, fig 3
Scott, W L 1951, 81-82, fig 2.29

Collection:
National Museum of Antiquities of Scotland EC 4

140. Accessory cup
North or South Ronaldsay, Orkney, Scotland

Accessory cup of biconical form with convex upper portion, but tapering from the shoulder to a dimpled or omphalos base. The shoulder is perforated by 2 diametrically opposed pairs of holes, 25 mm apart, made before firing. Ext ornamented with incised designs bordered by groups of 2 or 3 horiz lines: on the upper portion a pair of zig-zag lines; on the underside, a pattern of opposed and interlocking filled triangles. Ht 63-68 mm.

Circumstances of Discovery: Uncertain: said to have been 'found in a mound or tumulus enclosing the foundations of an "ancient ruin" in the island of Ronaldshay, Orkney'. There are two distinct islands by this name in the Orkney group, although Anderson does specify South Ronaldsay.

References:
Smith, J A 1872, 194-95, fig 2
Anderson, J 1886, 48
Scott, W L 1951, 80-81, fig 2.7

Collection:
National Museum of Antiquities of Scotland EC 1

141. Accessory cup
West Skichen Farm, Carmyllie, Angus, Scotland

Accessory cup. Bipartite and made in the form of a miniature vase-shaped food vessel, with neatly moulded rim, concave neck, well-defined shoulder and lower body tapering to narrow dished or omphalos base. Shoulder emphasised by a narrow groove spanned by 4 diametrically opposed stops, with horiz perforations. Ext profusely decorated with small jabs applied with a pointed tool, forming chevrons from the neck to below the shoulder. Transverse and oblique jabs encircle the rim, which has been emphasised by a grooved effect produced by applying the point deeply to form a continuous line of overlapping punctulations. Ht 53 mm.

Circumstances of Discovery: Found in 1897 on the farm of West Skichen in the side of a sand and gravel knoll at a point where the surface had given way. The cup lay inverted with its base just protruding from the soil.

References:
Proc Soc Antiq Scot, 32 (1897-98), 239, fig 1

Scott, W L 1951, 81-82, fig 2.20

Collection:
National Museum of Antiquities of Scotland EE 96

METALWORK HOARDS AND RELATED MATERIAL

142. Metalwork hoard
Arreton Down, Isle of Wight, England

142.1 Flanged axe of bronze with widely expanded cutting edge and rounded butt. The flanges are cast and the sides hammered to form 3 facets. Small stop bevel. L 202 mm. SL 743.

142.2 Flanged axe of bronze with widely expanded cutting edge which has recurving tips. Rounded butt. The flanges are cast and the sides hammered to form 3 facets. Small stop bevel. L 118 mm. Unreg (ex Ipswich Museum). (Not illustrated).

142.3 Flanged axe of bronze, widely expanded cutting edge with recurving tips one of which is broken. The butt is rounded with a flat facet on it. The flanges are cast and the sides hammered to form 3 facets. Small stop bevel. L 111 mm. SL 744.

142.4 Bronze dagger. Rounded midrib, outer furrow. Surface decorated with 3 grooved lines with punched dots on them, with 5 concave lines at the base of the hilt-plate, also with punched dots. Thick pointed tip, ogival, sharpened edge. Damaged hilt-plate with one rivet-hole surviving and remains of 3 others. Omega-shaped hilt-mark. L 229 mm. Gerloff's Hammersmith type. SL 745.

142.5 Bronze dagger. Decorated with 3 ribs which converge towards the tip. Thick, pointed tip and ogival, bevelled edge. Curved hilt with 3 rivet-holes retaining the rivets. L 240 mm. Sproughton type. 1908. 5-14.1. This is the dagger previously thought to be from Sproughton which gives its name to the type.

142.6 Tanged bronze spearhead. Lozenge-sectioned midrib with slight step, edge-bevelled blade. Rectangular-sectioned tang with broken rivet-hole at base. L 207 mm. Needham no 36. SL 747.

142.7 Tanged bronze spearhead. Rounded midrib. Edge-bevelled blade. Tang with dished faces and triple-broken off. L 201 mm. Needham no 37. SL 748.

142.8 Tanged bronze spearhead. Keeled midrib. Edge-bevelled blade. Tang with dished faces and triple-faceted sides. Rivet-hole at base with rivet still present. Base slightly bent. L 255 mm. Needham no 38. WG 2075.

142.9 Tanged bronze spearhead. Lozenge-sectioned midrib with 4 grooves outside it, 2 outer furrows and an edge bevel. Blade edge badly notched and tip slightly bent. Tang with rounded faces and dished sides and broken rivet-hole at base. L 249 mm. Needham no 41. 56.6-27.43.

142.10 Tanged bronze spearhead. Lozenge-sectioned midrib with 3 grooves outside it. Edge-bevelled blade. Tang with slightly dished faces and triple-faceted sides. Rivet-hole in end of tang. L 218 mm. Needham no 40. 56.6-27.44.

142.11 Tanged bronze spearhead. Lozenge-sectioned midrib with 4 grooves outside it and an edge bevel. Double arc of pointillé decoration across base of the blade. Rectangular-sectioned tang with rounded corners. Broken rivet-hole at base. L 262 mm. Needham no 39. SL 746.

142.12 Socketed bronze spearhead. Lozenge-sectioned midrib with 4 grooves outside it and an edge bevel. Base of blade enclosed by concave moulding with 3 grooves below. Oval socket with 4 grooves, transverse peg-hole and pair of bossed mock rivets. L 216 mm. Needham no 45. WG 2074.

142.13 Tanged bronze spearhead, originally collared. Lozenge-sectioned midrib, bevelled edges. Rectangular-sectioned tang with rivet-hole. Originally there was a separate collar and a rivet. The collar was round and the upper end 'V'-shaped. Both areas were decorated with incised lines and the surface was decorated with 5 pairs of bossed mock rivets, each with pointillé decoration below. L 245 mm. Needham no 44/69. 34674. (Not illustrated).

Associations: Another axe, 2 more tanged spearheads and a socketed spearhead.

Circumstances of Discovery: Found before 1735 c. 0.3 m below the ground surface during marl extraction. The pieces were arranged in rows with the axes on top of the spearheads.

References:
Britton 1963, 286-89, 317-18
Gerloff 1975, 133, no 221, 134, nos 223-24, pl 21
Needham 1979, 28-29, nos 36-46

Collection:
British Museum 56.6–27.43-44; 1908.5–14.1; WG 2074-75; SL 743-48; unreg (ex Ipswich Museum) Manchester Museum 34674

143. Metalwork hoard
Auchingoul, Banffshire, Scotland

143.1   Halberd of unalloyed copper; straight-sided almost symmetrical blade with well-developed midrib, tapering towards rounded point. Curving heel with no rivet-holes. L 256 mm. DJ 37.

143.2   Halberd of unalloyed copper; slightly asymmetrical blade with well-developed midrib; the sides, one ogival, one badly damaged, taper towards rounded point; edges bevelled. Straight hafting mark linking angular shoulders; 5 rivet-holes in curving heel. L 272 mm. DJ 38.

143.3   Halberd of unalloyed copper; nearly symmetrical blade with low midrib and slightly curving sides tapering to rounded point; edges bevelled. Arched heel with no rivet-holes. L 280 mm. DJ 39.

143.4   Halberd of unalloyed copper; slightly asymmetrical blade with one straight, one slightly curving side tapering from angular shoulder towards rounded point; well-developed midrib and margins of blade ornamented with grooves. No rivets in slightly arched heel, now damaged. L 293 mm. DJ 40.

Associations: The original find consisted of 7 or 8 halberds, but 3 or 4 were subsequently lost about the farmyard.

Circumstances of Discovery: Found during ploughing in Autumn 1939 in a field on a low terrace of the River Deveron about 0.4 km SE of the farmstead of Mains of Auchingoul, Inverkeithny, Banffshire.

References:
Edwards 1941, 208-09, pl XLIX
Coles, J M 1969, 37, fig 31.1-4; 104
Walker 1972, 76, fig 2.4-7; 115-16, Appendix XII, no 7

Collection:
National Museum of Antiquities of Scotland DJ 37-40

144. Metalwork hoard
Auchnacree Lodge, Fern, Angus, Scotland

144.1   Flat axe of bronze, with moderately expanded cutting edge, defective on one side, and slightly rounded butt. L 146 mm. Schmidt & Burgess' Migdale type. DQ 256.

144.2   Flat axe of bronze with expanded cutting edge, incomplete owing to damage; slightly rounded butt. L 137 mm. Migdale type. DQ 257.

144.3   Cutting edge of broken flat axe of bronze with slightly expanded blade. L 68 mm. Probably Migdale type. DQ 258.

144.4   Flat dagger of bronze with long broad tongue-shaped blade and arched heel, with indentations marking the locations of 9-11 rivet-holes or notches, only one of them now intact. Faintly bevelled edges. Traces of arched edge of the hilt-plate clearly visible. L 166 mm. Gerloff's Milston type. DQ 259.

144.5   Flat dagger/knife of bronze, with bevelled edges concave as a result of heavy whetting and 5 rivet-holes in sub-triangular butt. Arched line of hilt-plate visible. L 99 mm. East Kennet variant of Milston type. DQ 260.

144.6   Bronze bar armlet made from a solid rod of oval to D-shaped cross-section bent round so that the ends almost butt against each other. Diam 75 mm. DQ 261.

Associations: Found together with another complete flat axe, the butt-end of a broken flat axe, and a second butt-jointed armlet of D-shaped cross-section, all of which remain in private hands.

Circumstances of Discovery: Found in 1921 in the corner of a field near Auchnacree Lodge, while covering a potato pit with earth. The objects lay about 0.61 m below the surface. The site lies on the N side of a glen, at a height of about 213 m OD, with extensive views over Strathmore.

References:
Callander 1922, 351-56
Inventaria Archaeologica, GB 27
Coles, J M 1969, 65, fig 49.1-8, 103
Gerloff 1975, nos 60, 65, pls 5, 6, 43.D
Schmidt & Burgess 1981, nos 76, 104, 127, 278, 279, pls 7, 9, 11, 22

Collection:
National Museum of Antiquities of Scotland DQ 256-261

145. Metalwork hoard
Colleonard Farm, Banffshire, Scotland

145.1 Flat axe of bronze with expanded cutting edge and slightly rounded butt. Bevelled sides and punched 'rain' pattern decoration on both faces. L 131 mm. Schmidt & Burgess' decorated variant of Migdale type. DA 21.

145.2 Flat axe of bronze closely comparable to 145.1 and possibly from the same mould. L 134 mm. Decorated variant of Migdale type. DA 22.

145.3 Flat axe of bronze with slightly expanded cutting edge, rounded butt. Sides slightly hammer-flanged and punched 'rain' pattern decoration on two-thirds of each face. L 170 mm. Scrabo Hill type. DA 24.

145.4 Flat axe of bronze with expanded cutting edge and rounded butt. Bevelled sides and broad shallow fluting on both faces. All 4 lateral edges have a row of U-shaped notches. L 149 mm. Decorated variant of Migdale type. DA 20.

145.5 Flat axe of bronze with widely expanded cutting edge and apparently a rounded butt, although corrosion damage precludes certainty. Bevelled sides and broad shallow fluting on both faces. All 4 lateral edges have a row of shallow U-shaped notches. L 142 mm. Decorated variant of Migdale type. DA 19.

145.6 Fragment of flat axe of bronze lacking cutting edge and butt. Square sides and broad shallow fluting on each face. L 85 mm. Decorated variant of Migdale type. DA 25.

145.7 Fragment of flat axe of bronze with expanded cutting edge but lacking the butt. Sides slightly hammer-flanged but undecorated. L 81 mm. Migdale type. DA 23.

145.8 Pottery vessel of coarse brown ware. Conical in form with marginally splayed foot and inturned and int bevelled rim, part of which was missing at the time of discovery. Notching occurs on the rim, below which there is a row of irregular impressions. Slightly above the middle of the vessel there is an obliquely slashed cordon above which is a roughly incised zig-zag pattern which does not encircle the whole pot. Ht 182 mm. EA 18.

Circumstances of Discovery: Found during trenching operations in 1857 in a field N of Colleonard Farm sloping down towards the sea. The pot was *c.* 0.3 m below the surface, standing upright and protected by two vert stone slabs. The axes were packed inside the vessel with their cutting edges uppermost. The trenching operations may also have revealed a destroyed stone circle in the same field.

References:
Banffshire Journal, 24 February 1857, 5
Inventaria Archaeologica, GB 29
Schmidt & Burgess 1981, nos 74, 193-95, 199, 202, 342, pls 6, 16, 29, 132D

7.32 *Metalwork hoard from Gavel Moss, Renfrewshire (146)*

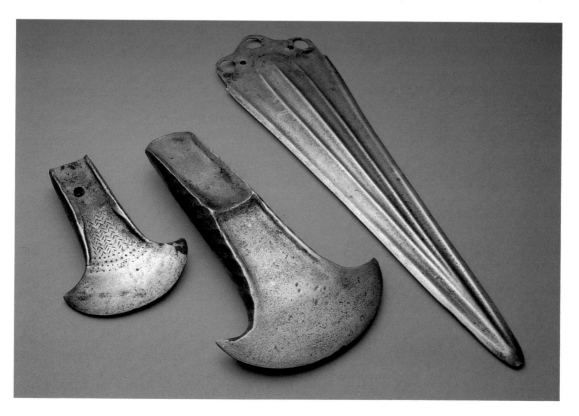

References:
Scott, J G 1951
Invertaria Archaeologica, GB 28
Britton 1963, 319 & pl XIX
Coles, J M 1969, 107-08, 67, fig 51
Gerloff 1975, no 225, pls 21 & 52A
Schmidt & Burgess 1981, nos 402-03, pl 33

Collection:
National Museum of Antiquities of Scotland DA 19-25; EA 18

Collection:
Glasgow Art Gallery & Museum A5920a-c

146. Metalwork hoard
Gavel Moss, Renfrewshire, Scotland

147. Metalwork hoard
Migdale, Creich, Sutherland, Scotland

146.1 Bronze flanged axe. The butt has been partly sawn-off, and there is a modern drill-hole through the face. Surviving sides diverge, gradually at first, then sharply to meet the widely splayed crescentic cutting edge. The margins of each face have low cast flanges and are ornamented with 3 vertical rows of 'ripple' pattern, the faces themselves being decorated with 10 vertical rows of incised chevrons above 4 curving rows of irregularly punched dots. The axe was mounted in a modern wooden haft while in private hands: periodic cleaning up to the edge of the haft accounts for the visible difference in surface condition and texture between blade and butt portions. L 153 mm. Schmidt & Burgess' Balbirnie type. A5920c.

146.2 Bronze flanged axe. The sides diverge from the curving butt, at first gradually and then sharply to meet the widely splayed crescentic cutting edges. The margins of each face have low cast flanges, ornamented with a cable or 'ripple' pattern, and on both surfaces there is a prominent cast stop-ridge. Variations in texture can be accounted for by differential cleaning (as in 146.1). L 95 mm. Balbirnie type. A5920b.

146.3 Large riveted bronze midrib dagger. The lobed heel rises from sharp offsets at the corners of the blade, and contains 3 large rivet-holes for plug-rivets, none of which survive. Beside these are 2 small holes, drilled in modern times in the course of fitting a hilt, in which the dagger was kept while in private hands. Just below them is an original hilt-mark with a semi-circular opening (showing as a darker area) and this should be distinguished from the straight line that links the corners of the blade. The latter is an effect of cleaning up to the lower edge of the modern hilt. The blade itself has an elongated triangular outline: on each face, and originally springing from the rounded opening in the hilt, is a triple midrib, whose lines converge towards the rounded tip of the blade, there to meet with 2 slight marginal ribs which run the length of the sides. L 258 mm. Gerloff's Sproughton type. A5920a.

Associations: There was a family tradition that 'armour' was also ploughed up with the find but was scrapped owing to its poor condition.

Circumstances of Discovery: Found together during ploughing in 1790, and thereafter preserved by descendants of the original owner.

147.1 Flat axe of bronze with expanded cutting edge and rounded butt: one face tin-enriched, the other much corroded. L 152 mm. Schmidt & Burgess' Migdale type. DQ 335.

147.2 Selection of composite tubular beads (not including fragments) of which there were originally at least 40 in the hoard: the beads consist of rectangular pieces of thin sheet bronze which have been folded into tubes around longitudinally perforated wooden cores. Portions of the cores survive in several cases. The beads may fall into as many as 5 groups by size but their incompleteness often leaves their original length uncertain. The beads certainly range from small examples with a diam of 4 mm and lengths of 18 and 24 mm (3 intact beads) to large examples with a diam of 6.5 mm and lengths from 33-35 mm (9 intact beads). However, the majority (22 intact beads) fall into a medium size group, with a diam of 5 mm and lengths from 21-28 mm. Stevenson has suggested that the beads may have been strung as a multi-strand necklace in a manner comparable to the jet/shale necklaces, whose component beads are also graduated by size. the different strands may have been separated by spacer-plates, of which 147.17 may represent the sole surviving example in the hoard. L 18-35 mm.

147.3 Cone of thin sheet bronze with an overlapping joint down one side and 2 small opposed perforations just above the edge. Damaged. Diam 23.5 mm. DQ 353.

147.4 Cone of thin sheet bronze with part of one perforation surviving; edge and point damaged. Diam 26.5 mm. DQ 354.

147.5 Cone of thin sheet bronze, beaten out to shape, with remains of 2 perforations; damaged around edge. Diam 22.5 mm. DQ 355.

147.6 Fragment of cone of thin sheet bronze; part of surviving edge has remains of perforation. L 22-23 mm. DQ 356.

147.7 Fragment of cone of thin sheet bronze, with remains of perforation on one edge. L 18 mm. DQ 357.

147.8 Part of basket earring of sheet bronze: a narrow hook for attachment expands into a thin broken plate just starting to curve at its lower edge. Glossy outer surface. L (surviving) 28 mm. DQ 358.

147.9-147.14 Bronze bar armlets made from D-shaped or oval sectioned rods with square-cut ends forming tightly fitting butt-joints. Ext diam given in each case.

147.9 D-shaped section. Diam 72 by 68 mm. DQ 338.

147.10 D-shaped section, ends unevenly cut. Diam 79 by 74 mm. DQ 339.

147.11 Slightly oval section. Diam 79 by 75 mm. DQ 340.

147.12 D-shaped section; glossy surface. Diam 81 by 75 mm. DQ 341.

147.13 Oval section; coppery colour; corroded around butt-joint. Diam 79 by 78 mm. DQ 342.

147.14 D-shaped section; at the joint, the ends have sprung and now overlap by *c.* 5 mm. Diam 74 by 70 mm. DQ 343.

147.15-147.16 Pair of bronze armlets made of strips of cast bronze with triple horiz mouldings around the ext, their square-cut ends bent together to form butt-joints. Between the moulded ridges in the intervening grooves are short closely-set vert lines, and round the outer edges, faint slanting nicks. 147.15 Diam 74 by 72 mm. DQ 336. 147.16 Butt-joint slightly out of alignment. Diam 73.25 by 72 mm. DQ 337.

147.17 Broken strip of thin sheet bronze bent into a rounded end so that the 2 faces lie parallel, 4 mm apart. Upper face decorated with a row of transverse lenticular bosses punched up from behind, outlined by and set against a background of traced lines. Along each margin, small bosses punched up from the back of the sheet. 2 pinholes in the undecorated lower surface and the overall shape of the fragment suggest that the complete strip originally bound a core (perhaps of wood, as with the tubular beads 147.2). Tentatively reconstructed as surviving part of a metal-bound wooden spacer-plate for a composite necklace. Total surviving L 57 mm. DQ 352.

147.18 Broken piece of sheet bronze, only the straight long edge being original; one surface tin-enriched. Possibly part of a second basket earring. L 42.5 mm. DQ 359.

147.19 Large conical V-bored jet/shale button, with very faint traces of marking-out lines for a cruciform design on upper surface; on the underside, an irregular encircling groove runs close to the edge. Diam 45 mm. DQ 360.

147.20 Slightly domed jet/shale button with very black and glossy upper surface; the V-boring has been broken through. Diam 38 mm. DQ 361.

147.21 V-bored jet/shale button with faint marking-out lines for a cruciform design on the upper surface; on the underside, irregular encircling groove runs close to the edge. Diam 35 mm. DQ 362.

147.22 Damaged V-bored jet/shale button; matt surfaces. Diam 30.5 mm. DQ 363.

147.23 V-bored jet/shale button, the upper surface rising into a pronounced boss; matt surface. Diam 28.5 mm. DQ 364.

147.24 Incomplete jet/shale button, damaged on lower surface and around much of circumference; only base of V-boring visible; matt surfaces. Estimated diam 33 mm. DQ 365.

Circumstances of Discovery: Hoard found in blasting the top of a granite knoll situated on the moor at the W end of Loch Migdale, on the Skibo Estate (owned by Andrew Carnegie).

References:
Anderson, J 1901
Stevenson 1956
Inventaria Archaeologica, GB 26
Britton 1963, 314, no 16
Coles, J M 1969, 50, fig 39, 108-109
Schmidt & Burgess 1981, no 157, pl 13, 133D

Collection:
National Museum of Antiquities of Scotland DQ 335-65

148. Metalwork hoard
Sluie, Moray, Scotland

148.1 Bronze flat axe. Expanded cutting edge, curved butt with flattened facet (? modern). Rounded sides. Tinned surface. L 149 mm. Schmidt & Burgess' Migdale type. DA 32.

148.2 Bronze flat axe. Expanded cutting edge worn asymmetrically. Curved and flattened butt. Triple-bevelled sides. Tinned surface. L 149 mm. Migdale type. DA 33.

148.3   Copper halberd. Rounded midrib leading to broad flattened area with slight furrow and edge bevel, broken tip, straight sharpish edge, curved butt with 4 rivet holes. L 276 mm. Ó Riordáin's type 6. DJ 4.

Circumstances of Discovery: Found in a cist on the Moor of Sluie in 1818. Ó Riordáin and others have cast doubt on the association of the axes and halberd, but Wilson clearly states that they were found together.

References:
Wilson 1851, 254
Smith, J A & Macadam 1872, 431
Ó Riordáin 1936, 202
Inventaria Archaeologica, GB 30
Schmidt & Burgess 1981, nos 92 & 156, pls 8, 13, 133B

Collection:
National Museum of Antiquities of Scotland DA 32-33; DJ 4

149.   Metalwork hoard
Knocknague, Co Galway, Ireland

149.1   Copper awl. Small, rectangular-sectioned with 2 sharp points, one slightly bent. Thickest part towards one end. L 46 mm. 1874:41.

149.2   Copper awl. Rectangular-sectioned with 2 sharp points. Thickest in centre. L 54 mm. 1874:42.

149.3   Copper awl. Large. Thick, square-sectioned with stout points. Thickest part slightly to one end. L 84 mm. 1874:43.

149.4   Flat axe of copper. Expanded cutting edge which is blunt and unsharpened. Quite thick flat butt. Sides have small, cast, undeveloped flanges. L 124 mm. Harbison's Lough Ravel type. 1874:37.

149.5   Flat axe of copper. Expanded cutting edge with sharpened blade. Slight bevel at end of body. Thickish flat butt and flat unmodified sides. L 110 mm. Lough Ravel type. 1874:38.

149.6   Flat axe of copper, miniature. Expanded cutting edge with sharpened blade. Slight bevel at end of body. Thinnish flat butt and flat unmodified sides. L 71 mm. Lough Ravel type, Ballybeg subtype. 1874:39.

149.7   Copper dagger/knife blade. Short flat blade with edge bevel, sharp edges and rounded tip. Large central tang at heel with half rivet-hole on either side. Shadow of omega-shaped hilt-plate at base of the blade. The edges of the tang are damaged and roughened and near its tip, the

blade is damaged with an undulating deformation. L 112 mm. Harbison's Knocknague type. 1874:40.

Circumstances of Discovery: Found in a bog in 1874.

References:
Coffey 1901, 276, pl 32.44-48
Harbison 1969a, 7, no 4
Harbison 1969b, 13, no 110-11, 20, no 382

Collection:
National Museum of Ireland 1874:37-43

150.   Bronze 'rapier'
Kimberley, Norfolk, England

Bronze 'rapier'. Lentoid section with expansions by the edges forming one side of the edge bevel. Within the edge bevel is a slightly raised dagger-shaped area which terminates in a line which runs through the tip. The blade edges and the tip are eroded on both sides. The hilt-plate is thin and flat and has shouldered edges. No rivet-holes. The blade is damaged near the hilt-plate. L 339 mm.

Circumstances of Discovery: Unknown.

References:
Greenwell 1902, 3-4
Butler & Sarfatij 1971, 309, fn 2

Collection:
British Museum WG 2062

151.   Bronze axe
? Banffshire, Scotland

Flat axe of bronze with expanded cutting edge and flattened butt. Both faces have been decorated with punched lines forming 7 rows of chevrons ending with a fringe of vertical strokes. Modern abrasion at butt end. L 154 mm. Schmidt & Burgess' decorated variant of Migdale type.

Circumstances of Discovery: ? Isolated find. Purchased in 1887 with material from Banffshire.

References:
Proc Soc Antiq Scot (1886-87), 288, no 12
Coles, J M 1969, 81
Walker 1972, 97, Appendix I, b
Schmidt & Burgess 1981, no 198, pl 16

Collection:
National Museum of Antiquities of Scotland DA 55

152. Bronze axe
Cornhill-on-Tweed, Berwickshire, Scotland

Axe of bronze with expanded and marginally recurved cutting edge and slightly rounded butt. Sides hammer-flanged, a process that has partly obscured the punched 'rain' pattern decoration on one side of one of the faces. The axe is decorated on both faces: at the butt end, the ornament consists of 5 lines of oblique dashes, but extending from the median bevel towards the blade there are over a dozen closely-set lines, terminating in a dashed zig-zag line at a point corresponding with the lower end of the flanges. L 146 mm. Schmidt & Burgess' Falkland type.

Circumstances of Discovery: Isolated find.

References:
Proc Soc Antiq Scot, 80 (1945-46), 151, no 6
Coles, J M 1969, 10, fig 8.2, 81
Schmidt & Burgess 1981, no 324, pl 28

Collection:
National Museum of Antiquities of Scotland DC 126

153. Bronze axe
Near Eildon, Roxburghshire, Scotland

Flat axe of bronze with expanded cutting edge, defective on one side, and narrow rounded butt; sides hammer-flanged. Profuse punched 'rain' pattern decoration on both faces although one surface now very badly corroded. L 179 mm. Schmidt & Burgess' Glenalla type.

Associations: Said to have been found with a spearhead (NMAS: DG 41 — *Nat Mus Antiq Scot Catalogue*, 1892) but this association is not documented elsewhere and must be treated as suspect. The spearhead is of a late bronze age type.

Circumstances of Discovery: Said to have been found under a large cairn near Eildon, Roxburghshire.

References:
Evans, J 1881, 57
Coles, J M 1969, 13, fig 10.5, 85, 104
Schmidt & Burgess 1981, no 318, pl 27

Collection:
National Museum of Antiquities of Scotland DA 9

154. Bronze axe
Lawhead, Lanarkshire, Scotland

Exceptionally large flat axe of bronze with narrow rounded butt and widely expanded cutting edge. Weight over 2000 g. L 348 mm. Schmidt & Burgess' Nairn type — a small group with the basic form of Migdale type axes but characterised by their much greater than average size.

Circumstances of Discovery: Isolated find, discovered during the digging of a drain on Lawhead Farm on the S side of the Pentland Hills, near Edinburgh.

References:
Proc Soc Antiq Scot, 7 (1866-68), 105-06
Evans, J 1881, 57, fig 20
Coles, J M 1969, 7, fig 5.1, 83
Schmidt & Burgess 1981, no 246, pl 20

Collection:
National Museum of Antiquities of Scotland DA 7

155. Copper halberd
Poltalloch Estates, Argyll, Scotland

Copper halberd. Rectangular midrib, flattened area beside this rib, with single groove and ridge, then furrow, and finally edge bevel. Rounded tip, relatively straight curved heel with 3 rivet-holes. L 267 mm. Ó Riordáin's type 4.

Circumstances of Discovery: Isolated find. Traditionally from Dunadd, but there is no documentary support for this.

References:
Ó Riordáin 1936, 311
Campbell & Sandeman 1962, 117

Collection:
National Museum of Antiquities of Scotland HPO 18

156. Copper halberd
Whiteleys, Wigtownshire, Scotland

Copper halberd. Flat midrib with deep groove and ridge, edge bevelled. Ogival blade. Shoulders at junction of blade and hilt-plate. 4 rivet-holes roughly in a square, rivets surviving. L 316 mm. Ó Riordáin's combination of types 2 & 5.

Circumstances of Discovery: Isolated find. Found in 1866 in a peat moss.

References:
Proc Soc Antiq Scot, 7 (1866-68), 423
Ó Riordáin 1936, 195

Collection:
National Museum of Antiquities of Scotland DJ 1

157. Bronze spearhead
Crawford Priory, Fife, Scotland

Tanged bronze spearhead. Lozenge-sectioned midrib with 5 grooves outside it, 4 of them closely set, and an edge bevel. Midrib filled with pointillé decoration. Rectangular tang with 2 opposed indentations near head, rivet-hole at base with surviving rivet. L 264 mm.

Circumstances of Discovery: Isolated find. Found *c.* 1873 near Walton Farm.

References:
Abercromby 1894
Needham 1979, 23, no 19

Collection:
National Museum of Antiquities of Scotland L.1974.1

158. Bronze spearhead
Whitehaugh Moss, Ayrshire, Scotland

Tanged bronze spearhead. Lozenge-sectioned midrib with 4-5 closely set grooves and an edge bevel. Rectangular-sectioned tang with rivet-hole at base and small nicks on either side. Base of tang slightly twisted. L 272 mm.

Circumstances of Discovery: Isolated find. Found 'some years' before 1884 *c.* 1.9 m down in Whitehaugh Moss, projecting from the side of a drain.

References:
Macdonald 1884
Needham 1979, 33, no 60

Collection:
National Museum of Antiquities of Scotland DG 88

COMPARATIVE MATERIAL FROM CONTINENTAL EUROPE

159. Beaker grave group
Lunteren, Gelderland, Netherlands

159.1 Flint arrowhead, triangular. L 24 mm.

159.2 Flint arrowhead, barbed and tanged. Broad tang. L 21 mm.

159.3 Flint arrowhead, hollow-based. L 29 mm.

159.4 Flint arrowhead, hollow-based, narrow. L 27 mm.

159.5 Flint arrowhead, hollow-based, broad. L 28 mm.

159.6 Flint arrowhead, barbed and tanged. Squared barbs one of which has broken off. L 31 mm.

159.7 Flint axe with partially polished surface. Bevelled cutting edge, thick irregular butt and roughly flattened sides. L 74 mm.

159.8 Cushion stone. Large and rectangular with 1 rough, 1 pecked and 4 polished surfaces, 1 with a shallow groove in it. L 145 mm.

159.9 Cushion stone. Small and rectangular with 6 polished surfaces. L 95 mm.

159.10 Stone hammer. Roughly rectangular elongated shape, with 4 polished facets. L 95 mm.

159.11 Whetstone. Elongated, flat rectangular shape. One surface has a smoothed, polished area with arcing grooves on it. L 186 mm.

159.12 Stone wristguard. Half of a flat wristguard with slightly rounded edges and slightly curving upper surface. 2 perforations remaining of the original 4. L 51 mm.

159.13 Copper awl of rectangular section with slight expansion near the middle and 2 pointed ends. L 78 mm.

159.14 Beaker. Int bevelled rim decorated ext with comb stamping to form 4 zones. The neck has 5 horiz bands of decoration each defined by 2 horiz lines. The topmost band consists of short vert strokes and those below it are a double row of running chevrons, short vert strokes, a triple row of running chevrons and a row of herring-bone decoration. The second zone consists of a series of undecorated panels with a running chevron inside which are bounded to the left and right by 2 vert bands infilled with chevrons or short horiz strokes separated by double lines and a single line of herring-bone decoration. The third zone has 4 horiz bands separated by double horiz lines and infilled with alternate bands of triple running chevrons and short vert strokes.

The fourth zone repeats the panelling of the second zone and the whole is completed by 3 horiz lines and vert strokes which reach the base. Ht 181 mm. Veluwe type.

Associations: Beaker of Veluwe type.

Circumstances of Discovery: Found in 1939 by Ruyter and excavated by Bursch. The objects came from a grave pit underneath a barrow and formed 2 concentrations within the grave: a. 159.1, 159.2, 159.7, 159.8, 159.13 & 159.14 and b. 159.3, 159.4, 159.5, 159.6, 169.9, 159.10, 159.11, 159.12 and the other Veluwe beaker. A second grave under the barrow contained a flint chisel, 7 flint arrowheads and a wristguard. A much later grave was set into the barrow, which was the more southerly of the 2 barrows at Lunteren.

References:
Butler & van der Waals 1966, 63-68, 125-31

Collection:
Rijksmuseum van Oudheden, Leiden 1958/56 1-22

160. ?Beaker grave group
Soesterberg, Utrecht, Netherlands

160.1 Cushion stone, rectangular with 2 pecked surfaces, 2 pecked and slightly polished surfaces and 2 polished surfaces, 1 of which is flat and the other flat in the centre with convex edges. L 142 mm. 7505.

160.2 Stone hammer, double headed, oval in section with a broad groove round the centre. The surfaces are pecked and slightly polished and the 2 hammer surfaces are convex. L 98 mm. 7506.

160.3 Stone hammer. Made from a broken oval-sectioned axe. The broken surface has been flaked and the working surface is flat and oval. L 82 mm. 7507.

160.4 2 boar's tusks, unworked. L (of chord) 79 & 77 mm. 7508 a-b.

Associations: Wristguard with 4 perforations; 'pot decorated with stripes and lines', perhaps a beaker.

Circumstances of Discovery: Found in 1942 during excavation of a sandhill to realign a railway. The objects were found 1.25 m below a large stone (*c.* 1 m diam).

References:
Butler & van der Waals 1966, 132-33

Collection:
Centraal Museum der Gemeente Utrecht (Museum van het Provinciaal Utrechts Genootschap voor Kunsten en Wetenschappen) 7505-8b

161. Gold neck-ring or diadem
Arlon, Luxembourg, Belgium

Neck-ring or diadem of gold composed of a circular-sectioned rod tapering at each end to spade-shaped expanded terminals with a gap between the terminals. Diam 125 mm. Taylor suggests this may be a blank for a lunula.

Circumstances of Discovery: Isolated find. Found in 1905 while digging up ground east of Arlon.

References:
De Loë 1906
De Loë 1931, 95, fig 42, 119-21
Butler 1956, 59-60
Taylor 1968, 259-61

Collection:
Musées Royaux d'Art et d'Histoire, Brussels

162. Gold neck-ring or diadem
Bennekom, Gelderland, Netherlands

Gold neck-ring now broken and comprising 2 lengths of twisted rectangular-sectioned wire with expanded oar-shaped terminals, each of which has embossed and repoussé decoration comprising dots around the outer edge and within them, 2 lines which enclose 3 more lines all of which join to form a triangle at the end of the terminal. L 192 & 202 mm. Originally the 2 pieces were joined and had an amber bead in the centre.

Associations: Veluwe beaker and an amber bead.

Circumstances of Discovery: Found *c.* 1890 in a barrow removed during gravel extraction. Normally interpreted as a grave group.

References:
Glasbergen 1956b
Butler 1956

Collection:
Biologisch-Archaeologisch Instituut, Groningen (on loan to Gemeentemuseum, Arnhem)

163. Dagger grave group
'La Motta', Lannion, Côtes-du-Nord, Brittany, France

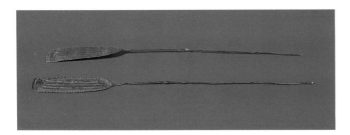

7.33 a. Gold neck-ring or diadem from Bennekom, Gelderland, Netherlands b. the Veluwe beaker (162)

163.1 7 flint arrowheads of 'long ogival' type, with convex sides, long drooping barbs, and long thin tapering tangs. Probably all the work of the same hand. L 37-47 mm.

163.2 Whetstone. Elongated oval whetstone of metamorphic crystalline schist with hour-glass perforation at one end; flattened oval cross-section; the slightly concave longitudinal profile and numerous striations indicate that it had been used prior to burial. L 367 mm.

163.3 Bronze sword. The curved heel has a small central languette or tongue. 4 of the original 6 rivets are still in place but the outermost 1 on each side has been torn. The blade is flat in cross-section and has a maximum thickness of only 3 mm: 2 sets of 3-4 lateral grooves follow the sinuous profile of its edges. Its present distorted shape is not original. L 492 mm.

163.4 Bronze dagger. Gently curving heel with 6 rivet-holes 2 of which retain peg-rivets, and just below them, traces of an omega-shaped hilt-mark; triangular blade with flattened cross-section and hollow-ground edges. L 108 mm.

163.5 Bronze dagger. Gently curving heel with central languette and an arrangement of 6 rivet-holes, retaining 2 intact peg-rivets and part of a third. Below them, traces of an omega-shaped hilt-mark. Triangular blade with flattened cross-section ornamented with 2 pairs of lateral grooves. Traces of sheath surviving as corrosion products. L 245 mm.

163.6 Bronze dagger. Gently curving heel, languette broken since discovery, with an arrangement of 6 rivet-holes; 4 rivets still in place, the outer ones on each side having been torn out. Below these, an omega-shaped hilt-mark. Triangular blade with flattened cross-section decorated with lateral grooves. Traces of composite sheath of wood and skin. L 222 mm.

163.7 Bronze dagger. Slightly angular heel with short rounded languette or tang, and an arrangement of 6 rivet-holes; 4 peg-rivets still in place, the outer ones on each

side having been torn out. Traces of wooden hilt around rivets and below them an omega-shaped hilt-mark. Triangular blade with a prominent tapering midrib, and 2 pairs of lateral grooves parallel to the sides. L 220 mm.

163.8 Bronze dagger. Gently curving heel with trapezoidal languette and arrangement of 6 rivet-holes, with all rivets in place. Below these, traces of an omega-shaped hilt-mark. The blade has a slightly thickened cross-section and ogival outline which is followed by 2 pairs of lateral grooves. Very fine condition. L 248 mm.

163.9 Bronze dagger. Very badly corroded; probably originally an arrangement of 6 rivet-holes but only 2 survive. Slightly thickened blade appears to have had lateral grooves. Probably originally similar in form to 163.8. L 245 mm.

163.10 Bronze flat axe. Slightly expanded cutting-edge and gently rounded butt. Low flanges run along the margins of each face. Differential patina suggests the axe had been hafted; traces of bovine hair preserved in the corrosion products. L 150 mm.

163.11 Bronze flat axe. Similar in form to 163.10. L 113 mm.

163.12 Gold 'box'-like pendant. Sub-rectangular pendant

with concave sides and convex surfaces made from 2 very thin sheets of gold folded and fitted together after the fashion of a miniature box, with 2 neat perforations for suspension. The int is filled with a simple jeweller's pitch, composed of roughly equal proportions of pine or fir resin mixed with powdered stone. The pitch would have acted as a former during the construction of the box, as a support during the application of the ornament and as reinforcement for the finished article, as the gold sheet was only 0.02 mm thick. After polishing, the outer surface was decorated, using a rounded point. On the base, there is a single impressed line parallel to each edge: this also serves a functional purpose by 'crimping' the 2 sheets of gold together. The upper surface is decorated with a line parallel to each edge, bordered int by a zig-zag along the longer sides and by a single large chevron at each end. L 6.8 mm.

Circumstances of Discovery: The tumulus of 'La Motta' was excavated in 1939 by Professor A E van Giffen. The barrow is situated on the edge of a plateau overlooking a river valley near the N coast of Brittany. It was 4.6 m high and would have been a conspicuous landmark in all directions. Excavation revealed, near the centre of a mound of clayey loam, an inner cairn protecting a carefully built cist, capped by a large slab of granite. The grave lay E of the centre of the barrow, orientated NW-SE and was composed of slabs of local schist set onto a large floor slab at the bottom of a prepared pit quarried in the natural rock. The careful construction of the cist had prevented infiltration of earth and stones, and when it was opened the surviving grave goods lay around the floor more or less in their original positions. No bones had survived. The sword (163.3) had been placed on a rectangular stone slab alongside and near the centre of the SW wall; the flint arrowheads (163.1) were also found by this edge. The daggers (163.4-9) were grouped in a rough circle opposite, but as with the remainder of the artefacts there appeared to be no obvious pattern in their layout. 2 of the daggers partly overlay each other and had in turn been partly covered by a rectangular stone slab. The larger axe (163.10) lay near the W corner, the smaller (163.11) near the diagonally opposite corner. The whetstone (163.2) was in the N corner parallel to the NE wall. Finally, the unique gold pendant (163.12) was recovered from an air-space beneath a gap in the floor slabs, suggesting that it must either have been deliberately deposited or been dislodged at some point in the process of interment.

References:
Butler & Waterbolk 1974
Taylor 1980, 47-48
Briard 1984, 218-220, fig 219

Collection:
Biologisch-Archaeologisch Instituut, Groningen.

164. Dagger fragment
Cosqueric, Priziac, Morbihan, Brittany, France

Fragment of bronze dagger blade with prominent tapering midrib and traces of triple lateral grooves. On either side of the midrib, and probably originally arranged in pairs, there have been inlaid a series of roundels of gold or electrum, of which 5 are still in place out of an original 8 on the fragment. L 97 mm.

Associations: Bronze metalwork, including a large and a small flat axe; a 'sword'; 3 almost complete dagger blades and parts of 2 others. The original contents of the grave are uncertain, however, owing to the circumstances of recovery.

Circumstances of Discovery: From a large barrow bulldozed and destroyed in 1973. Salvage excavations showed that the mound incorporated some soil brought to the site from a source *c.* 1-2 km distant.

References:
Le Roux 1975, 539
Briard 1976a, 564-65, fig 2.7
Briard 1984, 78, fig 46, 295

Collection:
Laboratoire d'Anthropologie, Université de Rennes

165. Dagger grave group
Brun-Bras, Saint-Adrien, Côtes-du-Nord, Brittany, France.

165.1 20 barbed and tanged flint arrowheads (selection from original assemblage of 45): 'short ogival' type with ogival sides, drooping squared barbs and tapering tang. L 30-37 mm.

165.2 Bronze flat axe, with low flanges along the margins of both faces. Found with traces of wooden ?haft. L 145 mm.

165.3 Small bronze dagger blade. Owing to its corroded state the original form is uncertain: as it survives, the heel has a large central languette or tang but no traces of any rivet-holes. An omega-shaped hilt-mark is visible. The triangular blade has had a prominent midrib and may have been decorated with lateral grooves. This dagger appears to have had a wooden hilt inlaid with tiny gold nails (0.3-1 mm in length); 5 roundels of gold (5-6 mm diam) were also found and these may either also have ornamented the hilt (as at Kernonen, Plouvorn) or been set into the blade (as at Cosqueric, Priziac). L 160 mm.

165.4 Bronze 'sword'. Hilt-plate badly corroded but

probably originally with an arrangement of 6 rivets. Blade with flat cross-section, ornamented with 2 lateral grooves. L 342 mm.

165.5 Silver handled cup, restored from fragments. The vessel consists of a lower portion in the form of a rounded bowl which has been riveted to an upper section with a concave profile. A flat handle would have sprung from the carination and been riveted to the outer edge of the flaring rim, which has traces of a line of pointillé decoration just below the lip. The face of the handle appears to have been similarly ornamented. Ht 122 mm.

Associations: Very fragmentary remains of the blade of a further 'sword' with traces of a composite sheath of wood and skin, and the very corroded remains of at least one other dagger dispersed around the floor of the grave. Traces of a hide 'shroud' with needle holes were also recovered.

Circumstances of Discovery: From the remains of a barrow originally 30 m in diam and 2 m high, excavated in 1974. A central cairn had covered a wooden mortuary structure 2.5 by 0.9 m, set in the subsoil and orientated E-W. Traces of a wooden box or coffin were found against the N wall of the tomb. It has been suggested that the body had been placed in the coffin with its head to the E: the cup (165.5) could have lain near the presumed position of the head, and the axe (165.2) at the feet. The bronze weapons (including 165.3-4) would then have been about waist level, with the exception of one of the 'swords' which lay outside the coffin towards the S wall of the grave. The arrowheads (165.1) lay side by side next to the weapons in a position suggesting that they had been placed in the grave in their shafts. A radiocarbon date of 1700 bc ± 35 (GrN — 7176) was obtained from the wood of the coffin.

References:
Le Roux 1975, 522-23
Briard 1978
Foltz 1978
Briard 1984, 225-26

Collection:
Laboratoire d'Anthropologie, Université de Rennes.

166. Dagger grave group
Saint-Fiacre, Melrand, Morbihan, Brittany, France

166.1 Bronze flat axe with gently curving butt and slightly expanded cutting edge; very low flanges run the length of the margin of both faces. Badly corroded. L 174 mm. 1926.131.

166.2 Bronze flat axe of similar form to 166.1, but with slightly asymmetrical cutting edge. L 156 mm. 1926.132.

166.3 Fragment of blade of bronze dagger; traces of edge bevel on one side. L 72 mm. 1926.133.

166.4 Fragment of the lower part of the blade of a bronze dagger; tapering central thickening, with traces of bevelled edges. Bent and damaged. L 88 mm. 1926.136.

166.5 Hilt and upper portion of blade of solid-hilted bronze dagger; hilt of oval cross-section with flat expanded terminal; 4 rivets arranged flush with the surface in a curve around the semi-circular opening formed by lower edge of hilt; blade corroded. L 142 mm. 1926.139.

166.6 Fragmentary dagger blade of bronze. Hilt-plate badly damaged, with traces of 4 rivet-holes surviving only as notches. Below these, there is a hilt-mark with semi-circular opening: descending from this there is a prominent midrib, tapering slightly towards the point. The blade, now badly corroded, has originally had 2 sets of double lateral grooves. L 188 mm. 1926.138.

166.7 Fragmentary dagger blade of bronze. The hilt-plate has an arched heel containing 2 rivet-holes, 1 of them now torn, the other distorted. Faint traces of a hilt-mark with semi-circular opening, with a further faint line of differential corrosion which may indicate upper edge of organic sheath. Blade with relatively flatt cross-section and bevelled edges. Badly corroded and distorted. L 143 mm. 1926.140.

166.8 Bronze dagger blade. Hilt-plate damaged, probably resulting in loss of tang or 'languette'. Rivet-holes set in gentle curve, 3 on either side of semi-circular hilt-mark: 1 complete, and parts of 2 broken peg-rivets still in place. The triangular blade has a flattened cross-section, with ground edges; both surfaces have double lateral grooves. Traces of ?skin sheath on surface of blade. Relatively good condition, consolidated by modern rivets. L 181 mm. 1926.141.

166.9 Lower part of the blade of a bronze dagger, with traces of 2 sets of double lateral grooves, converging near point. Blade virtually flat in cross-section but no original edges survive. Blackish substance adhering to blade possibly represents traces of skin sheath. L 150 mm. 1926.142.

166.10 Part of a bronze dagger blade: hilt-plate damaged, but faint traces of hilt-mark visible. Lateral grooves visible on corroded blade, adhering to which there is a blackish substance, possibly the remains of a sheath. L 197 mm. 1926.134.

166.11 2 bronze barbed and tanged arrowheads, now in fragmentary condition: the more complex example has 1 surviving drooping, squared barb and a thin tapering tang.

L 20 mm & 15 mm. These are the only examples of the type known from Brittany. 1926.144-45.

166.12 Amber pendant. Sub-rectangular in shape with concave sides; a perforation has been bored diagonally from the upper surface through each end. Almost intact apart from some damage to corners. L 60 mm. 1926.146.

Associations: Tiny fragment from the tip of a further blade (with central thickening); fragments of a silver vessel; tiny gold nails and fragments of wood from the hilt of one of the daggers; fragments of wood with traces of skin sheath.

Circumstances of Discovery: Well preserved barrow measuring 50 m in diam by 5 m in height, investigated in 1897. An earthen mound covered a central cairn enclosing a burial chamber built of dry-stone walling with a massive granite capstone. The W side of the cairn contained an unusual carefully constructed semi-circular kerb of upright slabs.

References:
Aveneau de la Grancière 1898
Gerloff 1975, 248, no 32, pl 55.B
Briard 1984, 292-93, fig 127

Collection:
Ashmolean Museum, Oxford 1926.131-46

167. Flint arrowheads
Creac'h Morvan, Saint-Thégonnec, Finistère, Brittany, France

6 barbed and tanged flint arrowheads (selected from total assemblage of 19): of 'long ogival' type in honey coloured flint; ogival sides with long drooping squared-off barbs and thin tapering tangs. L 32-42 mm.

Associations: 5 bronze daggers.

Circumstances of Discovery: Found during rescue excavation of a barrow in 1972. The earthen mound had covered a central cairn 6 m by 5 m enclosing a roughly constructed central dry-stone built 'chamber' 2.75 m by 0.9 m orientated NW-SE. 4 of the 5 daggers lay across the approximate middle of the grave, and nearly all of the arrowheads lay scattered around the NW half of the floor. The SE portion appears to have been nearly empty and may have contained the body.

References:
Giot 1973, 414
Briard 1984, 103-05, figs 61-62, 270, 272

Collection:
Laboratoire d'Anthropologie, Université de Rennes

168. Dagger grave group
Helmsdorf, Hettstedt, GDR

168.1 Stone battle axe with ridged cutting edge and flattened facet at the butt. Flat upper and lower surfaces and slightly rounded sides. Polished all over. L 120 mm.

168.2 Bronze flanged axe with expanded cutting edge and narrow thin butt. Flattened sides with slight flanges. Corroded surface. L 155 mm.

168.3 Bronze chisel with well rounded cutting edge and rounded butt. Flat sides and upper and lower surfaces which are all corroded. L 150 mm.

168.4 Bronze dagger with curved heel, irregular edges and blunt tip. The surfaces are flat and corroded. L 84 mm.

168.5 Gold arm-ring. Massive oval penannular ring with polished surface. The terminals are slightly expanded and have flat surfaces. Max diam 76 mm.

168.6 Gold bead in the shape of a spiral made from tightly wound gold wire. L 19 mm.

168.7 Gold hair-ring made from thick polished wire expanded in the middle and then bent to overlap the terminals and form a pear-shape. L 20 mm.

168.8 Gold hair-ring very similar to 168.7 but oval in shape. L 20 mm.

168.9 Gold pin with flat head which has a raised, rectangular, perforated expansion. The edge of the head is stepped, reducing in size to reach the shaft which is initially octagonal and then circular. The head and the octagonal part of the shaft have incised herring-bone decoration. At the junction between the octagonal and circular parts of the shaft is a double incised line with pendant triangles below. The shaft near the tip of the pin is bent. L 96 mm.

168.10 Gold pin with slightly rounded head with a simple transverse perforation. On both sides, below the perforation, are 2 bulbous, rounded expansions creating a cruciform head. Well polished surface all over. The shaft is circular in section and is slightly bent near the tip. L 85 mm.

Associations: Fragments of pottery and a male burial.

Circumstances of Discovery: The burial mound was excavated in 1906-07 by Grössler in the course of building a railway for a copper mine. Over earlier burials was erected a massive stone cairn enclosing a timber grave chamber. One end was paved, the other covered with reeds. On top of the paving lay a wooden bier with a wooden coffin containing a crouched male skeleton. All the grave goods were on the bier apart from the pot which was surrounded by a ring of stones and lay on the reeds. There was ash and signs of burning all over and it has been suggested that the whole wooden structure had been fired. The skeleton itself had been burnt in places. A radiocarbon determination from the coffin has given a date of 1663 bc ± 160 (Bln-248).

References:
Grössler 1907

Collection:
Museen der Lutherstadt Eisleben

169. Dagger grave group
Leubingen, Sömmerda, GDR

169.1 Stone pick with ridge-like cutting edge and square flat-faceted butt. The upper and lower surfaces and sides are polished flat and have longitudinal facets between them, giving the pick an octagonal section. L 308 mm.

169.2 Cushion stone. Rectangular with flattened, polished surfaces. L 212 mm.

169.3 Bronze axe with expanded bevelled cutting edge, broken butt and low side flanges. L 138 mm.

169.4 Bronze axe with expanded bevelled cutting edge which has slightly recurving tips. Low side flanges with a small stop bevel between. L 142 mm.

169.5 Bronze chisel with curved and expanded cutting edge and tanged, pointed butt. On both sides it expands in the middle. L 81 mm.

169.6 Bronze chisel with slightly expanded cutting edges at both ends. The sides are slightly flanged and expanded on both sides in the middle. L 153 mm.

169.7 Bronze chisel with rounded and expanded cutting edge and flat butt. The sides are flanged and the whole implement tapers towards the cutting edge. L 206 mm.

169.8 Bronze dagger. Flat blade, badly corroded, with curved heel and 3 rivets. The sides are now irregular and the top is broken. L 85 mm.

169.9 Bronze dagger. Flat blade with curved heel and 7 rivets. Omega shaped hilt-mark and decoration on the blade formed by a V-shape of 3 incised grooves. The tip is broken. L 116 mm.

169.10 Bronze dagger. Flat blade with curved heel and 6 rivets. The edges are slightly damaged and the top is broken. L 126 mm.

169.11 Bronze halberd. Rounded midrib with grooved edge becoming lozenge-shaped towards the tip which is rounded. The midrib is decorated with 2 sets of chevrons, one consisting of 4 grooves, the other of 3. The remains of a wooden haft set at right angles are clearly visible. Originally there were 3 rivets with high domed heads, but only 1 now remains. L 207 mm.

169.12 Gold arm-ring. Massive penannular ring with expanded flattened terminals with an incised line around each. The inner surface of the ring is undecorated and the outer has alternate grooves and ridges, there being 6 of the former and 5 of the latter. 3 of the ridges have an incised oblique stroke decoration. Max diam 82 mm.

169.13 Gold pin. Flat-headed pin with raised perforated eyelet and rounded stepping where it joins the shaft. The shaft is circular in section, has herring-bone decoration below the head and is bent above the tip. L 98 mm.

169.14 Gold pin. Very similar to 169.13. L 101 mm.

169.15 Gold hair-ring. Ring formed from thick gold wire folded back on itself and spiralled. Diam 22 mm.

169.16 Gold hair-ring. Very similar to 169.15. Diam 22 mm.

169.17 Gold spiral bead made from tightly wound gold wire. L 24 mm.

169.18 Pot. Flat-based pot with everted rim and globular form. The neck is black and burnished and has below it 2 horiz grooves above an area rusticated by oblique smearing with finger tips. This area is a reddish-buff in colour. 2 transversely perforated lugs are placed at the junction of the neck and body. Ht 395 mm.

Associations: Fragments of other pottery, a male skeleton and that of a '10-year old' child. There were traces of fastening on the pick, wooden hilts on the daggers (1 decorated with bronze wire), a haft on the halberd and, perhaps on 1 of the chisels. Remains of dagger sheaths were found — 1 wooden, the others leather.

Circumstances of Discovery: Excavated in 1877 by Klopfleish. There was a central massive timber mortuary structure with a wooden floor covered by a stone cairn, which had ditches at its edges, and had a very large earthen mound constructed over it. At a much later period the top of the mound was used as an inhumation cemetery. Within the mortuary chamber were placed the extended bodies of the man and the child laid with the child at right angles over the man's pelvis. The gold objects (169.12-169.17) lay between the shoulders of the 2 bodies on the man's right side. By his right leg lay the 3 chisels, the 2 axes laid across each other, the halberd and 1 of the daggers (169.10) with their blades at right angles and the other 2 daggers placed in the same way. At his feet were the pick and cushion stone and to the left of his left foot was the pot surrounded by a ring of stones.

References:
Höfer 1906

Collection:
Landesmuseum für Vorgeschichte, Halle

170. Bronze dagger
Bargeroosterveld, Drenthe, Netherlands

Bronze dagger with flat blade which has irregular edges. Attached originally by 4 bronze rivets is a horn hilt decorated with small tin nails, of which 22 survive. The hilt created a roughly omega-shaped edge with the blade, was carved on the left and right sides with grooves and ridges and had 4 tin nails on each side between the rivets. Just below the pommel was a circle of 14 tin nails. The pommel is flat-surfaced, expands from the hilt and has a groove around it. Just above the groove is a full circle of 26 tin nails and on the flat surface of the pommel is a cross formed by 17 tin nails. L 156 mm.

Circumstances of Discovery: Isolated find. Found in a peat bog in 1953.

References:
Glasbergen 1956a
Glasbergen 1960

Collection:
Provinciaal Museum van Drenthe, Assen 1955/VIII[1]

171. Gold cup
Eschenz, Thurgau, Switzerland

Gold cup. Sheet gold vessel with flaring rim, below which are 2 horiz rows of impressed dots. Below this are 11 horiz grooves with repoussé ridges between. At the base of this zone is a horiz line of small domed bosses with a groove and large repoussé ridge underneath. Below this is the second zone of decoration which comprises a row of larger 'pimpled' bosses with a groove and repoussé ridge below. The rest of the decoration consists of a horiz band of short oblique ridges and grooves, 4 horiz grooves with 3 ridges between and a zone divided into 4 panels by 4 vert

undecorated bands. Each panel has oblique ridging and grooving set at right angles to the neighbouring 2 panels. At the base are 2 ridges with a horiz band of small domed bosses between them. The base is now flat and is decorated with 5 concentric ridges with grooves between them and a probable sixth one at the centre which has a small central boss. Ht 111 mm.

Circumstances of Discovery: Discovered in the course of railway construction in 1916.

References:
Hardmeyer & Bürgi 1975
Bürgi & Kinnes 1975

Collection:
Historisches Museum des Kantons Thurgau, Frauenfeld

172. Necklace
Exloo, Odoorn, Drenthe, Netherlands

Necklace of tin, amber and faience beads of the following forms:
a. 25 tin beads of which 19 are globular, 5 segmented (having 4, 5, 5, 5 and 11 segments) and 1 is tubular.
b. 13 amber beads of which 2 are large, roughly rectangular and pierced at one end, 2 are small, roughly rectangular and pierced at one end, 7 are globular or disc-shaped, 1 is crescentic with a single perforation and 1 is tubular.
c. 4 faience beads all segmented, 3 having 3 segments and 1 having 4 segments.
d. 1 tubular 'clasp' of copper or bronze.
L a. tin, globular 3-5 mm; segmented 8-20 mm; tubular 9 mm. b. amber, rectangular 13-24 mm; globular/disc 3-7 mm; crescentic 10 mm; tubular 14 mm. c. faience 8-11 mm. d. clasp 13 mm.

Associations: Another amber bead.

Circumstances of Discovery: Found in a peat bog in 1881.

References:
Beck, H C & Stone 1935, 221, 243, pl 66.1

Collection:
Provinciaal Museum van Drenthe, Assen

173. Gold handled cup
Fritzdorf, Bonn, FRG

Sheet gold, biconical, handled cup with everted rim decorated with 2 rows of dots punched from the outside.

Concave neck with angular expanded shoulder below leading to a hemispherical base with omphalos. Ribbon handle attached to rim and top of shoulder in both cases with 4 rivets each of which has a lozenge-shaped washer. The handle is decorated with 3 grooves on each side. Ht 121 mm.

Associations: A pottery vessel.

Circumstances of Discovery: Found in 1954 near a turnip clamp, under a stone and lying within the pottery vessel which was broken during excavation. The excavation was arranged by Hermbrodt & Tholen after the discovery of the gold cup.

References:
von Uslar 1955
Gerloff 1975, 190-91

Collection:
Rheinisches Landesmuseum, Bonn

174. Metalwork hoard
Lessart or Landelles, near Pleudihen, La Vicomté-sur-Rance, Côtes-du-Nord, Brittany, France

174.1 Upper part of a large bronze rapier blade with expanded hilt-plate. The damaged heel has a curved arrangement of 4 rivet-holes, with 1 plug-rivet still in place; below these is an omega-shaped hilt-mark linking the angular shoulders. The centrally thickened blade has 2 sets of 5 finely drawn grooved lines, following the outlines of the sides. L 125 mm. 1884.119.276.

174.2 Bronze dagger blade. Expanded hilt-plate now badly damaged with only traces of the rivet-holes surviving; the line of an omega-shaped hilt-mark is visible. Traces of 2 sets of 4 finely grooved lines follow the outline of the blade. L 225 mm. 1884.119.275.

174.3 Bronze rapier blade. The damaged arched hilt-plate has an arrangement of 4 rivet-holes or notches, 1 of them still retaining a thin rivet with broad conical head; an omega-shaped hilt-mark is visible. The long narrow blade is centrally thickened, and has had bevelled edges. L 365 mm. A north European type. 1884.119.273.

174.4 Bronze rapier blade. Expanded hilt-plate now damaged but showing traces of 2 or more rivet-notches or holes. An omega-shaped line defined partly by differential corrosion and partly by fine cut-marks, indicates the lower edge of the now decayed hilt. L 292 mm. 1884.119.274.

174.5 Bronze flanged axe. From the flat butt, the slightly concave sides diverge to meet the expanded cutting edge; pronounced cast flanges. L 140 mm. 1884.119.125.

174.6 Small bronze flanged axe. From the flat butt the sides run nearly straight to meet the expanded cutting edge; pronounced cast flanges. L 86 mm. 1884.119.124.

174.7 Butt end only of a broken bronze flanged axe. Concave butt; low cast flanges along margins of each face. L 85 mm. 1884.119.123.

174.8 Bronze socketed spearhead with leaf-shaped blade. Socket decorated with very finely traced criss-cross lines arranged in 2 registers: the lower contains a series of filled triangles, the upper consists of 2 rows of opposed filled triangles enclosing an irregular zig-zag void. L 210 mm. 1884.119.345.

Associations: A further rapier (now in the Museé d'Antiquités Nationales, Saint-Germain, Paris). A socketed bronze axe (Pitt Rivers Museum: 1884.119.163) is also registered as part of the same accession.

Circumstances of Discovery: Hoard found in May 1877 under a large hollowed stone in a railway cutting between Dol and Dinan on the River Rance.

References:
Briard 1965, 83, fig 23.1, 5, 87, fig 25.6, 89, fig 26.1, 6, 8, 9, 307 (no 117)

Collection:
Pitt Rivers Museum, Oxford 1884.119.123-25; 1884.119.273-76; 1884.119.345

7.34 Metalwork hoard from Lessart, Côtes-du-Nord, Brittany, France (174)

175. Metalwork hoard
Bresinchen, Guben, GDR

175.1-175.103 103 flanged axes of bronze. All have expanded cutting edges some of which are bevelled. The flanges are cast but have occasionally been hammered to produce longitudinally faceted flanges. The butts are generally curved but a few are slightly flattened. A few of the axes have waisted sides and 8 of them, 175.96-175.103, have slight stop bevels. L 88-131 mm. 1954: 15/3-105.

175.104 Shaft-hole axe of bronze with blunt tip and butt and circular shaft-hole. There are 3 ridges on the top and bottom, the outer 2 close to the edges. L 216 mm. 1954: 15/106.

175.105 Metal-hilted dagger of bronze, solid cast. Flat central midrib and raised area beside the edge bevels. The tip is rounded and corroded. The cast hilt forms an omega-shaped hilt-plate and has 7 mock rivets in an arc and a further 4 which run up the hilt itself. The pommel is oval and expands from the hilt which is a very flattened ellipse in section. L 303 mm. 1954: 15/109.

175.106 Metal-hilted dagger of bronze, solid cast. Flat central midrib with ridge, furrow and then ridge leading to the edge-bevel. The triangular area of the blade formed by the midrib has an incised chevron decoration comprising 3 lines. The tip is broken. The cast hilt forms an omega-shaped hilt-plate with 5 mock rivets placed in an arc which is bounded by a ridge with nicks in it. The pommel is oval and expands from an oval hilt which has 3 bands of decoration — 2 groups of 3 grooves with a band of herring-bone between them. L 235 mm. 1954: 15/108.

175.107 Metal-hilted dagger of bronze, solid cast. Flat central midrib with furrow and flattened area leading to the edge-bevel. The tip is broken and part of the blade has been repaired. The cast hilt forms an omega-shaped hilt-plate with 7 mock rivets in an arc with a ridge below. From the central 'rivet' extends a line of a further 5 mock rivets running up the oval-sectioned hilt. The pommel is also oval and expands from the hilt which has, just below the pommel, 6 horiz grooves. L 258 mm. 1954: 15/110.

175.108 Metal-hilted dagger of bronze, solid cast. Central, thin linear midrib leading to flat area and edge-bevel. The tip is broken. The hilt forms an omega-shaped hilt-plate and has 7 mock rivets in an arc. The pommel is oval and expands from the oval-sectioned hilt which is decorated with 22 regularly spaced grooves. L 228 mm. 1954: 15/107.

175.109 Metal-hilted dagger of bronze, riveted hilt. Flat central surface on blade with furrow and edge bevel beyond. The tip is broken and worn. This area has a

triangular pattern of incised decoration. At the outside are 2 lines of offset, opposed and infilled triangles leaving an undecorated zig-zag area between. These meet at the tip where the decoration is rationalised to infill the apex. Within the triangle are 4 incised lines which form the sides of a smaller triangle whose base runs across the junction with the hilt-plate and is formed by an obliquely infilled band with 5 infilled pendant triangles springing from it. The hilt forms an omega-shaped hilt-plate and is attached with 7 rivets forming 2 groups of 3 rivets in a straight line with a single one above them. The hilt is oval in section and has 2 groups of 3 grooves decorating the surface and expands to form an oval pommel. L 316 mm. 1954: 15/113.

175.110 Metal-hilted dagger of bronze, riveted hilt. Flat central surface on blade with furrow and edge bevel beyond. The tip is broken. At the base of the blade is a narrow infilled transverse band with 2 outer incised lines from which spring 5 complete, and part of a sixth, pendant triangles formed by double lines. The hilt makes an omega-shaped hilt-plate and is riveted on with 3 rivets forming an arc with 2 mock rivets between. The hilt is oval in section and has a sub-circular pommel which is stepped where it joins the hilt. L 271 mm. 1954: 15/111.

175.111 Metal-hilted dagger of bronze, riveted hilt. Flat central surface on blade leading to furrow and edge bevel. The blade edges are badly corroded in places. At the base of the blade is an incised triangle composed of 4 lines. The hilt forms an omega-shaped hilt-plate and is attached by 5 rivets in an arc. The hilt is oval in section and leads to an expanded, oval-ended pommel. It is made from 2 pieces and held together at the pommel end by a single rivet (as well as the rivets through the blade). L 293 mm. 1954: 15/112.

175.112 Metal-hilted dagger of bronze, riveted hilt. Flat central surface on blade leading to the edge bevel. Tip slightly broken. The hilt forms an omega-shaped hilt-plate attached by 5 large and 4 small rivets and the blade itself is tanged, running through the centre of the hilt. The pommel has a raised mount with a lowered cruciform area on it through which the tang would have been attached. On the oval-sectioned hilt are 2 holes for rivets, again for fixing the tanged blade in place. In the middle of the hilt are 4 gold discs. L 315 mm. 1954: 15/114.

175.113 Metal-shafted halberd of bronze. The blade has a rounded tip, flat central midrib with a double groove outside leading to the edge bevel. This is mounted in an oval-sectioned shaft and secured wth 2 rivets flush with the surface, the shaft being also held together by a third rivet. There are 3 conical mock rivets on the shaft. The latter has a tapering top decorated with 2 grooves and again reduces in diam below the blade where it is decorated with 13 ridges. L (of blade) 235 mm. 1954: 15/116.

175.114 Metal-shafted halberd of bronze. The blade has

a rounded tip and a flat central midrib with a slight furrow outside it leading to the edge bevel. This is mounted in an oval shaft and secured by 2 rivets which are flush with the surface of the shaft on which there are also 3 conical mock rivets. The shaft is oval in section and is decorated at the top with an expanded ridge, with oblique incision, which tapers to form a hollow and then expands a little to another ridge decorated with oblique incisions. At the back of the shaft the surface rises to an angular point and then reduces in size again as the blade inside curves away. There is a ridge on the back which is decorated with small horiz incisions. A band of herring-bone decoration runs from the angular point to the central mock rivet and, on the other side of the rivet, runs an incised triangle with a splayed base which reaches the junction of the blade. Below this area are 3 ridges each with oblique incised decoration. L of blade 256 mm. 1954: 15/115.

175.115-175.124 10 neck-rings/ingot torcs of bronze with circular sections and tightly rolled terminals which leave a wide gap between them except in 2 instances where they overlap. Max diam 150-70 mm. 1954: 15/139-48.

175.125-175.128 4 heavy bronze rings. Oval and penannular with a small gap between the flat-ended terminals which are decorated with incised lines. The terminals are slightly tapered and the rings have a circular section. Max diam 124-42 mm. 1954: 15/135-38.

175.129-175.132 4 heavy bronze rings. Oval and penannular with a small gap between the flat-ended terminals which are slightly tapered. The rings have a circular section. Max diam 122-29 mm. 1954: 15/117, 132-34.

175.133 Heavy bronze ring. Oval and penannular with flat-ended terminals which taper slightly from a very thick circular-sectioned ring. Max diam 132 mm. 1954: 15/131.

175.134-175.135 2 large penannular rings. Almost circular with slightly tapering terminals which have flattened, expanded and slightly offset ends. The rings have a circular section. Max diam 165 mm & 173 mm. 1954: 15/127-28.

175.136-175.144 9 small penannular rings. Oval in shape with roughly circular sections tapering towards the terminals which are either flat-ended or have flattened slightly expanded ends. Max diam 80-104 mm. 1954: 15/118-24, 129-30.

175.145 Heavy, small penannular ring with stubby tapered terminals and a thick circular section. Max diam 105 mm. 1954: 15/125.

175.146 Heavy, small penannular ring with flat tapered terminals and faceted sub-rectangular section. Max diam 115 mm. 1954: 15/126.

175.147 Fragments of a flat-based pot with everted rim. The pot was globular and had a plain, smooth neck with 4 notched lugs below it. The rest of the surface was rusticated. Ht 278 mm. 1954: 15/2.

175.148 Fragments of a flat-based pot with simple flat rim. It was vase-shaped and had a plain smooth neck with 3 notched lugs below. The rest of the surface was rusticated. Ht 360 mm. 1954: 15/1.

Circumstances of Discovery: Found in 1954 during gravel extraction. One of the pots was 0.75 m below the ground surface and the 2 pots were 2 m from each other. In one of them were the axes and rings of different sizes and in the other were at least 1 halberd, all the daggers and several rings.

References:
Breddin 1969

Collection:
Museum für Ur- und Frühgeschichte Potsdam 1954: 15/1-148

176. Metalwork hoard
Dieskau II, Saalkreis, GDR

176.1-176.7 7 bronze penannular arm-rings. The terminals are expanded and have flat surfaces and the rings have a circular section. One is distorted so that the terminals overlap. Max diam 88-98 mm; distorted ring 64 mm.

176.8 Faceted bronze arm-ring. 'Leech'-shaped penannular ring with tapering flat-surfaced terminals and hexagonal faceted surface. Max diam 88 mm.

176.9 Bronze arm-ring. 'Leech'-shaped penannular ring with tapering flat-surfaced terminals and circular section. Max diam 100 mm.

176.10-176.11 2 heavy bronze penannular rings. Oval in form with terminals which are tapered and flat-surfaced and have a very small gap between them. The rings have a circular section. Max diam 134 mm.

176.12-176.13 2 heavy bronze penannular rings. Oval in form with flat-surfaced terminals which are decorated with 4 incised lines running round each one. The rings have a circular section. Max diam 132 mm.

176.14-176.17 4 heavy bronze annular rings. Oval in form, tapering on one side where there is a decorated area of 4 transverse ridges. The rings have a circular section. Max diam 140-48 mm.

176.18-176.19 2 bronze arm-spirals formed by tightly coiled thick bronze wire. 176.18 has 13 twists and 176.19 11 twists. The wire is oval in section. L 70 mm & 94 mm.

176.20 Flanged bronze axe with expanded cutting edge, curved thin butt and low flanges. There is a slight stop bevel and the surface between the bevel and the cutting edge has a punched 'rain' pattern. L 130 mm. Believed to be of Irish origin.

176.21 Shaft-hole axe of bronze. Wedge-shaped tip and butt and oval shaft-hole. Decorated with a raised ridge on the edges and on the middle of the upper and lower surfaces. L 305 mm.

176.22 Shaft-hole axe of bronze. Wedge-shaped tip and butt and circular shaft-hole. Decorated with raised ridges on the edges and with 3 raised ridges on the upper and lower surfaces which follow the shape of the axe. L 306 mm.

176.23 23 spiral bronze beads, each formed from tightly wound bronze wire. The lengths of the beads and thickness of the wire varies. L 30-70 mm.

176.24 Metal-shafted halberd of bronze cast in one piece. The blade has a rounded tip and a broad, flat midrib which expands markedly at the shaft. The heel of the halberd shaft has 3 conical mock rivets with short incised line decoration arranged radially at the base. Linking the 3 'rivets' is a rectilinear pattern of 2 and 3 incised lines. The junction between the blade and shaft is marked by short horiz nicks. The back of the heel is decorated with a double incised line and the shaft itself has a decorative banding reminiscent of binding and comprising 6 groups each with 3 ridges separated by grooves. L of blade 290 mm.

176.25 Metal-shafted halberd of bronze very similar to 176.24 except in decorative detail. Around the base of each 'rivet' is a circle of pointillé decoration. The 2 'rivets' nearest the blade have a semi-circle around each, consisting of a double line of pointillé decoration. The shape of the whole heel has been defined on the shaft by a double line of pointillé decoration and the shaft has decorative banding comprising 4 groups, each of 4 well-raised ridges. L of blade 280 mm.

176.26 Bronze halberd with fragmentary metal shaft, not cast in one. The blade has a rounded tip and a small flat midrib leading to a flat area with a furrow and edge bevel beyond. The base of the blade has a triangular pattern formed by 3 incised lines and within it, at the junction of the shaft, 5 small infilled triangles. The metal shaft encloses the heel of the blade and the 2 remaining conical rivets secure it in place. The rivets have stepped edges and the shaft has 3 incised lines at its top. L of blade 270 mm.

176.27-176.37 11 bronze halberd blades. 9 have broad, flat midribs and 2 have narrow rounded midribs. All the tips are rounded and all have edge bevels. 2 have an additional furrow. Where it survives, the heel is generally rounded though 176.30 is more angular. 176.27, 176.28, 176.31, 176.33, & 176.37 have 3 large rivet-holes (176.37 retaining 2 of the conical rivets). 176.30 has 3 small rivet-holes. 176.34, 176.35 & 176.36 have both large and small rivet-holes and 176.32 has too little of the heel remaining to be certain whether it had large rivet-holes in addition to the small ones which are visible. 176.32, 176.35 & 176.36 have additional incised decoration, all forming triangles at the junction of the blade and shaft. 176.32 has a triangle of 3 incised lines on the sides and 2 lines on the base from which spring 3 small infilled triangles. On either side of the large triangle, at the edge of the midrib and pointing inwards, are 4 small infilled triangles. 176.35 has a simple double chevron decoration each comprised of 2 incised lines. 176.36 has a triangle of 4 incised lines on the side with 2 lines on its base from which spring 5 small infilled triangles. L of blades 225-315 mm.

176.38-176.47 10 bronze neck-rings/ingot torcs. These are oval in form and have a wide gap between the 2 terminals which are tightly rolled spirals. The rings have a circular section. Max diam 122-46 mm.

176.48 3 bronze rivets, conical with fragments of sheet metalwork attached. From a halberd (or halberds). L 41 mm.

176.49 Small fragments of sheet bronze work with pointillé decoration. From a halberd.

176.50 One sherd of a large pottery vessel. L *c.* 162 mm.

176.51 Necklace of 106 amber beads, the surfaces of which are cracked in places, comprising:

a. 2 large trapezoidal beads with a longitudinal perforation. L 36 mm.

b. 3 rounded beads of irregular form, 2 with transverse perforations and 1 with a longitudinal perforation. L 28-43 mm.

c. 101 roughly spherical beads with central perforations. Diam 10-17 mm.

Associations: At least 14 more amber beads and the rest of the pottery vessel which was originally complete.

Circumstances of Discovery: Found in 1904 whilst digging a clamp. The hoard was within a pottery vessel, 0.75 m below the ground surface. The objects were carefully arranged in the pot with the amber beads and spiral beads at the bottom, the rings above them and the halberds and halberd blades on top.

References:
Förtsch 1905
von Brunn 1959, 55-56, pls 12-19

Collection:
Landesmuseum für Vorgeschichte, Halle

177. Metalwork hoard
   Wageningen, Gelderland, Netherlands

177.1   Stone axe with polished surface. Ridge-like cutting edge and flattened butt. Sides slightly faceted. L 136 mm. R.W.1.

177.2   Bronze flat axe. Expanded cutting edge and thinned slightly curved butt and double-faceted sides. L 115 mm. R.W.4.

177.3   Bronze dagger. Rounded tip, flat blade with 2 grooves of decoration leading to the edge bevel. Remains of omega-shaped hilt-plate visible with 2 of the original 3 rivets still in place in the curved heel. L 150 mm. R.W.3.

177.4   Bronze halberd. Rounded blunt tip; broad and low midrib with 2 furrows beyond it leading to the edge bevel. The remains of 3 rivet-holes are visible in the curved heel. L 210 mm. R.W.2.

177.5   Penannular ring of bronze made from square to round-sectioned wire. The ends of the ring are broken. Max diam 65 mm. This may be part of a spiral arm-ring. R.W.5a.

177.6   As 177.5. Max diam 67 mm. R.W.6b.

177.7   Fragment of ring of bronze wire. L (of chord) 64 mm. R.W.6.

177.8   As 177.7. L (of chord) 44 mm. R.W.7.

177.9   Bronze punch or awl. Rectangular cross-section. One end ground to a point, the other broken. L 103 mm. R.W.9a.

177.10   Ingot bar rolled into an irregular spiral. Wire of square cross-section. Max diam of spiral 70 mm. R.W.9b.

177.11   Fragment of bar of bronze wire. L 60 mm. R.W.8.

177.12   Bronze rivet. Octagonal cross-section with one face hammered. L 15 mm. R.W.10.

177.13   Bronze rivet roughly similar to 177.12 but unhammered. L 27 mm. R.W.11.

177.14   5 fragments of sheet bronze, some bent, all with 1 smoothed edge. L 28-56 mm. R.W.12, 13, 14a-c.

Circumstances of Discovery: Found in a moorland field in 1840 by a man digging trenches to plant trees. The objects were *c.* 0.6 m below the soil surface.

References:
Pleyte 1889, 49, pl XI.5-9
Inventaria Archaeologica, NL 11

Collection:
Rijksmuseum van Oudheden, Leiden R.W.1-14c

7.35 *Bronze 'sword' from Jutphaas,
Utrecht, Netherlands (179)*

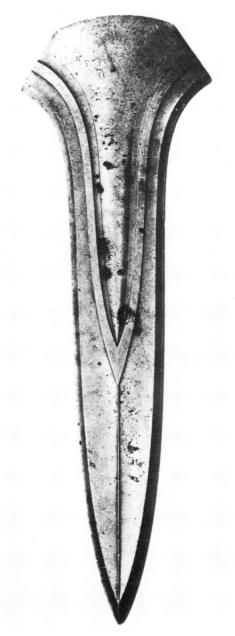

178. Bronze rapier/sword
Beaune, Côte d'Or, France

Large bronze 'sword'. Lentoid section. On the blade is a flat-surfaced raised area of decoration shaped like a dagger. From the tip of this runs a raised line to the tip of the blade. Blunt and rounded blade edges and tip. The hilt-plate is thin and flat and has shouldered edges. There is a notch on each blade edge near the hilt-plate. L 683 mm.

Circumstances of Discovery: Unknown.

References:
Greenwell 1902, 4-5
Butler & Bakker 1961, 201

Collection:
British Museum WG 2257

179. Bronze rapier/sword
Jutphaas, Utrecht, Netherlands

Large bronze 'sword'. Lentoid section. On the blade is a raised area of decoration with a flat surface shaped like a dagger with an incised line within it. From the tip of this runs a raised line to the tip of the blade. Around the edge where the edge bevel should be is a ridge. Blunt edges and tip. The hilt-plate is flat and has shouldered edges. L 423 mm.

Circumstances of Discovery: Found in 1946-47 during dredging work for an extension to the harbour at Utrecht.

References:
Butler & Sarfatij 1971

Collection:
Private collection

REFERENCES

Abbreviations used in this list are generally along the lines recommended in British Standard BS 4148: part 2, 1975. A list of the full titles of British and Irish periodicals is given in the Council for British Archaeology's *Signposts for archaeological publications*, 2nd edition, London, 1979, 25-31.

Abercromby, J 1894 Note on a tanged dagger or spear-head from Crawford Priory, Fife, *Proc Soc Antiq Scot*, 28 (1893-94), 219-25.

Acland, J E 1916 List of Dorset barrows opened by Mr E Cunnington, or described by him, *Proc Dorset Natur Hist Antiq Fld Club*, 37 (1916), 40-47.

Adkins, R & Jackson, R 1978 *Neolithic stone and flint axes from the River Thames: an illustrated corpus*. London. (= *Brit Mus Occas Pap*, 1).

Albrethsen, S E & Brinch Petersen, E 1976 Excavation of a mesolithic cemetery at Vedbaek, Denmark, *Acta Archaeol*, 47 (1976), 1-29.

Anderson, J 1866 Report on the ancient remains of Caithness, and results of exploration conducted, for the Anthropological Society of London, by Messrs Joseph Anderson and Robert Innes Shearer, in 1865, *Mem Anthrop Soc London*, 2 (1865-66), 226-56.

Anderson, J 1868 On the horned cairns of Caithness, their structural arrangement, contents of chambers, etc., *Proc Soc Antiq Scot*, 7 (1866-68), 480-512.

Anderson, J 1878 Notes on the character and contents of a large sepulchral cairn of the bronze age at Collessie, Fife, excavated by William Wallace, Esq, of Newton of Collessie, in August 1876 and 1877, *Proc Soc Antiq Scot*, 12 (1876-78), 439-61.

Anderson, J 1886 *Scotland in pagan times: the bronze and stone ages*. Edinburgh.

Anderson, J 1901 Notice of a hoard of bronze implements, and ornaments, and buttons of jet found at Migdale, on the Estate of Skibo, Sutherland, exhibited to the Society by Mr Andrew Carnegie of Skibo LLD, FSA Scot, *Proc Soc Antiq Scot*, 35 (1900-01), 266-75.

Anderson, J 1905 Description of sepulchral urns exhibited by Col Malcolm, CB, of Poltalloch, *Proc Soc Antiq Scot*, 39 (1904-05), 232-44.

Anderson, J 1909 Note on a group of perforated stone hammers remarkable for their similarity of form and ornamentation, *Proc Soc Antiq Scot*, 43 (1908-09), 377-84.

Anderson, R S G 1942 A cinerary urn from Sandmill Farm, Stranraer, Wigtownshire, *Proc Soc Antiq Scot*, 76 (1941-42), 79-83.

Annable, F K & Simpson, D D A 1964 *Guide catalogue of the neolithic and bronze age collections in Devizes Museum*. Devizes.

Anon 1901 Notes of the month [April 1901], *The Antiquary*, 37 (1901), 99.

ApSimon, A M 1954 Dagger graves in the "Wessex" bronze age, *Ann Rep Univ London Inst Archaeol*, 10 (1954), 37-62.

Arnal, J 1954 Les boutons perforés en V, *Bull Soc Préhist Fr*, 51 (1954), 255-68.

Arnold, D E 1981 A model for the identification of non-local ceramic distribution: a view from the present, *in* Howard, H & Morris, E L (eds), *Production and distribution: a ceramic viewpoint*, Oxford, 31-44. (= *Brit Archaeol Rep Int Ser*, 120).

Ashbee, P 1960 *The bronze age round barrow in Britain*. London.

Ashbee, P 1966 The Fussell's Lodge long barrow excavations, 1957, *Archaeologia*, 100 (1966), 1-80.

Ashbee, P 1970 *The earthen long barrow in Britain*. London.

Ashbee, P, Smith, I F & Evans, J G 1979 Excavation of three long barrows near Avebury, Wiltshire, *Proc Prehist Soc*, 45 (1979), 207-300.

Ashmore, P 1984 Callanish *in* Breeze, D J (ed), *Studies in Scottish antiquity presented to Stewart Cruden*, Edinburgh, 1-31.

Aspinall, A, Warren, S E, Crummett, J G & Newton, R G 1972 Neutron activation analysis of faience beads, *Archaeometry*, 14 (1972), 27-40.

Atkinson, J C 1863 Further researches in Cleveland grave-hills, *Gentleman's Mag*, 15 (1863), 548-52.

Atkinson, R J C 1965 Wayland's Smithy, *Antiquity*, 39 (1965), 126-33.

Atkinson, R J C 1968 Old mortality: some aspects of burial and population in neolithic England *in* Coles, J M & Simpson, D D A (eds), *Studies in ancient Europe: essays presented to Stuart Piggott*, Leicester, 83-94.

Atkinson, R J C 1970 Silbury Hill 1969-70, *Antiquity*, 44 (1970), 313-14.

Atkinson, R J C 1972 Burial and population in the British bronze age, *in* Lynch, F & Burgess, C (eds), *Prehistoric man in Wales and the west: essays in honour of Lily F Chitty*, Bath, 107-116.

Atkinson, R J C 1978 *Stonehenge and neighbouring monuments*. London.

Atkinson, R J C 1979 *Stonehenge*. Harmondsworth.

Atkinson, R J C, Piggott, C M & Sandars, N K 1951 *Excavations at Dorchester, Oxon. First report: Sites I, II, IV, V and VI with a chapter on henge monuments by R J C Atkinson*. Oxford.

Aveneau de la Grancière, P 1898 Le bronze dans le centre de la Bretagne-Armorique. Fouille du tumulus à enceinte semi-circulaire de Saint-Fiacre, en Melrand (canton de Baud, Morbihan), *L'Anthropologie*, 9 (1898), 134-43.

Barclay, G J 1983 Sites of the third millennium bc to the first millennium ad at North Mains, Strathallan, Perthshire, *Proc Soc Antiq Scot*, 113 (1983), 122-281.

Barfield, L H 1978 North Italian faience buttons, *Antiquity*, 52 (1978), 150-53.

Barnwell, E L 1860 Carved stone hammer [Maesmore], *Archaeol Cambrensis*, 6 (1860), 307-09.

Barton, T 1849 Letter from Thos Barton, Esq, to Henry Harrod, Esq dated 3rd July 1849 [describing discovery of burial at Little Cressingham]. Archaeology Dept, Norwich Castle Museum.

Barton, T 1852 Antiquities discovered at Little Cressingham, Norfolk, *Norfolk Archaeol*, 3 (1852), 1-2.

Bateman, T 1848 *Vestiges of the antiquities of Derbyshire*. London.

Bateman, T 1861 *Ten Years' digging in Celtic and Saxon grave hills in the counties of Derby, Stafford and York from 1848 to 1858*. London.

Bath-Bílková, B 1973 K problému původu hřiven, *Památky Archeol*, 64 (1973), 24-41.

Baynes, E N 1909 The excavation of two barrows at Ty'n-y-pwll, Llanddyfnan, Anglesey, *Archaeol Cambrensis*, 64 (1909), 312-32.

Beck, C W 1974 The provenience of amber in bronze age Greece, *Ann Brit Sch Athens*, 69 (1974), 170-72.

Beck, C W, Wilbur, E & Meret, S 1964 Infra-red spectra and the origin of amber, *Nature*, 201 (1964), 256-57.

Beck, C W, Wilbur, E, Meret, S, Kosove, M & Kermani, K 1965 The infra-red spectra of amber and the identification of Baltic amber, *Archaeometry*, 8 (1965), 96-109.

Beck, H C & Stone, J F S 1935 Faience beads of the British bronze age, *Archaeologia*, 85 (1935), 203-52.

Becker, C J 1954 A segmented faience bead from Jutland, with notes on amber beads from bronze age Denmark, *Acta Archaeol*, 25 (1954), 241-52.

Benson, D G & Clegg, I N I 1978 Cotswold burial rites, *Man*, N ser, 13 (1978), 134-37.

Benson, G 1905 Notes on an intrenchment on Holgate Hill, *Yorkshire Philosoph Soc Ann Rep for 1904*, (1905), 49-50.

Berry, L G, Mason, B & Dietrich, R V 1983 *Mineralogy, concepts, descriptions, determinations*. 2nd edition, San Francisco.

Binford, L R 1972 *An archaeological perspective*. New York & London.

Black, G F 1894 Descriptive catalogue of loan collections of prehistoric antiquities from the Shires of Berwick, Roxburgh, and Selkirk, *Proc Soc Antiq Scot*, 28 (1893-94), 321-41.

Boston, T 1884 Notes on three sepulchral mounds on the farm of Balmuick (the property of Col Williamson of Lawers), near Comrie, Perthshire, *Proc Soc Antiq Scot*, 18 (1883-84), 306-08.

Bradley, R 1982 Position and possession: assemblage variation in the British neolithic, *Oxford J Archaeol*, 1:1 (1982), 27-38.

Bradley, R 1984 *The social foundations of prehistoric Britain: themes and variations in the archaeology of power.* London.

Brailsford, J W 1953 *Later prehistoric antiquities of the British Isles.* London.

Braithwaite, M 1984 Ritual and prestige in the prehistory of Wessex c. 2200-1400 BC: a new dimension to the archaeological evidence *in* Miller, D & Tilley, C (eds), *Ideology, power and prehistory*, Cambridge, 93-110.

Breddin, R 1969 Der Aunjetitzer Bronzehortfund von Bresinchen, Kr Guben, *Veröffent Mus Ur- und Frühgesch Potsdam*, 5 (1969), 15-56.

Brewster, T C M 1980 *The excavation of Garton and Wetwang Slacks.* Malton.

Brewster, T C M 1984 *The excavation of Whitegrounds barrow, Burythorpe.* Wintringham.

Briard, J 1965 *Les dépôts Bretons et l'âge du bronze Atlantique.* Rennes.

Briard, J 1970 Un tumulus du bronze ancien Kernonen en Plouvorn (Finistère), *L'Anthropologie*, 74 (1970), 5-56.

Briard, J 1974 Bronze age cultures: 1800-600 BC *in* Piggott, S, Daniel, G & McBurney, C (eds), *France before the Romans*, London, 131-56.

Briard, J 1976a Les civilisations de l'âge du bronze en Armorique *in* Guilaine, J (ed), *Les civilisations néolithiques et protohistoriques de la France*, Paris, 561-74. (= *La Préhistoire Française*, Tome II).

Briard, J 1976b Acculturations néolithiques et campaniformes dans le tumulus armoricains *in* de Laet S J (ed) *Acculturation and continuity in Atlantic Europe, mainly during the neolithic period and the bronze age*, Brugge, 34-44 (= *Diss Archaeol Gandenses*, 16).

Briard, J 1978 Das silbergefäss von Saint-Adrien, Côtes-du-Nord, *Archäol Korrespondenzbl*, 8 (1978), 13-20.

Briard, J 1979 L'âge du bronze *in* Giot P-R, Briard J & Pape L, *Protohistoire de la Bretagne*, Rennes, 27-213.

Briard, J 1984 *Les tumulus d'Armorique.* Paris. (= *L'âge du bronze en France*, 3).

Briard, J & Mohen, J-P 1974 Le tumulus de la forêt de Carnoët à Quimperlé (Finistère), *Antiq Nationales*, 6 (1974), 46-60.

Britnell, W J & Savory, H N 1984 *Gwernvale and Penywyrlod: two neolithic long cairns in the Black Mountains of Brecknock.* Cardiff. (= *Cambrian Archaeol Monogr*, 2).

Britton, D 1961 A study of the composition of Wessex culture bronzes, *Archaeometry*, 4 (1961), 39-52.

Britton, D 1963 Traditions of metal-working in the later neolithic and early bronze age of Britain: part 1, *Proc Prehist Soc*, 29 (1963), 258-325.

Brown, J A 1981 The search for rank in prehistoric burials *in* Chapman, R, Kinnes, I & Randsborg, K (eds), *The archaeology of death*, Cambridge, 25-37.

Bruce, J R, Megaw, E M & Megaw, B R S 1947 A neolithic site at Ronaldsway, Isle of Man, *Proc Prehist Soc*, 13 (1947), 139-60.

von Brunn, W A 1959 *Die Hortfunde der frühen Bronzezeit aus Sachsen-Anhalt, Sachsen und Thüringen.* Berlin. (= *Deutsche Akad Wiss Berlin, Schr Sekt Vor- und Frühgesch*, Bd 7, Teil 1).

Bryce, T H 1902 On the cairns of Arran — a record of explorations, with an anatomical description of the human remains discovered, *Proc Soc Antiq Scot*, 36 (1901-02), 74-173.

Bryce, T H 1903 On the cairns of Arran — a record of further explorations during the season of 1902, *Proc Soc Antiq Scot*, 37 (1902-03), 36-67.

Bryce, T H 1904 On the cairns and tumuli of the Island of Bute. A record of explorations during the season of 1903, *Proc Soc Antiq Scot*, 38 (1903-04), 17-81.

Bryce, T H 1910 The sepulchral remains *in* Balfour, J A (ed), *The book of Arran: archaeology*, Glasgow, 33-155.

Burgess, C B 1974 The bronze age *in* Renfrew, A C (ed) *British prehistory: a new outline*, London, 165-232.

Burgess, C 1980 *The age of Stonehenge.* London.

Burgess, C 1984 Coupes à anse *in* MacSween, A & Burgess, C (eds), *Au temps de Stonehenge*, Tournai, 75-76.

Burgess, C & Cowen, J D 1972 The Ebnal hoard and early bronze age metal-working traditions *in* Lynch, F & Burgess, C (eds), *Prehistoric man in Wales and the west: essays in honour of Lily F Chitty*, Bath, 167-81.

Burgess, C & Shennan, S 1976 The beaker phenomenon: some suggestions *in* Burgess, C & Miket, R (eds), *Settlement and economy in the third and second millennia BC*, Oxford, 309-31. (= *Brit Archaeol Rep*, 33).

Bürgi, J & Kinnes, I 1975 A gold beaker from Switzerland, *Antiquity*, 49 (1975), 132-33.

Burl, A 1970 The recumbent stone circles of north-east Scotland, *Proc Soc Antiq Scot*, 102 (1969-70), 56-81.

Burl, A 1979 *Prehistoric Avebury.* London.

Burl, A 1981 'By the light of the cinerary moon'. Chambered tombs and the astronomy of death *in* Ruggles, C & Whittle, A W R (eds), *Astronomy and society in Britain during the period 4000-1500 BC*, Oxford, 243-74. (= *Brit Archaeol Rep Brit Ser*, 88).

Bushe-Fox, J P 1915 *Excavations at Hengistbury Head, Hampshire in 1911-12.* London. (= *Rep Res Comm Soc Antiq London*, 3).

Butler, J J 1956 The late neolithic gold ornament from Bennekom. II: the affiliations of the Bennekom ornament, *Palaeohistoria*, 5 (1956), 59-71.

Butler, J J 1963 Bronze age connections across the North Sea, *Palaeohistoria*, 9 (1963), 1-286.

Butler, J J & Bakker, J A 1961 A forgotten middle bronze age hoard with a Sicilian razor from Ommerschans (Overijssel), *Helinium*, 1 (1961), 193-210.

Butler, J J & Sarfatij, H 1971 Another bronze ceremonial sword by the Plougrescant-Ommerschans smith, *Ber Rijksdienst Oudheidkundig Bodemonderzoek*, 20-21 (1970-71), 301-09.

Butler, J J & van der Waals, J D 1966 Bell beakers and early metal-working in the Netherlands, *Palaeohistoria*, 12 (1966), 41-139.

Butler, J J & Waterbolk, H T 1974 La fouille de A E van Giffen à "La Motta", *Palaeohistoria*, 16 (1974), 107-67.

Callander, J G 1908 Notice of the discovery of a fourth cinerary urn containing burnt human bones and other relics at Seggiecrook, Kennethmont, Aberdeenshire, *Proc Soc Antiq Scot*, 42 (1907-08), 212-22.

Callander, J G 1922 Three bronze age hoards recently added to the National Collection, with notes on the hoard from Duddingston Loch, *Proc Soc Antiq Scot*, 56 (1921-22), 351-64.

Callander, J G 1931 Notes on (1) certain prehistoric relics from Orkney, and (2) Skara Brae: its culture and its period, *Proc Soc Antiq Scot*, 65 (1930-31), 78-114.

Callander, J G & Grant, W G 1934 A long stalled chambered cairn or mausoleum (Rousay Type) near Midhowe, Rousay, Orkney, *Proc Soc Antiq Scot*, 68 (1933-34), 320-50.

Callander, J G & Grant, W G 1935 A long, stalled cairn, the Knowe of Yarso, in Rousay, Orkney, *Proc Soc Antiq Scot*, 69 (1934-35), 325-51.

Callander, J G & Grant, W G 1936 A stalled chambered cairn, the Knowe of Ramsay, at Hullion, Rousay, Orkney, *Proc Soc Antiq Scot*, 70 (1935-36), 407-19.

Callander, J G & Grant, W G 1937 Long stalled cairn at Blackhammer, Rousay, Orkney, *Proc Soc Antiq Scot*, 71 (1936-37), 297-308.

Campbell, M & Sandeman, M L S 1962 Mid Argyll: a field survey of the historic and prehistoric monuments, *Proc Soc Antiq Scot*, 95 (1961-62), 1-125.

Campbell, M, Scott, J G & Piggott, S 1961 The Badden cist slab, *Proc Soc Antiq Scot*, 94 (1960-61), 46-61.

Care, V 1982 The collection and distribution of lithic raw materials during the mesolithic and neolithic periods in southern England, *Oxford J Archaeol*, 1 (1982), 269-85.

Case, H J 1966 Were Beaker people the first metallurgists in Ireland? *Palaeohistoria*, 12 (1966), 141-77.

Case, H 1969 Neolithic explanations, *Antiquity*, 43 (1969), 176-86.

Champion, T, Gamble, C, Shennan, S & Whittle, A 1984 *Prehistoric Europe.* London.

Chapman, R 1981 The emergence of formal disposal areas and the 'problem' of megalithic tombs in prehistoric Europe *in* Chapman, R, Kinnes, I & Randsborg, K (eds), *The archaeology of death*,

Cambridge, 71-81.

Cherry, J F 1978 Generalisation and the archaeology of the state *in* Green, D, Haselgrove, C & Spriggs, M (eds), *Social organisation and settlement*, Oxford, 411-37. (= *Brit Archaeol Rep Int Ser*, 47).

Chesterman, J T 1977 Burial rites in a Cotswold long barrow, *Man*, N ser, 12 (1977), 22-32.

Childe, V G 1930 Operations at Skara Brae during 1929, *Proc Soc Antiq Scot*, 64 (1929-30), 158-91.

Childe, V G 1931a Final report on the operations at Skara Brae, *Proc Soc Antiq Scot*, 65 (1930-31), 27-77.

Childe, V G 1931b *Skara Brae: a Pictish village in Orkney*. London.

Childe, V G 1952 Re-excavation of the chambered cairn of Quoyness, Sanday, on behalf of the Ministry of Works in 1951-52, *Proc Soc Antiq Scot*, (1951-52), 121-39.

Childe, V G & Grant, W G 1947 A stone age settlement at the Braes of Rinyo, Rousay, Orkney (second report), *Proc Soc Antiq Scot*, 81 (1946-47), 16-42.

Childe, V G & Paterson, J W 1929 Provisional report on the excavations at Skara Brae, and on finds from the 1927 and 1928 campaigns, *Proc Soc Antiq Scot*, 63 (1928-29), 225-80.

Chippindale, C 1983 *Stonehenge complete*. London.

Clarke, J G 1880 Notes on a gold lunette found at Auchentaggart, Dumfriesshire, and a massive silver chain found at Whitecleugh, Lanarkshire, exhibited by His Grace the Duke of Buccleuch, *Proc Soc Antiq Scot*, 14 (1879-80), 222-24.

Clarke, J G D 1952 *Prehistoric Europe: the economic basis*. London.

Clarke, J G D 1966 The invasion hypothesis in British archaeology, *Antiquity*, 40 (1966), 172-89.

Clarke, D L 1970 *Beaker pottery of Great Britain and Ireland*. Cambridge.

Clarke, D L 1976 The Beaker network — social and economic models *in* Lanting, J N & van der Waals, J D (eds), *Glockenbecher Symposium: Oberried 1974*, Bussum/Haarlem, 459-76.

Clarke, D V 1976a *The neolithic village at Skara Brae, Orkney. Excavations 1972-73: an interim report*. Edinburgh.

Clarke, D V 1976b Excavations at Skara Brae: a summary account *in* Burgess, C & Miket, R (eds), *Settlement and economy in the third and second millennia BC*, Oxford, 233-50. (= *Brit Archaeol Rep*, 33).

Clifford, E M 1936 Notgrove long barrow, Gloucestershire, *Archaeologia*, 86 (1936), 119-61.

Close-Brooks, J & Coles, J M 1980 Tinned axes, *Antiquity*, 54 (1980), 228-29.

Clough, T H McK & Cummins, W A (eds) 1979 *Stone axe studies: archaeological, petrological, experimental and ethnographic*. London. (= *Counc Brit Archaeol Res Rep*, 23).

Coffey, G 1901 Irish copper celts, *J Anthrop Inst*, 31 (1901), 265-79.

Coghlan, H H & Case, H 1957 Early metallurgy of copper in Ireland and Britain,

Proc Prehist Soc, 23 (1957), 91-123.

Cogné, J & Giot, P-R 1951 L'âge du bronze ancien en Bretagne, *L'Anthropologie*, 55 (1951), 425-44.

Coles, F R 1905 Notice of the exploration of the remains of a cairn of the bronze age at Gourlaw, Midlothian, *Proc Soc Antiq Scot*, 39 (1904-05), 411-18.

Coles, J M 1969 Scottish early bronze age metalwork, *Proc Soc Antiq Scot*, 101 (1968-69), 1-118.

Coles, J M & Harding, A F 1979 *The bronze age in Europe*. London.

Coles, J M, Heal, S V E & Orme, B J 1978 The use and character of wood in prehistoric Britain and Ireland, *Proc Prehist Soc*, 44 (1978), 1-45.

Coles, J M, Hibbert, F A & Orme, B J 1973 Prehistoric roads and tracks in Somerset: 3. The Sweet track, *Proc Prehist Soc*, 39 (1973), 256-93.

Coles, J M, Orme, B, Bishop, A C & Woolley, A R 1974 A jade axe from the Somerset Levels, *Antiquity*, 48 (1974), 216-20.

Coles, J M & Taylor, J 1971 The Wessex culture: a minimal view, *Antiquity*, 45 (1971), 6-14.

Connah, G 1965 Excavations at Knap Hill, Alton Priors, 1961, *Wiltshire Archaeol Natur Hist Mag*, 60 (1965), 1-23.

Conwell, E A 1866 Examination of the ancient sepulchral cairns on the Loughcrew Hills, County of Meath, *Proc Roy Ir Acad*, 9 (1864-66), 355-79.

Conwell, E A 1873 *Discovery of the tomb of Ollamh Fodhla*. Dublin.

Cowie, T G 1978 *Bronze age food vessel urns in northern Britain*. Oxford. (= *Brit Archaeol Rep*, 55).

Crabtree, D E 1972 *An introduction to flintworking*. Pocatello. (= *Occas Pap Idaho State Univ Mus*, 28).

Craw, J H 1930 Excavations at Dunadd and at other sites on the Poltalloch Estates, Argyll, *Proc Soc Antiq Scot*, 64 (1929-30), 111-46.

Crawford, O G S 1921 The ancient settlements at Harlyn Bay, *Antiq J*, 1 (1921), 283-99.

Cummins, W A 1979 Neolithic stone axes: distribution and trade in England and Wales *in* Clough, T H McK & Cummins, W A (eds), *Stone axe studies: archaeological, petrological, experimental and ethnographic*, London, 5-12 (= *Counc Brit Archaeol Res Rep*, 23).

Cummins, W A 1980 Stone axes as a guide to neolithic communications and boundaries in England and Wales, *Proc Prehist Soc*, 46 (1980), 45-60.

Cunningham, C 1981 *Victorian and Edwardian town halls*. London.

Cunnington, M E 1925 Prehistoric gold in Wilts, *Antiq J*, 5 (1925), 68-70.

Cunnington, M E 1929 *Woodhenge. A description of the site as revealed by excavations carried out there by Mr and Mrs B H Cunnington, 1926-7-8. Also of four circles and an earthwork enclosure south of Woodhenge*. Devizes.

Curle, A O 1916 Notes (1) on the discovery of a grave at Balneil, New Luce, Wigtownshire, containing a partially burnt interment, a cinerary urn, a bronze chisel, a bone pin,

and a bead of vitreous paste. (2) on a socketed axe of bronze found at Cambusmore, The Mound, Sutherlandshire, *Proc Soc Antiq Scot*, 50 (1915-16), 302-06.

Dalrymple, C E 1884 Notes of the excavation of the stone circle at Crichie, Aberdeenshire, *Proc Soc Antiq Scot*, 18 (1883-84), 319-25.

Darbishire, R D 1874 Notes on discoveries in Ehenside Tarn, Cumberland, *Archaeologia*, 44 (1873-74), 273-92.

Darvill, T C 1982 *The megalithic chambered tombs of the Cotswold-Severn region*. Highworth.

Dickson, F P 1981 *Australian stone hatchets, a study in design and dynamics*. London.

Dickson, J H 1978 Bronze age mead, *Antiquity*, 52 (1978), 108-13.

Dixon, P 1981 Crickley Hill, *Curr Archaeol*, no 76 (1981), 145-47.

Douglas, M 1982 Introduction to grid/group analysis *in* Douglas, M (ed), *Essays in the sociology of perception*, London, 1-8.

Drew, C D & Piggott, S 1936a The excavation of long barrow 163a on Thickthorn Down, Dorset, *Proc Prehist Soc*, 2 (1936), 77-96.

Drew, C D & Piggott, S 1936b Two bronze age barrows excavated by Mr Edward Cunnington, *Proc Dorset Natur Hist Archaeol Soc*, 58 (1936), 18-25.

Dymond, D P 1966 Ritual monuments at Rudston, E Yorkshire, England, *Proc Prehist Soc*, 32 (1966), 86-95.

Earle, T K 1982 Prehistoric economies and the archaeology of exchange *in* Ericson, J E & Earle, T K (eds), *Contexts for prehistoric exchange*, London, 1-12.

Edwards, A J H 1929 Excavations at Reay Links and at a horned cairn at Lower Dounreay, Caithness, *Proc Soc Antiq Scot*, 63 (1928-29), 138-50.

Edwards, A J H 1941 A hoard of bronze age halberds from Auchingoul, Inverkeithny Banffshire, *Proc Soc Antiq Scot*, 75 (1940-41), 208-09.

Edwardson, A R 1965 A spirally decorated object from Garboldisham, *Antiquity*, 39 (1965), 145.

Ehrich, R W 1966 Ceramics and man: a cultural perspective, *in* Matson, F R (ed), *Ceramics and Man*, London, 1-19.

Eluère, C 1982 *Les ors préhistoriques*. Paris (= *L'âge du bronze en France*, 2).

Eogan, G 1983 A flint macehead at Knowth, Co Meath, Ireland, *Antiquity*, 57 (1983), 45-46.

Eogan, G & Richardson, H 1982 Two maceheads from Knowth, County Meath, *J Roy Soc Antiq Ir*, 112 (1982), 123-38.

Ericson, J E & Purdy, B A 1984 *Prehistoric quarries and lithic production*. Cambridge.

Evans, J 1881 *The ancient bronze implements, weapons, and ornaments of Great Britain and Ireland*. London.

Evans, J 1897 *The ancient stone implements, weapons and ornaments of Great Britain*. 2nd edition, London.

Evans, J G with Atkinson, R J C, O'Connor, T & Green, H S 1984 Stonehenge — the environment in the late neolithic and early bronze age *and* a beaker-age burial, *Wiltshire Archaeol Natur Hist Mag*, 78

(1983), 7-30.

Farrer, J 1868 Note of excavations in Sanday, one of the north isles of Orkney, *Proc Soc Antiq Scot*, 7 (1866-68), 398-401.

Fenton, M B 1983 *Scottish battle-axes and axe-hammers: petrology, typology, manufacture and source.* Unpublished PhD thesis, Univ of Nottingham.

Fischer, A, Grønnow, B, Jönsson, J H, Nielsen, F O & Petersen, C 1979 *Stone age experiments in Lejre: internal organisation of the settlements.* Copenhagen. (= *Working Pap Nat Mus Denmark*, 8).

Fleming, A 1971 Territorial patterns in bronze age Wessex, *Proc Prehist Soc*, 27:1 (1971), 138-66.

Fleming, A 1972 Vision and design: approaches to ceremonial monument typology, *Man*, N set, 7 (1972), 57-73.

Fleming, A 1973a Tombs for the living, *Man*, N ser, 8 (1973), 177-93.

Fleming, A 1973b Models for the development of the Wessex culture *in* Renfrew, C (ed), *The explanation of culture change: models in prehistory*, London, 571-85.

Fogelson, R D 1977 Cherokee notions of power *in* Fogelson, R D & Adams, R N (eds), *The anthropology of power. Ethnographic studies from Asia, Oceania, and the New World*, New York, 1977, 185-94.

Foltz, E 1978 Restaurierung und rekonstruktion des frühbronzezeitlichen silbergefässes von Saint-Adrien, *Archäol Korrespondenzbl*, 8 (1978), 21-23.

Förtsch, O 1905 Ein Depotfund der älteren Bronzezeit aus Dieskau bei Halle, *Jahresschr Vorgesch sächsisch-thüringischen Länder*, 4 (1905), 3-33.

Foster, K P 1979 *Aegean faience of the bronze age.* New Haven & London.

Fox, C 1923 *The archaeology of the Cambridge Region.* Cambridge.

Fraser, D 1983 *Land and society in neolithic Orkney.* Oxford. (= *Brit Archaeol Rep Brit Ser*, 117).

Fraser, D & Kinnes, I A 1982 Comments on the archaeodemography of Isbister, *Scot Archaeol Rev*, 1 (1982), 144-47.

Frazer, W 1897 On gold lunulae, with descriptions of those contained in the Royal Irish Academy's Museum, and other collections; and on the source of the gold employed to make Irish gold ornaments, *J Roy Soc Antiq Ir*, 27 (1897), 53-66.

Gage, J 1836 A letter from John Gage Esq, FRS, Director, to Sir Henry Ellis, KH, FRS, Secretary, accompanying a gold British corselet exhibited to the Society, and since purchased by the Trustees of the British Museum, *Archaeologia*, 26 (1836), 422-31.

Gemmell, A M D & Kesel, R H 1979 Developments in the study of the Buchan flint deposits *in* Thoms, L M (ed), *Early man in the Scottish landscape*, Edinburgh, 66-77. (= *Scot Archaeol Forum*, 9).

Gerloff, S 1975 *The early bronze age daggers in Great Britain and a reconsideration of the Wessex culture.* Munich. (= *Prähistorische Bronzefunde*, VI/2).

Gifford, J, McWilliam, C & Walker, D 1984

The buildings of Scotland: Edinburgh. Harmondsworth.

Gimbutas, M 1956 *The prehistory of eastern Europe*, part 1. Cambridge, Massachusetts. (= *Bull Amer Sch Prehist Res, Peabody Mus, Harvard Univ*, 20)

Gimbutas, M 1965 *Bronze age cultures in central and eastern Europe.* The Hague.

Giot, P-R 1960 *Brittany.* London.

Giot, P-R 1973 Circonscription de Bretagne, *Gallia Préhist*, 16 (1973), 401-26.

Glasbergen, W 1956a De dolk van Bargeroosterveld. I. Vondstomstandigheden & beschrijving, *Nieuwe Drentse Volksalmanak*, 74 (1956), 191-98.

Glasbergen, W 1956b The late neolithic gold ornament from Bennekom. I. The discovery, *Palaeohistoria*, 5 (1956), 53-58.

Glasbergen, W 1960 De dolk van Bargeroosterveld. II. Herkomst & datering, *Nieuwe Drentse Volksalmanak*, 78 (1960), 190-98.

Glenn, E J nd *Early bronze age populations in Scotland.* (Priv circ typescript deposited in Prehistoric-Viking Dept, Nat Mus Antiq Scot).

Goldstein, L 1981 One-dimensional archaeology and multi-dimensional people: spatial organisation and mortuary analysis *in* Chapman, R, Kinnes, I & Randsborg, K (eds), *The archaeology of death*, Cambridge, 53-69.

Gourlay, R & Barrett, J 1984 Dail na Caraidh, *Curr Archaeol*, 8 (1983-84), 347-49.

Grant, W G 1939 Excavations on behalf of HM Office of Works at Taiverso Tuick, Trumland, Rousay, *Proc Soc Antiq Scot*, 73 (1938-39), 155-66.

Greaves, C S 1872 Remarks upon a runic comb, jet and glass beads, arrowheads and other objects of flint lately found near Whitby, *Archaeol J*, 29 (1872), 280-86.

Green, H S 1980 *The flint arrowheads of the British Isles.* Oxford. (= *Brit Archaeol Rep Brit Ser*, 75).

Greenwell, W 1866 An account of excavations in cairns near Crinan, *Proc Soc Antiq Scot*, 6 (1864-66), 336-51.

Greenwell, W 1890 Recent researches in barrows in Yorkshire, Wiltshire, Berkshire, etc, *Archaeologia*, 52 (1890), 1-72.

Greenwell, W 1902 On some rare forms of bronze weapons and implements, *Archaeologia*, 58 (1902), 1-16.

Greenwell, W & Rolleston, G 1877 *British barrows.* Oxford.

Gregory, C A 1982 *Gifts and commodities.* London.

Grimes, W F 1938 A barrow on Breach Farm, Llanbleddian, Glamorgan, *Proc Prehist Soc*, 4 (1938), 107-21.

Grimes, W F 1939 The excavation of Ty-isaf long cairn, Brecknockshire, *Proc Prehist Soc*, 5 (1939), 119-42.

Grinsell, L V 1957 Archaeological gazetteer *in* Pugh, R B & Crittall, E (eds) *A history of Wiltshire*, vol 1, pt 1, London, 21-279.

Grinsell, L V 1959 *Dorset barrows.* Dorchester.

Grinsell, L V 1974 Disc-barrows, *Proc Prehist Soc*, 40 (1974), 79-112.

Grössler, H 1907 Das Fürstengrab im grossen Galgenhügel am Paulsschachte bei Helmsdorf (im Mansfelder Seekreise), *Jahresschr Vorgesch sächsisch-thüringischen Länder*, 6 (1907), 1-87.

Guido, M, Henderson, J, Cable, M, Bayley, J & Biek, L 1984 A bronze age glass bead from Wilsford, Wiltshire: barrow G42 in the Lake group, *Proc Prehist Soc*, 50 (1984), 245-54.

Hajek, L 1957 Knoflíky Strédoevropské Skupiny Kultury Zvoncovitých Pohárů, *Památky Archeol*, 48 (1957), 389-424.

Hamilton, H McD 1983 *A survey of flint arrowheads from the NE of Scotland.* Unpub MA thesis, Dept of Archaeol, Univ Edinburgh.

Harbison, P 1969a *The daggers and the halberds of the early bronze age in Ireland.* Munich. (= *Prähistorische Bronzefunde*, VI/1).

Harbison, P 1969b *The axes of the early bronze age in Ireland.* Munich. (= *Prähistorische Bronzefunde*, IX/1).

Harbison, P 1973 The earlier bronze age in Ireland: late 3rd millennium-*c.* 1200 BC, *J Roy Soc Antiq Ir*, 103 (1973), 93-152.

Harbison, P 1980 Who were Ireland's first metallurgists? *in* Ryan, M (ed), *The origins of metallurgy in Atlantic Europe: proceedings of the 5th Atlantic Colloquium, Dublin 1978*, Dublin, 97-105.

Hardaker, R 1974 *A corpus of early bronze age dagger pommels from Great Britain and Ireland.* Oxford. (= *Brit Archaeol Rep*, 3).

Harding, A 1971 The earliest glass in Europe, *Archeol Rozhledy*, 23 (1971), 188-200.

Harding, A & Warren, S E 1973 Early bronze age faience beads from Central Europe, *Antiquity*, 47 (1973), 64-66.

Hardmeyer, B & Bürgi, J 1975 Der Goldbecher von Eschenz, *Zeitschr Schweiz Archäol Kunstgesch*, 32 (1975), 109-20.

Harrison, R J 1980 *The Beaker Folk.* London.

Harrison, R J 1984 Beaker cultures of Iberia, France and the west Mediterranean islands *in* Guilaine, J (ed), *L'âge du cuivre Européen: civilisations à vases campaniformes*, Paris, 187-207.

Hawkes, C F C 1954 Archaeological theory and method: some suggestions from the Old World, *Amer Anthrop*, 56 (1954), 155-68.

Hawkes, C F C 1966 British prehistory: the invasion hypothesis, *Antiquity*, 40 (1966), 297-98.

Hedges, J W 1982 An archaeodemographical perspective on Isbister, *Scot Archaeol Rev*, 1 (1982), 5-20.

Hedges, J W 1983 *Isbister: a chambered tomb in Orkney.* Oxford. (= *Brit Archaeol Rep Brit Ser*, 115).

Hedges, J W 1984 *Tomb of the eagles. A window on stone age tribal Britain.* London.

Hedges, J & Buckley, D 1978 Excavations at a causewayed enclosure, Orsett, Essex, 1975, *Proc Prehist Soc*, 44 (1978), 219-308.

Hemingway, J E, Wilson, V & Wright, C W 1968 *Geology of the Yorkshire coast.* Colchester. (= *Geol Assoc Guide*, 34).

Henshall, A S 1963 *The chambered tombs of Scotland.* Volume 1. Edinburgh.

Henshall, A S 1964a A dagger-grave and other cist burials at Ashgrove, Methilhill, Fife, *Proc Soc Antiq Scot*, 97 (1963-64), 166-79.

Henshall, A S 1964b Four early bronze age armlets, *Proc Prehist Soc*, 30 (1964), 426-29.

Henshall, A S 1968 Scottish dagger graves *in* Coles, J M & Simpson, D D A (eds), *Studies in ancient Europe: essays presented to Stuart Piggott*, Leicester, 173-95.

Henshall, A S 1972 *The chambered tombs of Scotland*. Volume 2. Edinburgh.

Henshall, A S 1985 The chambered cairns *in* Renfrew, C (ed), *The prehistory of Orkney*, Edinburgh, 83-117.

Henshall, A S & Wallace, J C 1963 A bronze age cist burial at Masterton, Pitreavie, Fife, *Proc Soc Antiq Scot*, 96 (1962-63), 145-54.

Herity, M 1974 *Irish passage graves*. Dublin.

Hewison, J K 1893 *The Isle of Bute in the olden time. Volume 1: Celtic saints and heroes.* Edinburgh & London.

Hoare, R C 1812 *The ancient history of south Wiltshire*. London.

Hodder, I 1982 *Symbols in action*. Cambridge.

Höfer, P 1906 Der Leubinger Grabhügel, *Jahresschr Vorgesch sächsisch-thüringischen Länder*, 5 (1906), 1-99.

Houlder, C H 1979 The Langdale and Scafell Pike axe factory sites: a field survey *in* Clough, T H McK & Cummins, W A (eds), *Stone axe studies: archaeological, petrological, experimental and ethnographic*, London, 87-89. (= *Counc Brit Archaeol Res Rep*, 23).

Howard, H 1981 In the wake of distribution: towards an integrated approach to ceramic studies in prehistoric Britain *in* Howard, H & Morris, E L (eds), *Production and distribution: a ceramic viewpoint*, Oxford, 1-30. (= *Brit Archaeol Rep Int Ser*, 120).

Hunter, D M 1971 Two groups of cists at Denovan near Dunipace, Stirlingshire, *Glasgow Archaeol J*, 2 (1971), 31-38.

Huntington, R & Metcalf, P 1979 *Celebrations of death.* Cambridge.

Hutcheson, A 1887 Notice of a burial place of the bronze age at Barnhill, near Broughty Ferry, *Proc Soc Antiq Scot*, 21 (1886-87), 316-24.

Hutcheson, A 1891 Notice of the discovery and examination of a burial cairn of the bronze age at the farm of Gilchorn, parish of Inverkeillor, Forfarshire, *Proc Soc Antiq Scot*, 25 (1890-91), 447-63.

Hutchins, A B 1845 [Description of barrow at Winterslow in proceedings of the central committee of the British Archaeological Association, March 13, 1844], *Archaeol J*, 1 (1845), 156-57.

Irving, G V 1855 On the ancient camps of the Upper Ward of Lanarkshire, *J Brit Archaeol Assoc*, 10 (1855), 1-32.

Jervise, A 1860 Notice of a stone coffin which contained an urn and jet ornaments, discovered near Pitkennedy, parish of Aberlemno, Forfarshire, *Proc Soc Antiq Scot*, 3 (1857-60), 78-79.

Jobey, G 1966 Excavations on palisaded settlements and cairnfields at Alnham,

Northumberland, *Archaeol Aeliana*, 4 ser, 44 (1966), 5-48.

Jobey, G 1980 Green Knowe unenclosed platform settlement and Harehope Cairn, Peeblesshire, *Proc Soc Antiq Scot*, 110 (1978-80), 72-113.

Junghans, S, Sangmeister, E & Schröder, M 1960 *Metallanalysen kupferzeitlicher und frühbronzezeitlicher Bodenfunde aus Europa*. Berlin. (= *Studien zu den Anfängen der Metallurgie*, 1).

Junghans, S, Sangmeister, E & Schröder, M 1968 *Kupfer und Bronze in der frühen Metallzeit Europas*. Berlin. (= *Studien zu den Anfängen der Metallurgie*, 2).

Keiller, A & Piggott, S 1938 Excavation of an untouched chamber in the Lanhill long barrow, *Proc Prehist Soc*, 4 (1938), 122-50.

Kenworthy, J 1977 A reconsideration of the 'Ardiffery' finds, Cruden, Aberdeenshire, *Proc Soc Antiq Scot*, 108 (1976-77), 80-93.

Kilbride-Jones, H E 1935 An account of the excavation of the stone circle at Loanhead of Daviot, and of the standing stones of Cullerlie, Echt, both in Aberdeenshire, on behalf of HM Office of Works, *Proc Soc Antiq Scot*, 69 (1934-35), 168-223.

Kinnes, I A 1976 Monumental function in British neolithic burial practices, *World Archaeol*, 7 (1975-76), 16-29.

Kinnes, I 1979 *Round barrows and ring-ditches in the British neolithic.* London. (= *Brit Mus Occas Pap*, 7).

Kinnes, I 1981 Dialogues with death *in* Chapman, R, Kinnes, I & Randsborg, K (eds), *The archaeology of death*, Cambridge, 83-91.

Kinnes, I A, Craddock, P T, Needham, S, & Lang, J 1979 Tin-plating in the early bronze age: the Barton Stacey axe, *Antiquity*, 53 (1979), 141-43.

Kinnes, I, Schadla-Hall, T, Chadwick, P & Dean, P 1983 Duggleby Howe reconsidered, *Archaeol J*, 140 (1983), 83-108.

Kirwan, R 1868 Memoir of the examination of three barrows at Broad Down, Farway, near Honiton, *Rep Trans Devonshire Assoc*, 2:2 (1868), 619-49.

Klejn, L S 1968 O date Karbunskogo Klada, *Problemi Arkheol*, 1 (1968), 5-74.

Kowiańska-Piaszykowa, M & Kurnatowski, S 1953 Kurhan kultury unietyckiej w Łękach Małych. pow. Kościan, *Fontes Archaeol Posnanienses*, 4 (1953), 43-76.

Lamberg-Karlovsky, C C 1963 Amber and faience, *Antiquity*, 37 (1963), 301-02.

Lanting, J N 1974 Chemical analysis of the filling of the Lannion gold box, *Palaeohistoria*, 16 (1974), 164-67.

Lanting, J N & van der Waals, J D 1972 British beakers as seen from the Continent. A review article, *Helinium*, 12 (1972), 20-46.

Lanting, J N & van der Waals, J D 1976 Beaker culture relations in the lower Rhine basin *in* Lanting, J N & van der Waals, J D (eds), *Glockenbecher Symposion: Oberried 1974*, Bussum/Haarlem, 1-80.

Larrain, J 1979 *The concept of ideology.* London.

Larrain, J 1982 On the character of ideology:

Marx and the present debate in Britain, *Theory, Culture & Society*, 1 (1982), 5-22.

Lawson, A J, Martin, E A & Priddy, D 1981 *The barrows of East Anglia.* Norwich. (= *East Anglian Archaeol Rep*, 12).

van der Leeuw, S E 1976 Neolithic beakers from the Netherlands: the potter's point of view *in* Lanting, J N & van der Waals, J D (eds), *Glockenbecher Symposion: Oberreid 1974*, Bussum/Haarlem, 81-139.

Lethbridge, T C 1950 Excavation of the Snailwell group of bronze age barrows, *Proc Cambridge Antiq Soc*, 43 (1949), 30-49.

Le Provost, F, Giot, P-R, Onnée, Y 1972 Prospections sur les collines de Saint-Nicolas-du-Pelem (Côtes-du-Nord) du chalcolithique à la protohistoire, *Annales de Bretagne*, 79 (1972), 39-48.

Le Roux, C-T 1975 Circonscription de Bretagne, *Gallia Préhist*, 18 (1975), 511-39.

Liddell, D 1935 Report on the excavations at Hembury Fort, *Proc Devon Archaeol Explor Soc*, 2 (1935) 134-75.

De Loë, A 1906 Présentation d'un ornement en or trouvé récemment à Arlon (Belgique), *Congrès international d'anthropologie et d'archéologie préhistoriques, 13e session*, Monaco, 294-95.

De Loë, A 1931 *Belgique ancienne II. Les âges du métal.* Brussels.

Londesborough, A D 1852 An account of the opening of some tumuli in the East Riding of Yorkshire, *Archaeologia*, 34 (1852), 251-58.

Longworth, I H 1983 The Whinny Liggate perforated wall cup and its affinities *in* O'Connor, A & Clarke, D V (eds) *From the stone age to the 'Forty-Five. Studies presented to R B K Stevenson.* Edinburgh, 65-86.

Longworth, I H 1984 *Collared urns of the bronze age in Great Britain and Ireland.* Cambridge.

Lowe, G & Anderson, J 1894 Notice of a cemetery of graves and cinerary urns of the bronze age, recently discovered at Kirkpark, Musselburgh, *Proc Soc Antiq Scot*, 28 (1893-94), 62-78.

Lowson, W 1882 Notes of a small cemetery of cists and urns at Magdalen Bridge, near Joppa, *Proc Soc Antiq Scot*, 16 (1881-82), 419-29.

Lucas, A 1962 *Ancient Egyptian materials and industries.* 4th edition, London.

Lynch, F 1970 *Prehistoric Anglesey.* Llangefni.

Lynch, F 1973 The use of the passage in certain passage graves as a means of communication rather than access *in* Daniel, G & Kjaerum, P (eds), *Megalithic graves and ritual: papers presented at the III Atlantic Colloquium, Moesgård 1969*, Aarhus, 147-61.

Macalister, R A S, Armstrong, E C R, & Praeger, R Ll 1912 Report on the exploration of bronze-age carns on Carrowkeel Mountain, Co Sligo, *Proc Roy Ir Acad*, 29C (1911-12), 311-47.

Macdonald, J 1884 Illustrated notices of the ancient bronze implements of Ayrshire, *Archaeol Hist Collect Ayr Wigtownshire*, 4 (1884), 47-54.

Machin, M L 1971 Further excavations of the enclosure at Swine Sty, Big Moor, Baslow, *Trans Hunter Archaeol Soc*, 10 (1971), 5-13.

MacKie, E W 1977 *Science and society in prehistoric Britain*. London.

MacLaren, A 1970 The decorated slab from Wester Yardhouses, Lanarkshire, *Trans Dumfriesshire Galloway Natur Hist Antiq Soc*, 47 (1970), 137-38.

Manby, T G 1974 *Grooved ware sites in the north of England*. Oxford. (= *Brit Archaeol Rep*, 9).

Manby, T G 1976 The excavation of the Kilham long barrow, East Riding of Yorkshire, *Proc Prehist Soc*, 42 (1976), 111-60.

Manby, T G 1979 Typology, materials and distribution of flint and stone axes in Yorkshire *in* Clough, T H McK & Cummins, W A (eds), *Stone axe studies: archaeological, petrological, experimental and ethnographic*, London, 65-81. (= *Counc Brit Archaeol Res Rep*, 23).

Mandeville, M D 1973 A consideration of the thermal pretreatment of chert, *Plains Anthrop*, 18 (1973), 177-202.

Mann, L Mc 1906 Notes on — (1) a drinking-cup urn, found at Bathgate; (2) a prehistoric hut in Tiree; (3) a cairn containing sixteen cinerary urns, with objects of vitreous paste and of gold, at Stevenston, Ayrshire; and (4) prehistoric beads of coarse vitreous paste, *Proc Soc Antiq Scot*, 40 (1905-06), 369-402.

Marshall, D N 1977 Carved stone balls, *Proc Soc Antiq Scot*, 108 (1976-77), 40-72.

Marwick, H 1925 Note on an incised stone found at Brogar, Stenness, *Proc Orkney Antiq Soc*, 3 (1924-25), 91.

Marwick, J G 1926 Discovery of stone cists at Stenness, Orkney, *Proc Soc Antiq Scot*, 60 (1925-26), 34-36.

Maryon, H 1936 Excavation of two bronze age barrows at Kirkhaugh, Northumberland, *Archaeol Aeliana*, 4 Ser, 13 (1936), 207-17.

Masters, L J 1973 The Lochhill long cairn, *Antiquity*, 47 (1973), 96-100.

Matthews, C L 1976 *Occupation sites on a Chiltern ridge. Part 1: neolithic, bronze age and early iron age*. Oxford. (= *Brit Archaeol Rep*, 29).

Mauss, M 1970 *The gift: forms and functions of exchange in archaic societies*. Paper edition. London.

McAdam, E 1974 *Some aspects of early bronze age short cists in Scotland*. Unpub MA Thesis, Dept of Archaeol, Univ Edinburgh.

McAdam, E & Watkins, T 1974 Experimental reconstruction of a short cist, *J Archaeol Sci*, 1 (1974), 383-86.

McInnes, I 1968 Jet sliders in late neolithic Britain *in* Coles, J M & Simpson, D D A (eds), *Studies in ancient Europe: essays presented to Stuart Piggott*, Leicester, 137-44.

McKerrell, H 1972 On the origins of British faience beads and some aspects of the Wessex-Mycenae relationship, *Proc Prehist Soc*, 38 (1972), 286-301.

Megaw, J V S 1960 Penny whistles and prehistory, *Antiquity*, 34 (1960), 6-13.

Megaw, J V S & Simpson, D D A (eds) 1979 *Introduction to British prehistory*. Leicester.

Meillassoux, C 1972 From reproduction to production, *Economy & Society*, 1 (1972), 93-105.

Meillassoux, C 1973 On the mode of production of the hunting band *in* Alexandre, P (ed), *French perspectives in African studies*, London, 187-203.

Mercer, R 1980 *Hambledon Hill, a neolithic landscape*. Edinburgh.

Mercer, R J 1981a Excavations at Carn Brea, Illogan, Cornwall, 1970-73 — a neolithic fortified complex of the third millennium bc, *Cornish Archaeol*, 20 (1981), 1-204.

Mercer, R J 1981b The excavation of a late neolithic henge-type enclosure at Balfarg, Markinch, Fife, Scotland, 1977-78, *Proc Soc Antiq Scot*, 111 (1981), 63-171.

Miles, H & Miles T J 1971 Excavations on Longstone Downs, St Stephen-in-Brannel and St Mewan, *Cornish Archaeol*, 10 (1971), 5-34.

Miller, D 1982 Structures and strategies: an aspect of the relationship between social hierarchy and cultural change *in* Hodder, I (ed), *Symbolic and structural archaeology*, Cambridge, 89-98.

Miller, D & Tilley, C (eds) 1984a *Ideology, power and prehistory*. Cambridge.

Miller, D & Tilley, C 1984b Ideology, power and prehistory: an introduction *in* Miller, D & Tilley, C (eds), *Ideology, power and prehistory*, Cambridge, 1-15.

Monkman, C 1869 On the finding of flint implements in the valley gravels and in the Hessle clay in York, *Yorkshire Archaeol J*, 1 (1869), 41-57.

Moore, C N 1979 Stone axes from the east Midlands *in* Clough, T H McK & Cummins, W A (eds), *Stone axe studies: archaeological, petrological, experimental and ethnographic*, London, 82-86. (= *Counc Brit Archaeol Res Rep*, 23).

Morgan, F de M 1959 The excavation of a long barrow at Nutbane, Hants, *Proc Prehist Soc*, 25 (1959), 15-51.

Morgan, R 1979 Tree-ring studies in the Somerset Levels: floating oak tree-ring chronologies from the trackways and their radiocarbon dating, *Somerset Levels Pap*, 5 (1979), 98-100.

Morgan, R 1984 Tree-ring studies in the Somerset Levels: the Sweet Track 1979-82, *Somerset Levels Pap*, 10 (1984), 46-64.

Morris, R W B 1977 *The prehistoric rock art of Argyll*. Poole.

Morrison, A 1979 A bronze age burial site near South Mound, Houston, Renfrewshire, *Glasgow Archaeol J*, 6 (1979), 20-45.

Morrison, J 1872 Remains of early antiquities, in and on the borders of the parish of Urquhart, Elgin, inclding hut circles, kitchen middens, stone cists with urns, stone weapons, etc, etc, *Proc Soc Antiq Scot*, 9 (1870-72), 250-63.

Mortimer, J R [1905] *Forty years' researches in the British and Saxon burial mounds of east Yorkshire*. London.

Moucha, V 1958 Faience and glassy faience beads in the Únětice culture in Bohemia, *Epitymbion Roman Hakon*, Prague, 1958, 44-49.

Munro, R 1892 On trepanning the human skull in prehistoric times, *Proc Soc Antiq Scot*, 26 (1891-92), 5-33.

Munro, R 1902 Notes on a set of five jet buttons found on a hill in Forfarshire, *Proc Soc Antiq Scot*, 36 (1901-02), 464-85.

Needham, S 1979 A pair of early bronze age spearheads from Lightwater, Surrey *in* Burgess, C & Coombs, D (eds), *Bronze age hoards*, Oxford, 1-39. (= *Brit Archaeol Rep Brit Ser*, 67).

Needham, S & Kinnes, I 1981 Tinned axes again, *Antiquity*, 55 (1981), 133-34.

Newall, R S 1929 Two shale cups of the early bronze age and other similar cups, *Wiltshire Archaeol Natur Hist Mag*, 44 (1927-29), 111-17.

Newbigin, N 1941 A collection of prehistoric material from Hebburn Moor, Northumberland, *Archaeol Aeliana*, 4 ser, 19 (1941), 104-16.

Newton, R G & Renfrew, C 1970 British faience beads reconsidered, *Antiquity*, 44 (1970), 199-206.

Noble, J V 1969 The techniques of Egyptian faience, *Amer J Archaeol*, 73 (1969) 435-39.

Norwich Castle Museum 1977 *Bronze age metalwork in Norwich Castle Museum*. Norwich.

Oakley, K 1965 Folklore of fossils: part II, *Antiquity*, 39 (1965), 117-25.

O'Kelly, M J 1982 *Newgrange: archaeology, art and legend*. London.

Olausson, D S 1982 Lithic technological analysis of the thin-butted flint axe, *Acta Archaeol*, 53 (1982), 1-87.

Olausson, D S 1983 Flint and groundstone axes in the Scanian neolithic, an evaluation of raw materials based on experiment, *Scripta Min Reg Soc Hum Litt Lundensis*, 2 (1982-83), 1-66.

O'Neil, H & Grinsell, L V 1960 Gloucestershire barrows, *Trans Bristol Gloucestershire Archaeol Soc*, 79 (1960), 1-149.

Ó'Riordáin, S P 1936 The halberd in bronze age Europe, *Archaeologia*, 86 (1936), 195-321.

Ó'Riordáin, S P 1955 A burial with faience beads at Tara, *Proc Prehist Soc*, 21 (1955), 163-73.

Otto, K-H 1955 *Die sozialökonomischen Verhältnisse bei den Stämmen der Leubinger Kultur in Mitteldeutschland*. Berlin. (= *Ethnog-archäol Forsch*, Bd 3, Teil 1).

Packard, V O 1957 *The hidden persuaders*. London.

Palmer, R 1976 Interrupted ditch enclosures in Britain: the use of aerial photography for comparative studies, *Proc Prehist Soc*, 52 (1976), 161-86.

Paton N 1870 Notice of two gold ornaments found at Orton on the Spey while cutting for the railway from Elgin to Keith in 1863, *Proc Soc Antiq Scot*, 8 (1868-70), 28-32.

Patterson, L W & Sollberger, J B 1979 Water treatment of flint, *Lithic Technol*, 8: 3 (1979), 50-51.

Peacock, D P S 1969 Neolithic pottery production in Cornwall, *Antiquity*, 43 (1969) 145-49.

Petersen, F, Shepherd, I A G & Tuckwell, A N 1974 A short cist at Horsbrugh Castle Farm, Peeblesshire, *Proc Soc Antiq Scot*, 105 (1972-74), 43-62.

Petrie, G 1860 Notice of a barrow at Huntiscarth in the parish of Harray, Orkney, recently opened, *Proc Soc Antiq Scot*, 3 (1857-60), 195.

Petrie, G 1868 Notice of ruins of ancient dwellings at Skara, Bay of Skaill, in the Parish of Sandwick, Orkney, recently excavated, *Proc Soc Antiq Scot*, 7 (1866-68), 201-19.

Phillips, B 1857 Discovery of a tumulus at Hove, near Brighton, containing an amber cup etc, *Sussex Archaeol Collect*, 9 (1857), 119-24.

Pierpoint, S 1980 *Social patterns in Yorkshire prehistory 3500-750 BC*. Oxford. (= *Brit Archaeol Rep Brit Ser*, 74).

Piggott, C M 1946 The late bronze age razors of the British Isles, *Proc Prehist Soc*, 12 (1946), 121-41.

Piggott, S 1938 The early bronze age in Wessex, *Proc Prehist Soc*, 4 (1938), 52-106.

Piggott, S 1939 Further bronze age 'dagger graves' in Brittany, *Proc Prehist Soc*, 5 (1939), 193-95.

Piggott, S 1940 A trepanned skull of the beaker period from Dorset and the practice of trepanning in prehistoric Europe, *Proc Prehist Soc*, 6 (1940), 112-32.

Piggott, S 1948 The excavations at Cairnpapple Hill, West Lothian, 1947-48, *Proc Soc Antiq Scot*, 82 (1947-48), 68-123.

Piggott, S 1954 *Neolithic cultures of the British Isles*. Cambridge.

Piggott, S 1958 Segmented bone beads and toggles in the British early and middle bronze age, *Proc Prehist Soc*, 24 (1958), 227-29.

Piggott, S 1962 *The West Kennet long barrow, excavations 1955-56*. London.

Piggott, S 1965 *Ancient Europe from the beginnings of agriculture to classical antiquity*. Edinburgh.

Piggott, S 1966 Mycenae and Barbarian Europe: an outline survey, *Sborník Národ Muz Praze*, 20 (1966), 117-25.

Piggott, S 1972 Excavations of the Dalladies long barrow, Fettercairn, Kincardineshire, *Proc Soc Antiq Scot*, 104 (1971-72), 23-47.

Piggott, S 1973 The Wessex culture of the early bronze age *in* Crittall, E (ed), *A history of Wiltshire*, volume 1:2, Oxford, 352-75.

Piggott, S & Powell, T G E 1949 The excavation of three neolithic chambered tombs in Galloway, 1949, *Proc Soc Antiq Scot*, 83 (1948-49), 103-61.

Piggott, S & Stewart, M 1958 Early and middle bronze age grave groups and hoards from Scotland, *Inventaria Archaeol*, GB 25-34.

Pleyte, W 1889 *Nederlandsche Oudheden van de Vroegste tijden tot op Karel den Groote. Gelderland*. Leiden.

Plunkett, T & Coffey, G 1898 Report on the excavation of Topped Mountain cairn, *Proc Roy Ir Acad*, 3 ser, 4 (1896-98), 651-58.

Pollard, A M, Bussell, G D & Baird, D C 1981 The analytical investigation of early bronze age jet and jet-like material from the Devizes Museum, *Archaeometry*, 23 (1981), 139-67.

Powell, T G E 1953 The gold ornament from Mold, Flintshire, North Wales, *Proc Prehist Soc*, 19 (1953), 161-79.

Radley, J 1969 A shale bracelet industry from Totley Moor, near Sheffield, *Trans Hunter Archaeol Soc*, 9 (1969), 264-68.

Radley, J 1970 The York hoard of flint tools, 1868, *Yorkshire Archaeol J*, 42 (1967-70), 131-32.

Rankin, D R 1874 Notice of a sculptured stone cist-lid and clay urn found in Carnwath Moor, *Proc Soc Antiq Scot*, 10 (1872-74), 61-63.

Rankine, W F 1952 Implements of coloured flint in Britain. Their distribution and the derivation of raw material, *Archaeol News Letter*, 4:10 (1952), 145-50.

RCAMS 1946 Royal Commission on the ancient monuments of Scotland, *Inventory of the ancient monuments of Orkney and Shetland. Volume 2. Inventory of Orkney*. Edinburgh.

RCAMS 1978 Royal Commission on the ancient and historical monuments of Scotland, *Lanarkshire: an inventory of the prehistoric and Roman monuments*. Edinburgh.

RCHME 1970 Royal Commission on historical monuments (England), *An inventory of historical monuments in the County of Dorset. Volume 2. South-East*. London.

RCHME 1979 Royal Commission on historical monuments (England), *Stonehenge and its environs*. Edinburgh.

Renfrew, C 1968 Wessex without Mycenae, *Ann Brit Sch Athens*, 63 (1968), 277-85.

Renfrew, C 1973 Monuments, mobilization and social organization in neolithic Wessex *in* Renfrew, C (ed), *The explanation of culture change: models in prehistory*, London, 539-58.

Renfrew, C 1976 Megaliths, territories and populations *in* De Laet, S J (ed), *Acculturation and continuity in Atlantic Europe, mainly during the neolithic period and the bronze age*, Brugge, 198-220. (= *Diss Archaeol Gandenses*, 16).

Renfrew, C 1977 Alternative models for exchange and spatial distribution *in* Earle, T K & Ericson, J E (eds), *Exchange systems in prehistory*, London, 71-90.

Renfrew, C 1979 *Investigations in Orkney*. London. (= *Rep Res Comm Soc Antiq London*, 38).

Renfrew, C (ed) 1985 *The prehistory of Orkney*. Edinburgh.

Renfrew, C & Buteux, S 1985 Radiocarbon dates from Orkney *in* Renfrew, C (ed) *The prehistory of Orkney*, Edinburgh, 263-74.

Richards, J 1982 The Stonehenge environs project: the story so far, *Scot Archaeol Rev*, 1 (1982), 98-104.

Richards, J 1984 The development of the neolithic landscape in the environs of Stonehenge *in* Bradley, R & Gardiner, J (eds), *Neolithic studies: a review of some current research*, Oxford, 177-87. (= *Brit Archaeol Rep Brit Ser*, 133/*Reading Stud Archaeol*, 1).

Ritchie, J N G 1976 The Stones of Stenness, Orkney, *Proc Soc Antiq Scot*, 107 (1975-76), 1-60.

Ritchie, J N G & Shepherd, I A G 1975 Beaker pottery and associated artifacts in south-west Scotland, *Trans Dumfriesshire Galloway Natur Hist Antiq Soc*, 50 (1975), 18-36.

Ritchie, P R 1968 The stone implement trade in third millennium Scotland *in* Coles, J M & Simpson, D D A (eds), *Studies in ancient Europe: essays presented to Stuart Piggott*, Leicester, 117-36.

Robbins, L H 1973 Turkana material culture viewed from an archaeological perspective, *World Archaeol*, 5 (1973), 209-14.

Roe, F E S 1966 The battle-axe series in Britain, *Proc Prehist Soc*, 32 (1966), 199-245.

Roe, F E S 1968 Stone mace-heads and the latest neolithic cultures of the British Isles *in* Coles, J M & Simpson, D D A (eds), *Studies in ancient Europe: essays presented to Stuart Piggott*, Leicester, 145-72.

Roe, F E S 1979 Typology of stone implements with shaftholes *in* Clough, T H McK & Cummins, W A (eds), *Stone axe studies: archaeological, petrological, experimental and ethnographic*, London, 23-48. (= *Counc Brit Archaeol Res Rep*, 23)

Rolleston, G 1876 On the people of the long barrow period, *J Anthrop Inst*, 5 (1876), 120-73.

Ruggles, C L N & Whittle, A W R (eds) 1981 *Astronomy and society in Britain during the period 4000-1500 BC*. Oxford. (= *Brit Archaeol Rep Brit Ser*, 88).

Sahlins, M 1974 *Stone age economics*. London.

Saville, A 1984 Preliminary report on the excavation of a Cotswold-Severn tomb at Hazleton, Gloucestershire, *Antiq J*, 54 (1984), 10-24.

Savory, H N 1961 Bronze age burials near Bedd Emlyn, Clocaenog, *Trans Denbighshire Hist Soc*, 10 (1961), 7-22.

Savory, H N 1980 *Guide catalogue of the bronze age collections* [National Museum of Wales]. Cardiff.

Schmidt, P K & Burgess, C B 1981 *The axes of Scotland and northern England*. Munich. (= *Prähistorische Bronzefunde*, IX/7).

Schon, D A 1971 *Beyond the stable state. Public and private learning in a changing society*. London.

Scott, J G 1948 Cinerary urn from Milngavie, Dunbartonshire, *Proc Soc Antiq Scot*, 82 (1947-48), 302-03.

Scott, J G 1951 A hoard of bronze weapons from Gavel Moss Farm, near Lochwinnoch, Renfrewshire, *Proc Soc Antiq Scot*, 85 (1950-51), 134-38.

Scott, J G 1964 The chambered cairn at Beacharra, Kintyre, Argyll, *Proc Prehist Soc*, 30 (1964), 134-58.

Scott, J G 1969 The Clyde cairns of Scotland *in*

Powell, T G E et al, Megalithic enquiries in the west of Britain, Liverpool, 175-222.

Scott, W L 1948 The chamber tomb of Unival, North Uist, Proc Soc Antiq Scot, 82 (1947-48), 1-49.

Scott, W L 1951 The colonisation of Scotland in the second millennium BC, Proc Prehist Soc, 17 (1951), 16-82.

Scudder, V (ed) 1910 Bede's Ecclesiastical history of the English nation. London.

Shanks, M & Tilley, C 1982 Ideology, symbolic power and ritual communication: a reinterpretation of neolithic mortuary practices in Hodder, I (ed), Symbolic and structural archaeology, Cambridge, 129-54.

Sharples, N forthcoming Excavations at Pierowall Quarry, Westray, Orkney, Proc Soc Antiq Scot, 114.

Shennan, S J 1982a Exchange and ranking: the role of amber in the earlier bronze age of Europe, in Renfrew, C & Shennan, S J (eds), Ranking, resource and exchange, Cambridge, 33-45.

Shennan, S J 1982b Ideology, change and the European early bronze age in Hodder, I (ed), Symbolic and structural archaeology, Cambridge, 155-61.

Shepard, A O 1956 Ceramics for the archaeologist. Washington DC.

Shepherd, I A G 1973 The V-bored buttons of Great Britain. Unpub MA thesis, Dept of Archaeol, Univ Edinburgh.

Shepherd, I A G 1974 The Balbirnie V-bored button in Ritchie, J N G, The excavation of a stone circle and cairn at Balbirnie, Fife, Archaeol J, 131 (1974), 17-18.

Shepherd, I A G 1981 Bronze age jet working in north Britain in Kenworthy, J (ed), Early technology in north Britain, Edinburgh, 43-51. (= Scot Archaeol Forum, 11).

Shepherd, I A G 1984 The Limefield V-bored button in MacLaren, A, A bronze age cairn at Limefield, Lanarkshire in Miket, R & Burgess, C (eds), Between and beyond the walls, Edinburgh, 112-13.

Shepherd, I A G & Cowie, T G 1977 An enlarged food vessel urn burial and associated artefacts from Kiltry Knock, Alvah, Banff and Buchan, Proc Soc Antiq Scot, 108 (1976-77), 114-23.

Shepherd, W 1972 Flint, its origin, properties and uses. London.

Simpson, D D A 1968 Food vessels: associations and chronology in Coles, J M & Simpson, D D A (eds), Studies in ancient Europe: essays presented to Stuart Piggott, Leicester, 197-211.

Simpson, D D A & Thawley, J E 1972 Single grave art in Britain, Scot Archaeol Forum, 4 (1972), 81-104.

Slater, E A 1985 Sources and resources for non-ferrous metallurgy in Phillips, P (ed), The archaeologist and the laboratory, London, 45-49. (= Counc Brit Archaeol Res Rep, 58).

Smellie, W 1782 Account of the institution and progress of the Society of the Antiquaries of Scotland. Edinburgh.

Smirke, E 1865 Notice of two golden ornaments found near Padstow, and communicated to the Institute by favour of HRH the Prince of Wales, KG, Archaeol J, 22 (1865), 275-77.

Smith, C R nd Collectanea antiqua, III. Privately printed, London.

Smith, I F 1965 Windmill Hill and Avebury. Excavations by Alexander Keiller 1925-1939. Oxford.

Smith, I F 1974 The jet bead from Fengate, 1972, in Pryor, F, Excavation at Fengate, Peterborough, England: the first report, Toronto, 40-42. (= Roy Ontario Mus Archaeol Monogr, 3).

Smith, J A 1872 Notice of a cinerary urn, containing a small-sized urn (in which were the bones of a child), discovered in Fife-shire; with notes of similar small and cup-like vessels, in the museum of the Society of Antiquaries of Scotland, Proc Soc Antiq Scot, 9 (1870-72), 189-207.

Smith, J A 1876 Notes of small ornamented stone balls found in different parts of Scotland, etc; with remarks on their supposed age and use, Proc Soc Antiq Scot, 11 (1874-76), 29-62.

Smith, J A & Macadam, S 1872 Notice of bronze celts or axe-heads, which have apparently been tinned; also of bronze weapons and armlets, found also with portions of metallic tin near Elgin in 1868, Proc Soc Antiq Scot, 9 (1871-72), 428-43.

Smith, M A 1955 The limitations of inference in archaeology, Archaeol News Letter, 6 (1955), 1-5.

Smith, W C 1963 Jade axes from sites in the British Isles, Proc Prehist Soc, 29 (1963), 133-72.

Startin, W & Bradley, R 1981 Some notes on work organisation and society in prehistoric Wessex in Ruggles, C L N & Whittle, A W R (eds), Astronomy and society in Britain during the period 4000-1500 BC, Oxford, 289-96. (= Brit Archaeol Rep Brit Ser, 88).

Stevens, F & Stone, J F S 1939 The barrows of Winterslow, Wiltshire Archaeol Natur Hist Mag, 48 (1937-39), 174-82.

Stevenson, R B K 1939 Two bronze age burials, Proc Soc Antiq Scot, 73 (1938-39), 229-39.

Stevenson, R B K 1953 Prehistoric pot-building in Europe, Man, 53 (1953), 65-68.

Stevenson, R B K 1956 The Migdale hoard bronze necklace, Proc Soc Antiq Scot, 89 (1955-56), 456-57.

Stewart, W B 1914 Notes on a further excavation of ancient dwellings at Skara, in the Parish of Sandwick, Orkney, made during August 1913, Proc Soc Antiq Scot, 48 (1913-14), 344-55.

Stone, J F S 1934 A middle bronze age urnfield on Easton Down, Winterslow, Wiltshire Archaeol Natur Hist Mag, 46 (1932-34), 218-24.

Stone, J F S & Thomas, L C 1956 The use and distribution of faience in the ancient East and prehistoric Europe, Proc Prehist Soc, 22 (1956), 37-84.

Stuart, J 1866 Notice of a group of artificial islands in the Loch of Dowalton, Wigtonshire, and of other artificial islands or "crannogs" throughout Scotland, Proc Soc Antiq Scot, 6 (1864-66), 114-78.

Sturrock, J 1880 Notice of a jet necklace and urn of the food-vessel type found in a cist at Balcalk, Tealing and of the opening of Hatton cairn, Parish of Inverarity, Forfarshire, Proc Soc Antiq Scot, 14 (1879-80), 260-67.

Tainter, J A 1978 Mortuary practices and the study of prehistoric social systems in Schiffer, M B (ed), Advances in archaeological method and theory, volume 1, New York, 105-41.

Talbot-Rice, D 1959 The art of Byzantium. London.

Taylor, J J 1968 Early bronze age gold neck-rings in western Europe, Proc Prehist Soc, 34 (1968), 259-65.

Taylor, J J 1970a Lunulae reconsidered, Proc Prehist Soc, 36 (1970), 38-81.

Taylor, J J 1970b The recent discovery of gold pins in the Ridgeway gold pommel, Antiq J, 50 (1970), 216-21.

Taylor, J J 1974 The gold box from "La Motta", Lannion, Palaeohistoria, 16 (1974), 152-63.

Taylor, J J 1978 The relationship of British early bronze age goldwork to Atlantic Europe in Ryan, M (ed), The origins of metallurgy in Atlantic Europe: proceedings of the 5th Atlantic Colloquium, Dublin 1978, Dublin, 229-50.

Taylor, J J 1979 The gold lunula from Auchentaggart, Trans Dumfriesshire Galloway Natur Hist Antiq Soc, 54 (1979), 12-19.

Taylor, J J 1980 Bronze age goldwork of the British Isles, Cambridge.

Taylor, J J 1983 An unlocated Scottish gold source or an experiment in alloying? in O'Connor, A & Clarke, D V (eds), From the stone age to the 'Forty-Five. Studies presented to R B K Stevenson, Edinburgh, 57-64.

Thom, A 1971 Megalithic lunar observatories. Oxford.

Thomas, N 1966 Notes on some early bronze age objects in Devizes Museum, Wiltshire Archaeol Natur Hist Mag, 61 (1966), 1-8.

Thorpe, I J 1983 Prehistoric British astronomy — towards a social context, Scot Archaeol Rev, 2 (1983), 2-10.

Thorpe, I J & Richards, C 1984 The decline of ritual authority and the introduction of beakers into Britain in Bradley, R & Gardiner, J (eds), Neolithic studies: a review of some current research, Oxford, 67-84. (= Brit Archaeol Rep Brit Ser, 133/Reading Stud Archaeol, 1).

Thorpe, O W & Thorpe, R S 1984 The distribution and sources of archaeological pitchstone in Britain, J Archaeol Sci, 11 (1984), 1-34.

Thurnam, J 1857 On a cromlech-tumulus called Lugbury, near Littleton Drew: and a note on the name Drew, Wiltshire Archaeol Mag, 3 (1857), 164-77.

Thurnam, J 1871 On ancient British barrows especially those of Wiltshire and the adjoining counties. Part II: round barrows, Archaeologia, 43 (1871), 285-544.

Tixier, J, Inizan, M L & Roche, H 1980 Préhistoire de la pierre taillée. 1: terminologie et technologie. Valbonne.

Treinen, F 1970 Les poteries campaniformes en France, *Gallia Préhist*, 13 (1970), 53-107, 263-332.

Turner, W 1903 An account of a chambered cairn and cremation cists at Taversöe Tuick, near Trumland House, in the island of Rousay, Orkney, excavated by Lieutenant-General Traill Burroughs, CB of Rousay in 1898, *Proc Soc Antiq Scot*, 37 (1902-03), 73-82.

Twohig, E S 1981 *The megalithic art of Western Europe*. Oxford.

Tylecote, R F 1980 Summary of results of experimental work on early copper smelting *in* Oddy, W A (ed), *Aspects of early metallurgy*, London, 5-12. (= *Brit Mus Occas Pap*, 17).

Tylecote, R F, Ghaznavi, H A, & Boydell, P J 1977 Partitioning of trace elements between the ores, fluxes, slags and metal during the smelting of copper, *J Archaeol Sci*, 4 (1977), 305-33.

Ucko, P 1969 Ethnography and archaeological interpretation of funerary remains, *World Archaeol*, 1 (1969), 262-80.

Ullrich, H 1972 *Das Aunjetitzer Gräberfeld von Grossbrembach. Teil 1 Anthropologische Untersuchungen zur Frage nach Entstehung und Verwandtschaft der thüringschen, böhmischen und mährischen Aunjetitzer*. Weimar.

von Uslar, R 1955 Der Goldbecher von Fritzdorf bei Bonn, *Germania*, 33 (1955), 319-23.

Vatcher, F de M 1961 The excavation of the long mortuary enclosure on Normanton Down, Wilts, *Proc Prehist Soc*, 27 (1961), 160-73.

Vatcher, F de M 1969 Two incised plaques near Stonehenge Bottom, *Antiquity*, 43 (1969), 310-11.

Vemming Hansen, P & Madsen, B 1983 Flint axe manufacture in the neolithic, *J Danish Archaeol*, 2 (1983), 43-59.

Wainwright, G J 1979 *Mount Pleasant, Dorset: excavations 1970-71*. London. (= *Rep Res Comm Soc Antiq London*, 37).

Wainwright, G J, Evans, J G & Longworth, I H 1971 The excavation of a late neolithic enclosure at Marden, Wilts, *Antiq J*, 51 (1971) 177-239.

Wainwright, G J & Longworth, I H 1971 *Durrington Walls: excavations 1966-1968*. London. (= *Rep Res Comm Soc Antiq London*, 29).

Wakeman, W F 1882 On some recent antiquarian discoveries at Toam and Killicarney, near Blacklion, in the County of Cavan, *J Hist Archaeol Assoc Ir*, 4 ser, 5 (1879-82), 193-200.

Walker, I C 1966 The counties of Nairnshire, Moray and Banffshire in the bronze age — part I, *Proc Soc Antiq Scot*, 98 (1964-66), 76-125.

Walker, I C 1972 The counties of Nairnshire, Moray and Banffshire in the bronze age — part II, *Proc Soc Antiq Scot*, 104 (1971-72), 71-120.

Warne, C 1866 *The Celtic Tumuli of Dorset*. London.

Watkins, T 1982 The excavation of an early bronze age cemetery at Barns Farm, Dalgety, Fife, *Proc Soc Antiq Scot*, 112 (1982), 48-141.

Watkins, T & Shepherd, I A G 1980 A beaker burial at Newmill, near Bankfoot, Perthshire, *Proc Soc Antiq Scot*, 110 (1978-80), 32-43.

Weisberger, G (ed) 1981 *5000 Jahre Feuersteinbergbau, Die Suche nach dem Stahl der Steinzeit*. Bochum.

Wells, C 1960 A study of cremation, *Antiquity*, 34 (1960), 29-37.

Whittick, A 1946 *War memorials*. London.

Wickham-Jones C R 1981 Flaked stone technology in northern Britain *in* Kenworthy, J (ed) *Early technology in north Britain*, Edinburgh, 36-42. (= *Scot Archaeol Forum*, 11).

Wilde, W R 1862 *Catalogue of the Museum of the Royal Irish Academy. Volume 2: a descriptive catalogue of the antiquities of gold in the Museum of the Royal Irish Academy*. Dublin.

Williams, A 1948 Excavations in Barrow Hills Field, Radley, Berkshire, 1944, *Oxoniensia*, 13 (1948), 1-17.

Wilson, D 1851 *The archaeology and prehistoric annals of Scotland*. 1st edition, London & Cambridge.

Wilson, D 1863 *Prehistoric annals of Scotland*. 2nd edition, London & Cambridge.

Windele, J nd *J Windele's miscellany*, Roy Ir Acad MSS 12/C/I.

Witts, G B 1883 *Archaeological handbook of the County of Gloucester*. Cheltenham.

Wood-Martin, W G 1888 *The rude stone monuments of Ireland*. Dublin.

Worth, R N (ed) 1880 Second report of the barrow committee, *Rep Trans Devonshire Assoc*, 12 (1880), 119-51.

Wulff, H E, Wulff, H S & Koch, L 1968 Egyptian faience, a possible survival in Iran, *Archaeology*, 21 (1968), 98-107.

Young, A 1951 A tripartite bowl from Kintyre, *Proc Soc Antiq Scot*, 85 (1950-51), 38-51.

INDEX